Brilliant Microsoft® Access

Steve Johnson

Perspection, Inc.

PEARSON
Prentice Hall

Harlow, England • London • New York • Boston • San Francisco • Toronto
Sydney • Tokyo • Singapore • Hong Kong • Seoul • Taipei • New Delhi
Cape Town • Madrid • Mexico City • Amsterdam • Munich • Paris • Milan

Pearson Education Limited
Edinburgh Gate
Harlow
Essex CM20 2JE
England

and Associated Companies throughout the world

Visit us on the World Wide Web at:
www.pearsoned.co.uk

Original edition, entitled MICROSOFT OFFICE ACCESS 2007 ON DEMAND, 1st edition, 0789736411
by JOHNSON, STEVE; PERSPECTION, INC., published by Pearson Education, Inc, publishing as
Que/Sams, Copyright © 2007 Perspection, Inc.

This UK edition published by PEARSON EDUCATION LTD, Copyright © 2007

This edition is manufactured in the USA and available for sale only in the United Kingdom, Europe,
the Middle East and Africa

The right of Steve Johnson to be identified as author of this work has been asserted
by him in accordance with the Copyright, Designs and Patents Act 1988.

ISBN: 978-0-132-05854-4

British Library Cataloguing-in-Publication Data
A catalogue record for this book is available from the British Library

10 9 8 7 6 5 4 3 2 1
10 09 08 07 06

Printed and bound in the United States of America

The publisher's policy is to use paper manufactured from sustainable forests.

Brilliant Guides

What you need to know and how to do it

When you're working on your PC and come up against a problem that you're unsure how to solve, or want to accomplish something in an application that you aren't sure how to do, where do you look?? Manuals and traditional training guides are usually too big and unwieldy and are intended to be used as an end-to-end training resource, making it hard to get to the info you need right away without having to wade through pages of background information that you just don't need at that moment – and helplines are rarely that helpful!

Brilliant guides have been developed to allow you to find the info you need easily and without fuss and guide you through the task using a highly visual, step-by-step approach – providing exactly what you need to know when you need it!!

Brilliant guides provide the quick easy to-access information that you need, using a detailed index and troubleshooting guide to help you find exactly what you need to know, and then presenting each task on one or two pages. Numbered steps then guide you through each task or problem, using numerous screenshots to illustrate each step. Added features include "See Also ..." boxes that point you to related tasks and information in the book, whilst "Did you know?..." sections alert you to relevant expert tips, tricks and advice to further expand your skills and knowledge.

In addition to covering all major office PC applications, and related computing subjects, the *Brilliant* series also contains titles that will help you in every aspect of your working life, such as writing the perfect CV, answering the toughest interview questions and moving on in your career.

Brilliant guides are the light at the end of the tunnel when you are faced with any minor or major task!

a

Acknowledgements

Perspection, Inc.

Brilliant Microsoft Access 2007 has been created by the professional trainers and writers at Perspection, Inc.

Perspection, Inc. is a software training company committed to providing information and training to help people use software more effectively in order to communicate, make decisions, and solve problems. Perspection writes and produces software training books, and develops multimedia and Web-based training. Since 1991, we have written more than 80 computer books, with several bestsellers to our credit, and sold over 5 million books.

This book incorporates Perspection's training expertise to ensure that you'll receive the maximum return on your time. You'll focus on the tasks and skills that increase productivity while working at your own pace and convenience.

We invite you to visit the Perspection Web site at:

www.perspection.com

Acknowledgements

The task of creating any book requires the talents of many hard-working people pulling together to meet impossible deadlines and untold stresses. We'd like to thank the outstanding team responsible for making this book possible: the writer, Steve Johnson; the technical editor, Alex Williams; the production team, Emily Atwood, Alex Williams, and Dori Hernandez; the editors and proofreaders, Emily Atwood and Holly Johnson; and the indexer, Katherine Stimson.

At Que publishing, we'd like to thank Greg Wiegand and Stephanie McComb for the opportunity to undertake this project, Michelle Newcomb for administrative support, and Sandra Schroeder for your production expertise and support.

Perspection

About The Author

Steve Johnson has written more than thirty-five books on a variety of computer software, including Microsoft Office 2003 and XP, Microsoft Windows XP, Apple Mac OS X Panther, Macromedia Flash MX 2004 and 8, Macromedia Director MX 2004, Macromedia Fireworks, and Adobe Photoshop CS and CS2. In 1991, after working for Apple Computer and Microsoft, Steve founded Perspection, Inc., which writes and produces software training. When he is not staying up late writing, he enjoys playing golf, gardening, and spending time with his wife, Holly, and three children, JP, Brett, and Hannah. When time permits, he likes to travel to such places as New Hampshire in October, and Hawaii. Steve and his family live in Pleasanton, California, but can also be found visiting family all over the western United States.

Contents

C

11 Importing and Exporting Information 279

12 Managing a Database 303

Introduction

Welcome to *Brilliant Microsoft Access 2007*, a visual quick reference book that shows you how to work efficiently with Microsoft Office Access. This book provides complete coverage of basic to advanced Access skills.

How This Book Works

You don't have to read this book in any particular order. We've designed the book so that you can jump in, get the information you need, and jump out. However, the book does follow a logical progression from simple tasks to more complex ones. Each task is presented on no more than two facing pages, which lets you focus on a single task without having to turn the page. To find the information that you need, just look up the task in the table of contents or index, and turn to the page listed. Read the task introduction, follow the step-by-step instructions in the left column along with screen illustrations in the right column, and you're done.

What's New

If you're searching for what's new in Access 2007, just look for the icon: **New!**. The new icon appears in the table of contents and through out this book so you can quickly and easily identify a new or improved feature in Access 2007. A complete description of each new feature appears in the New Features guide in the back of this book.

Keyboard Shortcuts

Most menu commands have a keyboard equivalent, such as Ctrl+P, as a quicker alternative to using the mouse. A complete list of keyboard shortcuts is available on the Web at *www.perspection.com*.

i

How You'll Learn

How This Book Works

What's New

Keyboard Shortcuts

Step-by-Step Instructions

Real World Examples

Workshop

Microsoft Office Specialist

Get More on the Web

Step-by-Step Instructions

This book provides concise step-by-step instructions that show you "how" to accomplish a task. Each set of instructions include illustrations that directly correspond to the easy-to-read steps. Also included in the text are time-savers, tables, and sidebars to help you work more efficiently or to teach you more in-depth information. A "Did You Know?" provides tips and techniques to help you work smarter, while a "See Also" leads you to other parts of the book containing related information about the task.

Real World Examples

This book uses real world examples files to give you a context in which to use the task. By using the example files, you won't waste time looking for or creating sample files. You get a start file and a result file, so you can compare your work. Not every topic needs an example file, such as changing options, so we provide a complete list of the example files used through out the book. The example files that you need for project tasks along with a complete file list are available on the Web at *www.perspection.com*.

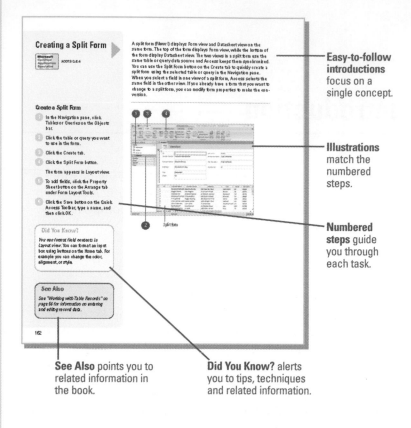

Easy-to-follow introductions focus on a single concept.

Illustrations match the numbered steps.

Numbered steps guide you through each task.

See Also points you to related information in the book.

Did You Know? alerts you to tips, techniques and related information.

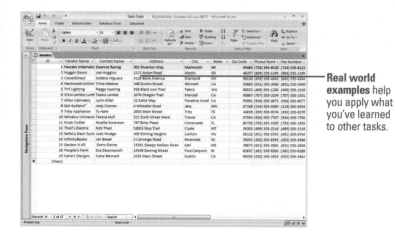

Real world examples help you apply what you've learned to other tasks.

Workshop

This book shows you how to put together the individual step-by-step tasks into indepth projects with the Workshop. You start each project with a sample file, work through the steps, and then compare your results with project results file at the end. The Workshop projects and associated files are available on the Web at *www.perspection.com.*

Workshop

Introduction

The Workshop is all about being creative and thinking outside of the box. These workshops will help your right-brain soar, while making your left-brain happy; by explaining why things work the way they do. Exploring possibilities is great fun; however, always stay grounded with knowledge of how things work.

Getting and Using the Project Files

Each project in the Workshop includes a start file to help you get started with the project, and a final file to provide you with the results of the project so you can see how well you accomplished the task.

Before you can use the project files, you need to download them from the Web. You can access the files at *www.perspection.com* in the software downloads area. After you download the files from the Web, uncompress the files into a folder on your hard drive to which you have easy access from your Microsoft Office program.

Project 1: Creating a Report with a Subreport

Skills and Tools: Create a report and add a subreport

A report is a summary of information from one or more tables. Reports allow you to include enhancements that a simple printout of records in a table would not provide. Within a report, you can add information from tables and queries. If you want to display additional information, you can add a subreport. The main report and the subreport provide separate information, yet they are displayed together. After you add information to a report, you can setup the page, add a header and footer, insert graphics and other related material, and format the page.

The Project

In this project, you'll learn how to create a comprehensive report, add a subreport, set up the page, add headers and footers, and then print out the report.

The Process

1. Open Access 2007, open Report_start.accdb, and then save it as Report_results.accdb.

The **Workshop** walks you through indepth projects to help you put Access to work.

Microsoft Certified Applications Specialist

This book prepares you for the Microsoft Certified Applications Specialist (MCAS) exam for Microsoft Office Access 2007. Each MCAS certification exam has a set of objectives, which are organized into broader skill sets. To prepare for the certification exam, you should review and perform each task identified with a MCAS objective to confirm that you can meet the requirements for the exam. Throughout this book, content that pertains to an objective is identified with the following MCAS logo and objective number next to it.

Microsoft Certified Applications Specialist

About the MCAS Program

The Microsoft Certified Applications Specialist (MCAS) certification is the globally recognized standard for validating expertise with the Microsoft Office suite of business productivity programs. Earning an MCAS certificate acknowledges you have the expertise to work with Microsoft Office programs. To earn the MCAS certification, you must pass a certification exam for the Microsoft Office desktop applications of Microsoft Office Word, Microsoft Office Excel, Microsoft Office PowerPoint, Microsoft Office Outlook, or Microsoft Office Access. (The availability of Microsoft Certified Applications Specialist certification exams varies by program, program version, and language. Visit *www.microsoft.com* and search on *Microsoft Certified Applications Specialist* for exam availability and more information about the program.) The Microsoft Certified Applications Specialist program is the only Microsoft-approved program in the world for certifying proficiency with Microsoft Office programs.

What Does This Logo Mean?

It means this book has been approved by the Microsoft Certified Applications Specialist program to be certified courseware for learning Microsoft Office Access 2007 and preparing for the certification exam. This book will prepare you for the Microsoft Certified Applications Specialist exam for Microsoft Office Access 2007. Each certification level has a set of objectives, which are organized into broader skill sets. Throughout this book, content that pertains to a Microsoft Certified Applications Specialist objective is identified with the following MCAS certification logo and objective number below the title of the topic:

Microsoft Certified Application Specialist	ACO7S-1.1 ACO7S-2.2

Logo indicates a task fulfills one or more MCAS certification objectives.

Get More on the Web

In addition to the information in this book, you can also get more information on the Web to help you get up to speed faster with Access 2007. Some of the information includes:

Transition Helpers

◆ **Only New Features.**
Download and print the new feature tasks as a quick and easy guide.

Productivity Tools

◆ **Keyboard Shortcuts.**
Download a list of keyboard shortcuts to learn faster ways to get the job done.

More Content

◆ **Photographs.** Download photographs and other graphics to use in your Office documents.

◆ **More Content.** Download new content developed after publication. For example, you can download a complete chapter on Office SharePoint Server 2007.

You can access these additional resources on the Web at *www.perspection.com*.

Working Together on Office SharePoint Documents

S

Introduction

Microsoft Windows SharePoint Services is a collection of products and services which provide the ability for people to engage in communication, document and file sharing, calendar events, sending alerts, tasks planning, and collaborative discussions in a single community solution.

Office SharePoint Server 2007 is a product that uses Windows SharePoint Services 3.0 or later technology to work effectively with Microsoft Office 2007 programs. You can create a slide library on a Office SharePoint site in PowerPoint 2007 (New!), use Office SharePoint list data to create reports in Access 2007, create a meeting workspace and synchronize calendar and contacts in Outlook 2007, design browser form templates in InfoPath 2007 (New!), and save worksheets on an Office SharePoint site in Excel 2007. In many of the Office 2007 programs, you can update properties for a server document in a Document Information Panel (New!), and participate in workflows (New!), which is the automated movement of documents or items through a sequence of actions or tasks, such as document approval.

Office 2007 programs use the Document Management task pane to access many Office SharePoint Server 2007 features. The Document Management task pane allows you to see the list of team members collaborating on the current project, find out who is online, send an e-mail message, and review tasks and other resources. You can also use the Document Management task pane to create document workspaces where you can collect, organize, modify, share, and discuss Office documents.

Before you can use Office SharePoint Server 2007 the software needs to be set up and configured on a Windows 2003 Server or later by your network administrator. You can view Office SharePoint Server sites using a Web browser or a mobile device (New!) while you're on the road.

What You'll Do

View and Navigate Office SharePoint Sites

Create a Document Workspace Site

Create a Document Library Site

Add and Upload Documents to a Site

Add Pages to a Site

Publish Slides to a Library

Saving a File to a Document Management Server

View Versions of Documents

Check Documents In and Out to Edit

Work with Shared Workspace

View Team Members

Create Lists

Create Events

Hold Web Discussions

Set Up Alerts

Customize Quick Launch or Top Link Bar

1

Additional content is available on the Web. You can download a chapter on SharePoint.

Getting Started with Access

Introduction

Microsoft Office Access 2007 is a database program that allows you to:

- Store an almost limitless amount of information.
- Organize information in a way that makes sense for how you work.
- Retrieve information based on selection criteria you specify.
- Create forms that make it easier to enter information.
- Generate meaningful and insightful reports that can combine data, text, graphics, and other objects.

Microsoft Office Access 2007 helps you start working with databases right away by providing template database applications you can use to store your own personal or business data. Access also offers a few samples that aid you in creating common business databases. These sample databases may give you some ideas for designing your own database for storing types of data not covered by the existing databases.

When you are working with an existing database, however, you don't need to worry about the complexities of database design. You just need to know how to move around the database you are using. The tasks that you are likely to perform with an existing database include entering and viewing data or subsets of data, creating and printing reports, and working efficiently with all the windows in front of you.

Understanding How Databases Store Data

Storing Data on a Computer

Some lists can serve a much more useful purpose when stored on a computer. For example, the names, addresses, and phone numbers you jot down on cards or in a paper address book are only used when you have the paper list in your hand. Suppose you currently store names and addresses on cards. All the information about a particular person is stored in one place.

If you store that list on a computer, however, you can do much more with it than just refer to it. For example, you can generate lists of your most important phone numbers to put next to every phone in the house, you can print mailing labels for greeting cards, you can create lists of this month's birthdays, and so on.

There are a number of ways to store lists on a computer. For example, you can store a list in a Microsoft Word table or on a Microsoft Excel spreadsheet.

If you place this information in a Word table or on an Excel spreadsheet, you are faced with a problem; you end up repeating some of the information. Consider what happens if a family moves or a last name is changed. You have to ensure that information is updated everywhere it's stored. For a small list that might not matter, but for a large list with information that requires constant updating (such as an address list), it is a huge task to keep data up-to-date in this way.

Storing Data in a Database

If, on the other hand, you save address information in an Access database, you can ensure that each piece of information is entered only once.

An Access database consists of objects, such as tables, forms, queries, reports, pages, macros, and modules.

- A **table** is a collection of related information about a topic, such as names and addresses. A table consists of fields and records. A field stores each piece of information in a table, such as first name, last name, or address. A record is a collection of all the fields for one person.

- A **form** provides an easy way to view and enter information into a database. Typically, forms display one record at a time.

- A **query** is a method to find information in a database. The information you find with a query is based on conditions you specify.

- **Reports** are documents that summarize information from the database.

- **Pages** enable you to access a database on the Internet using a Web browser; only backwards compatible for Access 2003 databases; not available in Access 2007.

- A **macro** saves you time by automating a series of actions into one action.

- **Modules** are programs you create in a programming language called Visual Basic for Applications (VBA), which extend the functionality of a database.

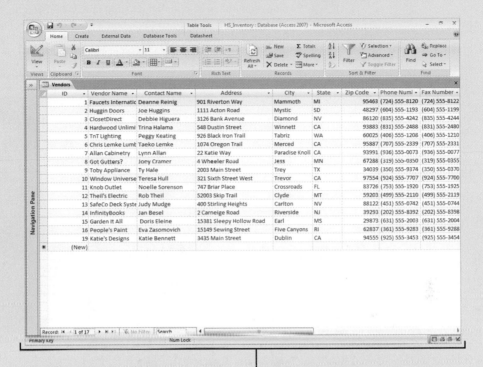

A database table with fields and records

Frequently Asked Questions

What is a Microsoft Access Project?

A Microsoft Office Access project is an Access data file (.adp) that provides access to a Microsoft SQL Server database through the OLE DB component architecture, which provides network and Internet access to many types of data sources. An Access project is called a project because it contains only code-based or HTML-based database objects: forms, reports, macros, and modules. Unlike an Access database, an Access project doesn't contain any data or data objects, such as tables, views, database diagrams, stored procedures, or user-defined functions. Working with an Access project is virtually the same as working with an Access database, except you need to connect to an SQL Server database, which stores the data. To create a new Access project, click the Office button, click Blank Database, click the Browse button (folder icon), type a name, click the Save as type list arrow, click Microsoft Office Access Project (*.adp), click OK, and then click Create.

Starting Access

You can start Access from the Start menu or the desktop. When you're choosing how to start Access, you need to decide if you want to create a new database or open an existing one. When you open Access from the Start menu, you make this choice from within Access. The Getting Started with Microsoft Office Access 2007 dialog box (**New!**) opens, displaying templates and recently opened databases.

Start Access from the Start Menu

1 Click the **Start** button on the taskbar.

2 Point to **All Programs**.

3 Click **Microsoft Office**.

4 Click **Microsoft Office Access 2007**.

If Microsoft Office asks you to activate the program, follow the instructions to complete the process.

TIMESAVER *To activate Microsoft Office later, click the Office button, click Access Options, click Resources, and then click Activate.*

If a Privacy dialog box appears, select the options you want, and then click OK.

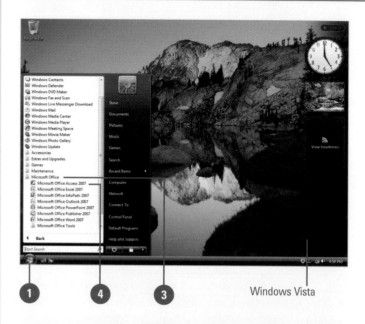

Windows Vista

Did You Know?

You can create a program shortcut from the Start menu to the desktop. Click the Start menu, point to All Programs, click Microsoft Office, right-click Microsoft Office Access 2007, point to Send To, and then click Desktop (Create Shortcut).

You can start Access and open a database from Windows Explorer. Double-clicking any Access database icon in Windows Explorer opens that file and Access.

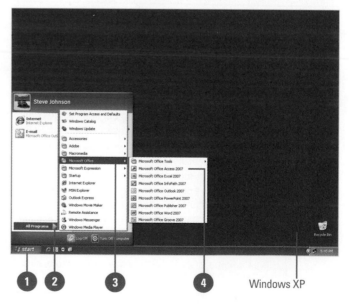

Windows XP

Get Started with Microsoft Office Access

1. Start Access, or click the **Office** button and then click **New**.

   The Getting Started with Microsoft Office Access 2007 dialog box (**New!**) opens, displaying templates and recently opened databases.

2. In the left pane, click a category.

3. Click an icon with the type of database you want to create.

4. Click the **Browse** button, click the **Save in** list arrow, select the location where you want to save the new database, select an Access database format, and then click **OK**.

5. Type in a name for the database.

6. Click **Create** or **Download**.

7. To close the database, click the **Close** button in the database window or click the **Office** button, and then click **Close Database**.

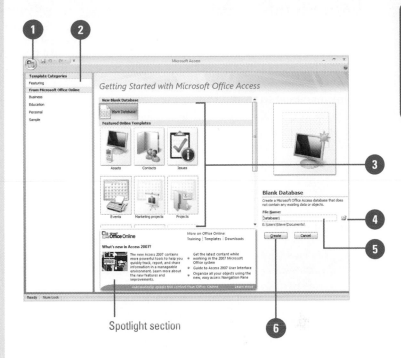

Spotlight section

Did You Know?

You can open a database from the Getting Started window. Click the Office button, click Open, select a location and a database file, and then click Open.

For Your Information

Getting Content from Microsoft Office Online

You can quickly access training, templates, and downloads from Microsoft Office Online in the Spotlight (**New!**) section of the Getting Started with Microsoft Office Access 2007 window. The Spotlight section highlights new content, which you can set to automatically update. When you click a link, Access opens your Web browser and displays the spotlight content on the Microsoft Office Online Web site.

Using the Ribbon

The **Ribbon** (New!) is a new look for Office 2007. It replaces menus, toolbars, and most of the task panes found in Office 2003. The Ribbon is located at the top of the document window and is comprised of **tabs** (New!) that are organized by task or objects. The controls on each tab are organized into **groups,** or sub-tasks. The controls, or **command buttons,** in each group execute a command, or display a menu of commands or a drop-down gallery. Controls in each group provide a visual way to quickly make document changes.

> **TIMESAVER** *To minimize the Ribbon, double-click the name of the tab that is displayed, or click the Customize Quick Access Toolbar list arrow, and then click Minimize the Ribbon. Click a tab to auto display it (Ribbon remains minimized). Double-click a tab to maximize it.*

If you prefer using the keyboard instead of the mouse to access commands on the Ribbon, Microsoft Office provides easy to use shortcuts. Simply press and release the [Alt] or [F10] key to display **KeyTips** (New!) over each feature in the current view, and then continue to press the letter shown in the KeyTip until you press the one that you want to use. To cancel an action and hide the KeyTips, press and release the [Alt] or [F10] key again. If you prefer using the keyboard shortcuts found in previous versions of Microsoft Office, such as Ctrl+P (for Print), all the keyboard shortcuts and keyboard accelerators work exactly the same in Microsoft Office 2007. Office 2007 includes a legacy mode that you can turn on to use familiar Office 2003 keyboard accelerators.

Tabs

Office provides three types of tabs on the Ribbon. The first type is called a **standard** tab—such as Home, Insert, Review, View, and Add-Ins—that you see whenever you start Office. The second type is called a **contextual** tab—such as Picture Tools, Drawing, or Table—that appears only when they are needed based on the type of task you are doing. Office recognizes what you're doing and provides the right set of tabs and tools to use when you need them. The third type is called a **program** tab—such as Print Preview—that replaces the standard set of tabs when you switch to certain views or modes.

Key Tip   Standard tabs   Contextual tab

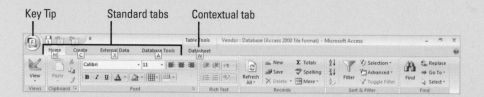

Choosing Commands

The Access commands are organized in groups on the Ribbon, Office menu (**New!**), Quick Access Toolbar, and Mini-Toolbar. The Office button opens to display file related menu commands, while the Quick Access Toolbar and Mini-Toolbar display frequently used buttons that you may be already familiar with from Access 2003. In addition to the Office menu, you can also open a **shortcut menu** with a group of related commands by right-clicking an Access element.

Choose a Command from the Office Menu

1 Click the **Office** button on the Ribbon.

2 Click the command you want.

If the command is followed by an arrow, point to the arrow to see a list of related options, and then click the option you want.

TIMESAVER *You can use a shortcut key to choose a command. Press and hold down the first key and then press the second key. For example, press and hold the Ctrl key and then press S (or Ctrl+S) to select the Save command.*

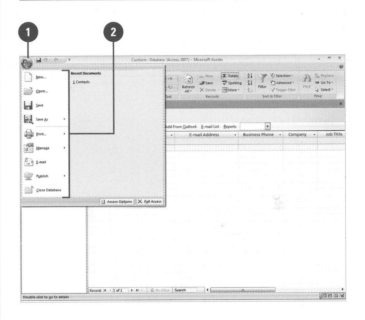

Choose a Command from a Shortcut Menu

1 Right-click an object or element.

TIMESAVER *Press Shift+F10 to display the shortcut menu for a selected command.*

2 Click a command on the shortcut menu. If the command is followed by an arrow, point to the command to see a list of related options, and then click the option you want.

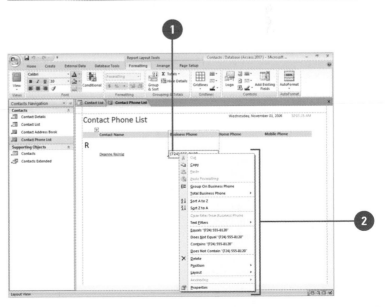

Working with Toolbars

Office includes its most common commands, such as Save and Undo, on the **Quick Access Toolbar (New!)**. Click a toolbar button to choose a command. If you are not sure what a toolbar button does, point to it to display a ScreenTip. When an Office program starts, the Quick Access Toolbar appears at the top of the window, unless you've changed your settings. You can customize the toolbar by adding command buttons or groups to it. You can also move the toolbar below or above the Ribbon so it's right where you need it. In addition to the Quick Access Toolbar, Office also displays the Mini-Toolbar when you point to selected text. The **Mini-Toolbar (New!)** appears above the selected text and provides quick access to formatting tools.

Choose a Command Using a Toolbar or Ribbon

◆ **Get command help**. If you're not sure what a button does, point to it to display a ScreenTip. If the ScreenTip includes *Press F1 for more help*, press F1.

◆ **Choose a command**. Click the button, or button arrow, and then click a command or option.

ScreenTip

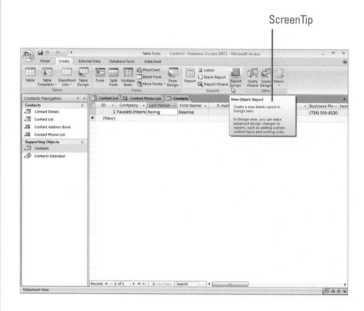

Did You Know?

You can move the Quick Access Toolbar to another location. Click the Customize Quick Access Toolbar list arrow, and then click Show Below the Ribbon or Show Above the Ribbon.

You can turn off or change ScreenTips. Click the Office button, click Access Options, click Popular, click the ScreenTip Scheme list arrow, click Don't show feature descriptions in ScreenTips or Don't show ScreenTips, and then click OK.

You can reset the Quick Access Toolbar to its original state. In the Options dialog box, click Customize, click Reset, and then click OK.

You can minimize the Ribbon. Click the Customize Quick Access Toolbar list arrow, and then click Minimize the Ribbon. Click a tab to maximize it.

Add or Remove Items from the Quick Access Toolbar

◆ **Add or remove a common button.**
Click the **Customize Quick Access Toolbar** list arrow, and then click a button name (checked item appears on the toolbar).

◆ **Add a Ribbon button or group.**
Right-click the button or group name on the Ribbon, and then click **Add to Quick Access Toolbar**.

◆ **Remove a button or group.** Right-click the button or group name on the Quick Access Toolbar, and then click **Remove from Quick Access Toolbar**.

Customize the Quick Access Toolbar

1️⃣ Click the **Customize Quick Access Toolbar** list arrow, and then click **More Commands**.

2️⃣ Click the **Choose commands from** list arrow, and then click **All Commands** or a specific Ribbon.

3️⃣ Click the **Customize Quick Access Toolbar** list arrow, and then click **For all documents (default)**.

Select the current document if you only want the commands available in the document.

4️⃣ Click the command you want to add (left column) or remove (right column), and then click **Add** or **Remove**.

TIMESAVER *Click <Separator>, and then click Add to insert a separator line between buttons.*

5️⃣ Click the **Move Up** and **Move Down** arrow buttons to arrange the order.

6️⃣ Click **OK**.

Customize Quick Access Toolbar list arrow   Click to add or remove frequently used buttons

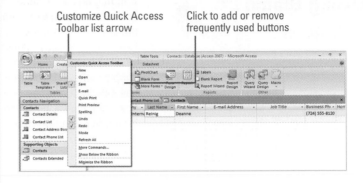

Right-click to add a button or group

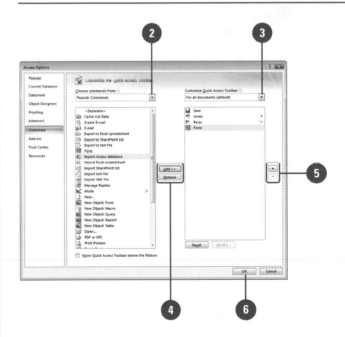

Choosing Dialog Box Options

A **dialog box** is a window that opens when you click a Dialog Box Launcher. **Dialog Box Launchers** (**New!**) are small icons that appear at the bottom corner of some groups. When you point to a Dialog Box Launcher, a ScreenTip with a thumbnail of the dialog box appears to show you which dialog box opens (**New!**). A dialog box allows you to supply more information before the program carries out the command you selected. After you enter information or make selections in a dialog box, click the OK button to complete the command. Click the Cancel button to close the dialog box without issuing the command. In many dialog boxes, you can also click an Apply button to apply your changes without closing the dialog box.

Choose Dialog Box Options

All dialog boxes contain the same types of options, including the following:

- **Tabs**. Each tab groups a related set of options. Click a tab to display its options.

- **Option buttons**. Click an option button to select it. You can usually select only one.

- **Up and down arrows**. Click the up or down arrow to increase or decrease the number, or type a number in the box.

- **Check box**. Click the box to turn on or off the option. A checked box means the option is selected; a cleared box means it's not.

- **List box**. Click the list arrow to display a list of options, and then click the option you want.

- **Text box**. Click in the box and type the requested information.

- **Button**. Click a button to perform a specific action or command. A button name followed by an ellipsis (...) opens another dialog box.

- **Preview box**. Many dialog boxes show an image that reflects the options you select.

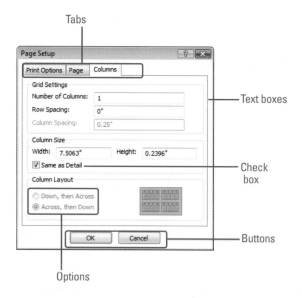

Using the Status Bar

The **Status bar** appears across the bottom of your screen and displays document information—such as cell mode, Office theme name, and current display zoom percentage—and some Office program controls, such as view shortcut buttons, zoom slider, and Fit To Window button. With the click of the mouse, you can quickly customize exactly what you see on the Status bar (**New!**). In addition to displaying information, the Status bar also allows you to check the on/off status of certain features (**New!**), such as Filtered, Extended Selection, View Shortcuts, Caps Lock, Num Lock, Scroll Lock, and much more.

Add or Remove Items from the Status Bar

◆ **Add Item**. Right-click the Status bar, and then click an unchecked item.

◆ **Remove Item**. Right-click the Status bar, and then click a checked item.

Did You Know?

You can show or hide the Status bar for the current database. Click the Office button, click Access Options, click Current Database in the left pane, select or clear the Display Status Bar check box, and then click OK.

You can show or hide the Status bar for all databases. Click the Office button, click Access Options, click Advanced in the left pane, select or clear the Status bar check box, and then click OK.

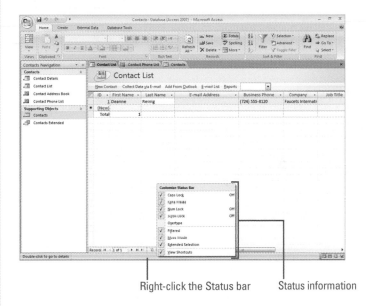

Right-click the Status bar   Status information

Creating a Database

Microsoft
Certified
Application
Specialist

AC07S-2.1.1,
AC07S-2.1.2

You can use a template to create a database, or you can create a custom database from scratch. The Access database templates help you create databases suited to your specific needs. Each template provides a complete out-of-the-box database with predefined fields, tables, queries, reports, and forms. If you need a custom database, you create a blank database, and then you can create the tables, forms, and reports that make up the inner parts of the database. When you create a database, you need to assign a name and location to your database. You can save an Access database in the .mdb format (for Access 2000 or 2002-2003) or .accdb format (for Access 2007) (**New!**).

Create a Blank Database

1 Start Access, or click the **Office** button and then click **New**.

The Getting Started with Microsoft Office Access 2007 dialog box (**New!**) opens, displaying templates and recently opened databases.

2 In the left pane, click **Featuring**.

3 Click **Blank Database**.

4 Click the **Browse** button, click the **Save in** list arrow, select the location where you want to save the new database, select an Access database format, and then click **OK**.

5 Type in a name for the database.

6 Click **Create**.

7 To close the database, click the **Close** button in the database window or click the **Office** button, and then click **Close Database**.

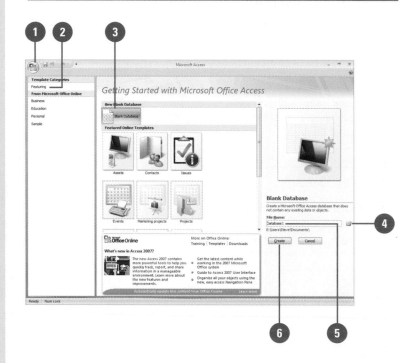

Did You Know?

You can open a sample database. Click the Office button, click New, click Sample in the left pane, click a sample database from the list, and then click Create or Download.

Create a Database Using a Template

1. Start Access, or click the **Office** button and then click **New**.

   The Getting Started with Office Access 2007 dialog box opens, displaying templates and recently opened databases.

2. In the left pane, click a template category.

3. Click the template you want.

4. Click the **Browse** button, click the **Save in** list arrow, select the location where you want to save the new database, select an Access database format, and then click **OK**.

5. Type in a name for the database.

6. Click **Create** or **Download** for those on the Web.

7. If a security warning appears, click **Options**, click the **Enable this content** option, and then click **OK**.

8. To close the database, click the **Close** button in the database window or click the **Office** button, and then click **Close Database**.

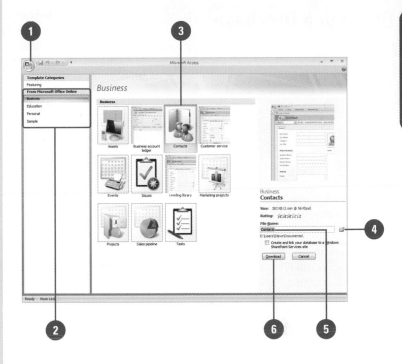

Did You Know?

You can open Access with the last used database. Click the Office button, click Access Options, click Advanced in the left pane, select the Open last used database when Access starts check box, and then click OK.

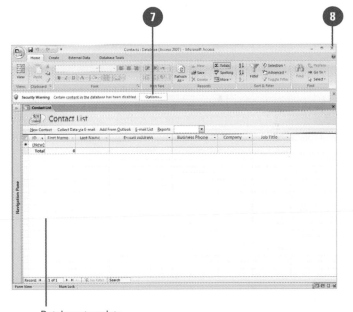

Database template

Opening a Database

Microsoft Certified Application Specialist

AC07S-6.1.1

You can open an Access database and start Office simultaneously, or you can open an Access database or file created in another program after you start an Office program. You can open an existing Access database by using the Office button. On the Office menu, you can choose the Open command to locate and select the document you want, or choose a recently used database from the Recent Documents list. Access shows the last nine databases (by default) in the Recent Documents list. If you want to change the number, you can make a change on the Advanced pane in Access Options.

Open a Database

1. Click the **Office** button, and then click **Open**, or click a recently used document.

2. If you want to open a specific file type, click the **Files of type** list arrow, and then click a file type.

3. If the file is located in another folder, click the **Look In** list arrow, and then navigate to the file.

4. Click the database file you want, and then click **Open**.

   ◆ To open a database in exclusive mode, click the Open button arrow, and then click Open Exclusive. This disables sharing and allows you to perform many database management functions.

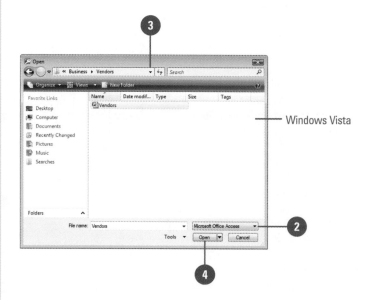

Windows Vista

See Also

See "Warnings About Macros and Add-Ins" on page 31 for information on security alerts that appear when you open a database.

See "Opening a Sample Database" on page 30 for information on opening the Northwind sample database.

See "Locking Database Records" on page 332 for information on opening a database using shared or exclusive mode.

Open a Recently Opened Database

1 Click the **Office** button.

2 Click the Access database you want to open on the Office menu.

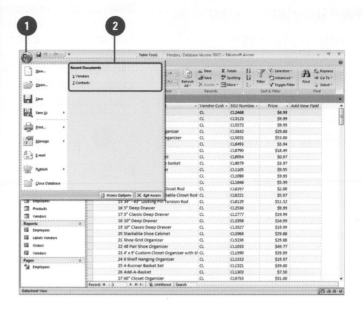

Did You Know?

You can change the number of recently opened files that appear on the Office menu. Click the Office button, click Access Options, click Advanced in the left pane, change the Show this number of Recent Documents box, and then click OK.

You can change the default file location of the Open dialog box. Click the Office button, click Access Options, click Popular in the left pane, enter a new location in the Default File Location box, and then click OK.

You can delete or rename a file in a dialog box. In the Open or Save As dialog box, right-click the file, and then click Delete or Rename.

You can move or copy a file quickly in a dialog box. In the Open or Save As dialog box, right-click the file you want to move or copy, click Cut or Copy, open the folder where you want to paste the file, right-click a blank area, and then click Paste.

Converting an Existing Database

When you open a database from Access 2000 or 2002-2003, Access 2007 goes into a compatibility mode (**New!**) where it disables new features that cannot be displayed or converted well by previous versions. When you save a database, Access 2007 saves Access 2000 or 2002-2003 files in their original format. The database stays in the original file format until you convert it to the Access 2007 file format.

Convert a Access 2000 or 2002 - 2003 Database to Access 2007

1. Open the Access 2000 or 2002-2003 database you want to convert to the Access 2007 file format

   The Access 2000 or 2002-2003 database opens in compatibility mode.

2. Click the **Office** button, and then click **Convert**.

3. Click **OK** to convert the file to new Access 2007 format.

   Access exits compatibility mode, which is only turned on when a previous version is in use.

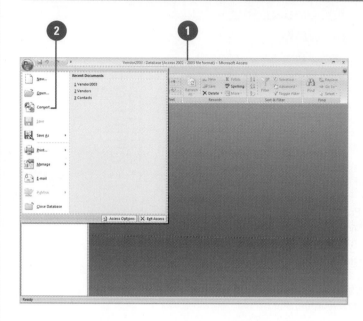

Did You Know?

You can display extensions in the Save and Open dialog boxes and Recent Documents list. Changing the Windows option using the Control Panel (Folder icon) also changes Access. In the Folder Options dialog box on the View tab, clear the Hide extensions for known file types check box.

Viewing the Access Window

When you open a database, the Access program window opens and displays a new look tab-based user interface, the Navigation pane and a switchboard (if available) for the database. The **Navigation pane** (**New!**) displays database objects. A **switchboard** is a window that gives easy access to the most common actions a database user might need to take.

Parts of the Access Window

◆ The **database title bar** displays the name of the open database and the database version.

◆ The **Ribbon** (**New!**) contains tabs that represent groups of related commands.

◆ The **Quick Access Toolbar** (**New!**) displays the most needed buttons that you can click to carry out commands.

◆ The **Navigation pane** (**New!**) displays data base objects, which replaces the Database window from earlier versions of Access.

◆ The **tabbed documents** (**New!**) displays tables, queries, forms, reports, and macros.

◆ The **View selector** (**New!**) displays view buttons.

◆ The **Status bar** displays information about the items you click or the actions you take.

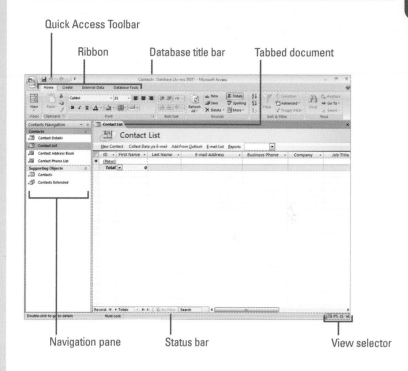

Quick Access Toolbar

Ribbon · Database title bar · Tabbed document

Navigation pane · Status bar · View selector

Did You Know?

You can customize Access startup. Click the Office button, click Access Options, click Current Database in the left pane, set the options you want under Applications Options, and then click OK. Close and open the database to see the new startup.

Arranging Windows

When you want to work with information in a database, or move or copy information between databases or programs, it's easier to move windows out of the way or display several windows at once. You can use the sizing button on the title bar or the pointer to resize and move windows around for easier viewing. You can also arrange two or more windows, from within Access or from different programs, on the screen at the same time.

Resize and Move a Window

All windows contain the same sizing buttons and mouse functionality:

◆ **Restore Down button**. Click to reduce a maximized window to a reduced size.

◆ **Maximize button**. Click to make a window fill the entire screen.

◆ **Minimize button**. Click to shrink a window to a taskbar button. To restore the window to its previous size, click the taskbar button.

◆ **Close button**. Click to shut a window.

◆ **Mouse pointer**. Position the pointer over the edge of a window (changes to a two-headed arrow), and drag to resize a window.

All windows contain a title bar which you can use to quickly move a window using the mouse:

◆ **Mouse pointer**. Position the pointer over the title bar of the window you want to move, and then Drag the window to a new location.

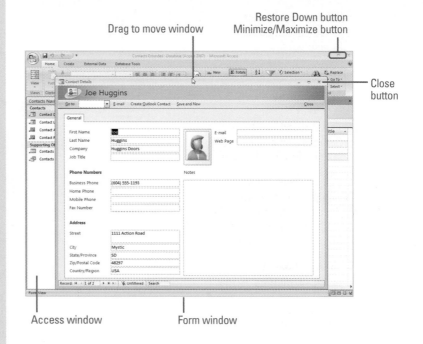

Drag to move window

Restore Down button
Minimize/Maximize button

Close button

Access window

Form window

Using Task and Window Panes

Task panes are separate windows that appear when you need them, such as Field List, or when you click a Dialog Box Launcher icon (**New!**), such as Clipboard. A task pane displays various options that relate to the current task. **Window panes** are sections of a window, such as the Navigation pane. If you need a larger work area, you can use the Close button in the upper-right corner of the pane to close a pane, move a border edge to resize a pane, or use the Shutter Bar Open/Close button to minimize a window pane (**New!**).

Work with Task and Window Panes

◆ **Open a Task Pane**. It appears when you need it or when you click a Dialog Box Launcher icon.

◆ **Close a Task or Window Pane**. Click the Close button in the upper-right corner of the pane.

◆ **Resize a Task Pane or Window Pane**. Point to the pane border edge until the pointer changes to double arrows, then drag the edge to resize it.

◆ **Minimize and Maximize a Window Pane**. Click the Shutter Bar Open/Close button (double arrows) in the upper right corner of the Window pane.

Click to open task pane

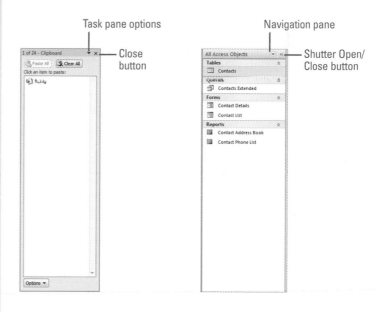

Task pane options

Navigation pane

Close button

Shutter Open/Close button

Getting Help While You Work

At some time, everyone has a question or two about the program they are using. The Office Help Viewer provides the answers and resources you need, including feature help, articles, tips, templates, training, and downloads. You can also access end-user and developer help (**New!**) from the same Help viewer window. By connecting to Microsoft Office Online, you not only have access to standard product help information, but you also have access to updated information over the Web without leaving the Help Viewer. The Web browser-like Help Viewer allows you to browse an extensive catalog of topics using a table of contents to locate information, or ask a question or enter phrases to search for specific information. When you use any of these help options, a list of possible answers is shown to you with the most likely answer or most frequently-used at the top of the list.

Using the Help Viewer to Get Answers

1 Click the **Help** button on the Ribbon.

> **TIMESAVER** *Press F1.*

2 Locate the Help topic you want.

- ◆ Click a Help category on the home page, and then click a topic (? icon).

- ◆ Click the **Table of Contents** button on the toolbar, click a help category (book icon) and then click a topic (? icon).

3 Read the topic, and then click any links to get Help information.

4 Click the **Back**, **Forward**, **Stop**, **Refresh**, and **Home** buttons on the toolbar to move around in the Help Viewer.

5 If you want to print the topic, click the **Print** button on the toolbar.

6 To keep the Help Viewer window (not maximized) on top or behind, click to toggle the **Keep On Top** button (pin pushed in) and **Not On Top** button (pin not pushed in) on the toolbar.

7 When you're done, click the **Close** button.

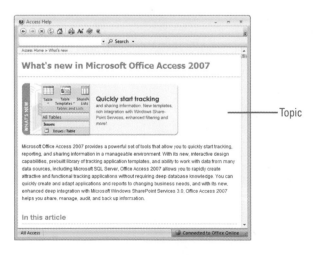

Topic

Search for Help

1. Click the **Help** button on the Ribbon.

2. Click the **Search button** list arrow below the toolbar, and then select the location and type of information you want.

3. Type one or more keywords in the Search For box, and then click the **Search** button.

4. Click a topic.

5. Read the topic, and then click any links to get information on related topics or definitions.

6. When you're done, click the **Close** button.

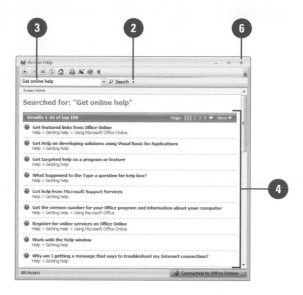

Check Help Connection Status

1. Click the **Help** button on the Ribbon.

2. Click the Connection Status at the bottom of the Help Viewer.

3. Click the connection option where you want to get help information:

   ◆ **Show content from Office Online** to get help from this computer and the internet (online).

   ◆ **Show content only from this computer** to get help from this computer only (offline).

   This setting is maintained for all Office 2007 program Help Viewers.

4. When you're done, click the **Close** button.

Saving a Database

Microsoft
Certified
Application
Specialist   AC07S-6.1.4

When you create an Access database, save it as a file on your computer so you can work with it later. When you want to save a copy of a database or change the database file format, use the Save As command. When you want to save the currently open database in the same format, use the Save button on the Quick Access Toolbar. When you save a document, Office Access 2007 saves 2000 or 2002-2003 files (.mdb) in their older format and 2007 files in a new format (.accdb) (**New!**). Access 2000 or 2002-2003 databases stays in their original file format until you convert it to the new 2007 file format.

Save a Database for Access 2007

1 Click the **Office** button, and then click **Save As**.

If necessary, click **Yes** to close any open tables.

TIMESAVER *Press Ctrl+S, or click the Office button, point to Save As, and then click the specific file format you want.*

2 Click the **Save in** list arrow, and then click the drive or folder where you want to save the file.

3 Type a document file name.

4 Click the **Save as type** list arrow, and then click **Microsoft Office Access 2007 Database**.

5 Click **Save**.

See Also

See "Saving a Database Object" on page 302 for information on making a copy of a database object or converting a database object to another type.

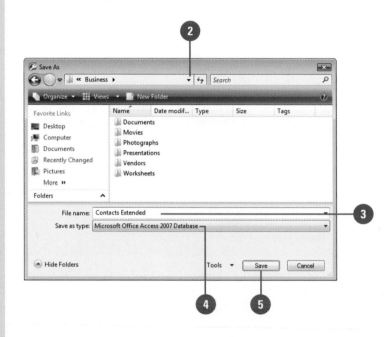

Access 2007 File Extensions

File Extension	Description
.accdb	The Office Access 2007 file format. This replaces .mdb
.accde	File format used in "execute only" mode. You can only execute VBA code, not modify it. This replaces .mde
.accdt	File format for Access Database templates
.accdr	File format used to open a database in runtime mode. By changing the file extension, from .accdb to .accdr you can create a locked database file. You can change the file extension back to .accdb to restore full functionality.

Save an Access 2000 or 2002 - 2003 Database in the Same Version

1. Open the Access 2000 or 2002-2003 database you want to continue to save in the same format.

   The database opens.

2. Click the **Save** button on the Quick Access Toolbar.

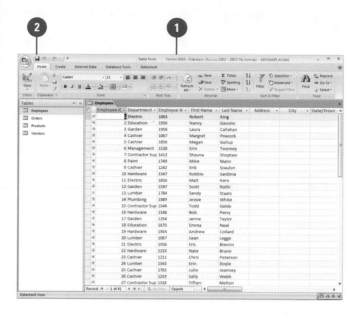

Set Save Options

1. Click the **Office** button, and then click **Access Options**.

2. In the left pane, click **Popular**.

3. Set the save options you want:

   ◆ **Default Save Format.** Click Save files in this format list arrow, and then click the default format you want.

   You need to close and reopen the current database for the option to take effect.

   ◆ **Default File Location.** Specify the complete path to the folder location where you want to save your document.

4. Click **OK**.

Saving a Database with Different Formats

Microsoft Certified Application Specialist

AC07S-6.1.4

Access 2007 allows you to save your database in previous Access file format versions. For example, you might want to save a database in an earlier 2000 or 2002-2003 version in case the people you work with have not upgraded to Office 2007. If you save a database to 2000 or 2002-2003 version (.mdb), some new features including attachments, multivalued fields, offline data and links to external data, are not supported by the new file format (.accdb). You can also use the Getting Started with Microsoft Office Access window (**New!**) to create a new database with different formats. In the window, you can use the Browse button (Folder icon) to select another format.

Save a Database with Different Formats

1. Click the **Office** button, point to **Save As**, and then click **Access 2000 Database** or **Access 2002 - 2003 Database**.

   If necessary, click **Yes** to close any open tables.

2. Click the **Save in** list arrow, and then click the drive or folder where you want to save the file.

3. Type a file name.

4. If necessary, click the **Save as type** list arrow, and then click the file format you want.

5. Click **Save**.

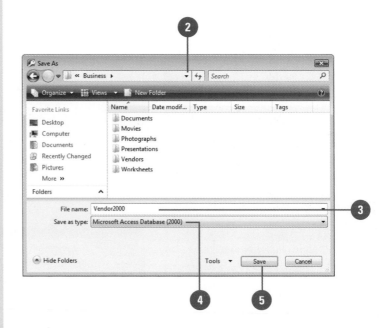

See Also

See "Creating a PDF Document" on page 300 or "Creating an XPS Document" on page 301 for information on using and saving a file with different formats.

Getting Updates on the Web

Access offers a quick and easy way to update Access with any new software downloads that improve the stability and security of the program. From the Resources area in the Options dialog box, simply click the Check for Updates button to connect to the Microsoft Update Web site to have your computer scanned for necessary updates, and then choose which Office updates you want to download and install.

Get Access Updates on the Web

1. Click the **Office** button, and then click **Access Options**.

2. In the left pane, click **Resources**.

3. Click **Check for Updates** to open the Microsoft Update Web site.

4. Click one of the update buttons to find out if you need updates, and then choose the updates you want to download and install.

Did You Know?

You can contact Microsoft for help. You can get support over the phone, chat, or e-mail messages. To get online help, click the Office button, click Access Options, click Resources in the left pane, and then click Contact Us. To get offline help, click the Office button, click Access Options, click Resources, click About, and then click Tech Support for contact information.

You can get better help information. At the bottom of a help topic, click Yes, No, or I don't know to give Microsoft feedback on the usefulness of a topic.

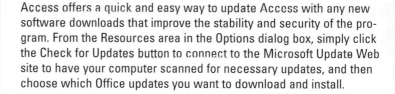

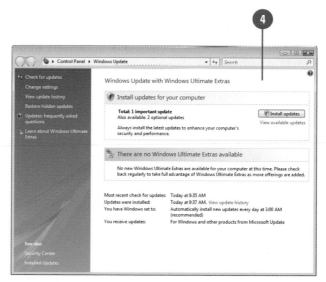

Diagnosing and Repairing Problems

At times you may determine that Access is not working as efficiently as it once did. This sometimes happens when you install new software or move files into new folders. Use the Diagnose command (**New!**) to improve performance by repairing problems, such as missing files from setup, corrupted file by malicious viruses, and registry settings. Note that this feature does not repair personal files like documents, presentations, or databases. If the Diagnose command does not fix the problem, you might have to reinstall Access. If you need to add or remove features, reinstall Access, or remove it entirely, you can use Office Setup's maintenance feature.

Diagnose and Repair Problems

1. Click the **Office** button, and then click **Access Options**.

2. In the left pane, click **Resources**.

3. Click **Diagnose**.

   TIMESAVER *In Windows, click Start, point to All Programs, click Microsoft Office, click Microsoft Office Tools, and then click Microsoft Office Diagnostics.*

4. Click **Continue**, and then click **Run Diagnostics**.

   Office runs diagnostics to determine and fix any problems. A report appears in your browser:

   ◆ **Setup.** Checks for corrupt files and registry settings.

   ◆ **Disk.** Checks error logs.

   ◆ **Memory.** Checks integrity of computer RAM.

   ◆ **Update.** Checks for Office updates on the Web.

   ◆ **Compatibility.** Checks for conflicts with Outlook.

   ◆ **Check for known solutions.** Checks data on Office program crashes on your computer.

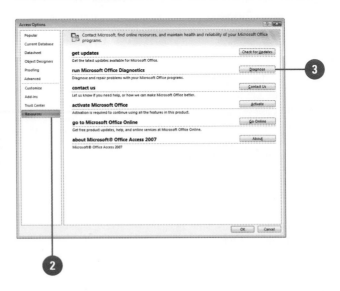

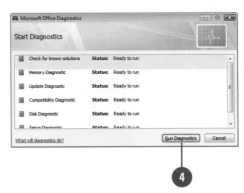

Perform Maintenance on Office Programs

1 Insert the Office CD in your drive.

2 In Windows Explorer, double-click the Setup icon on the Office CD.

3 Click one of the following maintenance buttons.

◆ **Add or Remove Features** to change which features are installed or remove specific features.

◆ **Repair** to reinstall or repair Microsoft Office 2007 to its original state.

◆ **Remove** to uninstall Microsoft Office 2007 from this computer.

4 Click **Continue**, and then follow the wizard instructions to complete the maintenance.

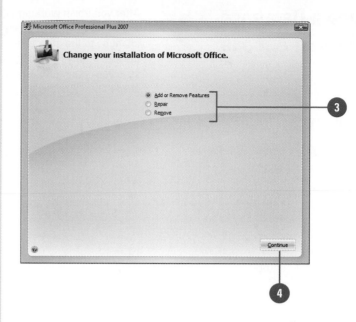

Add or Remove Features

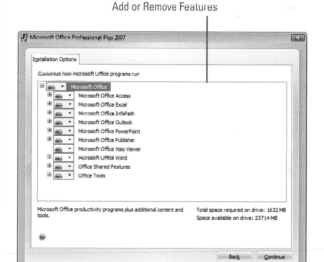

Closing a Database and Exiting Access

After you finish working in a database, you can close it. You can then choose to open another database or quit Access. If you made any changes to the structure of the database—for example, if you changed the size of any rows or columns in a table—Access prompts you to save your changes. Any changes you make to the data in a table are saved automatically as you make them.

Close a Database

① Click the **Office** button, and then click **Close Database**.

② If you have made changes to any open files since last saving them, a dialog box opens, asking if you want to save changes. Click **Yes** to save any changes, or click **No** to ignore your changes.

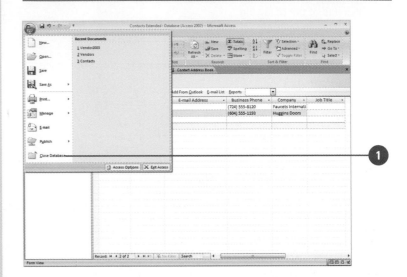

Exit Access

① Click the **Close** button on the Access window, or click the **Office** button, and then click **Exit Access**.

② If you have made changes to any open files since last saving them, a dialog box opens asking if you want to save changes. Click **Yes** to save any changes, or click **No** to ignore your changes.

Access window Close button

Touring Access Databases

2

Introduction

Microsoft Office Access 2007 helps you get started working with databases right away by providing sample database applications that you can use to store your own personal or business data. Access also offers a set of database wizards that aid you in creating common business databases. You can study these sample databases and wizards to get ideas for the databases you might want to design for other types of data that aren't covered by the existing samples and wizards.

When you are working with an existing database, however, you don't need to worry about the complexities of database design. You just need to know how to get around the database you are using. The tasks you are likely to perform with an existing database include entering and viewing data or subsets of data, creating and printing reports, and working efficiently with all the windows in front of you.

Opening a Sample Database

Access provides a sample database application called Northwind Traders—a database and project version—for you to explore. The Northwind Traders contains sample data and database objects for a specialty foods company. If you have specialized database needs, you can study the structure of the sample database, and then use them as models for your own.

Open a Sample Database

1. Start Access, or click the **Office** button and then click **New**.

   The Getting Started with Microsoft Office Access 2007 dialog box (**New!**) opens, displaying templates and recently opened databases.

2. In the left pane, click **Sample**.

3. Click **Northwind**.

4. If you want to change the save location, click the **Browse** button, click the **Save in** list arrow, select the location where you want to save the new database, select an Access database format, and then click **OK**.

5. Click **Download**.

6. If necessary, click **Continue** to download the template file.

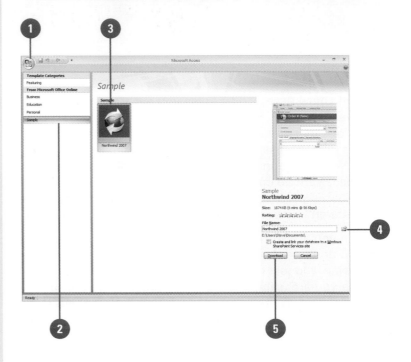

See Also

See "Warnings About Macros and Add-Ins" on page 31 for information on security alerts that appear when you open a database.

Did You Know?

You can switch to the Database window. *You can press F11 to switch to the Navigation pane from a switchboard or any other window.*

Warnings About Macros and Add-Ins

When you open a database or database template, you might be prompted with a security alert on the Message bar (**New!**) below the Ribbon. Databases can include potentially unsafe functions using additional programming code called macros, which can contain viruses. You can protect your computer from viruses by running up-to-date antivirus software and setting your macro security level to high for maximum protection or medium for less protection. When you set the macro security level to high, some database functionality, such as wizards, is disabled. If macro security is set to medium, database users will be prompted to enable macros. Prompts also might appear to block potentially unsafe functions.

Enable Macros When You Open a Database

1. Open a database with macros.

2. Click **Options** on the Message bar.

3. If you trust the content, click the **Enable external content** or **Trust all documents from this publisher** option (if available) to open it. If you don't trust it, click the **Help protect me from unknown content** option to block and disable the macros.

4. Click **OK**.

See Also

See "Setting Macro Security Options" on page 328 for information on setting security alerts that appear when you open a database.

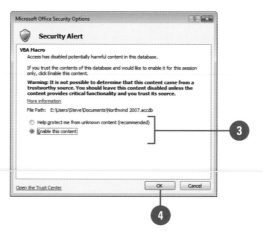

Using a Switchboard

The sample database that comes with Access employs a switchboard. A **switchboard** is a customized window that makes many features of a specific database available at the click of a button. The Address Book switchboard, for example, offers immediate access to printing mailing labels, merging addresses with a Word document, or locating an address quickly. Often, switchboard options open forms that allow you to view or enter data, reports that allow you to see summaries of data, or queries that allow you to view subsets of data.

Open and Use a Switchboard

1. Open the database. If the database contains a switchboard, it usually appears automatically when the database is opened.

2. If necessary, click the open the Navigation pane, and then double-click the switchboard you want to view.

3. Read the descriptions on the switchboard to find the task you need to perform.

4. Click the button that corresponds to the task you want to perform.

   Access opens or starts whatever database object will help you perform that task.

5. When you're done, click the **Close** button on the window for the database object.

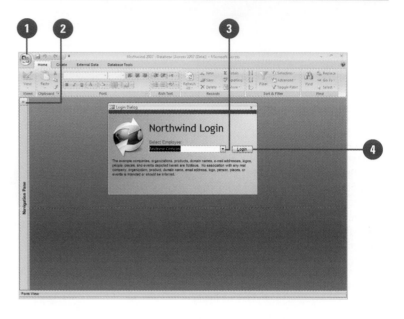

Changing the Navigation Pane Display

The Navigation pane (**New!**) is the container for all the objects in a database. These database objects work together to help you store and manage your data. Objects are organized into categories by object type in the Navigation pane. However, you can change the Navigation pane display. You can click Object bars on the Navigation pane to expand or collapse objects in categories, or click the Navigation pane title bar to select view options to change the way Access displays objects. If you need more space to work with database objects, you can quickly close and open the Navigation pane.

Change the Display of Objects in the Navigation Pane

1. Open the database you want to view.

2. If necessary, click the **Shutter Bar Open/Close** button (double arrows) to open the Navigation pane.

3. Click the Object bar you want to expand and view objects.

   ◆ When you click an Object bar, the object display expands or collapses.

4. Click the Navigation pane title bar, and then click the *Navigate To Category* item you want to display objects.

5. Click the Navigation pane title bar, and then click the *Filter By Group* criteria you want to display objects.

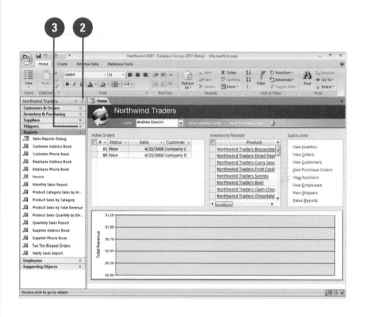

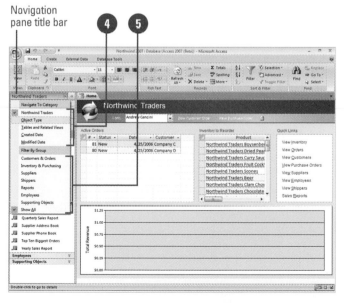

Navigation pane title bar

Working with Database Objects

The Navigation pane makes it easy to work with database objects, which help you store and manage your data. You can open, create, hide, group, rename, and delete database objects. If the predefined categories and groups don't meet your needs, you can create custom groups, which can also be used as a switchboard. You can create a simple object or a combination one based on the currently active object. For example, if a table is active and you click the Form button, Access creates a new form based on the active table.

Manage Database Objects

◆ **Open.** Double-click the object to open it for use, or right-click the object, and then click Design View to work with the object's design.

◆ **Create.** Click the Create tab, click the button (Table, Form, Report, Query Wizard, Macro, or Module) with the type of object you want. To create an object based on another, open and display the object before you click a button on the Create tab.

◆ **Delete.** Right-click the object, and then click Delete.

◆ **Rename.** Right-click the object, click Rename, type a new name, and then press Enter.

◆ **Hide** or **Unhide.** Right-click the object, and then click Hide in this Group or click Unhide this Group.

◆ **Import.** Right-click a table, point to Import, select the object type (a database table, text file, or Excel workbook), and then complete the wizard.

◆ **Close.** Click the Close button in the upper-right corner of the object.

Create tab

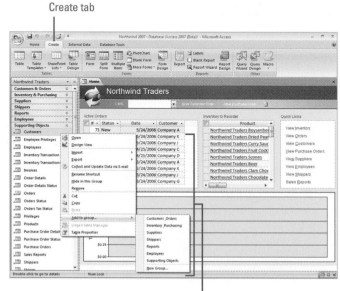

Right-click an object to perform management operations

Customize the Navigation Pane

1 Right-click the menu at the top of the Navigation pane, and then click **Navigation Options**.

2 Click a category, and then select or clear the item check boxes in Groups you want to show or hide.

3 To add, delete or rename a custom category, click **Add Item** and type a name, or select a custom category, and click **Rename Item** or **Delete Item**, or use **Up** or **Down** buttons to change order.

4 To create or change a group, click **Add Group** and type a name, or select a group and click **Rename Group** or **Delete Group**, or use **Up** or **Down** buttons to change order.

5 Select or clear check boxes to change the options you want.

   ◆ **Show Hidden Objects**. Select to show hidden objects as semi-transparent. (Default off).

   ◆ **Show System Objects**. Select to show system objects, such as system tables. (Default off).

   ◆ **Show Search Bar** (New!). (Default off).

6 Click the **Single-click** or **Double-click** option to open objects.

7 Click **OK**.

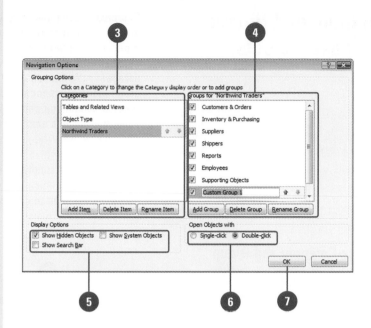

Did You Know?

You can use AutoCorrect to rename objects. When you rename an object, the Name AutoCorrect feature automatically fixes other Access objects that use the object you just renamed. Click the Office button, click Access Options, click Current Database in the left pane, and then select the Name AutoCorrect options you want.

Grouping and Hiding Database Objects

Objects are organized into groups and groups are organized into categories. You can create custom categories and groups to simplify and organize the objects in the Navigation pane. Categories and groups belong to the current database and cannot be transferred to other databases. When you create a custom category, Access creates a group in the custom category with all the objects called Unassigned Objects, which you can move to other groups. When you first create a custom group, it's empty until you populate it with shortcuts to the related objects. When you add an object to a group, you do not change the object's original location, nor are you creating a new object. Instead, you are simply creating a shortcut to an object that already exists. After you finish adding to a custom group, you can change the group filter to hide the Unassigned Objects group or any other groups you do not want to display. You can also hide objects in a group.

Create a Category and Group

1. Right-click the menu at the top of the Navigation pane, and then click **Navigation Options**.

2. Click **Add Item**, type a name, and then press Enter.

3. Select the custom category to which you want to add a group, click **Add Group**, type a name, and then press Enter.

4. To reorder a category or group in a list, select it, and then click the **Up** or **Down** buttons.

5. Click **OK**.

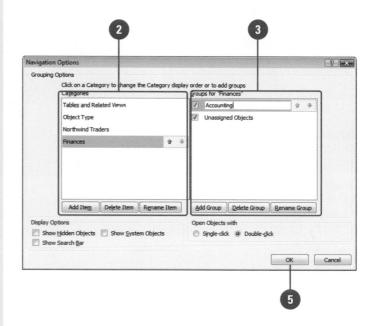

Did You Know?

You can delete or rename a custom group. In the Navigation pane, right-click the custom group you want to delete or rename, and then click Delete or Rename. When you rename a group, type a new name, and then press Enter.

Add Objects to a Custom Group

1. Right-click the object in a custom group you want to add to another custom group, and then point to **Add to group**.

   TIMESAVER *You can also drag an object from one custom group to another.*

2. Do either of the following:

   ◆ **Existing group.** Click the group name you want.

   ◆ **New group.** Click **New Group**, type a name, and then press Enter.

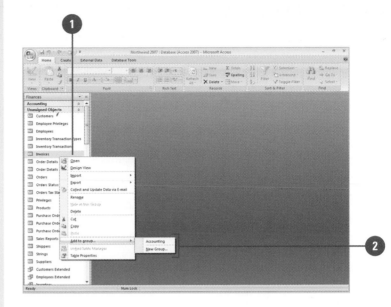

Hide and Unhide Objects

1. To hide an object in a group, right-click the object, and then click **Hide in this Group**.

2. To show hidden objects, right-click the menu at the top of the Navigation pane, click **Navigation Options**, select the **Show Hidden Objects** check box, and then click **OK**.

3. To unhide an object in a group, right-click the object (appears transparent), and then click **Unhide in this Group**.

Did You Know?

You can remove an object from a custom group. In the Navigation pane, display a custom group, right-click the object, and then click Remove.

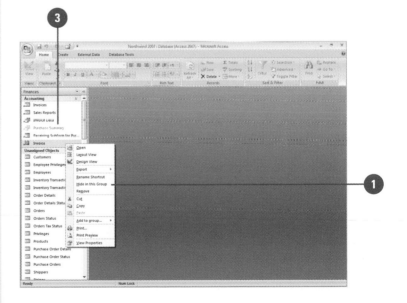

Touring a Table

A database is made up of groups of fields organized into tables. A **field** is a specific category of information, such as a name or a product. Related fields are grouped in tables. All the fields dealing with customers might be grouped in a Customer table, while fields dealing with products might be grouped in a Products table. You usually enter data into fields one entity at a time (one customer at a time, one product at a time, and so on). Access stores all the data for a single entity in a **record**. You can view a table in Datasheet or Design view. Design view allows you to work with your table's fields. Datasheet view shows a grid of fields and records. The fields appear as columns and the records as rows.

Open and View a Table

1 In the Navigation pane, click **Tables** on the Objects bar.

2 Double-click the table you want to open and view.

The table opens in Datasheet view.

3 Use the scroll bar to view the table:

◆ Drag the horizontal scroll box to scroll through the fields in a table.

◆ Drag the vertical scroll box to scroll through the records in a table.

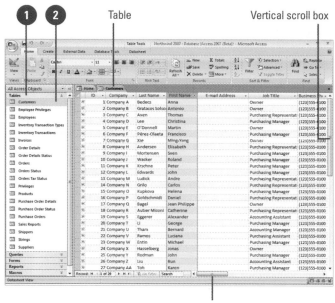

Table   Vertical scroll box

Horizontal scroll box

Did You Know?

You can select and resize a column. Click the column or row selector to select a column or row. Drag the border between the column or row selectors to resize a column or row. Each record has a unique identification number, which appears in the Specific Record box when that record is selected.

Enter a New Record in a Table

1. In the Navigation pane, click **Tables** on the Objects bar, and then double-click the table you want.

2. Click the **New Record** button.

3. Press Tab to accept the AutoNumber entry.

4. Enter the data for the first field. If you make a typing mistake, press Backspace.

5. Press Tab to move to the next field or Shift+Tab to move to the previous field.

6. When you reach the end of the record, click the **New Record** button or press Tab to go to the next record. Access saves your changes when you move to the next record.

Delete a Record from a Table

1. In the Navigation pane, click **Tables** on the Objects bar, and then double-click the table you want.

2. Click the row selector.

3. Click the **Home** tab.

4. Click the **Delete Record** button arrow, and then click **Delete Record**.

5. Click **Yes** to confirm the deletion.

Did You Know?

You can AutoNumber fields. The first field in a table is often an AutoNumber field, which Access uses to assign a unique number to each record. You can't select or change this value.

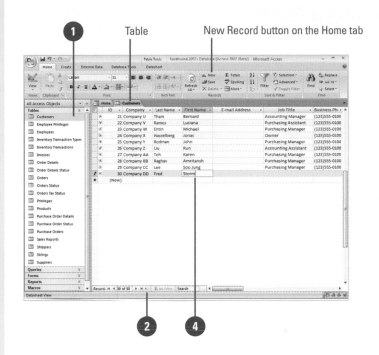

Table   New Record button on the Home tab

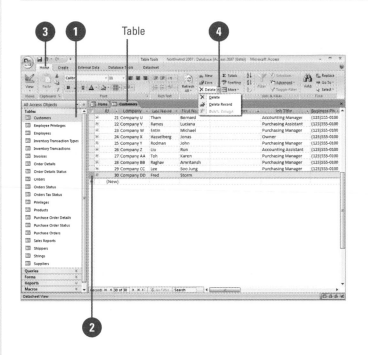

Table

Touring a Form

Database designers often display data in forms that mimic the paper forms used to record data. Forms facilitate data entry and record viewing. They can also contain buttons that allow you to perform other actions, such as running macros, printing, or creating labels. The options that appear on a form depend on what features the database designer included. A form directs you to enter the correct information and can automatically check your entries for errors. Access places the data you've entered in the form into the proper table or tables. You can open a form in Form view or Design view. Form view allows you to view all the information associated with a record; Design view allows you to modify the form's design.

Enter a New Record in a Form

1. In the Navigation pane, click **Forms** on the Objects bar, and then double-click the form you want.

2. Click the **New Record** button.

3. Enter the data for the first field.

4. Press Tab to move to the next field or Shift+Tab to move to the previous field.

5. When you have finished entering the data, you can close the form, click the **New Record** button to enter another record, or view a different record.

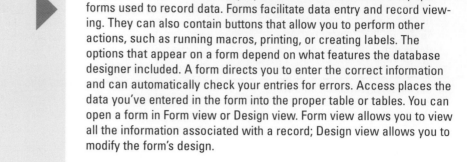

Form   New Record button on the Home tab

Did You Know?

You can delete a record from a form. Display the record you want to delete, click the Delete Record button on the Home tab, and then click Yes to confirm the deletion.

Entering Data

Normally you enter data into a form, because forms are specifically designed to facilitate data entry. You can, however, enter data into a table or a query. The methods are similar. How you enter data in a field depends on how the database designer created the field. Some fields accept only certain kinds of information, such as numbers or text. Some fields appear as check boxes or groups of option buttons; others appear as text boxes. Some text boxes only allow dates; others only allow certain predefined entries, such as a state or country. When you enter data, you don't have to click a Save button to save the data. Access automatically saves the data as you enter it.

Enter Data into a Field

① Open the query, table, page, or form into which you want to enter data.

② Activate the field into which you want to enter data.

 ◆ Click a field to activate it.

 ◆ Press Tab to move to the next field or Shift+Tab to move to the previous field.

③ Enter data in the active field.

 ◆ Click a list arrow, and then click one of the available choices (such as a category).

 ◆ Click a check box or option button.

 ◆ Type text in a box. When you click a box, a blinking insertion point appears, indicating where the text will appear when you type.

 ◆ Enter dates in the required format (such as month/day/year).

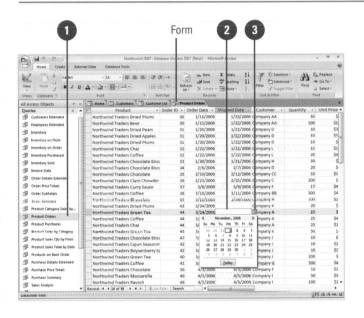

Form

Form in a window

Touring a Query

To locate and retrieve information in a table (or in multiple tables), you create a query. A **query** is simply a question that you ask a database to help you locate specific information. For example, if you want to know which customers placed orders in the last six months, you can create a query to examine the contents of the Order Date field and to find all the records in which the purchase date is less than six months ago. Access retrieves the data that meets the specifications in your query and displays that data in table format. You can sort that information or retrieve just a subset of its contents with still more specific criteria, so that you can focus on exactly the information you need—no more or less.

Open and Run a Query

 In the Navigation pane, click **Queries** on the Objects bar.

 Double-click the query you want to run.

The query opens in a table called a dynaset. The dynaset displays the records that meet the specifications set forth in the query.

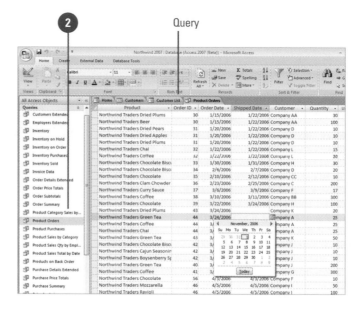

Query

Touring a Report

After you have retrieved and organized only the specific information you want, you can display and print this information as a report. In Access you can create a simple report that displays each record's information, or you can customize a report to include calculations, charts, graphics, and other features to really emphasize the information in the report. You can print a report, a table, a query, or any data in a single step using the Print button, in which case Access automatically prints a single copy of all pages in the report. If you want to print only selected pages or if you want to specify other printing options, use the Print command on the Office menu.

Create a Report

1. In the Navigation pane, click **Reports** on the Objects bar.

2. Double-click the report you want to view.

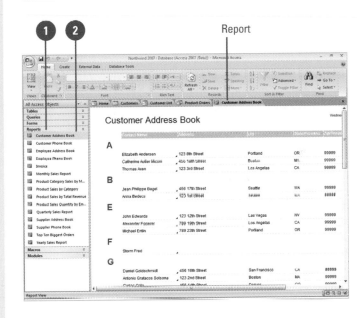

Report

Print Data

1. Click the **Office** button, point to **Print**, and then click **Print**.

2. If necessary, click the **Name** list arrow, and then select the printer you want to use.

3. To print selected pages in the report, click the **Pages** option, and then type the first page in the From box and the ending page in the To box.

4. Click **OK**.

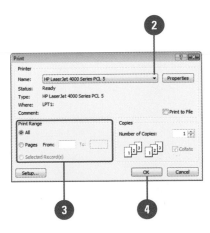

Switching Views

Access provides different views to help you work with and display information. To quickly switch between views—such as Form, Datasheet, Layout, Design, PivotTable, and PivotTable—you can use buttons on the view selector (**New!**) in the lower-right corner of the Program window. Datasheet view is the main view in Access. It lets you focus on entering, modifying, and managing your data. **Design view** lets you create forms and reports. **Layout view** (**New!**) combines Design view and Form or Report view to let you enter data and make basic changes without having to continually change views. In addition to the view selector, you can also use view buttons on the View tab to switch between views. The available views vary depending on the open object.

Switch Between Views

◆ **Use the View Selector.** Open the object you want to view, and then click any of the view buttons on the right-side of the Status bar.

  ◆ Form, Datasheet, Layout, Design, PivotTable, and PivotTable.

◆ **Use the View button.** Open the object you want to view, click the **Home** tab, and then click the **View** button arrow, and then click the view you want:

  ◆ Form, Datasheet, Layout, Design, PivotTable, and PivotTable.

TIMESAVER *The top of the View button displays the icon for the last view selected. You can click the top of the button to quickly display the view for the current object.*

View button

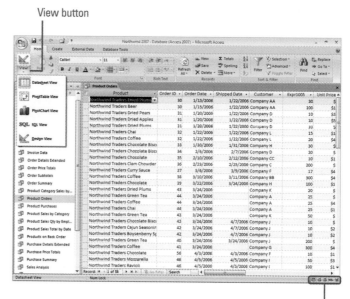

View Selector buttons

View a Query in Design View

1. In the Navigation pane, click **Queries** on the Objects bar.

2. Right-click the query you want to view, and then click **Open**.

3. Click the **Home** or **Design** tab.

4. Click the **View** button arrow, and then click **Design View**.

   TIMESAVER *Click the Design View button on the Status bar.*

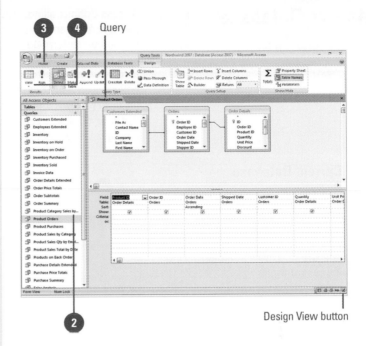

Query

Design View button

Changing Database Display Options

Access Options allows you to personalize what appears in the Access window. You can customize the way Access appears when you work on the currently opened database. You can specify a title and select an icon to create a database application, and select the form you want to display on startup. To customize the way you work with database objects, you can choose to display them as tabbed documents (**New!**) for easy access or overlapping windows for a custom interface. You can also display Layout view (**New!**), which allows you to make design changes while you browse a form or report.

Change Current Database Display Options

1. Open the database you want to customize.

2. Click the **Office** button, and then click **Access Options**.

3. In the left pane, click **Current Database**.

4. Enter a database application title and then click **Browse** to select an application icon (optional).

5. Click the **Display Form** list arrow, and then select the form object you want to display on startup.

6. Select or clear any of the check boxes to change the display options you want.

   ◆ **Display Status Bar.** Set to display the Status bar. (Default on).

   ◆ **Document Window Options.** Click the Overlapping windows or Tabbed documents (**New!**) option to hide or show tabs.

   ◆ **Enable Layout View for this database** (**New!**). (Default on).

   ◆ **Enable design changes for tables in Datasheet view for this database.** (Default on).

7. Click **OK**.

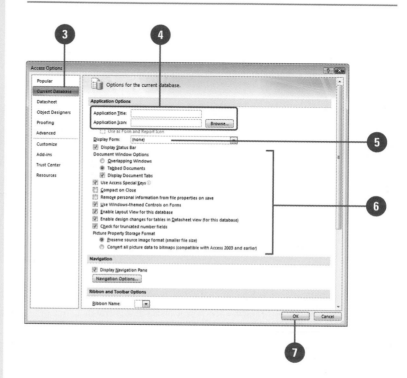

Planning and Creating a Custom Database

3

Introduction

The Microsoft Office Access 2007 database wizards make creating databases easy, but you may need to create a database that does not fit any of the predefined template choices. In that situation, you may need to create the database "from scratch."

Creating a database from scratch involves careful planning. You must:

◆ Determine the purpose and scope of your data base.

◆ Decide what tables your database will contain and what the content of those tables will be.

◆ Define how data in one table is related to data in another table.

When you create a database from scratch, you can take advantage of the tools that Access provides. If you don't plan to create a database from scratch but instead plan to use only existing Access databases, you might not need the information in this chapter. Understanding database design concepts, however, will help you better understand how to create effective queries later on.

Creating a Custom Database Template

When you create a blank database in the Getting Started with Microsoft Office Access 2007 dialog box, Access uses a database file called Blank.accdb for Access 2007 or Blank.mdb for earlier versions of Access located in the templates folder. If you want to create a custom blank template, you can save your own database file with the name Blank in the templates folder. The new custom blank template can contain any object type you want, such as forms, reports, macros, or additional tables. If you no longer want to use a custom blank database, delete or rename the file named Blank, and Access creates a new default blank database for you.

Create a Custom Blank Template Database

1. Start Access, or click the **Office** button and then click **New**.

2. In the left pane, click **Featuring**.

3. Click **Blank Database**.

4. Click the **Browse** button.

5. Click the **Save in** list arrow, and then select one of the following locations:

   ◆ **System template folder.** C:\Program Files\Microsoft Office\Templates\1033\Access.

   A template in the System folder overrides a template in the User folder.

   ◆ **User template folder.** C:\Users*user name*\Documents (Vista), or C:\Documents and Settings*user name*\App Data\Microsoft\Templates (XP).

6. Click the **Save as type** list arrow, and then click a file type.

7. Type **Blank.accdb** (or **Blank.mdb**, if you are creating an earlier-version template) in the File name box.

8. Click **OK**.

9. Click **Create**.

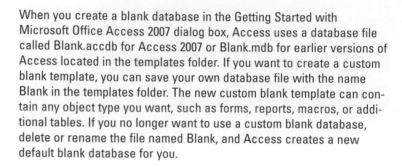

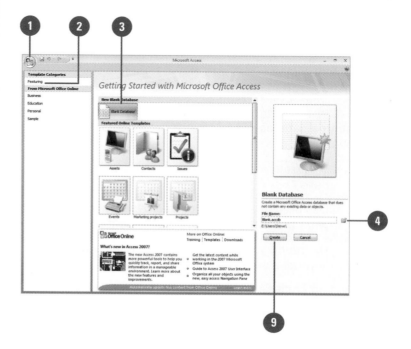

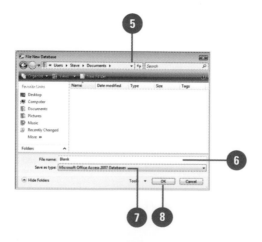

Create a Custom Template Database from an Existing Database

1. Start Access, click the **Office** button and then click **Open**.

2. Click the **Files of type** list arrow, and then click a file type.

3. If the file is located in another folder, click the **Look in** list arrow, and then navigate to the file.

4. Click the database file you want to use as a blank template.

5. Click **Open**.

6. Click the **Office** button, click **Save As**, and then select the format you want: **Access 2007 Database**, **Access 2002 - 2003 Database**, or **Access 2000 Database**.

7. Click the **Save in** list arrow, and then select one of the following locations:

   ◆ **System template folder.** C:\Program Files\Microsoft Office\Templates\1033\Access.

   ◆ **User template folder.** C:\Users*user name*\Documents (Vista), or C:\Documents and Settings*user name*\App Data\Microsoft\Templates (XP).

8. Type **Blank.accdb** (or **Blank.mdb**, if you are creating an earlier-version template) in the File name box.

9. Click **Save**.

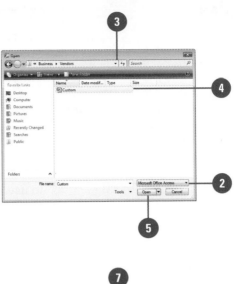

Planning Tables

Microsoft Certified Application Specialist   AC07S-1.3.1, AC07S-1.3.2

Although you can always make changes to your database when necessary, a little planning before you begin can save time later on. When you plan a database, consider how you will use the data. What kind of data are you collecting? What kind of data are you entering? How are data values related to one another? Can your data be organized into separate, smaller groups? What kinds of safeguards can you create to ensure that errors do not creep into your data? As you consider these questions, you should apply the answers as you structure your database.

Plan Tables

Tables are one of the fundamental building blocks of a database. Database planning begins with deciding how many and what kinds of tables your database will contain. Consider organizing your database information into several tables—each one containing fields related to a specific topic—rather than one large table containing fields for a large variety of topics. For example, you could create a Customers table that contains only customer information and an Orders table that contains only order information. By focusing each table on a single task, you greatly simplify the structure of those tables and make them easier to modify later on.

Choose Data Types

When you create a table, you must decide what fields to include and the appropriate format for those fields. Access allows you to assign a data type to a field, a format that defines the kind of data the field can accept. Access provides a wide variety of data types, ranging from text and number formats to object-based formats for images, sound,

video clips, and embedded macros (**New!**). Choosing the correct data type helps you manage your data and reduces the possibility of data-entry errors. To make it easier to create fields, Access provides the Add New Field column (**New!**) in Datasheet view so you can quickly enter a field name. If you already have a defined field in the database that you want to use again, you can drag the existing field from the Field List pane (**New!**) on to the datasheet and Access automatically creates a relationship or guides you through the process. You can also use field templates (**New!**) for creating new fields. A **field template** is a design for a field, complete with a name, data type, length, and predefined properties. You can drag field templates onto the datasheet. Field templates are XSD based so that you can set up standard definitions for shared use. If you create a field for numbers, you can use the Totals row (**New!**) to calculate values using functions such as sum, count, average, maximum, minimum, standard deviation, or variance.

Specify a Primary Key

You should also identify which field or fields are the table's primary keys. Primary keys are those fields whose values uniquely identify each record in the table. A social security number field in a personnel table could be used as a primary key, since each employee has a unique social security number. A table with time-ordered data might have two primary keys—a date field and a time field (hours and minutes), which together uniquely identify an exact moment in time. Although primary keys are not required, using them is one way of removing the possibility of duplicate records existing within your tables.

Creating Tables in a Database

Microsoft Certified Application Specialist

AC07S-1.2.2

After creating a database file, you need to create the tables that will store the data. There are several ways to create a new table: in Datasheet view, in Design view, with Table Templates, SharePoint Lists, or by importing a table or linking to the data in a table from another Access database. Depending on the method you choose, creating a table can involve one or more of the following:

- Specifying the fields for the table
- Determining the data type for each field
- Determining the field size (for text and number fields only)
- Assigning the primary key
- Saving and naming the table

Methods for Creating a Table

Type	Method	Description
Datasheet	Table button on the Create tab	When you create a table in Datasheet view, you can start viewing and entering data right away. Access automatically assigns a data type based on the kind of information you entered in the field, and it assigns a default field size for text and number fields. After you close and save the table, Access prompts you to identify a primary key or to allow Access to designate one for you.
Table Template	Table Templates button on the Create tab	When you create a table using table templates, you select the type of table you want. Access provides several table templates, including Contacts, Tasks, Issues, Events, and Assets.
Design	Design View button on the Create tab	In Design view, you must specify the fields, specify the data type for each field, assign the size (for text and number fields), assign the primary key, and save the table yourself.
SharePoint	SharePoint Lists button on the Create tab	When you create a table using data from a SharePoint list, you select the type of table you want. Access provides several table types, including Contacts, Tasks, Issues, Events, Custom, and Existing SharePoint List.
Importing	Access button on the External Data tab	If you want to use data from another Access database in the database you are creating, you can import it. When you import a table, all the field names and data types are retained with the imported data. However, you must name the new table and identify the primary key or have Access create a primary key for you. Also, you may need to change the field size and other properties after importing.
Linking	Access button on the External Data tab	When you link a table, the data is retrieved from a table in another database. Linking a table saves disk space because there is only one table rather than multiple tables with the same data. Linking a table saves time because there is no need to update the same information in more than one table.

Creating a Table by Entering Data

Access allows you to display many of its objects in multiple viewing modes. Datasheet view displays the data in your tables, queries, forms, and reports. Design view displays options for designing your Access objects. You can create a new table in both views. When you create a table in Datasheet view, you enter data and Access creates the table as you type. Access determines the data type of each field based on the data you enter (**New!**). When you finish entering data, Access will prompt you for the name of the table you've just created.

Enter Data to Create a Table

1 Click the **Create** tab.

2 Click the **Table** button.

3 Enter the data.

Press Tab to move from field to field or click in a cell.

4 To change a field name, double-click the field name, type the new name, and then press Enter.

5 Click the **Save** button on the Quick Access Toolbar.

6 Type a table name.

7 Click **OK**.

8 To have Access set the primary key, click **Yes**.

9 Click the **Close** button in the Table window.

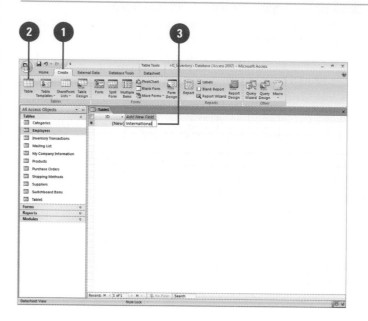

Did You Know?

You can select or resize a column or row like in Excel. To select a column or row in a table, click the Column or Row selector. To resize a column or row, drag the border between the Column or Row selector. You can also click the Home tab, and then click the More button to access commands to resize columns and rows.

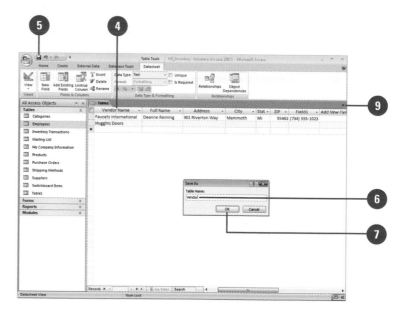

Creating a Table Using a Template

AC07S-2.2.3

A table template is a predefined table with fields you can quickly insert and use in a database. Access provides several table templates (**New!**) including: Contacts, Tasks, Issues, Events, and Assets. You can use the Create tab to quickly insert a table template. After you insert a table template, you can change fields to meet your own needs, and then name and save the table in the database.

Create a Table Using a Template

1. Click the **Create** tab.

2. Click the **Table Templates** button.

3. Click the table template (**Contacts**, **Tasks**, **Issues**, **Events**, or **Assets**) you want.

4. To change a field name, double-click the field name, type the new name, and then press Enter.

5. Click the **Save** button on the Quick Access Toolbar.

6. Type a table name.

7. Click **OK**.

8. To have Access set the primary key, click **Yes**.

9. When you're done, click the **Close** button in the Table window.

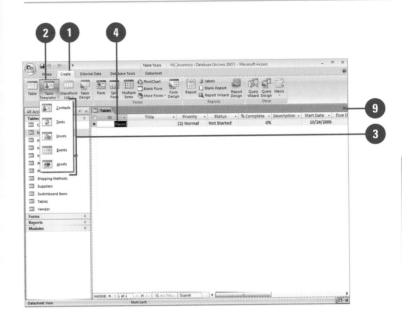

Did You Know?

You can insert a subdatasheet in a table. In the Datasheet view of a table, click the Home tab, click the More button, point to Subdatasheet, and then click Subdatasheet. Click the Tables tab, click the table, specify the foreign key in the Link Child Fields box and the primary key in the Link Master Fields box, and then click OK.

You can view a subdatasheet. In the Datasheet view of a table, click the plus box next to the record to display the subdatasheet. Click the minus box to hide the subdatasheet.

Importing Data into Tables

You can create new tables from other Access databases by importing and linking tables. When you import a table, you copy data from a table in one Access database and place it in a new table in your database. You can also import data from other programs. After you select the table you want to import during the import process, you have the option of saving the import steps for use again in the future.

Import a Table from a Database

1. Click the **External Data** tab.

2. Click the **Import Access Database** button.

3. Click **Browse**, locate and select the database file that contains the data you want to import, and then click **Open**.

4. Click the **Import tables, queries, forms, reports, macros, and modules into the current database** option.

5. Click **OK**.

6. Click the tables you want to import. To deselect a table, click the table again.

7. Click **OK**.

8. To save import steps, select the Save import steps check box, enter a name and description, and then click **Save Import**.

   Otherwise, click **Cancel**.

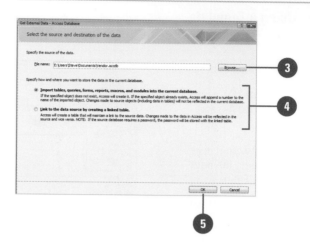

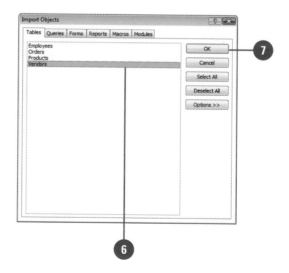

Linking to Data in Tables

You can create new tables from other Access databases by importing and linking tables. When you link a table, the data stays in its original location, but you can display and access that data from within your database. If data in the original database changes, the changes will appear in your linked database, too. After you select the table you want to link during the linking process, you have the option of saving the import steps for use again in the future.

Link to Data from a Database

1. Click the **External Data** tab.

2. Click the **Import Access Database** button.

3. Click **Browse**, locate and select the database file that contains the data you want to import, and then click **Open**.

4. Click the **Link to the data source by creating a linked table** option.

5. Click **OK**.

6. Click the tables you want to import. To deselect a table, click the table again.

7. Click **OK**.

8. To save import steps, select the Save import steps check box, enter a name and description, and then click **Save Import**.

   Otherwise, click **Cancel**.

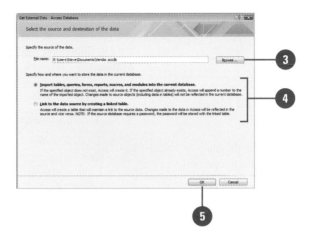

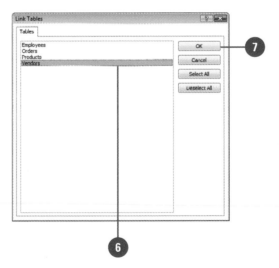

Working with Table Records

Microsoft
Certified
Application
Specialist

AC07S-1.3.1, AC07S-3.1
AC07S-3.2

A **database** is made up of groups of fields organized into tables. A **field** is a specific category of information, such as a name or a product. Related fields are grouped in tables. You usually enter data into fields one entity at a time (one customer at a time, one product at a time, and so on). Access stores all the data for a single entity in a record. You can view a table in Datasheet or Design view. Design view allows you to work with your table's fields. Datasheet view shows a grid of fields and records. The fields appear as columns and the records as rows. The first field in a table is often an **AutoNumber** field, which Access uses to assign a unique number to each record. You can't select or change this value. You can use Record buttons at the bottom of the table in Datasheet view to quickly move around and search for data in a table.

Enter a New Record and Move Around in a Table

1. In the Navigation pane, double-click the table you want to open.

2. Click the **New Record** button.

3. Press Tab to accept the AutoNumber entry.

4. Enter the data. If you make a typing mistake, press Backspace.

5. Press Tab to move to the next field or Shift+Tab to move to the previous field.

6. When you reach the end of the record, click one of the Record buttons:

   ◆ **First Record** button.

   ◆ **Previous Record** button.

   ◆ **Specific Record** box. Enter a record number in the box, and then press Enter.

   ◆ **Next Record** button.

   ◆ **Last Record** button.

   TIMESAVER *You can also use buttons in the Records group on the Home tab to perform the same commands.*

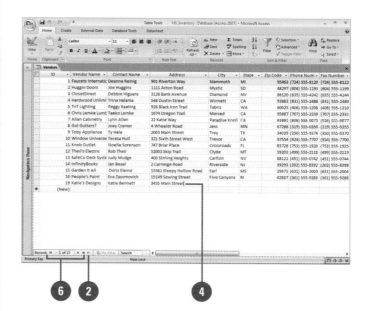

Search for Records

1. In the Navigation pane, double-click the table you want to open.

2. If you want, click in the table field where you want to start the search.

3. Click in the Search box.

4. Type the text you want to find in the table.

5. Press Enter to find the first instance of the text you want to find.

6. Press Enter again to find the next instance of the text you want to find.

7. When you're done, delete the text in the Search box.

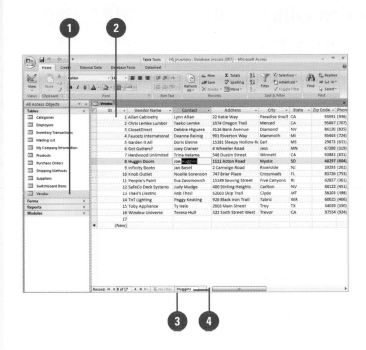

Delete a Record from a Table

1. In the Navigation pane, double-click the table you want to open.

2. Right-click the row selector with the record you want to delete.

3. Click **Delete Record**, and then click **Yes** to confirm.

   TIMESAVER *Click the row selector, click the Home tab, and then click the Delete button.*

Working with a Table in Design View

Most Access objects are displayed in Design view, which allows you to work with the underlying structure of your tables, queries, forms, and reports. To create a new table in Design view, you define the fields that will comprise the table before you enter any data. In Design view for tables, each row corresponds to a field. You can edit, insert, and delete fields in your database tables in Design view. You insert a field by adding a row, while you delete a field by removing a row. You can also change field order by dragging a row selector to a new position.

Create or Modify a Table in Design View

1. Click the **Create** tab, and then click the **Table Design** button, or select the table you want to modify in the Navigation pane, and then click the **Design View** button.

2. Click in a **Field Name** cell, and then type a modified field name.

3. Click in a **Data Type** cell, click the Data Type list arrow, and then click a data type.

4. Click in a **Description** cell, and then type a description. If the **Property Update Options** button appears, select an option, if necessary.

5. To insert a field, click the row selector below where you want the field, and then click the **Insert Rows** button on the Ribbon.

6. To delete a field, click the row selector for the field you want to delete, and then click the **Delete Rows** button on the Ribbon.

7. Click the **Save** button on the Quick Access Toolbar, and then if necessary, enter a table name and click **OK**.

8. When you're done, click the **Close** button in the Table window.

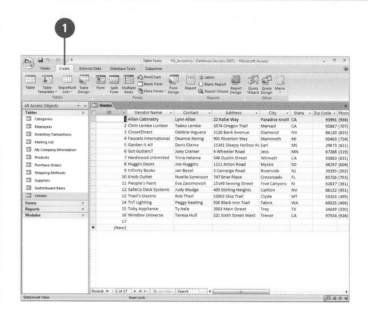

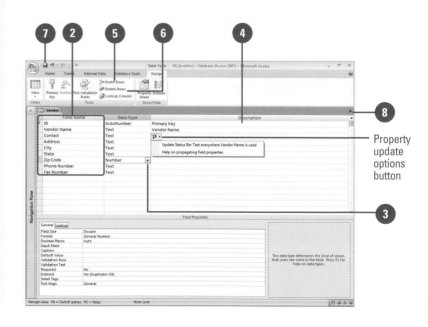

Property update options button

Specifying a Primary Key in Design View

A primary key is one or more fields in a table that provide a unique identifier for every row. You use the primary key in other tables to refer back to the table with the primary key. In Design view, you can use the Primary Key button to assign or remove the primary key designation for the selected field or fields. When you create a new table in Datasheet view, Access automatically creates a primary key and assigns it the field name "ID" and the data type AutoNumber. When you create a table in Design view, you can specify more than one field as a primary key, known as a composite key, so you are responsible for determining the data type of the primary key. Whatever data type you choose, values for the primary key must be unique for each table record.

Specify a Primary Key

1. In Design view, create a field that will be that table's primary key, and then select an appropriate data type.

   ◆ If you choose the AutoNumber data type, Access assigns a value to the primary key for a new record that is one more than the primary key in the previous record.

   ◆ If you choose any other data type, such as Text, Number, or Date/Time, during data entry, you must enter a unique value in the appropriate format for the primary key of each new record.

2. Click the row selector of that field.

   ◆ To create more than one primary key, press and hold Ctrl, and then click the additional row selector for each field.

3. Click the **Primary Key** button.

4. To remove a primary key, delete any table relationships associated with the primary key, select the row selector for the Primary key, and then click the **Primary Key** button.

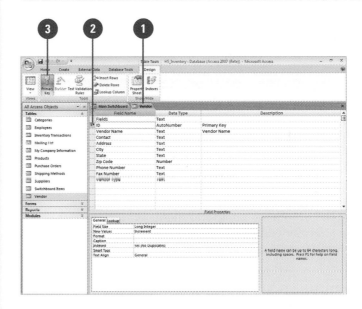

Planning Table Relationships

Microsoft Certified Application Specialist   AC07S-1.2.1, AC07S-1.2.2

When you place data into separate tables, you need some way of merging this data together for forms and reports. You can do this by establishing table relationships that indicate how data in one table relates to data in another.

Specifying Common Fields

Data from several different tables is related through the use of common fields. A common field is a field existing in two or more tables, allowing you to match records from one table with records in the other tables. For example, the Customers table and the Orders table might both contain a Customer ID field, which functions as a primary key that identifies a specific customer. Using Customer ID as a common field allows you to generate reports containing information on both the customer and the orders the customer made. When you use a primary key as a common field, it is called a **foreign** key in the second table.

Building Table Relationships

Once you have a way of relating two tables with a common field, your next task is to express the nature of that relationship. There are three types of relationships: one-to-one, one-to-many, and many-to-many.

A table containing customer names and a second table containing customer addresses exist in a one-to-one relationship if each customer is limited to only one address. Similarly, a one-to-many relationship exists between the Customers table and the Orders table because a single customer could place several orders. In a one-to-many relationship like this, the "one" table is called the **primary**

Table Relationships	
Choice	**Description**
One-to-one	Each record in one table is matched to only one record in a second table, and visa versa.
One-to-many	Each record in one table is matched to one or more records in a second table, but each record in the second table is matched to only one record in the first table.
Many-to-many	Each record in one table is matched to multiple records in a second table, and visa versa.

table, and the "many" table is called the **related table**.

Finally, if you allow several customers to be recorded on a single order (as in the case of group purchases), a many-to-many relationship exists between the Customers and Orders tables.

Maintaining Referential Integrity

Table relationships must obey standards of **referential integrity**, a set of rules that control how you can delete or modify data between related tables. Referential integrity protects you from erroneously changing data in a primary table required by a related table. You can apply referential integrity when:

♦ The common field is the primary table's primary key.

♦ The related fields have the same format.

♦ Both tables belong to the same database.

Referential integrity places some limitations on you.

- Before adding a record to a related table, a matching record must already exist in the primary table.

- The value of the primary key in the primary table cannot be changed if matching records exist in a related table.

- A record in the primary table cannot be deleted if matching records exist in a related table.

Access can enforce these rules by cascading any changes across the related tables. For example, Access can automatically copy any changes to the common field across the related tables. Similarly, if a record is deleted in the primary table, Access can automatically delete related records in all other tables.

As you work through these issues of tables, fields, and table relationships, you will create a structure for your database that will be easier to manage and less prone to data-entry error.

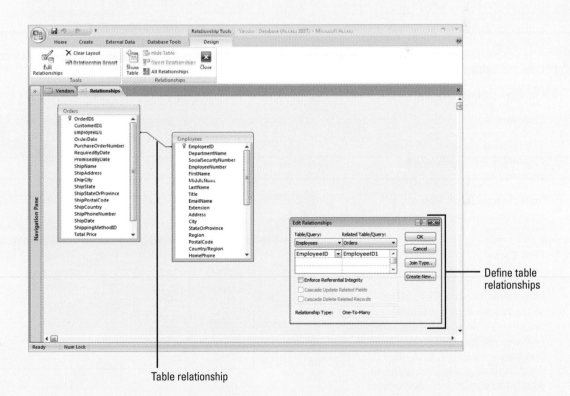

Table relationship

Define table relationships

Defining Table Relationships

Microsoft
Certified
Application
Specialist

AC07S-1.2.1, AC07S-1.2.2
AC07S-4.2.3

You can define table relationships in several ways. After you create tables in your database, you can define table relationships between them. You can define and manage relationships using buttons on the Database Tools tab. This gives you control over your table relationships and also gives you a quick snapshot of all the relationships in your database. After you define a relationship, you can double-click the connection line to modify or add to the relationship.

Define Table Relationships

1. Click the **Database Tools** tab.

2. Click the **Relationships** button.

   If relationships are already established in your database, they appear in the Relationships window. In this window you can create additional table relationships.

3. If necessary, click the **Show Table** button to display the Show Table dialog box.

4. Click the **Tables** tab.

5. Click the table you want.

6. Click **Add**.

   The table or query you selected appears in the Relationships window.

   Repeat steps 5 and 6 for each table you want to use in a relationship.

7. Click **Close**.

8. Drag the common field in the first table to the common field in the second table. When you release the mouse button, a line appears between the two tables, signifying that they are related. Also, the Edit Relationships dialog box opens, in which you can confirm or modify the relationship.

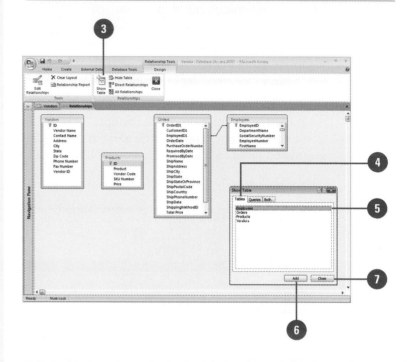

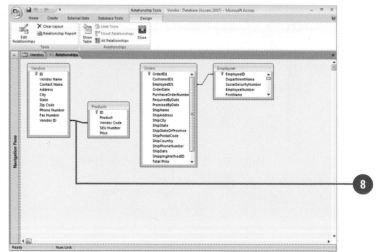

9 Click the **Join Type** button if you want to specify the join type. Click **OK** to return to the Edit Relationships dialog box.

10 Click **Create** to create the relationship.

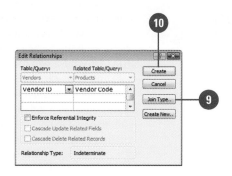

Did You Know?

You can view the relationships you want to see. Click the Design tab under Relationship Tools, click the Show Direct Relationships button to see tables that are directly related to each other. Click the All Relationships button to see all the relationships between all the tables and queries in your database.

You can print the Relationships window. Click the Design tab under Relationship Tools, click the Relationships Report button the Relationships window you want to print, click the Print button, select the print settings you want, and then click OK.

You can delete a table relationship. In the Relationships window, right-click the line that joins the tables that you no longer want related to one another, and then click Delete. In the message box, click Yes to confirm that you want to permanently delete this relationship. You will not be able to undo this change.

Join Types	
Join Types	**Description**
Include rows only where the joined fields from both tables are equal	Choose this option if you want to see one record in the second table for every record that appears in the first table. The number of records you see in the two tables will be the same.
Include ALL records from "xxx" (the first table) and only those records from "yyy" (the second table) where the joined fields are equal	Choose this option if you want to see all the records in the first table (even if there is no corresponding record in the second table) as well as the records from the second table in which the joined fields are the same in both tables. The number of records you see in the first table might be greater than the number of records in the second table.
Include ALL records from "yyy" (the second table) and only those records from the "xxx" (the first table) where the joined fields are equal	Choose this option if you want to see all the records in the second table (even if there is no corresponding record in the first table) as well as the records from the first table in which the joined fields are the same in both tables. The number of records you see in the second table might be greater than the number of records in the first table.

Creating and Printing a Table Relationship Report

Microsoft
Certified
Application
Specialist

AC07S-1.2.3

After you create a table relationship, you can create and print a report. In the Relationships window, the Relationship Report button creates a report with the currently displayed relationship and switches to Print Preview, where you can print the report. When you close Print Preview, the report appears in Design view. If you want, you can make changes to the report. To complete the process, you need to save and name the report or close it without saving it. Instead of printing the report, you can also use exporting tools in Print Preview to save the report in another format, including a PDF or XPS document.

Create and Print a Table Relationship Report

1. Click the **Database Tools** tab.

2. Click the **Relationships** button.

   If relationships are already established in your database, they appear in the Relationships window.

3. Do any of the following to display the table relationships you want to use to create a report:

   - **Hide tables.** Click the table you want to hide, and then click the **Hide Table** button.

   - **Add tables.** Click the **Tables** tab, click the table you want, click **Add**, and then click **Close**.

4. Click the **Relationship Report** button.

   The report appears in Print Preview.

5. To print the report, click the **Print** button, specify the settings you want, and then click **OK**.

6. Click the **Close Print Preview** button.

   The relationship report appears in Design view.

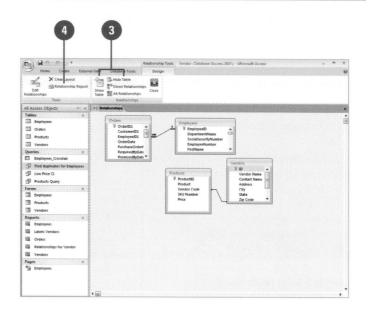

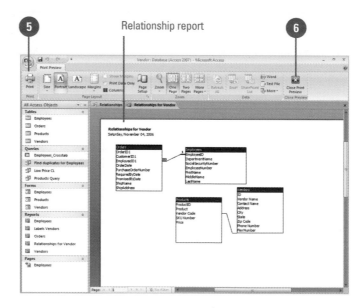

Relationship report

⑦ Click the **Save** button on the Quick Access Toolbar.

⑧ Type a name for the relationship report.

⑨ Click **OK**.

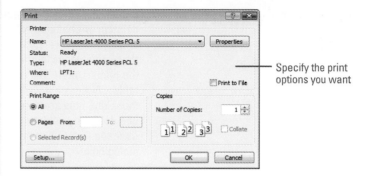

Specify the print options you want

Did You Know?

You can show direct relationships. In the Relationships window, click the Direct Relationships button to display only tables that relate to each other.

You can clear relationships. In the Relationships window, click the Clear Layout button, and then click Yes to remove the layout of the Relationships window.

See Also

See "Creating a PDF Document" on page 300 or "Creating an XPS Document" on page 301 for information on using and saving a file with different formats.

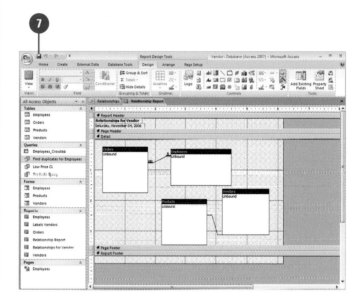

Did You Know?

You can show direct relationships. In the Relationships window, click the Direct Relationships button to display only tables that relate to each other.

Ensuring Referential Integrity

Microsoft Certified Application Specialist AC07S-1.2.2

Referential integrity in table relationships keeps users from accidentally deleting or changing related data. If a primary table contains a list of employees and related tables contain additional information about those employees, and an employee quits, his record is removed from the primary table. His records should also be removed in all related tables. Access allows you to change or delete related data, but only if these changes are cascaded through the series of related tables. You can do this by selecting the Cascade Update Related Fields and Cascade Delete Related Records check boxes in the Edit Relationships dialog box.

Ensure Referential Integrity

1. Click the **Database Tools** tab.

2. Click the **Relationships** button.

3. Click the join line for the relationship you want to work with.

4. Click the **Edit Relationships** button.

5. Select the **Enforce Referential Integrity** check box to ensure that referential integrity always exists between related tables in the database.

6. If you want changes to the primary field of the primary table automatically copied to the related field of the related table, select the **Cascade Update Related Fields** check box.

7. If you want Access to delete records in the related tables whenever records in the primary table are deleted, select the **Cascade Delete Related Records** check box.

8. Click **OK**.

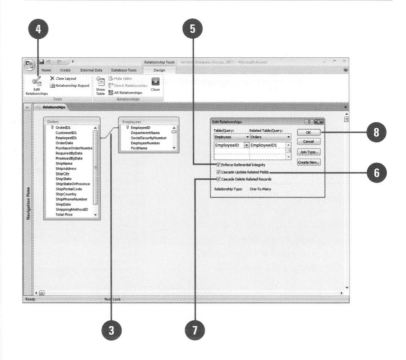

Identifying Object Dependencies

Microsoft
Certified
Application
Specialist

AC07S-6.2.4.1

As you develop a database, you create a relationship between objects to share data and provide the information in forms and reports. When you make changes to one object, it might affect another object. For example, if you no longer need a field in a table, instead of deleting it right away and possibly creating problems, you can check object dependencies to make sure that the field you want to delete is not used in another table. Checking for object dependencies helps you save time and avoid mistakes. Access generates dependency information by searching name maps maintained by the Name AutoCorrect feature. If Track Name AutoCorrect Info is turned off on the Current Database pane in the Options dialog box, you cannot view dependency information.

View Dependency Information

1. In the Navigation pane, click the database object in which you want to view dependencies.

2. Click the **Database Tools** tab.

3. Click the **Object Dependencies** button.

4. Click the **Objects that depend on me** or **Objects that I depend on** option.

    The Object Dependencies task pane shows the list of objects that use the selected object.

5. To view dependency information for an object listed in the pane, click the **Expand** icon (+) next to it.

6. When you're done, click the **Close** button on the task pane.

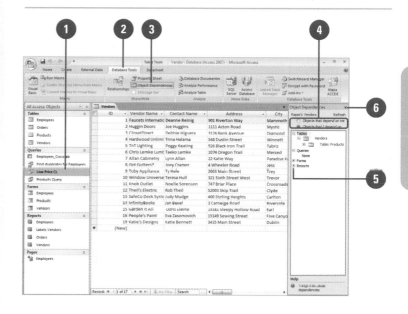

Did You Know?

You can view a list of database objects. Click the Office button, click point to Manage, click Database Properties, and then click the Contents tab. When you're done, click OK.

Dependency Information

Object	Dependent	Description
Table	Table or query	A relationship is defined between the objects
Table	Form	Fields in the selected table look up values
Query	Table or query	Query is bound to the table or query
Form	Table or query	Form is bound to the table or query
Form	Form	Form includes the other form as a subform
Report	Table or query	Report is bound to the table or query
Report	Form	Report includes the form as a subform
Report	Report	Report include the other report as a subreport

Modifying Object Dependencies

Modify Dependency Information

1 In the Navigation pane, click the database object in which you want to view and modify dependencies.

2 Click the **Database Tools** tab.

3 Click the **Object Dependencies** button.

4 Click the **Objects that depend on me** or **Objects that I depend on** option.

The Object Dependencies task pane shows the list of objects that use the selected object.

5 Click the **Expand** icon (+) next to an object to view dependency information.

6 Click the object you want to open in Design view.

7 Modify the object in Design view, and then click the **Close** button in the Design view window.

8 When you're done, click the **Close** button on the task pane.

As you view dependencies for an object in the Object Dependencies task pane and determine you can make changes without effecting other objects, you can open an object in Design view directly from the Object Dependencies task pane and modify it. If you need to look at other objects, you can open more than one from the Object Dependencies task pane. If you are having problems viewing dependency information, you need to turn on the Track Name AutoCorrect Info option on the Current Database pane in Access Options.

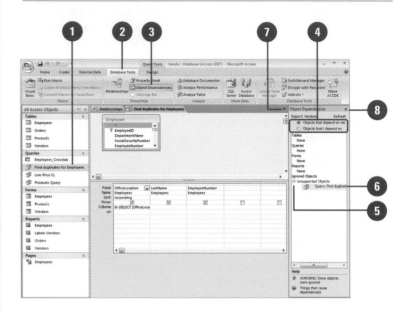

Working with Fields

4

Introduction

An important part of creating your own database is field design. How you design your fields determines how accurately they will be able to store data. Microsoft Office Access 2007 provides flexibility and control in field design. You can design fields so that they allow you to:

◆ Assign a data type so the field accepts and displays the data in the appropriate format.

◆ Include input masks that guide users during data entry.

◆ Specify whether data must be entered into certain fields.

◆ Include a default value for a field.

◆ Include validation checks to ensure that correct data is entered.

◆ Accommodate data whose values are taken from lookup lists.

By taking advantage of these tools during the database design stage, you can save yourself and your database users a lot of trouble later on. By properly designing your fields, you can remove many sources of data-entry error and make your database more simple to manage.

Inserting Fields

Microsoft
Certified
Application
Specialist

AC07S-2.4.2,
AC07S-2.7.1

To make it easier to create fields, Access provides the Add New Field column (**New!**) in Datasheet view so you can quickly enter a field name. If you already have a defined field in the database that you want to use again, you can drag the existing field from the Field List pane (**New!**) on to the datasheet and Access automatically creates a relationship or steps you through the process. You can also use field templates (**New!**) for creating new fields. A field template is a design for a field, complete with a name, data type, length, and predefined properties. You can drag field templates on the datasheet. If you are working in Datasheet or Design view, you can also use the Insert Column or Insert Rows button to create a new field.

Insert Fields Using the Field List Pane and Field Templates

1. In the Navigation pane, click **Tables** on the Objects bar, double-click the table you want to open.

2. Click the **Datasheet** tab under Table Tools.

3. To insert fields, use either of the following methods.

   ◆ **Field Templates.** Click the **New Field** button, and then drag the field you want on to the datasheet between the headers of existing fields.

   ◆ **Field List pane.** Click the **Add Existing Fields** button, and then drag the field you want on to the datasheet between the headers of existing fields.

Did You Know?

Field descriptions appear in the status bar. Access displays the description in the Status bar, giving your users more information during data entry.

Field Templates fields

Field List pane fields

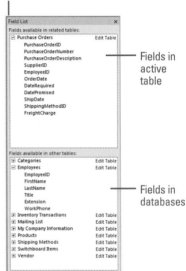

Fields in active table

Fields in databases

Insert a Field in Datasheet View

1. In the Navigation pane, click **Tables** on the Objects bar, double-click the table you want to insert a new field.

2. Click the **Datasheet** tab under Table Tools.

3. Do either of the following:
   - **Add New Field**. Click in the Add New Field, and then type the field name you want.
   - **Insert Column**. Click the column header to the right of where you want to insert a field, and then click the Insert Column button.

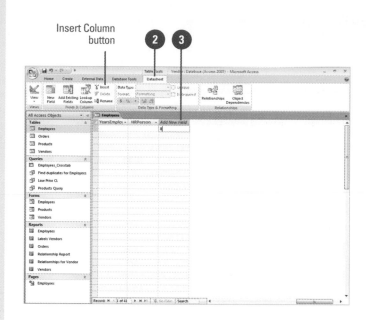

Insert Column button

Insert a Field in Design View

1. In the Navigation pane, click **Tables** on the Objects bar, double-click the table you want to insert a new field, and then click the **Design View** button.

2. Click the row selector for the field that will be below the new field you want to insert.

3. Click the **Insert Rows** button.

   A new blank row appears above the row you selected.

4. Click the Field Name cell for the row you inserted, type the name of the new field.

5. Click the list arrow in the Data Type column, click the data type you want to assign to the field.

6. Click the Description cell, and then type a brief description.

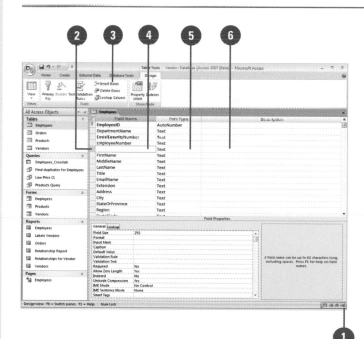

Working with Fields

You can insert, delete, and edit fields in your database tables in Datasheet and Design views. In Datasheet view, each column corresponds to a field. In Design view for tables, each row corresponds to a field. You can add a field by inserting a new column or row that contains the field name, data type, and other properties. You can delete a field by removing a column or row. You can also change field order by re-ordering the columns or rows to better suit your data entry needs.

Delete a Field

① Display the table in Datasheet or Design view.

② Click the column header in Datasheet view, or row selector in Design view for the field you want to delete.

③ Click the **Delete** button in Datasheet view or **Delete Rows** button in Design view.

If any records in the table contain data for this field, a message informs you that deleting this field will also delete any data in the field.

④ Click **Yes** to confirm you want to continue, or click **No** to cancel the deletion.

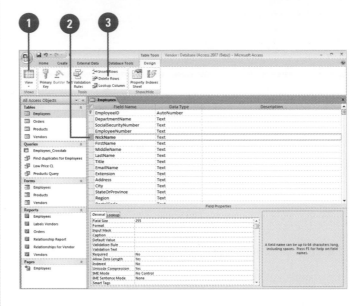

Rename a Field

1. Display the table in Datasheet or Design view.

2. Double-click the column header in Datasheet view, or Field Name cell in Design view for the field you want to rename.

    TIMESAVER *In Datasheet view, you can also click the column header, and then click the Rename button.*

3. Type a new field name, and then press Enter.

Change the Order of Fields in a Table

1. Display the table in Datasheet or Design view.

2. Click the column header in Datasheet view, or row selector in Design view for the field you want to move.

3. Click the column header or row selector again, and then press and hold the mouse button.

4. Drag the column or row to the new position where you want the field to appear, and then release the mouse button.

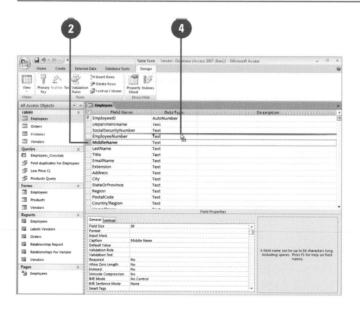

Specifying Data Types and Field Properties

Microsoft Certified Application Specialist

AC07S-1.1.1, AC07S-1.1.2, AC07S-2.4.1

Access provides different **data types**— field formats that define the kind of data the field can accept—which cover a wide variety of data. When you choose a data type for a field, Access will accept data entered only in the format specified by the data type. Selecting the appropriate data type makes it easier for users to enter and retrieve information in the database tables. It also acts as a check against incorrect data being entered. For example, a field formatted to accept only numbers removes the possibility that a user will erroneously enter text into the field.

You can change the data type for a field even after you have entered data in it. However, you might need to perform a potentially lengthy process of converting or retyping the field's data when you save the table. If the data type in a field conflicts with a new data type setting, you may lose some or all of the data in the field.

Once you've selected a data type, you can begin to work with field properties. A **field property** is an attribute that defines the field's appearance or behavior in the database. The number of decimal places displayed in a numeric field is an example of a property that defines the field's appearance. A property that forces the user to enter data into a field rather than leave it blank controls that field's behavior. For the Date/Time field, a calendar button (**New!**) automatically appears next to the field to make it easy to find and choose a date. In Design view for tables, Access provides a list of field properties, called the **properties list**, for each data type.

Data Types

Data Type	Description
Text (default)	Text or combinations of text and numbers, as well as numbers that don't require calculations, such as phone numbers. Limited to 255 characters.
Number	Numeric data used in mathematical calculations.
Date/Time	Date and time values for the years 100 through 9999. An automatic calendar for data picking appears next to a date field (**New!**).
Currency	Currency values and numeric data used in mathematical calculations involving data with one to four decimal places. Values are accurate to 15 digits on the left side of the decimal separator.
AutoNumber	A unique sequential number (incremented by 1) or a random number Access assigns whenever you add a new record to a table. AutoNumber fields can't be changed.
Yes/No	A field containing only one of two values (for example, Yes/No, True/False, On/Off).
OLE Object	An object (such as a Microsoft Excel spreadsheet) linked to or embedded in an Access table.
Hyperlink	A link that, when clicked, takes the user to another file, a location in a file, or a site on the Web.
Lookup Wizard	A wizard that helps you to create a field whose values are chosen from the values in another table, query, or list of values.

Viewing Field Properties

Microsoft Certified Application Specialist

AC07S-1.1.1, AC07S-1.1.2, AC07S-2.4.2

Text Field Properties

Field	Action
Field Size	Specify the maximum number of characters (up to 255) that can be entered in the field.
Format	Specify how the data for the field will appear on the screen.
Input Mask	Specify a format or pattern in which data must be entered.
Caption	Enter a label for the field when used on a form. If you don't enter a caption, Access uses the field name as the label.
Default Value	Specify a value that Access enters automatically.
Validation Rule	Enter an expression that limits the values that can be entered in this field.
Validation Text	Enter an error message that appears when a value prohibited by the validation rule is entered.
Required	Indicate whether data entry is required.
Allow Zero Length	Specify if field allows zero length text strings.
Indexed	Indicate whether Access will keep an index of field values.
Unicode Compression	Indicate whether you want Access to save space if only plain text is entered.

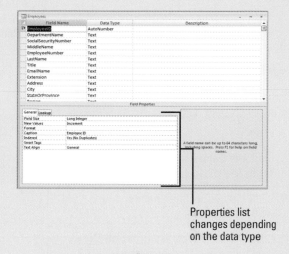

Properties list changes depending on the data type

Changing Field Properties

Microsoft Certified Application Specialist
AC07S-2.4.1, AC07S-2.4.2

After you create fields in a table, you can specify properties that define the field's appearance or behavior in Datasheet or Design view. In Datasheet view, you can quickly set the field data type and format (**New!**). If you want to set more detailed properties, you need to use Design view. In Design view for tables, Access provides a list of field properties for each data type. The properties list changes depending on the data type. Some of the field text properties include Field Size, Format, Input Mask, Caption, Default Value, Validation Rule, Validation Text, Required, Allow Zero Length, and Smart Tags.

Change Field Properties in Datasheet View

1. Display the table in Datasheet view.

2. Click the **Datasheet** tab under Table Tools.

3. Click the field column header you want to change.

4. Click the **Data Type** list arrow, and then select the field data type you want.

5. If available, click any of the formatting buttons, or click the **Format** list arrow, and then select format.

6. To make this a unique field, select the **Unique** check box.

7. To make this a required field, select the **Is Required** check box.

8. Click the **Save** button on the Quick Access Toolbar.

9. When you're done, click the **Close** button in the Table window.

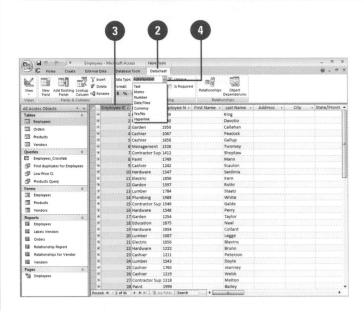

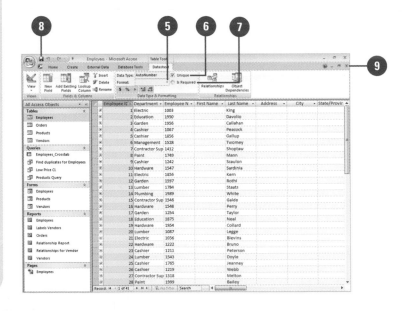

Change Field Properties in Design View

1. Display the table in Design view.

2. Click the field you want to change.

3. Click the field property box you want to change.

4. Type or change the value, or click the list arrow, and then select a value or option.

5. Click the **Save** button on the Quick Access Toolbar.

6. When you're done, click the **Close** button in the Table window.

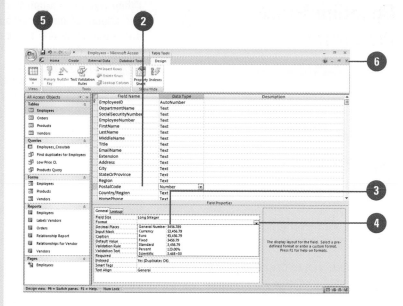

Did You Know?

You can set the number of decimal places. Another way to set the number of decimal places for numeric fields is to specify the number of decimal places in the Decimal Places box in the list of field properties.

You can use different formats for different values. Access allows you to specify different formats for positive, negative, zero, and null values within a single field. Use online Help for more information.

Updating Field Properties

When you make property changes to a field in Table Design view, you can choose to update the corresponding property of controls on forms and reports that are bound to the field. When a bound control inherits a field property change, the Property Update Options button appears in Table Design view, where you can choose the Update command. If a bound control doesn't inherit the field's property change, Access doesn't update the control's property.

Update Field Properties

1 Display the table in Design view.

2 Click the field property box you want to change.

3 Click the **General** or **Lookup** tab, and then change a property.

  If you changed the value of an inherited property, the Property Update Options button appears.

4 Click the **Property Update Options** button, and then click an update command.

5 Select the forms or reports that contain the controls needed to be updated, and then click **Yes**.

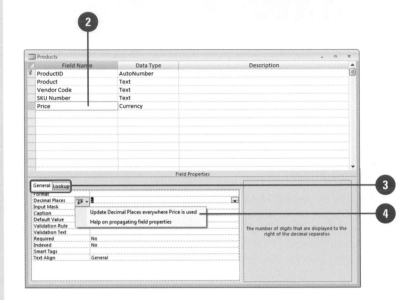

Did You Know?

You can turn off Property Update. Click the Office button, click Access Options, click Object Designers in the left pane, clear the Show Property Update Options Buttons check box, and then click OK.

Setting Field Size

For Text, Number, and AutoNumber data types, you can use the Field Size property to set the maximum size of data stored in the field. In the case of text data, this property specifies the number of characters allowed (from 0 to 255). Numeric field sizes include Byte, Integer, and Long Integer options for integer values, and Single and Double options for decimals. The difference between these sizes lies in the amount of storage space they use and the range of possible values they cover. If your integers will cover only the range 0 to 255, you should use Byte, but for a larger range you should use Integer or Long Integer.

Specify Field Size

1. Display the table in Design view.

2. Click the text or numeric field in the field list.

3. Click the **Field Size** box in the properties sheet, and then either type the Field Size value (for text fields) or choose the value from the drop-down list (for numeric fields).

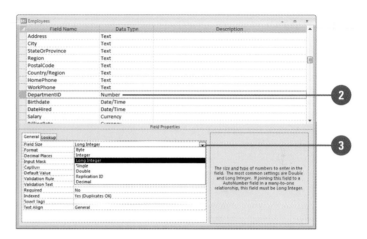

Numeric Field Sizes

Field Size	Range	Storage
Byte	Integers from 0 to 255	1 byte
Integer	Integers from -32,768 to 32,767	2 bytes
Long Integer	Integers from -2,147,483,648 to 2,147,483,647	4 bytes
Single	from -3.402823E38 to -1.401298E-45 (negative values) and 1.401298E-45 to 3.402823E38 (positive values)	4 bytes
Double	from -1.797693E308 to -4.940656E-324 (negative values) and 1.797693E308 to 4.940656E324 (positive values)	8 bytes
Replication ID	Values used to establish unique identifiers	16 bytes

Formatting Text Values

A **format** is a property that determines how numbers, dates, times, and text are displayed and printed. Access provides custom formats for dates and times, but you can also create your own formats using formatting symbols. **Formatting symbols** are symbols that Access uses to control how it displays data values. For example, the formatting symbol "<" forces Access to display text characters in lowercase, while the symbol ">" displays those same characters in uppercase. Formatting may also include use of **literals**, which are text strings that are displayed exactly as they appear in format. Formatting only affects the way the data is displayed. It does not affect the data itself.

Format Text Data

1. Display the table in Design view.

2. Click a text field for which you want to set formatting values.

3. Click the **Format** box, and then enter a text format for all data values in the text field.

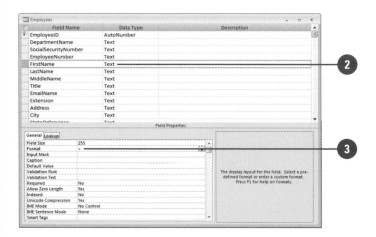

General and Text Formatting Symbols

Symbol	Data	Format	Display
!	321	!	321
<	Today	<	today
>	News	>	NEWS
"ABC"	20	&"lbs."	20lbs.
(space)	16	& "oz."	16 oz.
\	10	&\k	10k
@	5551234	@@@-@@@@	555-1234
&	Mr	&\.	Mr.
*	Hello	&*!	Hello!!!!!!
[color]	Alert	[gray]	Alert

Formatting Memo Text with Rich Text

In previous versions of Access, you could only use plain text. With Access 2007, you can format memo text using the Rich Text format (**New!**). You can format text with common formatting options—such as bold, italic, fonts, and colors—or Rich Text specific options—such as numbering, bullets, text highlight and text direction—and store it in the database. The rich text formatting is stored in a compatible HTML-based format. For a field with the Memo data type, you set the Text Format property to Rich Text, select a field or record in Datasheet view, and then use formatting buttons on the Home tab.

Format Memo Text with Rich Text

1. Display the table in Design view, and then click a memo field for which you want to set formatting values.

2. Click the **Text Format** box.

3. Click the list arrow in the cell to the right, and then click **Rich Text**.

4. If necessary, click **Yes** to convert the contents of the field to Rich Text.

5. Click the **Datasheet View** button.

6. Select the memo field or record you want to format.

7. Click the **Home** tab.

8. Click any of the Rich Text specific formatting buttons (**Decrease List Level**, **Increase List Level**, **Left-to-Right Text Direction**, **Numbering**, **Bullets**, **Text Highlight Color**).

9. Click any of the formatting buttons (**Bold**, **Italic**, **Underline**, **Font Color**, **Font**, or **Font Size**) you want.

Formatting Date and Time Values

Access provides formatting symbols and predefined formats for date and time values that allow you to display different combinations of the time, date, and day. The predefined formats include a general form, which displays the date and time, as well as short, medium, and long forms of the date and time. To help you find and choose a date, the Date/Time field automatically displays a calendar button (**New!**).

Specify a Date and Time Format

① Display the table in Datasheet or Design view.

② Click a date and time field.

③ Click the **Format** list arrow on the Datasheet tab or in the Data Type cell in Design view.

④ Select a format from the predefined list of formats.

Predefined Date Formats	
Format	**Display**
General Date	1/1/05 12:35:15 PM
Long Date	Saturday, January 1, 2005
Medium Date	01-Jan-05
Short Date	1/1/05
Long Time	12:35:15 PM
Medium Time	12:35 PM
Short Time	12:35

Find and Choose a Date

1. In the Navigation pane, double-click the table you want to open.

2. Select a date field.

   TROUBLE? *If the date field contains an input mask, the date picker doesn't appear.*

3. Click the calendar button.

4. Click the **Next** and **Previous** button to find the month you want, and then click the date you want.

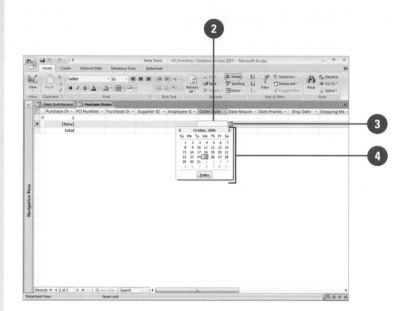

Formatting Number and Currency Values

If a field has a Number or Currency data type, Access provides a list of predefined formats to display the data values in Datasheet or Design view. In Design view, you can also create your own format using formatting symbols applicable to numeric values and currency.

Choose a Predefined Numeric or Currency Format

1. Display the table in Datasheet or Design view.

2. Click a numeric or currency field.

3. Click the **Format** list arrow on the Datasheet tab or in the Data Type cell in Design view.

4. Select a format from the predefined list of formats, or enter the appropriate formatting symbols.

   TIMESAVER *In Datasheet view, you can also click number and currency buttons.*

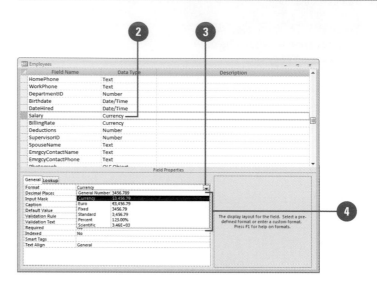

Did You Know?

You can set the number of decimal places. Another way to set the number of decimal places for numeric fields is to specify the number of decimal places in the Decimal Places box in the list of field properties.

You can use different formats for different values. Access allows you to specify different formats for positive, negative, zero, and null values within a single field. Use online Help for more information.

Numeric and Currency Formatting Symbols

Symbol	Data	Format	Display
#	15	#	15
0	20.1	#.00	20.10
.	15	#.	15.
,	92395	#,###	92,395
$	19.3	$#.00	$19.30
%	0.75	#%	75%
E-,E+,e-,e+	625971	#.00E+00	625E+05

Performing a Total Calculation

AC07S-2.3.5

If you create a field for numbers, you can use the Totals row (**New!**) to calculate values using functions such as sum, count, average, maximum, minimum, standard deviation, or variance. To perform a calculation, select the field you want to use in a table, use the Totals button on the Home tab, select the Total row field, and then select the function you want to use.

Use the Total Row to Perform a Calculation

① In the Navigation pane, double-click the table you want to open.

② Click the field with the numbers you want to use in a calculation.

③ Click the **Home** tab.

④ Click the **Totals** button to insert the Totals row at the bottom of the table.

⑤ Click the Total row field in the column with the numbers you want to use in a calculation.

⑥ Click the list arrow, and then select the function you want to use.

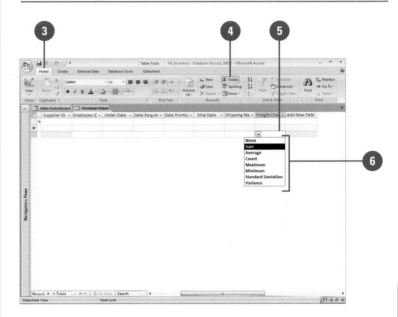

Creating Input Masks

An **input mask** allows you to control what values a database user can enter into a field. Input masks consist of literal characters, such as spaces, dots, parentheses, and placeholders. A **placeholder** is a text character, such as the underline symbol (_), that indicates where the user should insert values. An input mask for a phone number field might appear as follows: (_ _ _) _ _ _ - _ _ _ _ . The parenthesis and dash characters act as literal characters, and the underscore character acts as a placeholder for the phone number values. Access provides several predefined input masks, which cover most situations, but you can create your own customized masks, if necessary. The **Input Mask Wizard** is available only for text and date fields. If you want to create an input mask for numeric fields, you must enter the formatting symbols yourself.

Specify an Input Mask

1. Display the table in Design view, and then click a field for which you want to specify an input mask.

2. Click the **Input Mask** box.

3. Click the **Build** button to start the **Input Mask Wizard**.

4. Scroll thru the predefined list to find an input mask form.

5. Type some sample values to see how the input mask affects your sample values.

6. Click **Next** to continue.

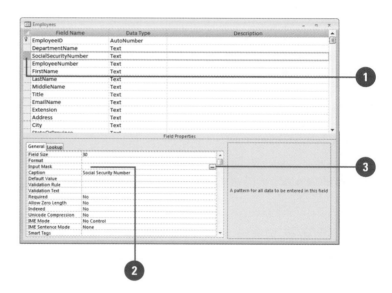

Click to modify or add input masks to the predefined list.

7 If you change the input mask, type new formatting codes.

8 If you want to display a different placeholder, click the Placeholder list arrow, and select the placeholder you want to use.

9 Enter values to test the final version of your input mask, and then click **Next** to continue

10 Indicate whether you want to store the input mask symbols along with the data values.

11 Click **Next** to continue, and then click **Finish**.

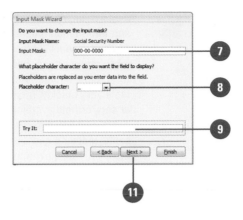

Did You Know?

You can use the Input Mask Wizard. The Input Mask Wizard is available only for text and date fields. If you want to create an input mask for numeric fields, you must enter the formatting symbols yourself.

You can create a password mask. For sensitive data, choose the password input mask from the Input Mask Wizard. Any text the user types will be saved as the text, but displayed as an asterisk (*).

Input Mask Symbols

Symbol	Description
0	Digital 0 to 9 (required)
9	Digital 0 to 9 (optional)
A	Letter or digit (required)
a	Letter or digit (optional)
#	Digit or space
&	Any character or space (required)
C	Any character or space (optional)
L	Letter A-Z (required)
?	Letter A-Z (optional)
>	Make following characters uppercase
<	Make following characters lowercase

Creating Indexed Fields

Just like an index in a book, an index in Access helps you locate and sort information quickly, especially in a very large table. An **index** in Access is an invisible data structure that stores the sort order of a table based on the indexed field or fields. When you sort a large table by an indexed field, Access consults the index and is able to sort the table very quickly. It can be helpful to index fields you frequently search or sort, or fields you join to fields in other tables in queries. If a field contains many different values, rather than many values that are the same, indexing can significantly speed up queries. After indexing a field, you can view and then modify indexes as necessary.

Create a Field Index

1. Display the table in Design view.

2. Click a field you want as an index.

3. Click the **Indexed** box.

4. Click the list arrow, and then select one of the following.

   ◆ **Yes (Duplicates OK)** option if you want to allow multiple records to have the same data in this field.

   ◆ **Yes (No Duplicates)** option if you want to ensure that no two records have the same data in this field.

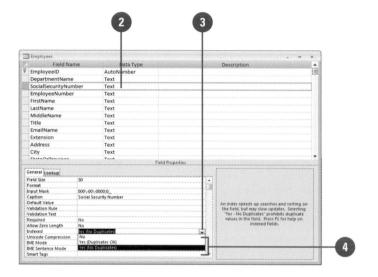

View or Edit Indexes

1. Display the table in Design view.

2. Click the **Indexes** button.

3. Type a name for the index.

4. Select a field to act as an index.

5. Click the list arrow, and then select **Ascending** or **Descending** to indicate the index sort order.

6. Click the **Close** button.

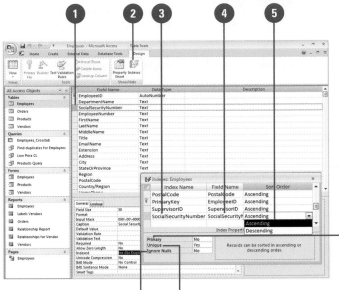

Click to make the index the primary key

Click to remove null values from the index

Click if every value in the index must be unique

Did You Know?

You can index data types. You don't have to index all data types, and there are some data types you cannot index. For example, you do not need to index the primary key of a table, because it is automatically indexed. You can index a field only if the data type is Text, Number, Currency, or Date/Time. You cannot index a field whose data type is Memo or OLE Object.

You can create a multiple-field index. If you think you'll often search or sort by two or more fields, create a multiple-field index by adding additional fields in the Field Name column for each index name.

Specifying Required Fields and Default Values

Some fields contain essential information. For example, social security numbers are required for employees in order to process payroll and other reports. You set fields like these as **required fields**, which means that Access refuses to accept a record until you enter an acceptable value for that field. You can also set a **default value** for a field, a value Access uses unless a user enters a different one. If a field usually has the same value, such as a city or state if most contacts are local, you could assign that value as the default in order to speed up data entry.

Create a Required Field

1. Display the table in Design view, and then click a field that you want to be a required field.

2. Click the **Required** box.

   TIMESAVER *In Datasheet view on the Datasheet tab, you can also select the Is Required check box.*

3. Click the list arrow, and then click **Yes**.

Specify a Default Value

1. Display the table in Design view, and then click a field for which you want to set a default value.

2. Click the **Default Value** box.

3. Enter the default value for the field in the box.

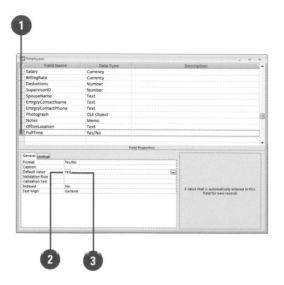

Adding a Caption to a Field

A field **caption** is text displayed alongside a field to better describe its purpose and content. You can add a caption to a field, and later when you create forms and reports that use this field, Access automatically displays the caption you specify. Captions can contain up to 2,048 characters, including spaces. If you don't specify a caption, Access uses the field name as the field caption in any forms or reports you create.

Set the Caption Property

① Display the table in Design view, and then click a field for which you want to set a caption.

② Click the **Caption** box.

③ Type text you want to appear as the field's caption.

Did You Know?

You can set zero-length strings. Text and Memo data type fields allow you to control whether or not a user can leave a field blank. To ensure that some text is entered, set the Required property to Yes.

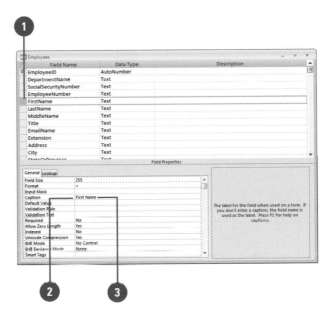

Validating Field Values

When you need explicit control over data entered in a field, such as a range of numbers or dates, you can enforce a **validation rule**, which causes Access to test values a user enters in a field. If the value doesn't satisfy the validation rules criteria, Access refuses to enter the value and displays an error message. You can specify the text of the error message yourself. You can use the Expression Builder to create a validation rule by selecting the functions, constants, and operators you need for your rule from a list of options.

Create a Validation Rule

1. Display the table in Design view, and then click a field that you intend to validate.

2. Click the **Validation Rule** box, and then click the **Builder** button to open the Expression Builder.

3. Create an expression by clicking the appropriate elements in the Expression Builder dialog box.

4. Click **OK**.

As you select options and type variables, the expression appears in this pane.

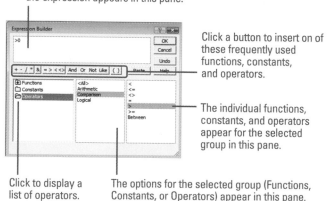

Click a button to insert on of these frequently used functions, constants, and operators.

The individual functions, constants, and operators appear for the selected group in this pane.

Click to display a list of operators.

The options for the selected group (Functions, Constants, or Operators) appear in this pane.

Specify Validation Text

1. Display the table in Design view, and then click a field.

2. Click the **Validation Text** box.

3. Type the text that Access will display when the user tries to enter incorrect data for the field.

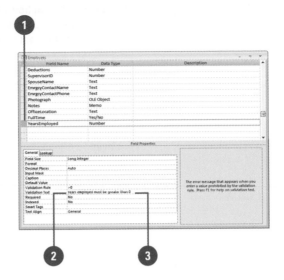

Check Validation Rules

1. Display the table in Design view.

2. Click the **Test Validation Rules** button.

   A validation alert appears, indicating the results of the test or the need to continue the process.

3. If necessary, click **Yes** to continue.

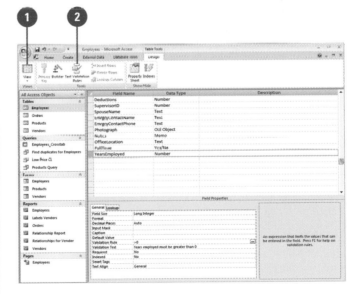

Creating a Lookup Field

The **Lookup Wizard** helps you create a field that displays either of two kinds of lists during data entry: a **Lookup** list that displays values looked up from an existing table or query, or a **Value** list that displays a fixed set of values you enter when you create the field. Because values are limited to a predefined list, using Lookup fields helps you avoid data entry errors in situations where only a limited number of possible values are allowed. The lists are not limited to a single column. You can include additional columns that could include descriptive information for the various choices in the list. However, only a single column, called the **bound column**, contains the data that is extracted from the list and placed into the Lookup field.

Create a Field Based on a Lookup List

1. Display the table in Design view, enter a new field, click the **Data Type** list arrow, and then click **Lookup Wizard**.

   ◆ You can also open a table in Datasheet view, select a field, click the **Datasheet** tab under Table Tools, and then click the **Lookup Column** button.

2. Click the **I want the lookup column to look up the values in a table or query** option, and then click **Next** to continue.

3. Specify the number of columns you want in the Value list.

4. Enter the values in the list. Resize the column widths, if necessary. Click **Next** to continue.

5. Choose which column will act as the bound column, and then click **Next** to continue.

6. Enter a label for the Lookup column.

7. Click **Finish**.

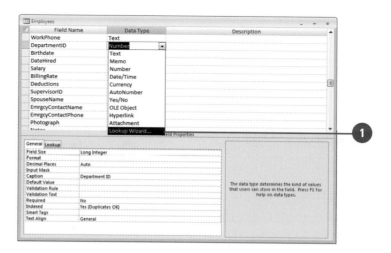

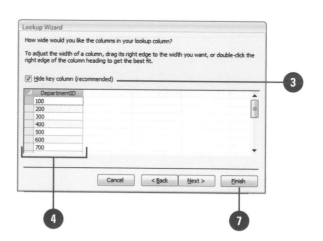

Create a Field Based on a Value List

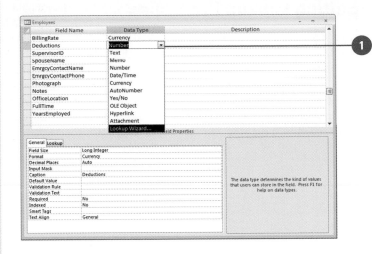

1. Display the table in Design view, enter a new field, click the **Data Type** list arrow, and then click **Lookup Wizard**.

2. Click the **I will type in the values that I want** option, and then click **Next** to continue.

3. Specify the number of columns you want in the Value list.

4. Enter the values in the list. If necessary, resize the column widths, and then click **Next** to continue.

5. Choose which column will act as the bound column, and then click **Next** to continue.

6. Enter a label for the Lookup column.

7. Click **Finish**.

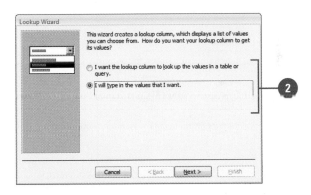

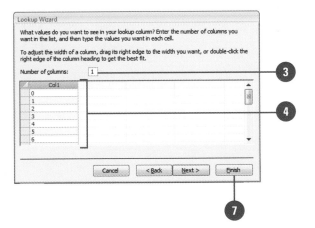

Setting Lookup Properties

If you want to create a Lookup field manually or make changes to the field created by the wizard, you can do so by changing the values in the Lookup properties. These properties allow you to specify the type of drop-down list Access will display, the source of the values in the list, the appearance of the list, and the column that will act as the bound column. You can also indicate whether the user is limited to the choices in the list or can enter other values during data entry.

Specify the type of source for the Lookup data.

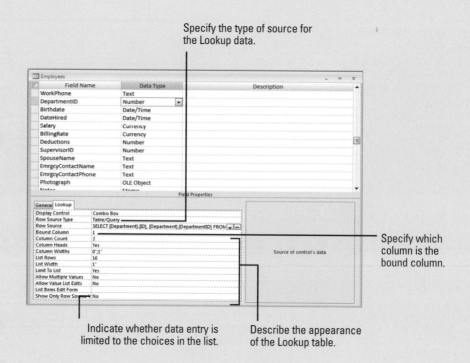

Specify which column is the bound column.

Indicate whether data entry is limited to the choices in the list.

Describe the appearance of the Lookup table.

Creating a Multivalued Field

Microsoft Certified Application Specialist

AC07S-2.4.3

Sometimes you want to store multiple values in a field. For example, you want to assign a task or responsibility to more than one person. In Access 2007, you can create a multivalued field (**New!**) that lets you select more than one value. When you click a multivalue field, check boxes appear next to each available value. You can select or clear items in the list, and then click OK on the menu. To create a multivalue field, you use the Lookup Wizard, and then select the Allow Multiple Values check box on the last wizard screen. The Lookup Wizard helps you create a field that displays either of two kinds of lists during data entry: a Lookup list that displays values looked up from an existing table or query, or a Value list that displays a fixed set of values you enter when you create the field. Because values are limited to a predefined list, using Lookup fields helps you avoid data entry errors in situations where only a limited number of possible values are allowed.

Create a Multivalued Field

1. Display the table in Design view, enter a new field, click the **Data Type** list arrow, and then click **Lookup Wizard**.

   ◆ You can also open a table in Datasheet view, select a field, click the **Datasheet** tab under Table Tools, and then click the **Lookup Column** button.

2. Click the **I want the lookup column to look up the values in a table or query** or **I will type in the values that I want** option, and then click **Next** to continue.

3. Follow the Lookup Wizard instructions depending on how you specified the lookup column values until you get to the final wizard screen.

4. Select the **Allow Multiple Values** check box.

5. Click **Finish**.

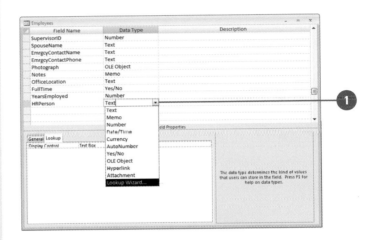

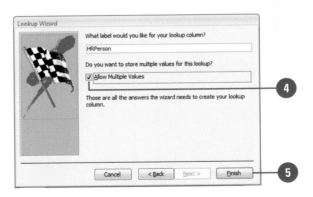

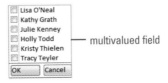

multivalued field

Attaching Files to Field Records

In earlier versions of Access, you needed to use the OLE data type to store images and documents in a database. In Access 2007, you can create a field in a table with the Attachments field and then store multiple files in a single record (**New!**). You can attach a maximum of two gigabytes of data in a database. Individual files cannot exceed 256 megabytes. After you set the data type to Attachments, you cannot change it. A table with the Attachments field display a paper clip in each record where you can attach files. When you double-click a paper clip, the Attachments dialog opens, where you can add, edit, and manage attachments. Access automatically compresses any attached files in a database to optimize it. You can also view and add attachment files in Forms or Reports view.

Create an Attachment Field

① Display the table in Datasheet or Design view.

② Click a blank field name, and then type a field name.

③ Click the **Data Type** list arrow on the Datasheet tab or in the Data Type cell in Design view.

④ Click **Attachment** from the list.

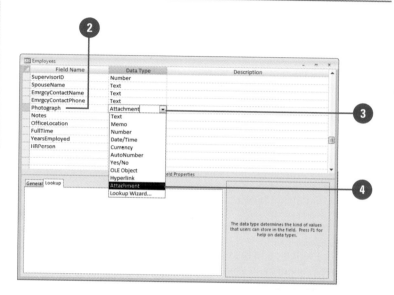

Attachment field

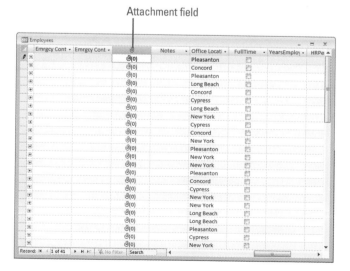

Attach Files in a Record

1. Display the table in Datasheet view.

2. Double-click the record with the paper clip icon where you want to attach a file.

3. Click **Add**.

4. If you want to open a specific file type, click the **Files of type** list arrow, and then select a file type.

5. If the file is located in another folder, click the **Look In** list arrow, and then navigate to the file.

6. Click **Open**.

7. To add more than one file to this record, click **Add**, select the file, and then click **Open**.

8. Click **OK**.

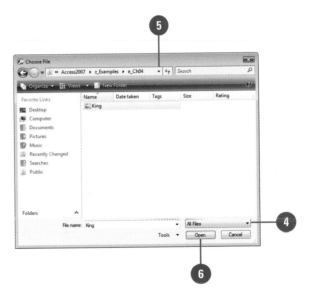

Manage Attachment Files in a Record

1. Display the table in Datasheet view.

2. Double-click the record with the attachments you want to manage.

3. To open an attachment, select it, and then click **Open**.

4. To remove an attachment, select it, and then click **Remove**.

5. To save an attachment, select it, and then click **Save As**. To save all attachments, click **Save All**.

6. Click **OK**.

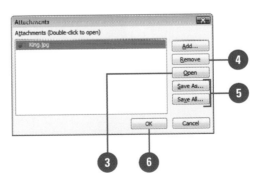

Setting Table Properties

Microsoft
Certified
Application
Specialist

AC07S-2.3.1

Set Table Properties

1. Display the table in Design view.

2. Click the **Design** tab under Table Tools.

3. Click the **Property Sheet** button.

4. Click the box for the property you want to set, and then type a setting for the property.

5. Click the **Close** button on the Property Sheet.

In addition to setting field properties, you can also set table properties. Table properties apply to the entire table and to entire records. The Table Properties task pane displays a list of all available properties, which includes DefaultView, ValidationRule, ValidationText, Filter, OrderBy and SubdatasheetExpanded. You can open a table in Design View, and then use the Property Sheet button on the Design tab to open the Table Properties task pane.

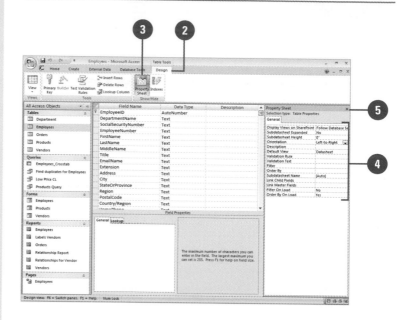

Common Table Properties	
Property	**Description**
DefaultView	Set default view when you open a table
ValidationRule	Specify an expression that must be true to add or change a record
ValidationText	Enter text that appears when a record fails the ValidationRule
Filter	Specify criteria to display only matching rows
OrderBy	Select fields to specify the default sort order
FilterOnLoad	Apply filter when you open table in Datasheet view
OrderByOnLoad	Apply sort criteria when you open table in Datasheet view
Subdatasheet Expanded	Expand all subdatasheets when you open table open

100

Working with Tables

5

Introduction

Tables are the storage containers of your data. To help you work effectively with tables, Microsoft Office Access 2007 provides features that assist you not only in entering and editing the data in your tables but also in locating the information you need.

- ◆ You can locate records based on the text they contain with the Find feature.

- ◆ You can enter and edit data more accurately with features like AutoCorrect, copy, collect, paste, and language features.

- ◆ You can display records in either ascending or descending order based on the contents of a specific field.

- ◆ You can arrange records and columns so your information is listed in the order you want, and adjust the size of your rows and columns to show more or less of the information displayed in any of the fields. You can also view subdatasheets that show groups of data related to the records in your tables.

- ◆ To focus on certain records in a table, you can apply a filter to change which records are displayed. With a filter, you describe characteristics or contents of the records you want to view.

Working with Tables

A database is made up of groups of fields organized into tables. As you develop a database, you continually need to work with tables to change, update, and manage information. Instead of creating a new table everytime you need one, you can also copy an existing table, and then make changes to it. During the copy and paste process, you can select options to create table a with or without data, or append data into another table. If you want to change a table name, you can quickly change it the same way you rename a file or folder name. If you no longer need a table, you can remove it and its data.

Copy a Table

1. In the Navigation pane, click **Tables** on the Objects bar, and then select the table you want to copy.

2. Click the **Home** tab.

3. Click the **Copy** button.

4. Click the **Paste** button.

5. Type a name for the copied table.

6. Click the **Structure Only** or **Structure and Data** option you want.

7. Click **OK**.

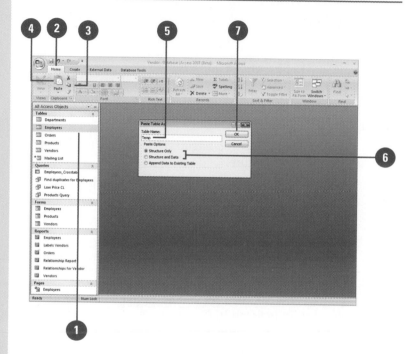

Did You Know?

You can delete a table. Select the table you want to delete in the Navigation pane, click the Delete button on the Home tab, and then click Yes to confirm. You can also right-click a table, and then click Delete.

Rename a Table

1. In the Navigation pane, click **Tables** on the Objects bar.

2. Right-click the table you want to rename, and then click **Rename**.

3. Type a name, and then press Enter.

Append Data to Table

1. In the Navigation pane, click **Tables** on the Objects bar, and then select the table you want to get data.

2. Click the **Home** tab.

3. Click the **Copy** button.

4. Click the **Paste** button.

5. Type the name of the table to which you want to append data.

6. Click the **Append Data to Existing Table** option.

7. Click **OK**.

8. Click **Yes**.

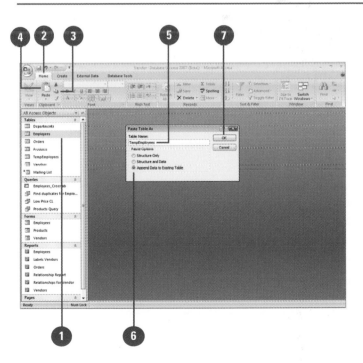

Repairing Renaming Errors

Access can correct errors that commonly occur when you rename forms, reports, tables, queries, text boxes, or other controls in a database. When Access detects a change in the name of one of these objects, it automatically corrects all the other objects that use that name. You can set Access to track renaming without taking action, to apply changes if you rename an object, and to log any changes it makes. Although Name AutoCorrect eliminates errors for database objects that don't employ Visual Basic for Applications (VBA) code, it doesn't repair renaming errors under some circumstances, such as in replicated databases and OBDC linked tables.

Enable and Log Name AutoCorrect

1. Click the **Office** button, and then click **Access Options**.

2. In the left pane, click **Current Database**.

3. Select the **Track name AutoCorrect info** check box to allow Access to maintain the information it needs to perform Name AutoCorrect but not take any action.

4. Select the **Perform name AutoCorrect** check box to perform Name AutoCorrect as changes are applied to the database.

5. To log name AutoCorrect changes, you need to select all three Name AutoCorrect check boxes: **Track name AutoCorrect info**, **Perform name AutoCorrect**, and **Log name AutoCorrect changes**.

   You can view the name changes in a table called AutoCorrect Log.

6. Click **OK**.

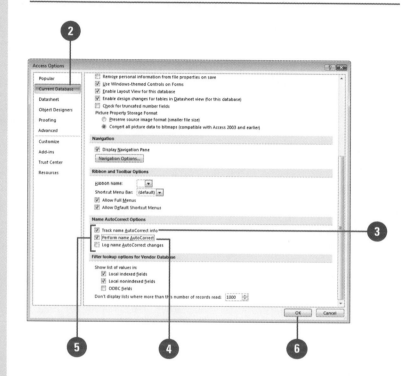

Managing Linked Tables

Update Linked Tables

1. Click the **Database Tools** tab.

2. Click the **Linked Table Manager** button.

3. Select or clear the check box next to the table you want to enable or disable.

4. Click **OK**.

When you link a table from one Access database to another it's important to keep track of where the source database resides and whether the data in the source table changes. A linked table appears in the Navigation pane with a diamond to the left of the name. The Linked Table Manager allows you to enable and disable the linked tables you want to update. If you need to locate a linked table, the Table Manage displays the complete path to the table so you can find it.

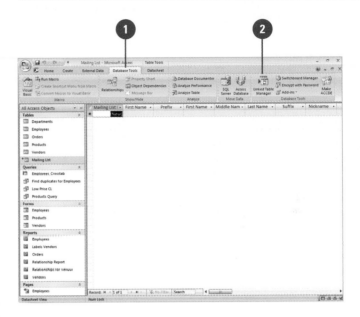

Working with the Clipboard

The Office Clipboard is available from within any Office program and holds information, any or all of which you can paste to a new location. As you cut or copy information, Office collects it in the Office Clipboard. You can use the Office Clipboard task pane to manage the information and use it in Office documents. The Office Clipboard allows you to collect multiple items and paste them quickly. When you paste an item, the Paste Options button appears below it. When you click the button, a menu appears with options to specify how Office pastes the information. The available options differ depending on the content you are pasting.

Paste Items from the Office Clipboard

1. Click the **Home** tab.

2. Click the **Clipboard Dialog Box Launcher**.

3. Click where you want to insert the text.

4. Click any icon on the Clipboard task pane to paste that selection. If there is more than one selection you can paste all the selections at once, by clicking **Paste All**.

5. When you're done, click the **Close** button on the task pane.

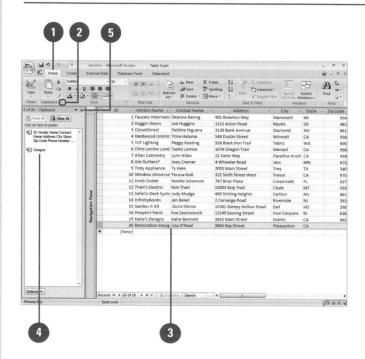

Did You Know?

You can copy and paste a new record. In Datasheet view, select the row selector for the row you want to copy, click the Copy button on the Home tab, select the empty row selector for the new record row, and then click the Paste button.

You can paste information in a different format. Select the object or text, click the Copy button on the Home tab, click to indicate where you want to paste the object, click the Paste button arrow, click Paste Special, click the object type you want, and then click OK.

Delete Items from the Office Clipboard

1. Click the **Home** tab.

2. Click the **Clipboard Dialog Box Launcher**.

3. Click the list arrow of the item you want to paste, and then click **Delete**.

4. To erase all items in the Office Clipboard, click **Clear All**.

5. When you're done, click the **Close** button on the task pane.

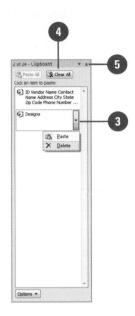

Change Clipboard Options

1. Click the **Home** tab.

2. Click the **Clipboard Dialog Box Launcher**.

3. Click **Options**, and then click to select any of the following options:

   ◆ **Show Office Clipboard Automatically.**

   ◆ **Show Office Clipboard When Ctrl+C Pressed Twice.**

   ◆ **Collect Without Showing Office Clipboard.**

   ◆ **Show Office Clipboard Icon On Taskbar.**

   ◆ **Show Status Near Taskbar When Copying.**

4. When you're done, click the **Close** button on the task pane.

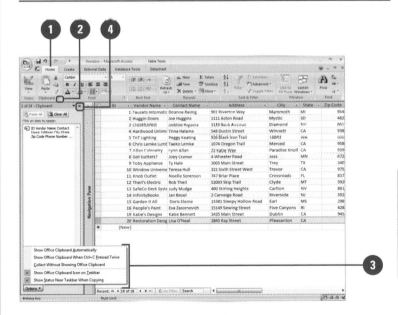

Editing Text

Before you can edit text, you need to highlight, or select, the text you want to modify. You can edit text you enter in a record by selecting the text you want to change and then performing an action. When you want to insert or delete text one character at a time, you point between two characters or words and then click to place the **insertion point**, a vertical cursor that indicates your location in a section of text. When you want to change the entire contents of a table cell, you select the cell. After you select the items you want, you can delete, replace, move (cut), or copy text within Access objects or between different programs. In either case, the steps are the same.

Select and Edit Text and Cell Contents

1. Select the text or cell contents you want to edit.

   - ◆ Double-click a word.

   - ◆ Drag to select multiple words.

   - ◆ Click the border of a table cell to select its entire contents in Datasheet view.

   - ◆ Point to the border of a table cell, and then drag to select multiple cells in Datasheet view.

2. Perform one of the following editing commands:

   - ◆ To replace text, type your text.

   - ◆ To delete text, press the Backspace key or the Delete key.

Did You Know?

You can undo a mistake. If you insert or delete something by mistake, you can click the Undo button on the Quick Access Toolbar to reverse the action.

Insert and Delete Text and Cell Contents

1 Click in the field to place the insertion point where you want to make the change.

◆ To insert text, type your text.

◆ To delete text, press the Backspace key or the Delete key.

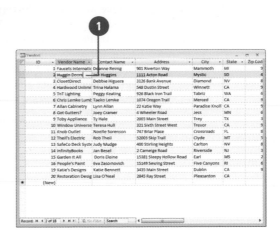

Move or Copy Text and Cell Contents

1 Select the text you want to move or copy.

2 Click the **Home** tab.

3 Click the **Cut** or **Copy** button.

4 Click where you want to insert the text.

5 Click the **Paste** button.

◆ To paste the text with another format, click the Home tab, click the Paste button arrow, click Paste Special, click a format option, and then click OK.

Entering Data Accurately with AutoCorrect

As you enter data in tables, you might occasionally make typing mistakes. For certain errors, Access will correct the errors as soon as you type them and then press the Spacebar or Enter. For example, if you type compnay when you meant to type company, the AutoCorrect feature will correct the error automatically. You can easily customize the preset AutoCorrect options or add errors that you commonly make to the list of AutoCorrect entries.

Set AutoCorrect Options

1 Click the **Office** button, and then click **Access Options**.

2 In the left pane, click **Proofing**, and then click **AutoCorrect Options**.

3 Select the **Replace text as you type** check box to enable AutoCorrect.

4 Select or clear the **Show AutoCorrect Options buttons** check box to show or hide it.

5 Select the check boxes with the additional options you want:

- ◆ **Correct two initial capital letters so that only the first letter is capitalized.**

- ◆ **Always capitalize the first word in a sentence.**

- ◆ **Capitalize the names of days.**

- ◆ **Correct accidental use of the Caps Lock key.**

6 Click **OK**, and then click **OK** again.

Did You Know?

You can replace text as you type. To correct incorrect capitalization or spelling errors automatically, simply continue to type and AutoCorrect will make the required correction.

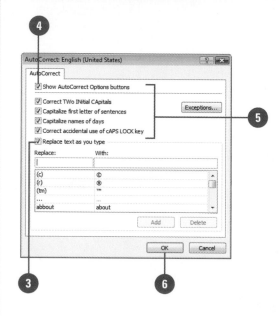

Examples of AutoCorrect Changes

Type of Correction	If You Type	AutoCorrect Inserts
Capitalization	cAP LOCK	Cap Lock
Capitalization	TWo INitial CAps	Two Initial Caps
Capitalization	thursday	Thursday
Common typos	can;t	can't
Common typos	windoes	windows

Add or Edit an AutoCorrect Entry

① Click the **Office** button, and then click **Access Options**.

② In the left pane, click **Proofing**, and then click **AutoCorrect Options**.

③ To edit an entry, select the entry you want to change.

④ To add an entry, type a word or phrase that you often mistype or misspell.

⑤ Type the correct spelling of the word.

⑥ Click **Add** or **Replace**.

⑦ Click **OK**, and then click **OK** again.

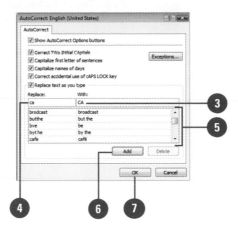

Change Correction as You Type

① After an AutoCorrect correction, point to the AutoCorrect Options button.

② Click the **AutoCorrect Options** button.

③ Click any of the following options:

   ◆ **Change Back To**.

   ◆ **Stop Automatically Correcting**.

   ◆ **Control AutoCorrect Options to change the AutoCorrect settings**.

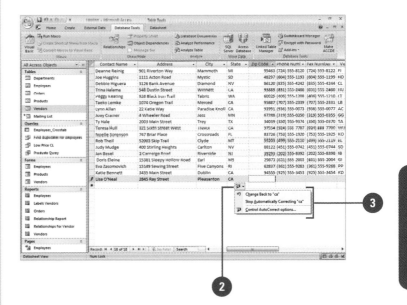

Using Smart Tags

Smart Tags help you integrate actions typically performed in other programs directly in Access. For example, you can add a person's name and address in a database to the contacts list in Microsoft Outlook, or copy and paste information with added control. Access analyzes the data you type and recognizes certain types that it marks with Smart Tags. You can add a smart tag to a field or control by setting the Smart Tag property. Once you have added a smart tag and activate the cell, the Smart Tag Actions button appears, where you can click the button to perform actions. The AutoCorrect Options button is a smart tag. Another smart tag is the Error Indicator button, which helps you correct common errors.

Show or Hide Smart Tags

1. Click the **Office** button, and then click **Access Options**.

2. In the left pane, click **Advanced**.

3. Select or clear the **Show Smart Tags on Forms and Reports** check box.

4. Select or clear the **Show Smart Tags on Datasheets** check box.

5. Click **OK**.

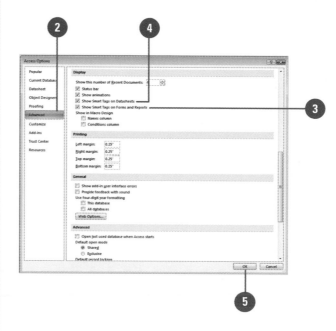

Did You Know?

You can find new smart tags on the Web. In the Smart Tags dialog box, click More Smart Tags to access the Web where you can find information about the latest smart tags.

Add a Smart Tag

1. Select a location where you want to add a smart tag.

   ◆ Open the table or query, and then select the field you want to add a smart tag.

   ◆ Open the form or report, add or select a text box, and then click the **Property Sheet** button.

2. Click the **Build** button in the Smart Tags property box.

3. Select the check boxes for the smart tags you want.

4. Click **OK**, and then save your changes.

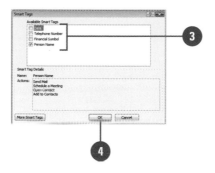

Use a Smart Tag

1. Open the table, query, form, or report with the smart tag.

2. Point to the purple triangle in the cell or text box to display the Smart Tag button.

3. Click the **Smart Tag Options** button, and then click the list arrow next to the button.

4. Click the smart tag option you want; options vary depending on the data.

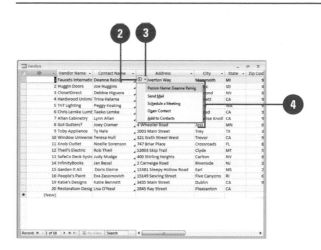

Finding and Replacing Text

To locate one or more records in which you expect to find specific text, you can use the Find feature. In the Find dialog box, you enter the text you want to find, and specify whether Access should search the current field or the entire table, and whether the text you enter should match part of the field or the whole field. You can also indicate whether Access should look for matching capitalization. When Access finds the first record that contains the specified text, it selects that record. You can then move to the next matching record or cancel the search. You can also use the Find and Replace feature to automatically replace specified text with new text. You can review and change each occurrence individually, or replace all occurrences at once.

Search for Text in the Current Field

1. Display the table in Datasheet view.

2. Click the insertion point anywhere in the field (column) where you want to search.

3. Click the **Home** tab.

4. Click the **Find** button.

5. Type the text you want to find in either uppercase or lowercase letters.

6. Click the **Look in** list arrow to specify whether Find should search the current field or the entire table.

7. Click the **Match** list arrow, and indicate whether you want the text you typed to match the whole field or part of the field.

8. Click **Find Next** as many times as necessary to view all the records that contain the specified text.

9. When you're done, click the **Close** button.

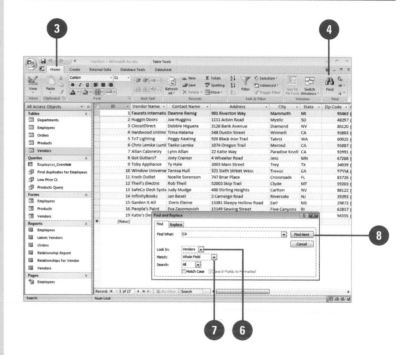

Find and Replace Text

1. Display the table in Datasheet view.

2. Click the insertion point anywhere in the field (column) where you want to search.

3. Click the **Home** tab.

4. Click the **Replace** button.

5. Type the text you want to find, and then press Tab.

6. Type the replacement text.

7. Click **Find Next**.

8. Click **Replace** to replace the first occurrence with the replacement text, or click **Replace All** to replace all occurrences with the replacement text, or click **Find Next** to skip to the next occurrence.

9. Click the **Close** button.

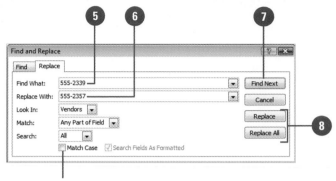

Select the Case check box to search for records matching the case of the text you type.

Did You Know?

You can use wildcards to search for data. When you recall only part of a record data, type an asterisk (*) for two or more unknown characters.

You can search for formatted text. You might need to find information that has been assigned a specific data format, such as a date format, without entering the information in the specified format. For example, if dates are displayed in the format 05-Jan-08, you can locate that number by typing 1/5/08. Select the Search Fields As Formatted check box to only search for the text as formatted. Be aware that searching this way can be slow.

Checking Spelling

The Spelling feature helps you proofread your data by identifying potentially misspelled words and suggesting possible spellings to use instead. You can correct the spelling, ignore the word, add the word to the dictionary, or create an AutoCorrect entry. Microsoft Office 2007 programs share a common spell checker and dictionary, so you only need to make additions and changes once (**New!**). In addition, you can control the kinds of spelling errors Access identifies by specifying the spelling options you want in effect. If the text in your database is written in more than one language, you can automatically detect languages or designate the language of selected text so the spelling checker uses the right dictionary.

Check the Spelling in a Table

1. Display the table in Datasheet view, click the row selector for the record or select the field you want to check. Drag to select additional rows.

2. Click the **Home** tab.

3. Click the **Spelling** button. If Access identifies any misspelled words, it opens the Spelling dialog box.

4. Correct or ignore the identified words, as appropriate.

   ◆ Click **Ignore** to ignore the word and retain its spelling. Click **Ignore All** to ignore all instances of the word.

   ◆ Click **Add** to add the word to the dictionary so the spelling checker won't identify it as a misspelled word.

   ◆ Click a word in the Suggestions list, and then click **Change** to spell the word with the selected spelling. Click **Change All** to change all instances of the word to the selected spelling.

   ◆ Click **AutoCorrect** to add the word to the AutoCorrect list.

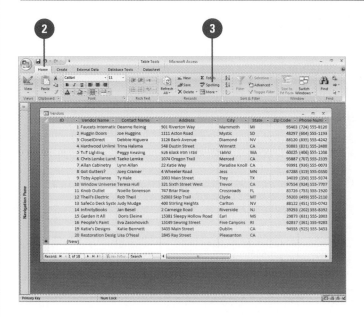

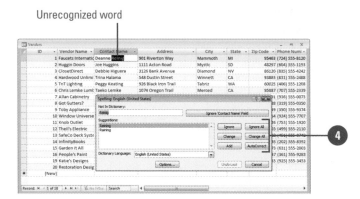

Unrecognized word

Customize Spelling Options

1. In the Spelling dialog box, click **Options**, or click the **Office** button, click **Access Options**, and then click **Proofing**.

2. Select or clear the Microsoft Office spelling options you want.

   ◆ **Ignore words in UPPERCASE**.

   ◆ **Ignore words that contain numbers**.

   ◆ **Ignore Internet and file addresses (New!)**.

   ◆ **Flag repeated words (New!)**.

   ◆ **Enforce accented uppercase in French (New!)**.

   ◆ **Suggest from main dictionary only (New!)**. Select to exclude your custom dictionary.

3. Click **OK**.

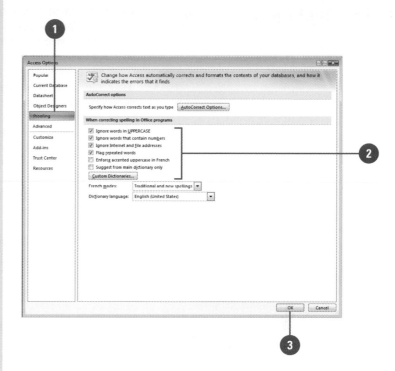

See Also

See "Using Multiple Languages" on page 353 for information on using different languages in Access.

Using Custom Dictionaries

Before you can use a custom dictionary, you need to enable it first. You can enable and manage custom dictionaries by using the Custom Dictionaries dialog box (**New!**). In the dialog box, you can change the language associated with a custom dictionary, create a new custom dictionary, or add or remove an existing custom dictionary. If you need to manage dictionary content, you can also change the default custom dictionary to which the spelling checker adds words, as well as add, delete, or edit words. All the modifications you make to your custom dictionaries are shared with all your Microsoft Office programs, so you only need to make changes once (**New!**). If you mistakenly type an obscene or embarrassing word, such as *ass* instead of *ask*, the spelling checker will not catch it because both words are spelled correctly. You can avoid this problem by using an exclusion dictionary (**New!**). When you use a language for the first time, Office automatically creates an exclusion dictionary. This dictionary forces the spelling checker to flag words you don't want to use.

Use a Custom Dictionary

1. Click the **Office** button, and then click **Access Options**.

2. In the left pane, click **Proofing**.

3. Click **Custom Dictionaries**.

4. Select the check box next to **CUSTOM.DIC (Default)**.

5. Click the **Dictionary language** list arrow, and then select a language for a dictionary.

6. Click the options you want:

    ◆ Click **Edit Word List** to add, delete, or edit words.

    ◆ Click **Change Default** to select a new default dictionary.

    ◆ Click **New** to create a new dictionary.

    ◆ Click **Add** to insert an existing dictionary.

    ◆ Click **Remove** to delete a dictionary.

7. Click **OK** to close the Custom Dictionaries dialog box.

8. Click **OK**.

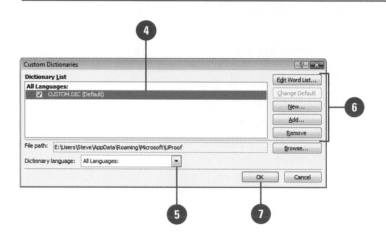

Formatting a Datasheet

If you want to print a datasheet, you can use formatting tools to make it look better than the standard display. You can apply special effects to cells, change the background and gridline color, and modify border and line styles. If you don't want to show the gridlines, you can hide either the horizontal or vertical gridlines, or both. The default display for a datasheet is to display the columns from left to right. If you prefer, you can change the column display to appear from right to left.

Format a Datasheet

1. Open the datasheet you want to format.

2. Click the **Home** tab.

3. Click the **Font Dialog Box Launcher**.

4. Click a cell effect option.

5. Select or clear the **Horizontal** or **Vertical** check box to show or hide gridlines.

6. Click the **Background Color**, **Alternate Background Color**, or **Gridline Color** list arrow, and then select a color.

7. Click the **Border and Line Styles** list arrow, and then select the styles you want.

8. Click a display direction option.

9. Click **OK**.

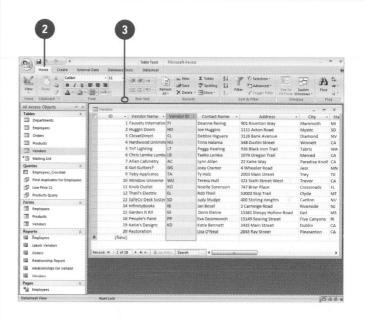

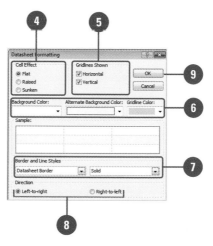

Did You Know?

You can change the formatting in a datasheet using formatting buttons on the Home tab. Open the datasheet you want to format, click the Home tab, click the formatting buttons you want to use, such as Font, Font Style, Font Color, Bold, Italic, or Underline.

Arranging Columns

The order in which columns appear in the Table window in Datasheet view is initially determined by the order established when you first designed the table. If you want to temporarily rearrange the order of the columns in a table, you can do so without changing the table design. You can arrange columns in the order you want by selecting and then dragging columns to a new location. You can also hide columns you do not want to view. The **freeze column** feature allows you to "freeze" one or more of the columns on a datasheet so that they are visible regardless of where you scroll.

Move a Column

1. In Datasheet view, click the column selector of the column you want to move.

2. Drag the selected column to its new location.

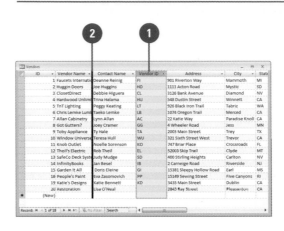

Hide a Column

1. In Datasheet view, select the column or columns you want to hide.

2. Click **Home** tab.

3. Click the **More** button, and then click **Hide Columns**.

   TIMESAVER *Right-click the column you want to hide, and then click Hide Columns.*

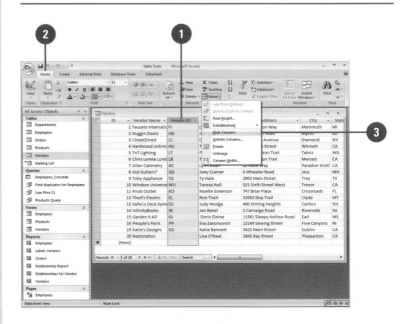

Display a Hidden Column

① In Datasheet view, click the **Home** tab.

② Click the **More** button, and then click **Unhide Columns**.

③ Select the names of the columns that you want to show.

④ Click **Close**.

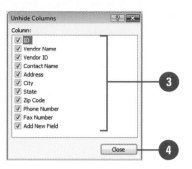

Freeze or Unfreeze Columns

① In Datasheet view, select the column(s) you want to freeze or unfreeze.

② Click **Home** tab.

③ Click the **More** button, and then click **Freeze** or **Unfreeze**.

TIMESAVER *Right-click a column or the selected columns, and then click Freeze Columns or Unfreeze All Columns.*

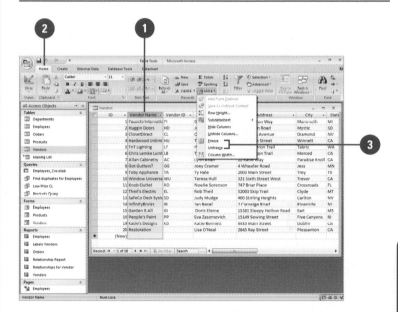

Changing the Size of Rows and Columns

If some of the text in a column is hidden because the column is too narrow, you can increase the width of the column. You can also change the height of the rows to provide more space for the text. Unlike changing the column width, which affects only the selected column or columns, changing the row height affects all the rows in the table. You can adjust the size of columns and rows by using commands or by dragging the borders between columns or rows.

Change Column Width

◆ Point to the border between two field selectors, and then drag the border left or right.

◆ Right-click a field selector or select a column and click the **More** button on the Home tab, and then click **Column Width**. Click **Best Fit**, or enter a new width, and then click **OK**.

Drag to resize

Change Row Height

◆ Point to the border between two row selectors, and then drag the border up or down to adjust the height of all the rows in the table.

◆ Right-click a row selector or select a row and click the **More** button on the Home tab, and then click **Row Height**. Enter a new height, and then click **OK**.

> ### Did You Know?
>
> ***You can format columns in other Access objects.*** These formatting steps also work for columns in queries, forms, views, or stored procedures.

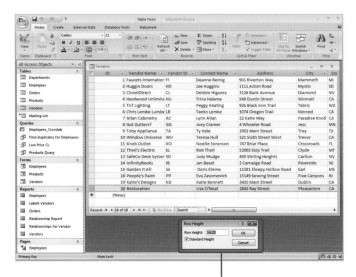

Enter row height information

Managing Columns in Datasheet View

You can quickly add, remove, and rename columns from within Datasheet view. If you remove a column, Access deletes all the data it contains, so delete a column only if you are sure you no longer require its data. If other database objects contain references to a deleted field, such as a query, Microsoft automatically updates those references.

Insert a Column

1 In Datasheet view, right-click the column selector to the right of where you want to add the new column.

◆ You can also select a column and then click the **Insert** button on the Datasheet tab.

2 Click **Insert Column**.

The column is inserted with the name Field1, which you can rename.

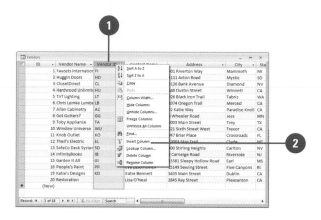

Delete a Column

1 In Datasheet view, right-click the column selector(s) for the column(s) you want to delete.

◆ You can also select a column and then click the **Delete** button on the Datasheet tab.

2 Click **Delete Column**.

3 Click **Yes** to confirm the deletion.

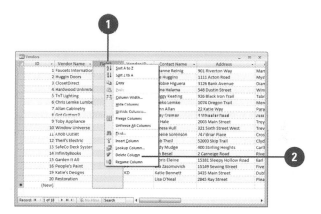

Did You Know?

You can rename a column. In Datasheet view, right-click the selector for the column you want to rename, click Rename Column, type the name you want, and then press Enter.

You can't delete a column in a relationship. You must delete the relationship first before you can delete a column.

Sorting Records

Microsoft
Certified
Application
Specialist

AC07S-5.1.1, AC07S-5.1.2,
AC07S-5.1.3, AC07S-5.1.4

You can change the order in which records appear in a table, query results, forms, or reports by sorting the records. You can select a field and then sort the records by the values in that field in either ascending or descending order. Ascending order means that records appear in alphabetical order (for text fields), from most recent to later, (for date fields), or from smallest to largest (for numeric fields). In Descending order, the order is reversed. You might also want to sort records by more than one field; this is referred to as a **secondary sort**. For example, in a table containing information about products, you might need to view information about specific prices for each product. You can sort the records first by product and then, in records with the same product, sort the records by price.

Sort Records

1. In the Datasheet view, display the table, query results, form, or report in which you want to sort records.

2. To sort multiple columns, drag the column headers to rearrange them to be adjacent.

3. Click the column selector of the column you want to sort. To select another column, press and hold Shift, and then click the column selector.

4. Click the **Home** tab.

5. Click the **Sort Ascending** button (A to Z), or click the **Sort Descending** button (Z to A).

   The list arrow displays an arrow icon indicating the field is sorted. The direction of the arrow indicates the sort direction.

6. To clear all sorts in the current table, click the **Clear All Sorts** button.

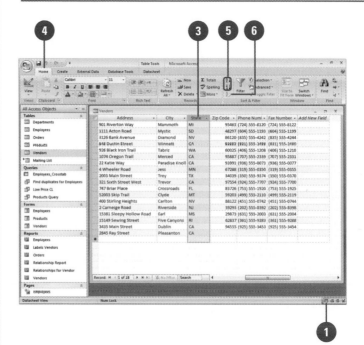

Change the Order of Records Based on Multiple Fields

1. Display the table in Datasheet view.

2. Because multiple fields that you want to sort must be adjacent and in the order of sort priority, rearrange columns if necessary.

3. Click the column selector of the first column you want to sort, and then before you release the mouse button, drag the mouse to the right to select the adjacent columns fields.

4. Click the **Home** tab.

5. Click the **Sort Ascending** button (A to Z), or click the **Sort Descending** button (Z to A).

   The list arrow displays an arrow icon indicating the field is sorted. The direction of the arrow indicates the sort direction.

6. To clear all sorts in the current table, click the **Clear All Sorts** button.

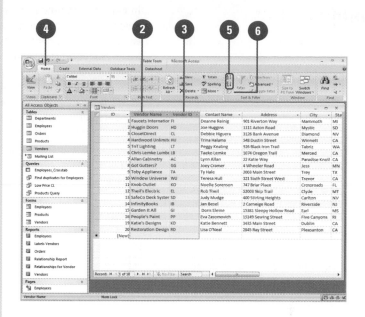

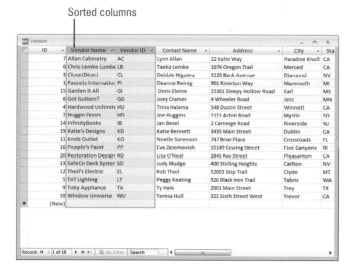

Sorted columns

Did You Know?

You can specify a sort order when designing a table. Changing the order of records displayed in a table is not the same as specifying the sort order when you first design the table. Use the Sort feature when designing a table to display records in the order that you are likely to use most often, and then use the Sort Ascending and Sort Descending buttons to handle the exceptions when you display the table in Datasheet view.

Viewing a Subdatasheet

In a table that has a one-to-many relationship with another table, a given record might have multiple related items. For example, a customer in a Customers table might have many products in a Products table. Access allows you to view the products related to that customer from the Customers table. You can open a **subdatasheet**, a list of the records from the "many" table that relate to a single record from the "one" table in a one-to-one or one-to-many relationship. Subdatasheets help you browse related data in tables, queries, forms, and subform datasheets. For any related tables, Access automatically creates subdatasheets. You can also insert a sub-datasheet in a table or query to view related data.

Insert a Subdatasheet in a Table

1. Display the table or query in Datasheet view.

2. Click the **Home** tab.

3. Click the **More** button, point to **Subdatasheet**, and then click **Subdatasheet**.

4. Click the tab corresponding to the object you want to insert as a subdatasheet.

5. Click a table or query in the list.

6. Select the field you want to use as a foreign key.

7. Select the field you want to use as a primary key.

8. Click **OK**.

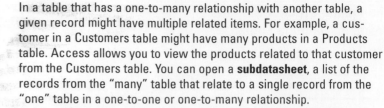

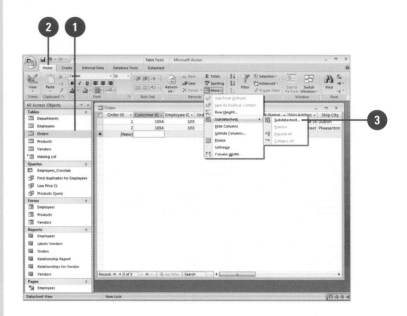

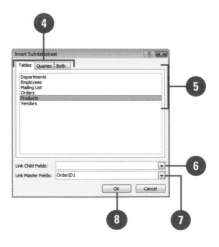

Display or Hide a Subdatasheet

① In Datasheet view of the table, click the plus sign next to the record for which you want to see related information.

② To hide the subdatasheet, click the minus sign next to the record whose subdatasheet you want to hide.

Remove a Subdatasheet

① Display the table or query in Datasheet view with the subdatasheet you want to remove.

② Click the **Home** tab.

③ Click the **More** button, point to **Subdatasheet**, and then click **Remove**.

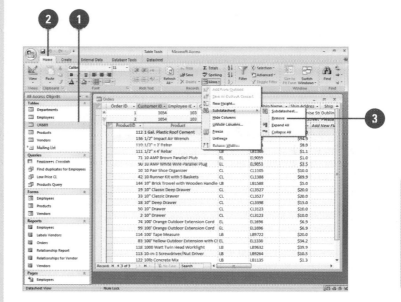

Filtering Out Records

Microsoft Certified Application Specialist

AC07S-4.1.6, AC07S-5.2.1, AC07S-5.2.2, AC07S-5.2.3, AC07S-5.2.4

Instead of displaying all the records in a table, you can use a **filter** to display only those records that you want to see. You can display records based on a specific value in one field or on multiple values in multiple fields. You can filter by selecting quick AutoFilter options (**New!**) for the field values on which to base the filter in Datasheet view or by using Filter By Form to help you create more complex filters involving multiple field values. After you apply a filter, Access displays only those records that match your specifications. You can remove a filter to return the datasheet to its original display.

Filter a Table

1. Display the table in Datasheet view.

2. Click the list arrow for the field you want to filter.

3. Select the check boxes with the items that records must match in order to be included in the table.

4. To use built-in filters, point to **<Column Name> Filters**, and then select a filter option, such as Equals, Begins With, or Contains.

5. Repeat steps 2 through 4, as necessary, to filter out more records using additional fields, and then click **OK**, if necessary.

   The list arrow displays an icon indicating the field is filtered. Also, *Filter* appears in the Status bar.

Did You Know?

You can quickly clear a filter from a table. Display the filtered table in Datasheet view, click the Toggle Filter button.

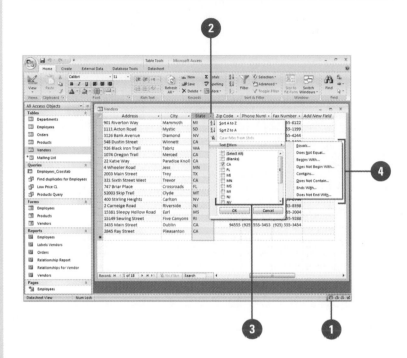

Sorted records

Save a Filter as a Query

1. Display the filtered table in Datasheet view.

2. Click the **Home** tab.

3. Click the **Advanced** button, and then click **Advanced Filter/Sort**.

   The details of the filter appear in Design view.

4. Click the **Save** button on the Quick Access Toolbar.

5. Type the name you want to assign to the query. If you enter the name of an existing query, Access will ask if you want to overwrite the existing query. Be sure to answer "No" if you want to retain the original query, so you can give the new query a different name.

6. Click **OK** to save the filter as a query.

   The query you have just saved appears in the Queries list in the Navigation pane.

7. If necessary, click **OK**.

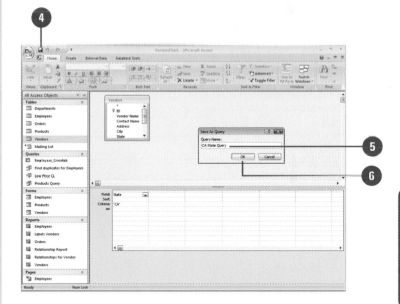

Creating Complex Filters Using Forms

The Filter By Form feature allows you to create a more complex filter. Adding criteria on a particular tab in the form restricts the filter so that records must match all the criteria on the form for the records to be displayed; this is called an AND filter. To expand the filter to include more records, you can create an OR filter by specifying criteria on the subsequent Or tab in the Filter By Form grid. To be displayed, a record needs to match only the criteria specified on the Look For tab or the criteria specified on any one of the Or tabs.

Create an AND or OR Filter

1. Click the **Home** tab.

2. In Datasheet view, click the **Advanced** button, and then click the **Filter By Form**.

3. Click in the empty text box below the field you want to filter.

4. Click the list arrow, and then click the field value by which you want to filter the records.

5. For each field by which you want to filter, click the list arrow, and select the entry for your filter. Each new field in which you make a selection adds additional criteria that a record must match to be included.

6. If you want to establish Or criteria, click the **Or** tab at the bottom of the form to specify the additional criteria for the filter. If not, proceed to step 7.

7. Click the **Toggle Filter** button to turn the filter on or off.

Did You Know?

You can clear previous filters. If necessary, click the Home tab, click the Advanced button, and then click Clear All Filters to clear the previous filter.

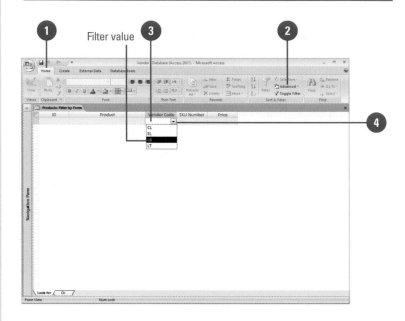

Filter value

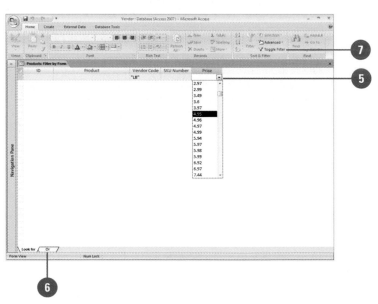

Locating Specific Information Using a Query

6

Introduction

A **query** is a description of the records you want to retrieve from a database. As the name implies, a query helps answer specific questions about the information in your database—for example, "Which customers have placed orders in the last six months?" or "Who sent us greeting cards over the holidays in the last two years?" The description of the records you want to retrieve identifies the names of the fields and the values they should contain; this description is called the **selection criteria**. With a Microsoft Office Access 2007 query you can:

◆ Focus on only the information you need by displaying only a few fields from a large table.

◆ Apply functions and other expressions to fields to arrive at calculated results.

◆ Add, update, or delete records in tables; or create entirely new tables.

◆ Summarize and group values from one table and display the result in a table.

◆ Save a query definition that Access will treat as a table for the purpose of creating forms and reports.

◆ Retrieve information stored in multiple tables, even if the tables are not open.

Understanding Types of Queries

Access offers several types of queries that help you retrieve the information you need— select queries, crosstab queries, action queries, and parameter queries.

- A select query retrieves and displays records in the Table window in Datasheet view.

- A crosstab query displays summarized values (sums, counts, and averages) from one field in a table, and groups them by one set of fields listed down the left side of the datasheet and by another set of fields listed across the top of the datasheet.

- An action query performs operations on the records that match your criteria. There are four kinds of action queries that you can perform on one or more tables: delete queries delete matching records; update queries make changes to matching records; append queries add new records to the end of a table; and make-table queries create new tables based on matching records.

- A parameter query allows you to prompt for a single piece of information to use as selection criteria in the query. For example, instead of creating separate queries to retrieve customer information for each state in which you do business, you could create a parameter query that prompts the user to enter the name of a state, and then continues to retrieve those specific records from that state.

Creating Queries in Access

As with most database objects you create in Access, there are several ways to create a query. You can create a query from scratch or use a wizard to guide you through the process of creating a query.

With the Query Wizard, Access helps you create a simple query to retrieve the records you want. All queries you create and save are listed under Queries in the Navigation pane. You can then double-click a query to run it and display the results. When you run a select query, the query results show only the selected fields for each record in the table that matches your selection criteria. Of course, once you have completed a query, you can further customize it in Design view. As always, you can begin creating your query in Design view without using the wizard at all. Queries are not limited to a single table. Your queries can encompass multiple tables as long as the database includes a field or fields that relate the tables to each other.

Query Wizard

Creating a Query in Design View

AC07S-4.1.1

Although a wizard can be a big help when you are first learning to create a query, you do not need to use a wizard. If you prefer, you can create a query without the help of a wizard. Instead of answering questions in a series of dialog boxes, you can start working in Design view right away. As you create a query, you can include more than one table or even another query in Design view. You can use comparison operators, such as >, <, or =, to compare field values to constants and other field values in the Criteria box. You can also use logical operators to create criteria combining several expressions, such as >1 AND <5.

Create a Query in Design View

1. Click the **Create** tab.

2. Click the **Query Design** button.

3. Select the table or query you want to use.

4. Click **Add**.

5. Repeat steps 3 and 4 for additional tables or queries, and then click **Close**.

6. Double-click each field you want to include in the query from the field list.

7. In the Design grid, enter any desired search criteria in the Criteria box.

8. Click the list arrow in the Sort box, and then specify a sort order.

9. Click the **Save** button, type a name for the query, and then click **OK**.

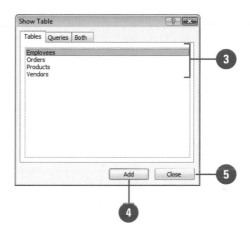

Did You Know?

You can show or hide table names in query properties. Open your query in Design view, and then click the Table Names button on the Design tab under Query Tools. The tables field toggles on and off when you click the Table Names button.

Click to run the query   Click to add more tables

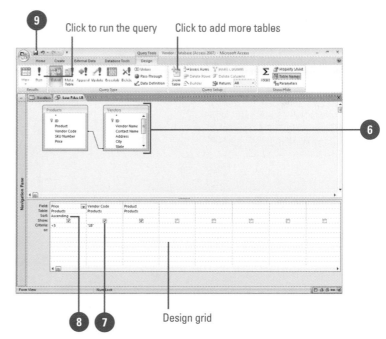

Design grid

Getting Information with a Query

Access saves and lists the queries you create on the Queries bar in the Navigation pane. You can double-click a query to run it and display the results. When you run a query, the query results show only the selected fields for each record in the table that matches your selection criteria. After you run a query, you can close it for use again later.

Run a Query

1. In the Navigation pane, click **Queries** on the Objects bar to display the available queries in the database.

2. Double-click the query you want to run.

   TIMESAVER *You can also drag the object or objects onto the Access work area.*

   The query opens in a table called a dynaset. The dynaset displays the records that meet the specifications set forth in the query.

3. To close the query, click the **Close** button.

Results of query

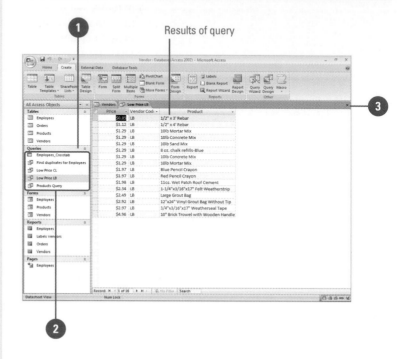

Did You Know?

You can make a query display only records with top or bottom values, or recent or older values. Display the query in Design view, click the Design tab, click the Return list arrow, and then select an option: 5, 25, 100, 5%, 25%, or All.

Modifying a Query in Design View

Once you have completed a query, you can further customize it in Design view. However, you can also create a query in Design view without using the wizard. Queries are not limited to a single table. Your queries can encompass multiple tables as long as the database includes a field or fields that relate the tables to each other. You can create a query using specific criteria and sort the results. If you no longer want to include a table or field, you can remove it from the query. In some cases you might want to hide a field from the query results while keeping it part of the query design for selection design purposes.

Modify a Query in Design View

1. In the Navigation pane, click the **Queries** bar to display the available queries in the database.

2. Click the query you want to modify.

3. Click the **Design View** button.

4. Double-click or drag each field you want to include in the query from the field list.

5. In the Design grid, enter any search criteria in the Criteria box.

6. Click the list arrow in the Sort box, and then specify a sort order.

7. To hide a field, clear the **Show** check box.

8. To delete a field, select the field, and then press Delete.

9. Click the **Save** button on the Quick Access Toolbar.

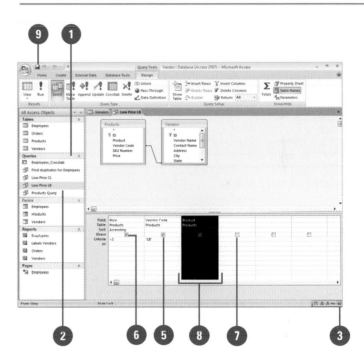

Did You Know?

You can sort the retrieved records. Display the query in Datasheet view, select the field in which you want to sort, and then click the Sort Ascending or Sort Descending button on the Home tab.

You can remove a table. In the query, right-click the table, and then click Remove Table.

Creating a Query Using a Wizard

Microsoft
Certified
Application
Specialist

AC07S-4.1.2, AC07S-4.1.5
AC07S-4.2.5

A query is a simple question you ask a database to help you locate specific information within the database. When you create a query with the **Query Wizard**, you can specify the kind of query you want to create and type of records from a table or existing query you want to retrieve. When you use an existing query to create a new query, the existing one is known as a **subquery**. The Query Wizard guides you through each step; all you do is answer a series of questions, and Access creates a query based on your responses. All queries you create are listed under Queries in the Navigation pane.

Create a Query or Subquery Using the Query Wizard

1 Click the **Create** tab.

2 Click the **Query Wizard** button.

3 Click **Simple Query Wizard**, and then click **OK**.

4 Select a table or existing query.

5 Click to select the fields that you want included in the query.

6 Click **Next** to continue.

7 If you selected numeric or date fields in step 5, indicate whether you want to see detail or summary information.

8 If you choose Summary, click **Summary Options** to specify the calculation for each field, and then click **OK**.

9 Click **Next** to continue.

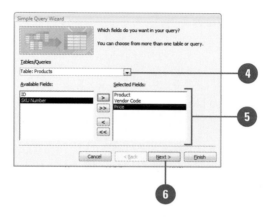

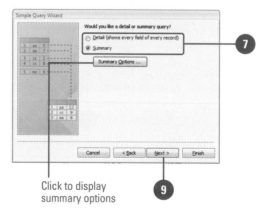

Click to display summary options

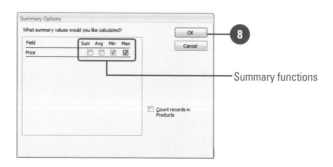

Summary functions

10 In the final wizard dialog box, type the name of the query.

11 Choose whether you want to view the results of the query or modify the query design in Design view.

12 Click **Finish**.

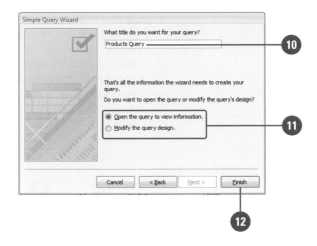

Did You Know?

You can include fields from another source. Click the Tables/Queries list arrow if you want to include a field from another source.

You can create aliases for a table name. An alias makes it easier to work with tables. For example, you can create an alias "e" for a table name Employees, and then refer to the table as "e" throughout the rest of the query. Open the query you want to change in Design view, right-click the table for which you want to create an alias, select Properties, and then enter an alias in the Alias box in the Property Sheet.

Name of query   Results of query

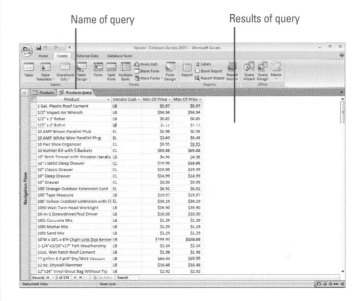

Changing the Query Fields

Microsoft Certified Application Specialist

AC07S-4.1.1, AC07S-4.1.2, AC07S-4.2.1

In Design view, you can add or remove fields in your query design to produce different results. You can also include fields from other tables in your database. In some cases you might want to hide a field from the query results while keeping it part of the query design for selection criteria purposes. When you remove a field from the query design grid, you're only removing it from the query specifications. You're not deleting the field and its data from the underlying table. When you hide a field by clearing the Show check box, the field remains part of the query; it just won't be displayed to the user.

Add a Field to a Query

1. Display the query in Design view.

2. Double-click a field name from the field list to place the field in the next available column in the design grid, or drag a field to a specific column in the design grid.

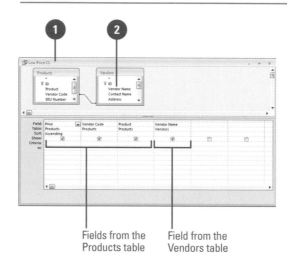

Fields from the Products table   Field from the Vendors table

Remove a Field from a Query

1. Display the query in Design view.

2. Select the field you want to remove from the query.

3. Press Delete, or click the **Design** tab under Query Tools, and then click the **Delete Columns** button.

Did You Know?

You can get field properties. Display the query in Design view, select the field you want to view, and then click the Property Sheet button.

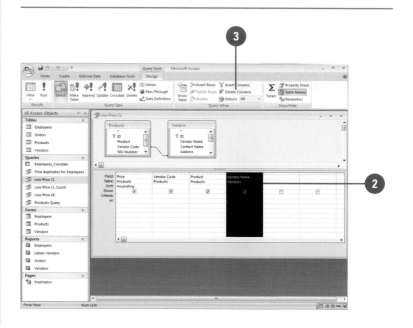

138

Add a Field from Another Table to a Query

1. Display the query in Design view.

2. Click the **Design** tab under Query Tools.

3. Click the **Show Table** button.

4. Select the table that contains the fields you want to include in the query.

5. Click **Add**.

6. Repeat steps 4 and 5 for each table you want to include.

7. Click **Close**.

8. Double-click or drag the fields you want to include to the design grid.

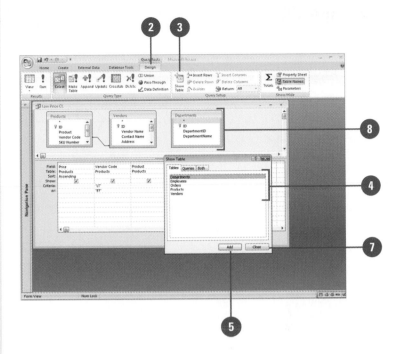

Did You Know?

You can remove a table from the Query design grid. To remove a table, right-click its field list in the top portion of the Query Design View window, and then click Remove Table.

You can change the order of fields in a query. In the design grid, point at the column selector for the column you want to move. (The column selector is the thin gray box at the top of a column.) When the pointer changes to a small black arrow, click to select the column. When the black arrow changes back, use the mouse pointer to drag the selected column to a new position.

Specifying Criteria for a Single Field

For each field you include in a query, you can specify criteria that a record must match to be selected when you run the query. For example, you can create a query to retrieve toys of a certain type, such as infant toys, from a toys database. You do this by entering a criterion's value in the Query Design window. Access allows you to add multiple criteria values for a single field so that the query retrieves records that meet either (or both) of the criteria you specify.

Specify Criteria for a Single Field in a Query

1. Display the query in Design view.

2. Click the **Design** tab under Query Tools.

3. Click the field's Criteria box.

4. Enter a criterion value for the field.

5. If additional values of the field are allowed, enter them into the Or box listed below the Criteria box.

6. Click the **Run** button.

Did You Know?

You can specify text to search for in your selection criteria. When the criterion is a text value, it must be enclosed in quotation marks. Access inserts quotation marks after you type the value and press Tab or Enter.

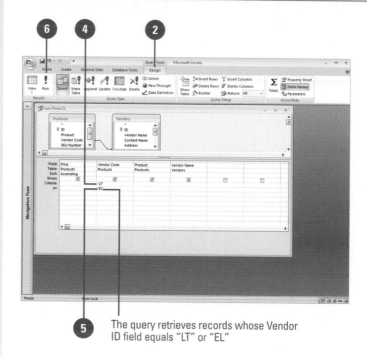

The query retrieves records whose Vendor ID field equals "LT" or "EL"

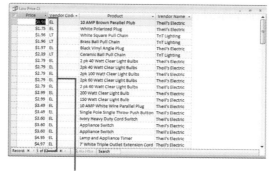

The query retrieves products by vendor LT and EL

Specifying Criteria for Multiple Fields

Microsoft
Certified
Application
Specialist

AC07S-4.2.2

You can specify several query fields. If the criteria for the fields occupy the same row in the Query Design window, Access retrieves records for which **all** of the criteria are satisfied. For example, if you specify the vendor ID as "LT" (TnT Lighting) and the product price equal to "9.99," only products equal to $9.99 by LT will be retrieved. On the other hand, if the criteria are entered into different rows, Access retrieves records for which **any** of the criteria are satisfied. For example, placing "LT" and "9.99" in different rows will cause Access to retrieve either LT products or products with the price $9.99.

Specify Criteria for Multiple Fields in a Query

1. Display the query in Design view.

2. Click the **Design** tab under Query Tools.

3. Enter the criteria value or values for the first field.

4. Enter a criteria value or values for additional fields.

5. Click the **Run** button.

Did You Know?

You can format a query field. To modify the appearance of a query field, click anywhere within the query field's column, and then click the Property Sheet button. You can then specify the format, caption, input mask, and other features of the query field.

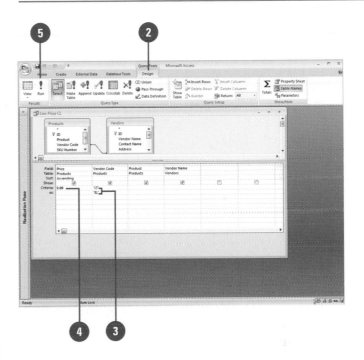

The query retrieves products with a price of $9.99 for LT or any price for EL

Creating Queries with Comparison and Logical Operators

You can use the Expression Builder to create more complicated queries. For example, you can use **comparison operators**, such as >, <, or =, to compare field values to constants and other field values. For example, you can use the greater-than operator (>) to create a query that retrieves records in which more than 1 toy is ordered. You can also use logical operators to create criteria combining several expressions. For example, you can use the AND operator to retrieve records in which the number of toys ordered is greater than 1 AND less than 5. You can also use **logical operators** to negate expressions. For example, you could run a query that retrieves toy records that are NOT infant toys.

Use a Comparison Operator

1. Display the query in Design View.

2. Click the **Design** tab under Query Tools.

3. Click the Criteria box for the field.

4. Click the **Builder** button.

5. Click the appropriate comparison operator button.

◆ To see additional comparison operators, click the Operators folder, click Comparison, and then choose the comparison operator you want from the list on the right.

6. Enter a value or click a field whose value you want to compare.

7. Click **OK**.

8. Click the **Run** button.

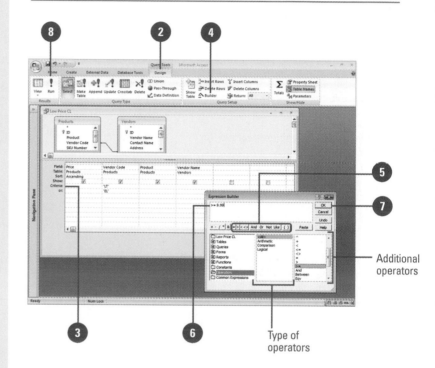

Additional operators

Type of operators

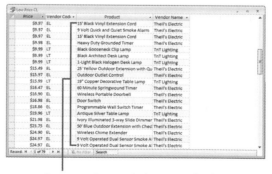

Access retrieves only those records whose price is greater then or equal to $9.99 for LT or any price for EL

Use a Logical Operator

1 Display the query in Design view.

2 Click the **Design** tab under Query Tools.

3 Click the Criteria box for the field.

4 Click the **Builder** button.

5 Click the appropriate logical operator button.

◆ To see additional comparison operators, click the Operators folder, click Logical, and then choose the logical operator you want from the list on the right.

6 Enter any values needed to complete the expression.

7 Click **OK**.

8 Click the **Run** button.

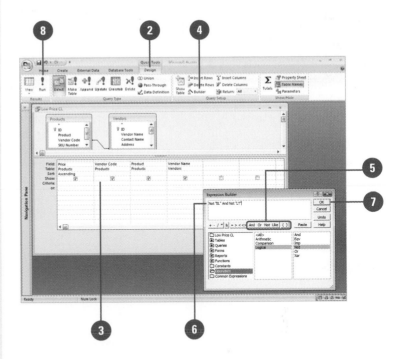

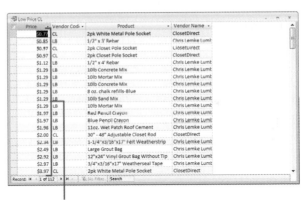

Access retrieves only those records in which the vendor is not EL and LT

Did You Know?

You can fine-tune selection criteria. To fine-tune your selection criteria, combine logical and comparison operators in the same expression.

You can compare one field with another. To create an expression that compares one field with another, use the Expression Builder and look within the Tables folder to locate the table and field of interest. Double-click the field name to add it to the expression. The expression should contain the table name and field name in brackets, separated by an exclamation point. For example, to choose records where the value of the OnOrder field in the Orders table is greater than the value of the InStock field, the expression is: [Orders]![OnOrder]>[Orders]![InStock].

Performing Calculations in Queries

Microsoft Certified Application Specialist

AC07S-2.6.5, AC07S-4.2.4, AC07S-4.2.5, AC07S-4.2.6

In addition to the built-in functions you can use to compare values in a query, you can use the **Expression Builder** to create your own calculations using arithmetic operators. By clicking the operator buttons you want to use and entering constant values as needed, you can use the Expression Builder to include expressions in a query. For example, to determine fees based on a contract amount, you can create an arithmetic expression in your query to compute the results. When you run the query, Access performs the required calculations and displays the results. You can also insert functions, such as AVG and Count, to perform other operations. When you insert a function, <<expr>> appears in parentheses, which represents an expression. Select <<expr>> and replace it with a field name, which you can select in Expression Builder. To create subtotals across groups of records, you can create a totals query, which calculates grand totals for column data.

Create a Calculated Field Using Expression Builder

1. In Query Design view, position the insertion point in the Field row of a blank column in the Design grid.

2. Click the **Design** tab under Query Tools.

3. Click the **Builder** button.

4. Double-click the field (or fields) you want to use in the calculation, and then build an expression using the operator buttons and elements area.

    ◆ Click the button corresponding to the calculation you want.

    ◆ Click the Operators folder, click the Arithmetic folder, and then click the operator you want.

    ◆ Click the Functions folder, click Built-In Functions, and then click the function you want.

5. Type any other values (constants) you want to include in the expression.

6. Click **OK**.

7. Click the **Run** button.

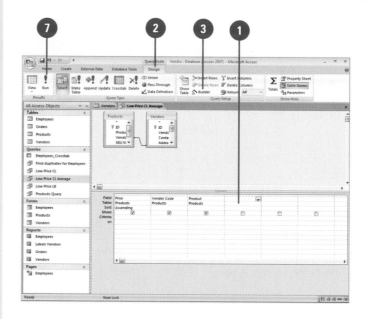

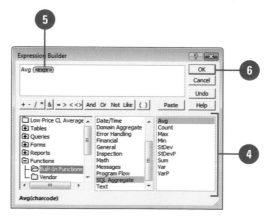

144

Calculate Grand Totals by Using a Query

1. Display the query in Design View.

2. Click the **Design** tab under Query Tools.

3. Click the **Totals** button.

   The Total box appears in query properties with the *Group By*.

4. Click the Total box you want to create a calculated field.

5. Click the list arrow, and then click the function you want to use: Sum, Avg, Min, Max, Count, StDev, Var, First, Last, Expression, or Where.

6. Click the **Run** button.

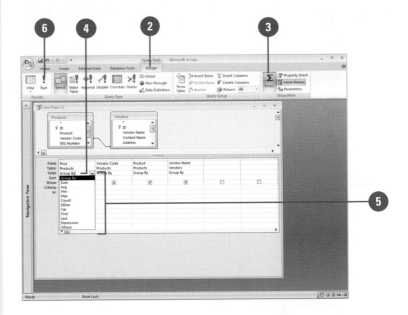

Calculated Average

Did You Know?

You can use aggregate functions in a field. In the Expression Builder under Built-In Functions, you can use an aggregate function, such as Sum, Count, Avg, or Max, to calculate totals. In writing expressions and in programming, you can use SQL aggregate functions (including the four listed here) and domain aggregate functions to determine various statistics.

You can create aliases for column names. An alias makes it easier to work with column names, calculations, and summary values. Open the query you want to change in Design view, right-click the field name in a table which you want to create an alias, select Properties, and then enter an alias in the Alias box in the Property Sheet.

Creating a Parameter Query

When you need to change the criterion value for a query, you either must edit the old query or create a new one. However, if the change involves simply altering a value, you might consider using a parameter query. A **parameter query** prompts the user for the value of a particular query field, rather than having the value built into the query itself. For example, if you want to display the records for particular toy types, a parameter query can prompt you for the type, saving you from creating a separate query for each type.

Create a Parameter Query

1. In Query Design view, click the Criteria box.

2. Click the **Design** tab under Query Tools.

3. Enter the text of the prompt surrounded by square brackets; you can enter multiple criteria in a field (use AND), or use different fields.

4. Click the **Run** button.

5. Enter a criteria value in response to the prompt.

6. Click **OK**.

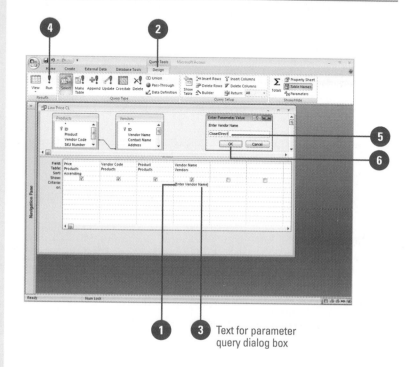

Text for parameter query dialog box

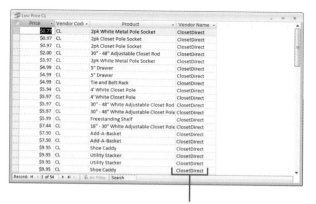

Access retrieves records with ClosetDirect Vendor

Create a Custom Parameter Query

1. Display the query you want to customize with parameters in Query Design view.

2. Click the **Design** tab under Query Tools.

3. Click the **Parameters** button.

4. In the Parameter box, enter the text of the prompt surrounded by square brackets; you can enter multiple criteria in a field (use AND), or use different fields.

5. In the Data Type box, click the list arrow, and then select a data type.

6. When you're done, click **OK**.

7. Click the **Run** button.

8. Enter a criteria value in response to the prompt, and then click **OK** until you're done.

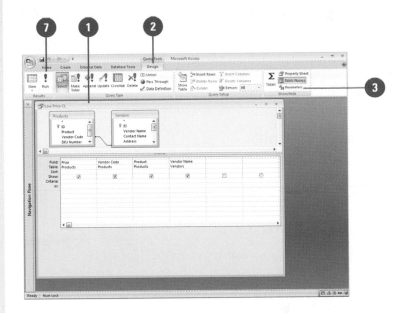

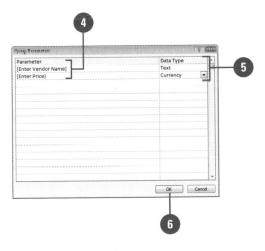

Did You Know?

You can control parameter order and data type. To control the order in which the Enter Parameter Value dialog boxes appears, use the Query Parameters dialog box. To open the Query Parameters dialog box, first open your query in Design view, and then click the Parameters button on the Design tab under Query Tools. The values you enter in the Query Parameters dialog box control the order in which to display the parameters, and the data type to expect for each parameter. When you run your parameter query, Access uses the data types you chose in the Query Parameters dialog box to validate the data that is entered.

Finding Duplicate Fields

In some tables, you need to find records that have duplicate values in particular fields. For example, in a table of employees, you might want to discover which employees work at the same location. You can create a query that retrieves all the records from the Employees table that have duplicate values for the Office Location field. Access provides the Find Duplicate Query Wizard to guide you through each step to help you create the query.

Find Duplicate Records

1. Click the **Create** tab.

2. Click the **Query Wizard** button.

3. Click **Find Duplicates Query Wizard**, and then click **OK**.

4. Choose the table or query that you want to search for duplicate records.

5. Click **Next** to continue.

6. Select the field or fields that might contain duplicate information.

7. Click **Next** to continue.

8. Select any other fields that you want displayed in the query.

9. Click **Next** to continue.

10. Enter a name for the new query.

11. Specify whether you want to view the query results or further modify the query design.

12. Click **Finish**.

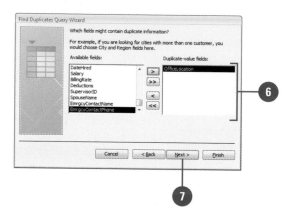

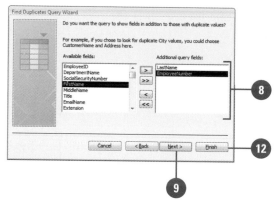

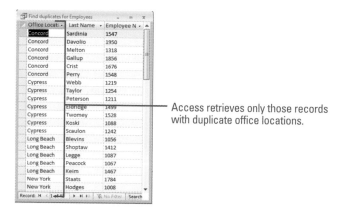

Access retrieves only those records with duplicate office locations.

Finding Unmatched Records

Microsoft Certified Application Specialist

AC07S-4.1.2

When you have related tables, you might want to find which records in one table have no match in the other table. For example, if you have a table of products and a table of customer orders, you might need to know whether there are products that have no match in the Orders table. In other words, are there some products that no customer has yet purchased? Access provides a query wizard to help you answer questions of this type.

Find Unmatched Records

① Click the **Create** tab.

② Click the **Query Wizard** button.

③ Click **Find Unmatched Query Wizard**, and then click **OK**.

④ Choose the table or query whose values you want displayed in the query.

⑤ Click **Next** to continue.

⑥ Choose the related table or query.

⑦ Click **Next** to continue.

⑧ Specify the field that matches records in the first table to records in the second.

⑨ Click **Next** to continue.

⑩ Choose which fields from the first table to display in the query results.

⑪ Click **Next** to continue.

⑫ Enter a name for the new query.

⑬ Specify whether you want to view the query results or further modify the query design.

⑭ Click **Finish**.

Table displayed in the query results

Related links

Matching field

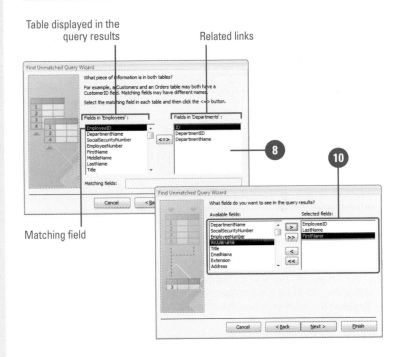

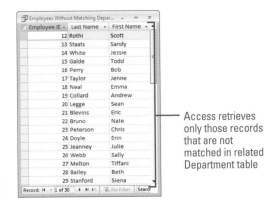

Access retrieves only those records that are not matched in related Department table

Creating New Tables with a Query

Create a New Table with a Query

1. In Query Design view, create a select query, including any combination of fields, calculated fields, or criteria.

2. Click the **Design** tab under Query Tools.

3. Click the **Make Table** button.

4. Type the name of the table you want to create, or click the list arrow, and then select a table from the list if you want to replace the existing one.

5. Click the **Current Database** option if the table is in the currently open database, or click the **Another Database** option and type the name of another database (including the path, if necessary).

6. Click **OK**.

7. Click the **Run** button.

8. Click **Yes** when Access asks if you're sure you want to create the new table.

9. Open the new table to view the records resulting from the query.

The data that appears after you run a query appears in table form and Access allows you to work with those results like tables. However, query results are not tables. If you want to place the results of a query into a separate table, you can use the **make table query**. This query directs Access to save the results of your query to a new table in either the current database or a different database.

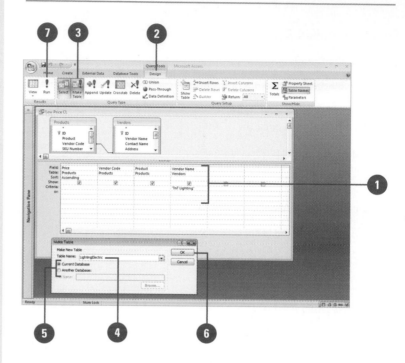

New table

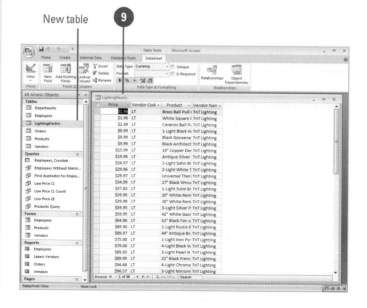

Adding Records with a Query

You can use a query to add records to a table by creating an **append query**. If the fields you've selected have the same name in both tables, Access automatically fills the matching name in the Append To row in the design grid. If the fields in the two tables don't have the same name, enter the names of the fields in the Append To row in the design grid. If the table you are appending records to includes a primary key field, the records you are appending must have the same field or an equivalent field of the same data type. Access won't append any of the records if either duplicate or empty values would appear in the primary key field.

Add Records with a Query

1. In Query Design view, create a select query.

2. Click the **Design** tab under Query Tools.

3. Click the **Append** button.

4. Type the name of the table to which you want to append the records, or click the list arrow, and then choose one.

5. Click the **Current Database** option, or click the **Another Database** option and type the name of another database (including the path, if necessary).

6. Click **OK**.

7. Specify which fields will contain the appended values by entering the field names in the Append To row of the design grid.

8. Click the **Run** button.

9. Click **Yes** when Access asks if you're sure you want to append records to the table.

10. Open the table to view the appended records.

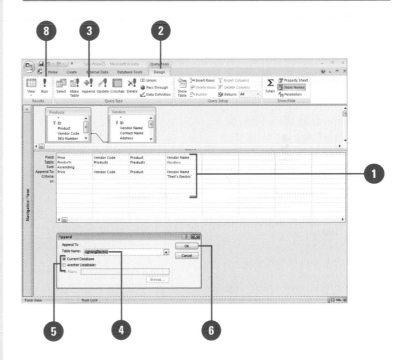

Appended new records to the table

Deleting Records with a Query

If you want to remove records from a table based on a criterion or criteria, you can do so with a **delete query**. The delete query searches the table you specify and removes all records that match your criteria. Because Access permanently deletes these records, use caution before you run a delete query. You can preview the results before you actually run the query. By clicking the Datasheet View button, you can see which records will be deleted before you actually run the query.

Create a Query to Delete Records

1. In Query Design view, create a select query.

2. Click the **Design** tab under Query Tools.

3. Click the **Delete** button.

4. Click the **Datasheet View** button to preview the list of deleted records.

5. If you're satisfied that the appropriate records would be deleted, click the **Design View** button to return to Query Design view.

6. Click the **Run** button.

7. Click **Yes** when Access asks if you're sure you want to delete records from the table.

8. Open the table to view the remaining records.

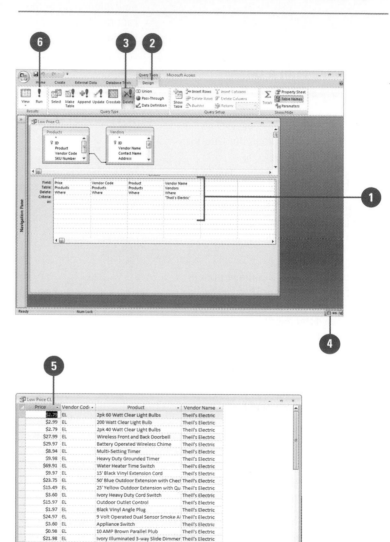

) Unmatched query, can search tbl-copy & give a result if no matching record found in tbl-rentals then it would mean the game is in stock.

. Search for obsolete member details.

2) Search for the copy-ID (exact copy of the game) to put in the rentals tbl.

4. Search for " Game_ID, & a list of the it's details comes up.

5. Search for rental_ID via member ID?

. Search for date due 'ie Today's date' (search for any loans out that are due back at today's date'

6. Search for the price per night of a particular copy of a game.

8. Search for the 'date out' of the game so that the particular price & info can be placed into the letter.

9. Create a query that is less than £4.99 pn, AND available to loan.

10. Grand total query.

11) Increasing all games under the platform 'PS3' by £1 cs

Updating Records with a Query

An **update query** allows you to make changes to a set of records that match your query's criteria. For example, if you want to increase the unit price of board games in a toy product table by $3, you can construct a query that will locate those records and update them to the new value. Make sure you preview the changes to the records before you run the query, because once the records are changed you can't easily change them back.

Create a Query to Update Records

① Display a new query in Query Design view. Add the fields or fields you intend to update and any fields that you want to use for the selection criteria.

② Click the **Design** tab under Query Tools.

③ Click the **Update** button.

④ Enter an expression to update the selected field.

⑤ Enter a criterion, if needed, to indicate which records should be updated.

⑥ Click the **Datasheet View** button to preview the list of deleted records.

⑦ If you're satisfied that the appropriate records would be updated, click the **Design View** button to return to Query Design view.

⑧ Click the **Run** button.

⑨ Click **Yes** when Access asks if you're sure you want to update the records.

⑩ Open the table to view the remaining records.

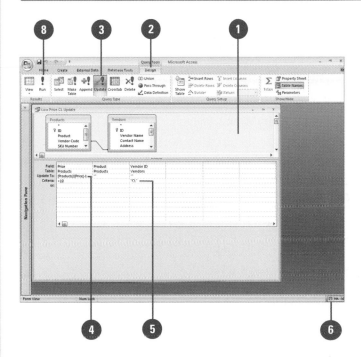

Access decreases the price by $1 for every product by CL over $10

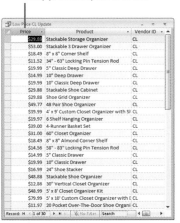

Summarizing Values with a Crosstab Query ▶

Microsoft Certified Application Specialist

ACO7S-4.1.4

A **crosstab query** allows you to summarize the contents of fields that contain numeric values, such as Date fields or Number fields. In this type of query, the results of the summary calculations are shown at the intersection of rows and columns. For example, you can use a crosstab query to calculate the total number of toy products on sale, broken down by toy type. Crosstab queries can also involve other functions such as the average, sum, maximum, minimum, and count. You cannot update crosstab queries. The value in a crosstab query cannot be changed in order to change the source data.

Create a Crosstab Query

1. Click the **Create** tab.

2. Click the **Query Wizard** button.

3. Click **Crosstab Query Wizard**, and then click **OK**.

4. From the list at the top of the dialog box, select the table or query that contains the records you want to retrieve.

5. Click the view option you want: **Tables**, **Queries**, or **Both**.

6. Click **Next** to continue.

7. Double-click the field(s) you want to use in the crosstab query.

8. Click **Next** to continue.

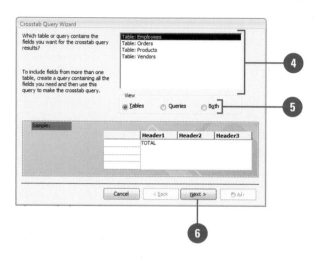

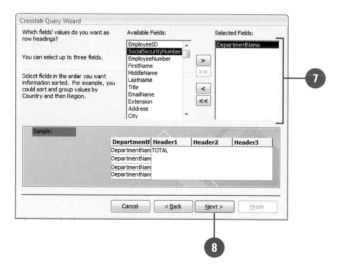

9 Select the field for the columns in the crosstab query.

10 Click **Next** to continue.

11 Click the field whose values you want to be calculated and displayed for each row and column intersection.

12 Click the function you want for the calculation to be performed.

13 Select the **Yes, include row sums** check box if you want to see a total for each row, or clear the check box if you do not want to see a total for each row.

14 Click **Next** to continue.

15 Enter a name for your query.

16 Indicate whether you want to immediately view the query or modify the design.

17 Click **Finish**.

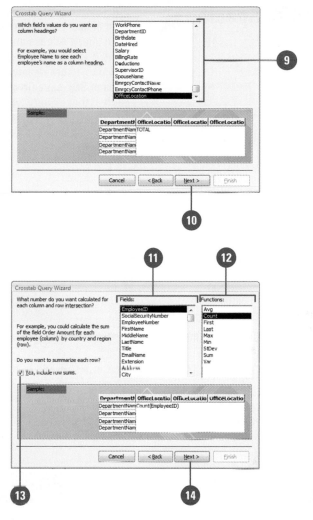

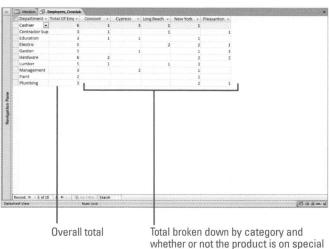

Overall total

Total broken down by category and whether or not the product is on special

Creating SQL-Specific Queries

SQL (Structured Query Language) is a powerful database language used in querying, updating, and managing relational databases. For each query, Access automatically creates an equivalent SQL statement. If you know SQL, you can edit this statement, or write an entirely new one, to create new, more powerful queries. Access supports three kinds of SQL-specific queries: union, pass-through, and data-definition. Each of these query types fulfills a different need.

Create a SQL-Specific Query

1. Click the **Create** tab.

2. Click the **Query Design** button.

3. In the Show Table dialog box, click **Close**.

4. Click the **Union**, **Pass-Through**, or **Data Definition** button.

   The query switches from Design view to SQL view.

5. In SQL view, enter SQL commands to create the query.

   ◆ **Union example.** Type SELECT, followed by a list of fields from the first table. Type FROM, followed by the name of the first of the tables. If you want, type WHERE followed by criterion. Type UNION, and then press Enter. Use the same format for the second table. Type a semicolon (;) to indicate the end of the query. See the illustration for specifics.

6. Click the **Run** button.

7. Save and view the query.

Did You Know?

You can view a query in SQL. To see what your query looks like in SQL, click the View button arrow on the Home tab and then click SQL View.

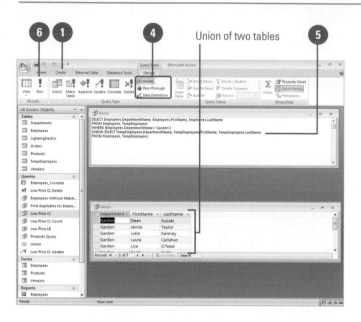

Union of two tables

Types of SQL-Specific Queries

Type	Definition
Union	A query that combines related fields from multiple tables into one field, thus combining the data from several tables.
Pass-Through	A query that sends SQL commands directly to an SQL database server. This allows you to work with tables on the server instead of linking the tables to your Access database.
Data Definition	A query that creates, deletes, or alters tables, or creates indexes in a database table. For example, the following data-definition query uses the CREATE TABLE statement to create a table.
Subquery	A SELECT statement nested inside a SELECT, SELECT...INTO, INSERT...INTO, DELETE, or UPDATE statement or inside another query.

Simplifying Data Entry with Forms

7

Introduction

Forms allow a database designer to create a user-friendly method of data entry in Microsoft Office Access 2007. Instead of entering records in the grid of rows and columns in Datasheet view, you can use a form that can represent a paper form. Such a form can minimize data-entry errors because it closely resembles the paper-based form containing the information you want to enter in your table. A form can include fields from multiple tables, so you don't have to switch from one table to another when entering data. You can use one of the form buttons available on the Create tab (**New!**) to quickly create a basic form, split form, tabular form using multiple items, blank form, and PivotChart.

If your table contains fields that include graphics, documents, or objects from other programs, you can see the actual objects in Form view. (In Datasheet view, the object is identified with text or with an icon.) You can open a form in Form, Design, or Layout view. Form view allows you to view all the information associated with a record; Design view allows you to modify the form's design; and Layout view (**New!**) allows you to view information associated with the record and make changes to the form. To make it even easier to enter and maintain data, you can also include instructions and guidance on the form so that a user of the form knows how to complete it. You can add borders and graphics to the form to enhance its appearance.

The Windows operating system offers you several themes. If you have chosen a theme other than the default, Access will apply the chosen theme to views, dialog boxes, and controls. You can prevent form controls from inheriting themes from the operating system by setting an option in the database or project.

What You'll Do

Create Forms

Work with Form Controls

Create a Form

Create a Form Using a Wizard

Create a Split Form

Create a Datasheet Form

Create a Multiple Items Form

Create a Blank Form

Create a Dialog Form

Create a PivotChart and PivotTable Form

Enter and Edit Data in a Form

Work with a Form in Layout View

Work with a Form in Design View

Modify a Form

Add and Modify Controls

Use the Control Wizards

Create a Subform

Use Windows Themes on Forms

Creating Forms

As with most objects you create in a data-base, you have several choices when creating a form.

- ◆ You can use the **Form** button on the Create tab to create a simple form that contains all the fields in the currently selected table or query.

- ◆ You can use the **Split Form** button on the Create tab to create a form that contains all the fields and a datasheet in the currently selected table or query.

- ◆ You can use the **Multiple Items** button on the Create tab to create a tabular form that contains all the fields in the currently selected table or query.

- ◆ You can use the **Blank Form** button on the Create tab to create a form that contains the fields you want.

- ◆ You can use the **PivotChart** button or **PivotTable** command (More button) on the Create tab to create a PivotChart or PivotTable form.

- ◆ You can use the **Modal Dialog** command (More button) on the Create tab to create a dialog box form that contains the fields you want.

- ◆ You can use the **Datasheet** command (More button) on the Create tab to create a datasheet form.

- ◆ With the Form Wizard, you can spec-ify the kind of form you want to cre-ate and the wizard guides you through each step of the process. You answer a series of questions about your form, and Access creates a form using your formatting preferences.

Of course, once you have completed a form, you can further customize it in Layout or Design view.

Use to create forms

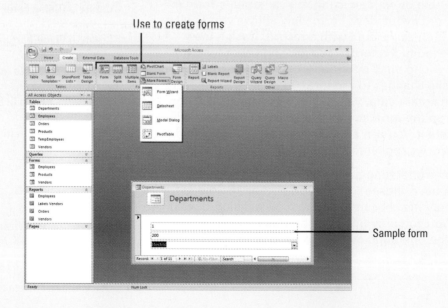

Sample form

Working with Form Controls

Each item on a form, such as a field name, a field value, and the form title, is called a control. When you create a form with a wizard, the wizard takes care of arranging and sizing the controls to make a form according to the selections you provided to the wizard. If you want to modify a form, you can do so in Design view by:

- Moving and sizing controls.

- Changing control properties.

- Changing the appearance of controls with borders, shading, and text effects such as bold and italics.

- Inserting new controls.

- Organizing controls using group boxes.

Types of Form Controls

There are three kinds of controls you can use in a form:

- **Bound controls** are fields of data from a table or query. A form must contain a bound control for each field that you want to appear on the form. You cannot create a calculation in a bound control.

- **Unbound controls** are controls that contain a label or a text box. Typically, you use unbound controls to identify other controls or areas on the form. You can create calculations from an unbound control.

- **Calculated controls** are any values calculated in the form, including totals, subtotals, averages, percentages, and so on.

To create a control, you click the control button for the kind of control you want to create and then drag the pointer over the area where you want the control to appear. The control buttons are available on the Design tab in Design view.

In Design view, you see two parts for every control: the control itself and its corresponding label. When you drag a control to position it, its corresponding label moves with it (and visa versa). You cannot separate a label from its control.

If you are unsure of how to create controls, you can click the Control Wizard button on the Design tab to activate the Control Wizards. With the Control Wizards active, a wizard guides you through the process of creating certain types of controls. For example, if you create a list box control with the Control Wizards button active, the wizard appears, providing information about this type of control. It also prompts you to enter a name for the control label. To turn off the Control Wizards, click the Control Wizards button again (so that it is no longer indented).

Each type of form control has specific characteristics you can change using the Properties feature. You simply select the control you want to modify and then click the Property Sheet button on the Arrange tab under Form Layout Tools or on the Design tab under Form Design Tools. In the control property sheet, you can specify the characteristics you want to change.

After you add fields, you can use the Tab Order button on the Arrange tab under Form Layout Tools to change the selection order when you tab through fields in a form.

Creating a Form

Microsoft
Certified
Application
Specialist

AC07S-2.5.8

To create a simple form in Access, you can use one of the form buttons available on the Create tab (**New!**). You can create a basic form, split form (**New!**), tabular form using multiple items, blank form, and PivotChart. These buttons quickly arrange the fields from the selected table or query into an attractive form. The new form is based on the active object. For example, if a table is active and you click the Form button, Access creates a new form based on the active table. After you create a form, you can save and name it so that you can use it again.

Create a Form

1 In the Navigation pane, click **Tables** or **Queries** on the Objects bar, and then click the table or query you want to use in the form.

2 Click the **Create** tab.

3 Click the any of the following form button:

- **Form.** Creates a columnar form displaying a single record.

- **Split Form.** Creates a columnar form and includes the table datasheet.

- **Multiple Items.** Creates a tabular form displaying multiple records.

- **PivotChart.** Creates a form with a PivotChart based on the table datasheet.

- **Blank Form.** Creates a blank form.

- **More Forms.** Displays a menu with additional options: Form Wizard, Datasheet, Modal Dialog, and PivotTable.

The form appears in Layout view.

4 Click the **Save** button on the Quick Access Toolbar, type a name, and then click **OK**.

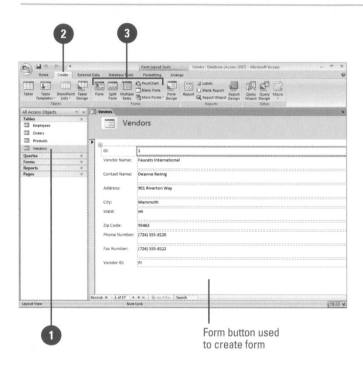

Form button used to create form

Creating a Form Using the Form Wizard

If you need a more custom form, you can use the Form wizard to select the information you want to include from a variety of places. The Form wizard takes you step by step through the form creation process. During the process, you select the data source (tables or queries, and then specific fields), determine the arrangement of information on the form, specify the style of the form, and indicate the view.

Create a Custom Form Using the Form Wizard

1. Click the **Create** tab.

2. Click the **More Forms** button, and then click **Form Wizard**.

3. Click the list arrow for choosing a table or query on which to base the form, and then click the name of the table or query you want.

4. Specify the fields that you want included in the form by double-clicking the fields.

5. Click **Next** to continue.

6. Determine the arrangement and position of the information on the form (Columnar, Tabular, Datasheet, or Justified). Click **Next** to continue.

7. Specify the style of the form, which affects its formatting and final appearance. In the preview area of the dialog box, you can see a preview of the selected style.

8. Click **Next** to continue.

9. Enter a name for your form.

10. Indicate whether you want to open the form or display it in Design view.

11. Click **Finish**.

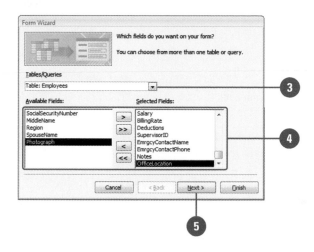

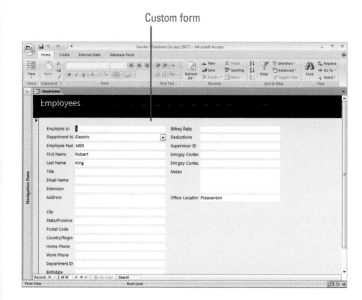

Custom form

Creating a Split Form

A split form (**New!**) displays Form view and Datasheet view on the same form. The top of the form displays Form view, while the bottom of the form display Datasheet view. The two views in a split form use the same table or query data source and Access keeps them synchronized. You can use the Split Form button on the Create tab to quickly create a split form using the selected table or query in the Navigation pane. When you select a field in one view of a split form, Access selects the same field in the other view. If you already have a form that you want to change to a split form, you can modify form properties to make the conversion.

Create a Split Form

1 In the Navigation pane, click **Tables** or **Queries** on the Objects bar.

2 Click the table or query you want to use in the form.

3 Click the **Create** tab.

4 Click the **Split Form** button.

The form appears in Layout view.

5 To change properties, click the **Property Sheet** button on the Arrange tab under Form Layout Tools.

6 Click the **Save** button on the Quick Access Toolbar, type a name, and then click **OK**.

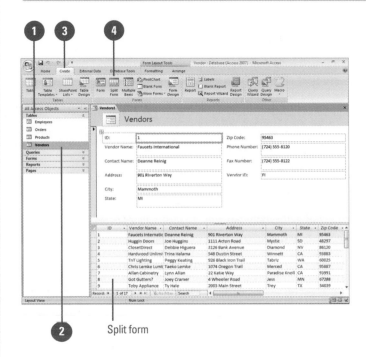

Split form

Did You Know?

You can format field contents in Layout view. You can format an input box using buttons on the Home tab. For example you can change the color, alignment, or style.

See Also

See "Working with Table Records" on page 56 for information on entering and editing record data.

Create an Existing Form into a Split Form

1. In the Navigation pane, click **Forms** on the Objects bar.

2. Double-click the form you want to change into a split form.

3. Click the **Design View** button.

4. Click the **Design** tab under Form Design Tools.

5. Click the **Property Sheet** button.

6. Click the list arrow at the top of the Property Sheet, and then click **Form**.

7. Click the **Format** tab on the Property Sheet.

8. Click the **Default View** list arrow, and then click **Split Form**.

9. Click the **Close** button on the Property Sheet.

10. Click the **Save** button on the Quick Access Toolbar.

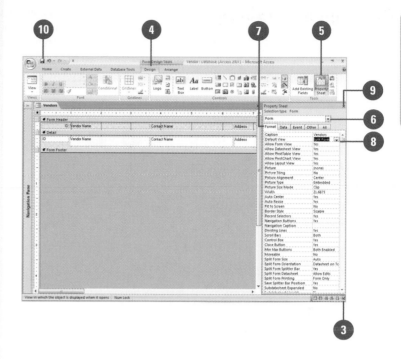

Common Split Form Properties

Property	Description
Split Form Orientation (set in Design view)	Select the location of the datasheet: Top, Bottom, Left, or Right.
Split Form Datasheet	Allow or prevent edits on the datasheet.
Split Form Splitter Bar (set in Design view)	Allow or prevent the splitter bar between the form and datasheet to resize.
Save Splitter Bar Position (set in Design view)	Opens the splitter bar in the same position or hides it.
Split Form Size	Specifies the exact height or width of the split form. Type Auto to set size using the splitter bar in Layout view
Split Form Printing	Define which portion of the form prints: Forms Only or Datasheet Only.

Creating a Datasheet Form

Microsoft
Certified
Application
Specialist

AC07S-2.5.2

Datasheet view is an easy way to scroll through information in a table. Access provides the ability to create a datasheet form, which you can use in the same way as a table. You can use the More button on the Create tab to select the Datasheet command to quickly create a datasheet form using the selected table or query in the Navigation pane.

Create a Datasheet Form

1. In the Navigation pane, click **Tables** or **Queries** on the Objects bar.

2. Click the table or query you want to use in the form.

3. Click the **Create** tab.

4. Click the **More Forms** button, and then click **Datasheet**.

   The form appears in Datasheet view.

5. Click the **Save** button on the Quick Access Toolbar, type a name, and then click **OK**.

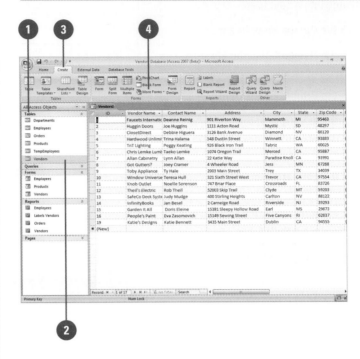

Creating a Multiple Items Form

Microsoft Certified Application Specialist AC07S-2.5.3

Create a Multiple Items Form

1. In the Navigation pane, click **Tables** or **Queries** on the Objects bar.

2. Click the table or query you want to use in the form.

3. Click the **Create** tab.

4. Click the **Multiple Items** button.

   The form appears in Layout view.

5. To change properties, click the **Property Sheet** button on the Arrange tab under Form Layout Tools.

6. Click the **Save** button on the Quick Access Toolbar, type a name, and then click **OK**.

When you create a form using the Form button on the Create tab, Access creates a form that display a single record at a time. If you need to display multiple records in a form, you can use the Multiple Items button (**New!**) on the Create tab to quickly create a tabular form using the selected table or query in the Navigation pane. A multiple items form shows multiple records in a datasheet, with one record per row. The data on the form appears in rows and columns.

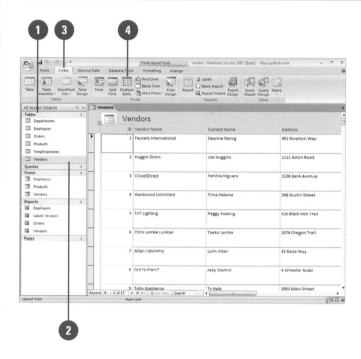

Creating a Blank Form

Microsoft Certified Application Specialist

AC07S-2.5.7

If you plan to use only a few fields in a form, the Blank Form tool makes it easy to quickly drag-and-drop fields from any table in the database. You can use the Blank Form button on the Create tab to quickly create a blank form in Layout view. When you create a blank form, the Field List opens, where you can drag the fields you want onto the blank form. After you add fields in Layout view, you can switch to Design view, and add controls. In Design and Layout views, you can add pictures, titles, pages numbers, date and time, and format the appearance of the form.

Create a Blank Form

1. Click the **Create** tab.

2. Click the **Blank Form** button.

   The form appears in Layout view along with the Field List.

3. Drag fields from the Field List onto the blank form where you want to place them to create a form.

   If necessary, click **Show all tables** in the Field List to display available tables.

4. To show only fields in the current record source, click the link at the bottom of the Field List.

5. Click the **Save** button on the Quick Access Toolbar, type a name, and then click **OK**.

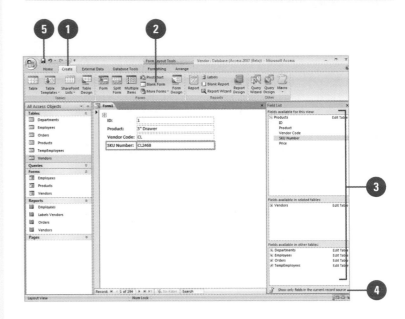

Creating a Dialog Form

If you need to make sure information is entered in a form, the Modal Dialog tool requires you to close the window before you can move on. You can use the More button on the Create tab to select the Modal Dialog command to quickly create a dialog form in Design view. When you create a dialog form, the Field List opens, where you can drag-and-drop fields from any table in the database onto the form in Design view. After you add fields in Design view, you can add controls, pictures, titles, pages numbers, date and time, and then format the appearance of the form.

Create a Dialog Form

1. Click the **Create** tab.

2. Click the **More Forms** button, and then click **Modal Dialog**.

   The form appears in Design view along with the Field List.

3. Drag fields from the Field List onto the blank form where you want to place them to create a form.

   If necessary, click **Show all tables** in the Field List to display available tables.

4. To show only fields in the current record source, click the link at the bottom of the Field List.

5. Click the **Save** button on the Quick Access Toolbar, type a name, and then click **OK**.

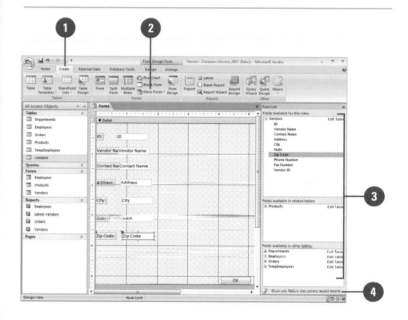

Creating a PivotChart and PivotTable Form

When you want to summarize information in a lengthy list using complex criteria, use the **PivotTable** to simplify your task. Without the PivotTable, you would have to manually count or create a formula to calculate which records met certain criteria, and then create a table to display that information. You can use the PivotTable layout to determine what fields and criteria you want to use to summarize the data and how you want the resulting table to look (**New!**). Sometimes a PivotTable is hard to read. To help you present PivotTable data, you can create a chart. A chart of a PivotTable is called a **PivotChart**. You can use the PivotChart button or PivotTable command (on the More button) on the Create tab in Access to create a blank PivotChart or PivotTable form. In PivotChart or PivotTable view, you can quickly drag-and-drop fields onto the form to create a PivotChart or PivotTable.

Create a PivotChart Form

1. Click the **Create** tab.

2. Click the **More Forms** button, and then click **PivotTable**.

   The form appears in PivotChart view.

3. Click the **Design** tab under PivotChart Tools

4. If necessary, click the **Field List** button to display the Chart Field List.

5. Click the **Expand** icon (+) to display Field items.

6. Drag field items to the **Drop x Fields Here** boxes to create a PivotChart.

7. To add a legend, click the **Legend** button.

8. To change the chart type, click the **Change Chart Type** button, click a chart, and then click **OK**.

9. To refresh the pivot data, click the **Refresh Pivot** button.

10. Click the **Save** button on the Quick Access Toolbar, type a name, and then click **OK**.

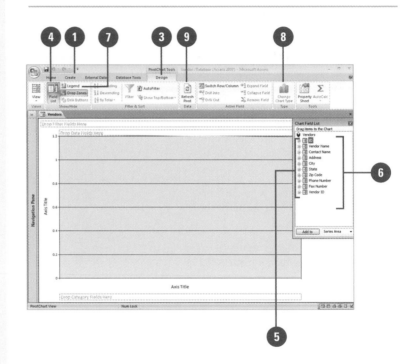

Create a PivotTable Form

1 Click the **Create** tab.

2 Click the **PivotChart** button.

The form appears in PivotTable view.

3 Click the **Design** tab under PivotTable Tools

4 If necessary, click the **Field List** button to display the PivotTable Field List.

5 Click the **Expand** icon (+) to display Field items.

6 Drag field items to the **Drop x Fields Here** boxes to create a PivotTable.

7 To refresh the pivot data, click the **Refresh Pivot** button.

8 Click the **Save** button on the Quick Access Toolbar, type a name, and then click **OK**.

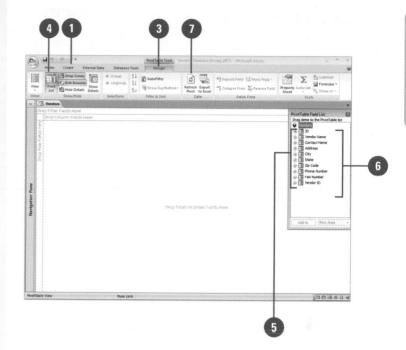

Entering and Editing Data in a Form

Database designers often display data in forms that mimic the paper forms used to record data. Forms facilitate data entry and record viewing. They can also contain buttons that allow you to perform other actions, such as running macros, printing reports, or creating labels. The options that appear on a form depend on what features the database designer included. A form directs you to enter the correct information and can automatically check your entries for errors. Access places the data you've entered in the form into the proper table. You can open a form in Form, Design, or Layout view. Form view allows you to view all the information associated with a record; Design view allows you to modify the form's design; and Layout view (**New!**) allows you to view information associated with the record and make changes to the form.

Enter a New Record in a Form

1. In the Navigation pane, click **Forms** on the Objects bar.

2. Double-click the form you want to open.

3. Click the **Form View** or **Layout View** button.

4. Click the **New Record** button.

5. Enter the data for the first field.

6. Press Tab to move to the next field or Shift+Tab to move to the previous field.

   When you have finished entering the data, you can close the form, click the New Record button to enter another record, or view a different record.

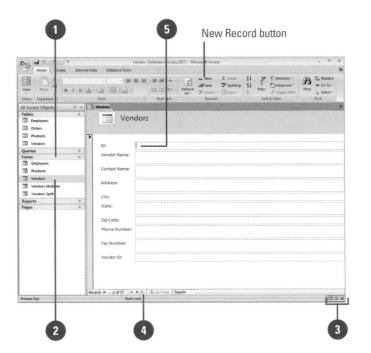

New Record button

Edit a Record in a Form

1. In the Navigation pane, click **Forms** on the Objects bar.

2. Double-click the form you want to open.

3. Click the **Form View** or **Layout View** button.

4. Click in the field you want to edit to place the insertion point, and then edit the text.

5. Press Tab to move to the next field or Shift+Tab to move to the previous field.

Did You Know?

You can delete a record from a form.
In Form view, display the record you want to delete, click the Home tab, click the Delete Record button, and then click Yes.

Working with a Form in Layout View

After you create a form, you can fine-tune the design by working in Layout view (**New!**) , where you can view actual form data as a guide while you make common changes. Since you can view actual form data, Layout view is very useful for sizing controls and fields and changing the appearance of the form. You can also enter and edit data like you can in Form view. If you need to add controls or make more detailed changes to a form, you need to switch to Design view where you can work with the structure of a form. If Layout view is not available, you can enable it for the current database by selecting an option in Access Options.

View a Form in Layout View

① In the Navigation pane, click **Forms** on the Objects bar.

② Click the table you want to use in the form.

③ Click the **Layout View** button.

Switch Between Views

1. Display the form you to view.

2. Do either of the following:

   ◆ **View Selector**. Click the Form, Layout, or Design View button you want.

   ◆ **View button**. Click the Home tab, click the View button arrow, and then click the view you want (Form, Layout, or Design).

   Views vary depending on the form type. Others include Datasheet, PivotChart, PivotTable, or SQL.

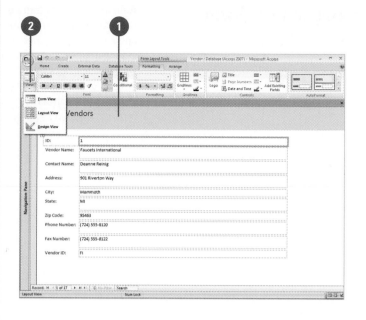

Enable Layout View for the Current Database

1. Click the **Office** button, and then click **Access Options**.

2. In the left pane, click **Current Database**.

3. Select the **Enable Layout View for this database** check box.

4. Click **OK**.

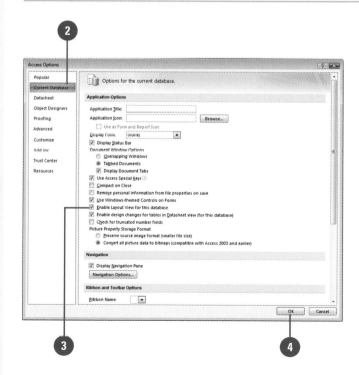

Working with a Form in Design View

Although a wizard can be a big help when you are first learning to create a form, you can create a form without the help of a wizard if you have a good idea of how you want the form to look. Instead of answering questions in a series of dialog boxes, you can start working in Design view right away. Design view is useful for working with the structure and development of a form. You can create, modify, move, and format controls to create the exact form you want. In Design view, form data doesn't appear like it does in Layout view.

Create a Form in Design View

1. Click the **Create** tab.

2. Click the **Form Design** button.

3. Click the **Design View** button.

4. If necessary, click the **Add Existing Field** button on the Design tab under Form Design Tools to add a bound control.

5. Select the field you want to add to the form, drag the field to the location in the form where you want the field to appear, and then release the mouse button to position the field.

6. Create new controls as needed; use any of the control buttons on the Design tab under Form Design Tools, drag to create the control and then follow the wizard.

7. Format the text in the form, as needed.

8. Click the **Save** button on the Quick Access Toolbar to name the form, and then save it in the database.

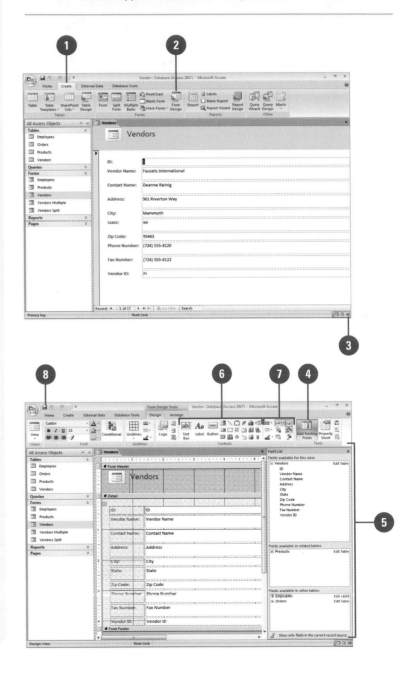

Modify a Form in Design View

1. In the Navigation pane, click **Forms** on the Objects bar, and then double-click the form you want to change.

2. Click the **Design View** button.

3. If necessary, click the **Add Existing Field** button on the Design tab under Form Design Tools to add a bound control.

4. Select the field you want to add to the form, drag the field to the location in the form where you want the field to appear, and then release the mouse button to position the field.

5. Create new controls as needed; use any of the control buttons on the Design tab under Form Design Tools, drag to create the control and then follow the wizard.

6. Format the text in the form, as needed.

7. Click the **Save** button on the Quick Access Toolbar to name the form, and then save it in the database.

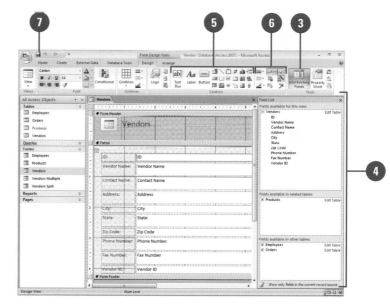

Modifying a Form

Microsoft
Certified
Application
Specialist

AC07S-2.7.1

Controls can make a form easier to use and improve its appearance. Controls also allow you to display additional information on your forms. To create a control on a form, you click the appropriate control button on the Design tab under Form Design Tools. With the control pointer, drag in the form where you want the control to appear. When you release the mouse for some controls, such as the Combo box or List box, the Control Wizard starts, which steps you through the creation process. You can also edit controls to change text and delete controls that you no longer want.

Add Fields and Controls to a Form

1. In the Navigation pane, click **Forms** on the Objects bar, and then double-click the form you want to open.

2. Click the **Design View** button.

3. Click the button on the Design tab under Form Design Tools for the type of control you want to create.

4. In the Form window, drag the pointer to draw a box in the location where you want the control to appear.

5. If you want to switch to Layout view, click the **Layout View** button.

6. Click the **Add Existing Fields** button to display the Field List.

7. Select the field you want to add to the form, drag the field to the location in the form where you want the field to appear, and then release the mouse button to position the field.

8. If a smart tag appears indicating an error, click the **Smart Tag Options** button, and then click an option.

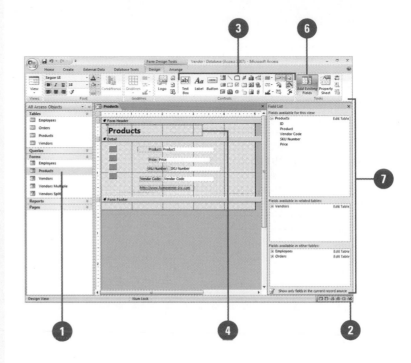

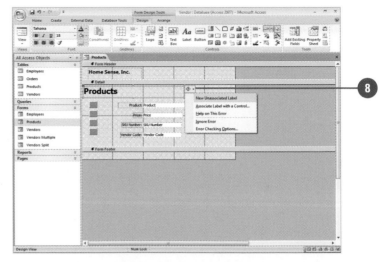

Edit Controls and Modify Properties in a Form

1. Open the form in which you want to edit controls in Design view or Layout view.

2. Click the **Design** tab in Design view or **Layout** tab in Layout view.

3. Click the control you want to edit.

   Small boxes, called handles, appear around the control to indicate it is selected. You can use them to resize the control.

4. To remove the control, press Delete.

5. To edit the control, click the control to place the insertion point, and then use the Backspace or Delete key to remove text or type to insert text.

6. To change control properties, click the **Property Sheet** button, enter the property information you want to add or change, and then click the **Close** button.

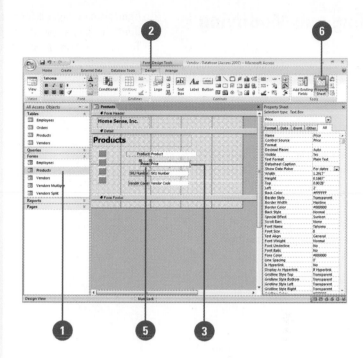

Adding and Modifying Controls

Microsoft Certified Application Specialist

AC07S-2.7.1

Controls can make a form easier to use and improve its appearance. Controls also allow you to display additional information on your forms. To create a control on a form, you click the appropriate control button in the Controls group on the Ribbon. With the control pointer, drag in the form where you want the control to appear. You can also edit controls to change text and delete controls that you no longer want.

Add Controls to a Form

1. Open the form in which you want to add controls in Design view, and then click the **Design** tab under Form Design Tools.

2. Click the button in the Control group for the type of control you want to create.

3. In the Form window, drag the pointer to draw a box in the location where you want the control to appear.

4. Select the field you want to add to the form.

5. Drag the field to the location in the form where you want the field to appear, and then release the mouse button to position the field.

6. If a smart tag appears indicating an error, click the **Smart Tag Options** button, and then click an option.

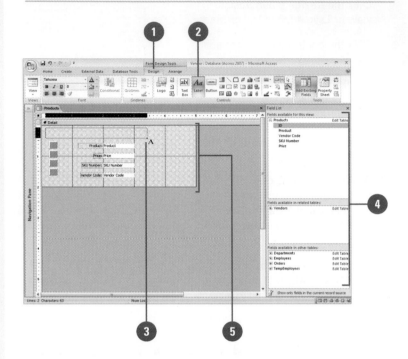

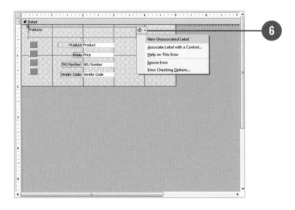

> ### Did You Know?
>
> *You can change the tab order in a form.* Tab order determines the sequence when move between fields using the Tab key. To change the tab order, open the form you want to change in Design view, click the Arrange tab under Form Design Tools, click Tab Order, click a section option, drag selected row to a new tab order, and then click OK.

Edit Controls in a Form

① Open the form in which you want to edit controls in Design view, and then click the **Design** tab under Form Design Tools.

② Click the **Select** button.

③ Click the control you want to edit.

Small boxes, called handles, appear around the control to indicate it is selected. You can use them to resize the control.

④ To remove the control, press Delete.

⑤ To edit the control, click the control to place the insertion point, and then use the Backspace or Delete key to remove text or type to insert text.

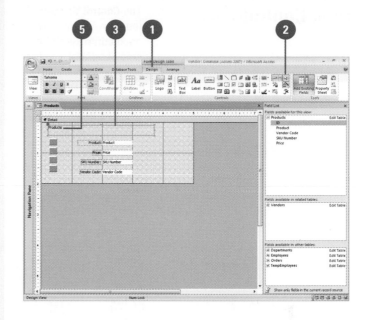

Modify Control Properties

① Open the form or report in which you want to modify controls in Design view, and then click the **Design** tab.

② Click the control you want to view properties.

③ Click the **Property Sheet** button.

TIMESAVER *Double-click the object or its edge (control, section, or form) to open the object's property sheet.*

④ Enter the property information you want to add or change.

⑤ Click the **Close** button on the Property Sheet.

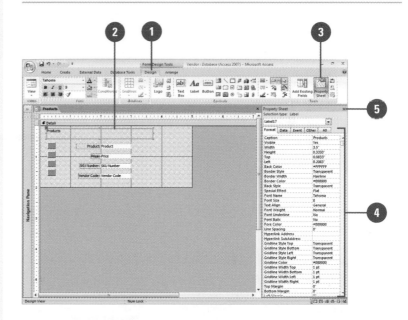

Using the Control Wizards

The **Control Wizards** help you create controls on your form. Although there are many controls you can create, the procedures for creating each control are quite similar, with minor variations depending on the type of control. For example, when you want to include a list of valid options for a field on a form, you can create either a **combo box** or **list box** control. Both controls provide a list from which a user can choose when entering data. The easiest way to create either of these controls is with a Control Wizard, which includes additional sorting options.

Create a List Box or Combo Box

1. Display the form in Design view, click the **Design** tab under Form Design Tools, and then if necessary, click the **Control Wizards** button.

2. Click the **Combo Box** or **List Box** button.

3. In the Form window, drag a rectangle in the location where you want the control to appear. When you release the mouse button, the wizard dialog box for the selected control appears.

4. Specify whether you want the control to get its values from a table or query, from what you type in the box, or from what value is selected in the list or combo box. Click **Next** to continue.

5. If applicable, select the table that contains the values you want displayed in the list or combo box. Click **Next** to continue.

6. Select the field that contains the values you want displayed in control. Click **Next** to continue.

7. Select the first sort list arrow, select a table to sort, and then click the **Sort** button. If you want, select additional sorts. Click **Next** to continue.

8. Adjust the width of the columns for the list box as necessary. Click **Next** to continue.

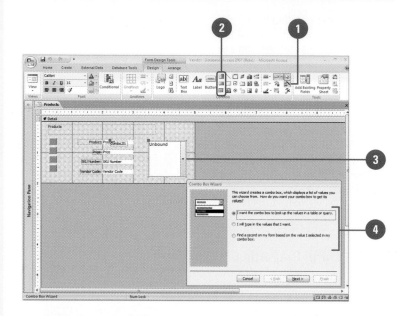

⑨ If necessary, specify which column contains the value that will be stored in the list box control. Click **Next** to continue.

⑩ Specify whether you want Access merely to display the column value (for later use to perform a task) or to store the value in a field in a table.

⑪ If you choose to store the value in a field, specify the field.

⑫ Click **Next** to continue.

⑬ Enter a label for the new control, and then click **Finish**.

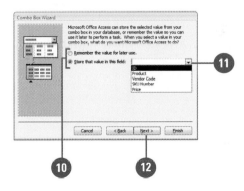

Did You Know?

You can create a list box with custom values. If you want specific values (rather than values from a table) to populate the list box, click the I will type in the values that I want option in the wizard's first step, and then enter the values manually when you are prompted by the wizard.

You can create a list box to display a specific record. If you want your list box to cause Access to retrieve records, click the Find a record on my form based on the value I selected in my list box option in the wizard's first step. The wizard then prompts you for the field from which the list box will receive its values. When the list box is added to the form, choosing a specific value causes Access to retrieve the matching record.

You can display Help on customizing the combo box. Click to select the check box at the bottom of the wizard dialog box, where you label your list or combo box.

Creating a Subform

Microsoft
Certified
Application
Specialist   AC07S-2.5.5

Some forms use fields from multiple tables. One of the most common forms involves a one-to-many relationship between two tables. For example, an order form would include a single order date and customer, but the order might involve several different products. Thus there are two tables involved: an orders table with information about the order and a detailed orders table with data about the products purchased. The user should not have to enter the order date for each product. This can be avoided with a **subform**, a form embedded within a **main form**. The user enters the order date and other general information in the main form, and the individual products are listed in the subform. Access then stores the appropriate data in each table without the user being aware that multiple tables are involved.

Create a Subform

1. Display the form you want to add a subform in Design view.

2. Click the **Design** tab under Form Design Tools.

3. Click the **Subform/subreport** button.

4. Drag to create a frame for the subform.

   The Subform wizard opens, asking you to step through the process.

5. Select the data option you want, and then click **Next** to continue.

6. Click the **Tables/Queries** list arrow, and then select the table that will appear in the main form.

   The table contains general information (the *one* table).

7. Select the fields from the table that will appear in the main form. Make sure you include the common field that links the one table to the many table.

8. On the same wizard screen, click the **Tables/Queries** list arrow, and then select the table that will appear in the subform.

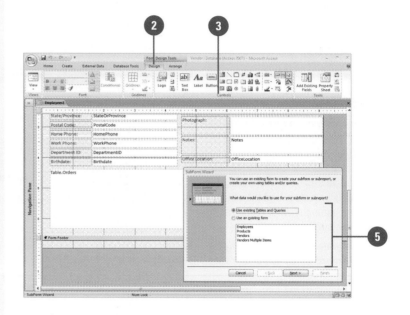

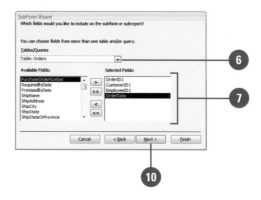

The table contains detailed information (the *many* table).

⑨ Select the fields from the table that will appear in the subform. Do not include the common field you entered in the previous step, since this will appear in the main form.

⑩ Click **Next** to continue.

⑪ Click the option to view the data by the one table.

⑫ Click **Next** to continue.

⑬ Specify whether you want the subform to be laid out in tabular or datasheet format. Click **Next** to continue.

⑭ Specify a style for the form. Click **Next** to continue.

⑮ Enter a name for the subform.

⑯ Click **Finish**.

The form and subform are ready for data entry or further editing.

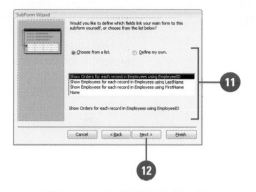

Did You Know?

You can create a form with tables in a one-to-one relationship. If the tables have a one-to-one relationship, use the Form Wizard to create the form, including the common field only once in the field list. The wizard will create a single form, combining the fields from both tables.

You can create a linked form. If you want a linked form instead of a subform (so that the form appears in response to the user clicking a button), click the Linked Forms option when the Form Wizard asks you how you want to view your data.

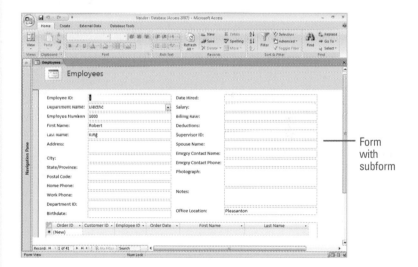

Form with subform

Using Windows Themes on Forms

The Microsoft Windows operating system offers you several themes. If you have chosen a theme other than the default, Access applies the selected theme to views, dialog boxes, and controls. However, you can prevent form controls from taking on themes from the operating system by setting an option on the database or project.

Enable or Disable Windows Themes in Forms

1. Click the **Office** button, and then click **Access Options**.

2. In the left pane, click **Current Database**.

3. Select or clear the **Use Windows-themed Controls on Forms** check box.

4. Click **OK**.

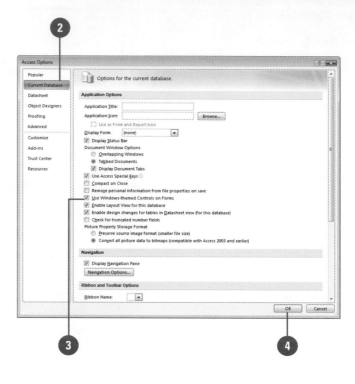

Change a Windows Visual Theme

◆ **Windows Vista.** Right-click the desktop, click **Personalize**, click **Theme**, click the **Theme** list arrow, select a theme, and then click **OK**.

◆ **Windows XP.** Right-click the desktop, click **Properties**, click the **Themes** tab, click the **Theme** list arrow, select a theme, and then click **OK**.

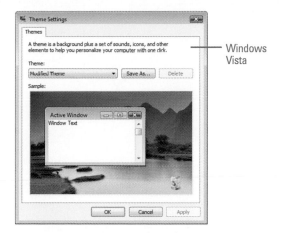

Windows Vista

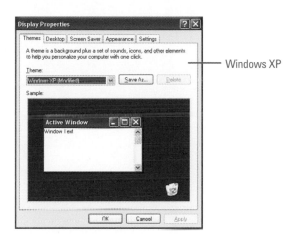

Windows XP

Creating Reports to Convey Information

8

Introduction

You can use print commands on the Office menu to print a simple list of the records in your table. But if you want to include calculations, graphics, or a customized header or footer, you can create a report. A report is a summary of information in one or more tables. Reports allow you to include enhancements that a simple printout of records in a table would not provide. In many cases a report answers important questions about the contents of your database. For example, a report might tell you how many movies in several different categories (such as drama, comedy, and western) have been rented each month or the amount of catalog sales made to customers in Canada in the last quarter. In addition to providing detailed and summary information that can include calculations, reports also provide these features:

◆ Attractive formatting to help make your report easier to read and understand.

◆ Headers and footers that print identifying information at the top and bottom of every page.

◆ Grouping and sorting that organize your information.

◆ Graphics to enhance the appearance of a report with clip art, photos, or scanned images.

Exploring Different Ways to Create a Report

As with most objects you create in a database, you have several ways to create a report—by using Report buttons, Report wizard or by creating it from scratch in Design view.

Quick Reports

With the Report button, Access creates a simple report based on the data in the currently selected table or query. You can create a report using a column format.

Report Wizard

With the Report Wizard you can specify the kind of report you want to create, and the Report Wizard guides you through each step of the process. All you do is answer a series of questions about your report, and Access builds a report with your data, using your formatting preferences. Creating a report with the Report Wizard allows you to select the fields you want to include from available tables and queries.

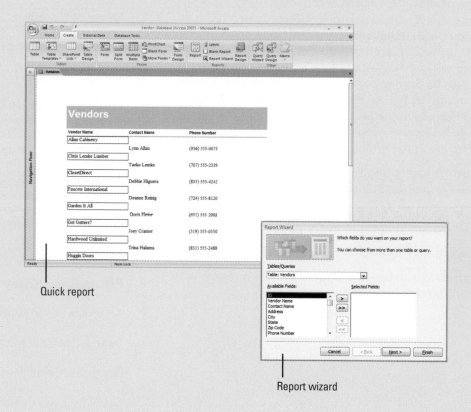

Quick report

Report wizard

Design View

Once you have completed a report, you can further customize it in Design view. As always, you can also begin creating your report in Design view without using a wizard.

When you work with a report in Design view, Access displays not the report data, but rather the individual parts, or controls, that make up the report, including titles, fields whose data appear in the report, labels that clarify the report contents, and objects such as headers and footers.

Previewing a Report

Once you have created your report and finalized its design, you can preview it using two views: Print Preview and Layout Preview. Print Preview displays the report as it will print, in a "what you see is what you get" format. Layout Preview displays a sample of the report as it will print, with just a few rows of data, so you can get a feel for the report's appearance without having to view all the data in the report.

Report in Design view

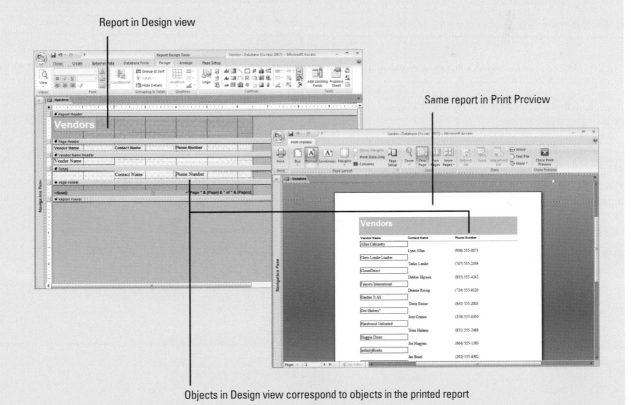

Same report in Print Preview

Objects in Design view correspond to objects in the printed report

Creating a Report

Microsoft Certified Application Specialist

AC07S-2.6.1,
AC07S-2.6.2

To quickly create a simple report in Access, you can use one of the form buttons available on the Create tab (**New!**). You can create a basic report, blank report, and labels. These buttons quickly arrange the fields from the selected table or query into an attractive report. The new report is based on the active object. For example, if a table is active and you click the Report button, Access creates a new report based on the active table. After you create a report, you can save and name it so that you can use it again. You can also create a report using the **Report Wizard**, which allows you to select the fields and information you want presented and to choose from available formatting options that determine how the report will look.

Create a Report

1. In the Navigation pane, click the **Reports** on the Objects bar, and then click the table you want to use in the report.

2. Click the **Create** tab.

3. Click the any of the following form button:

   ◆ **Report.** Creates a columnar report.

   ◆ **Labels.** Creates a columnar report of labels.

   ◆ **Blank Report.** Creates a blank report.

   Access displays the form in Print Preview, but you can switch to Design view, save, print, or close the report.

4. Click the **Save** button on the Quick Access Toolbar, type a name for your report, and then click **OK**.

Report Wizard

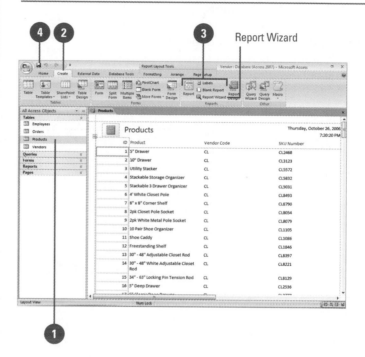

Create a Report Using the Report Wizard

1. Click the **Create** tab.

2. Click the **Report Wizard** button.

3. Click the list arrow for choosing a table or query on which to base the form, and then click the name of the table or query you want.

4. Select the fields you want to include, indicating the source of any fields you want to include from other tables or queries. Click **Next** to continue.

5. If necessary, specify any groupings of the records, choosing any or all of the selected fields (up to ten). Click **Next** to continue.

6. Specify the order of records within each group, sorting by up to four fields at a time, and then specify ascending or descending order. Click **Next** to continue.

7. Determine the layout and orientation of your report. Click **Next** to continue.

8. Specify the style of the report, which affects its formatting and final appearance. Click **Next** to continue.

9. In the final wizard dialog box, name your report, and then indicate whether you want to preview the report or display it in Design view. Click **Finish**.

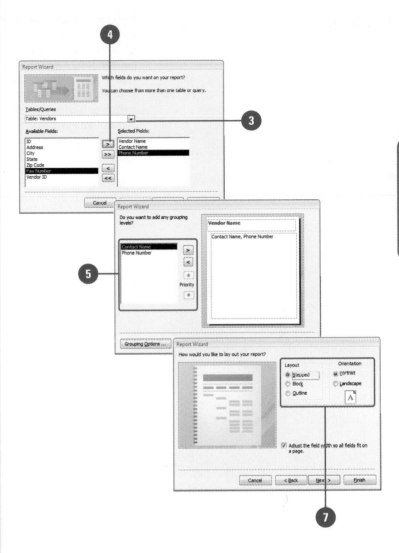

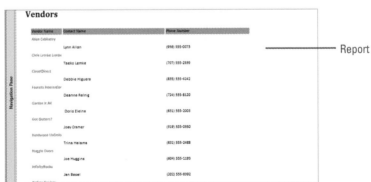

Report

Creating a Blank Report

If you plan to use only a few fields in a report, the Blank Report tool makes it easy to quickly drag-and-drop fields from any table in the database. You can use the Blank Report button on the Create tab to quickly create a blank report in Layout view. When you create a blank report, the Field List opens, where you can drag the fields you want onto the blank report. After you add fields in Layout view, you can switch to Design view, and add controls. In Design and Layout views, you can add pictures, titles, pages numbers, date and time, and format the appearance of the report.

Create a Blank Report

① Click the **Create** tab.

② Click the **Blank Report** button.

The form appears in Layout view along with the Field List.

③ Drag fields from the Field List onto the blank form where you want to place them to create a form.

If necessary, click **Show all tables** in the Field List to display available tables.

④ To show only fields in the current record source, click the link at the bottom of the Field List.

⑤ Click the **Save** button on the Quick Access Toolbar, type a name, and then click **OK**.

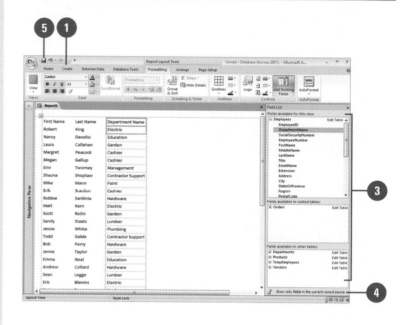

Did You Know?

You can create a subreport. In the Navigation pane, click Reports on the Objects bar, and then double-click the report you want to add a subreport, click the Design tab under Report Design Tools, click the Subform/subreport button, drag to create a frame for the subreport, and then follow the wizard instructions.

Creating Mailing Labels

AC07S-2.6.7

Access provides a **Label Wizard** to help you create mailing labels quickly. The wizard supports a large variety of label brands and sizes. You can also create customized labels for brands and sizes not listed by the wizard, provided you know the dimensions of your labels and label sheets. You can create labels by drawing data from any of your tables or queries. In addition to data values, labels can also include customized text that you specify.

Create Mailing Labels

1. In the Navigation pane, click the **Tables** on the Objects bar, and then click the table you want to use.

2. Click the **Create** tab.

3. Click the **Labels** button.

4. Select the type of mailing label you're using. Click **Next** to continue.

5. Specify the font style and color for the label text. Click **Next** to continue.

6. Double-click the field names in the Available Fields list to place them on your mailing labels. Type any text that you want to accompany the field values. Click **Next** to continue.

7. If necessary, select a field to sort your labels by. Click **Next** to continue.

8. Enter a name for your mailing labels report, and then choose whether to preview the printout or modify the label design.

9. Click **Finish**.

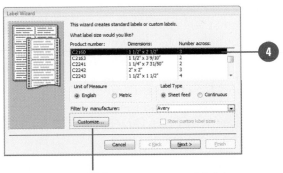

Click to create your own label size.

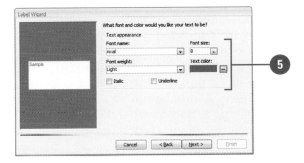

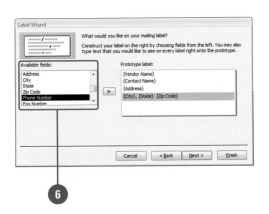

Using Sections in Design View

Microsoft Certified Application Specialist AC07S-2.6.4

When Access displays a report or a form in Design view, it divides the report or form into sections, individual parts that control what elements appear and how they are formatted.

Each section has a **selector**, a box to the left of its heading, that you can click to select the section. Any formatting changes you make then affect just that section. Clicking the selector in the upper-left corner selects the entire report or form. To set section properties, double-click the selector, and then change properties, such as Force New Page or Visible, you want on the Property sheet.

Header and footer sections come in pairs. **Headers** in a report display text at the top of each page or at the top of the report. **Footers** appear at the bottom of the page. Headers and footers can also appear at the start and end of records you have grouped together. A group header is useful for displaying a title for a group, while a group footer is useful for summarizing data in a group. You can create a group using the Report Wizard button on the Create tab or the Group & Sort command on the Design tab under the Report Design Tools in Layout or Design view. As with other sec-

tions in a report, you can add controls to headers and footers that include text, expressions, page numbers, and the date and time.

Design View Sections

Section	Description
Report Header	Text that appears at the top of the first page of a report, such as a title, logo, or introduction.
Page Header	Text that appears at the top of each page of a report, such as page numbers or report date.
Group Header	Text that appears before each group of records, such as a vendor name.
Detail	Contains the main body of the report, the fields that display values.
Group Footer	Text that appears at the end of a group of records, such as totals.
Page Footer	Text that appears at the bottom of each page of a report, such as page numbers.
Report Footer	Text that appears at the end of the report, such as report totals or other summary information.

Design view sections

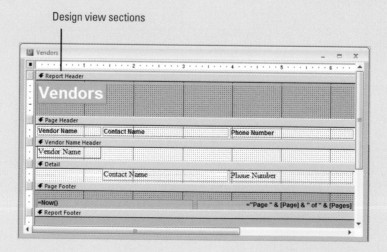

Working with Controls

Microsoft Certified Application Specialist AC07S-2.7.1, AC07S-2.7.2

Each item in a report or form—such as a field name, a field value, and the report title—is represented in Design view by a control. When you create a report or form with a wizard, the wizard arranges and sizes the controls to make the report according to the selections you provided. If you want to modify a report, you can do so in Design view by:

- ◆ Creating and deleting controls

- ◆ Moving and sizing controls

- ◆ Changing control properties

- ◆ Formatting the contents and appearance of controls

Types of Report Controls

There are three kinds of controls you can use in a report:

- ◆ **Bound controls** are fields of data from the table or query. You cannot create a calculation in a bound control.

- ◆ **Unbound controls** are controls that contain a label or a text box. They don't have a source of data (a field or expression). You can create calculations in an unbound control.

- ◆ **Calculated controls** are any values calculated in the report, including totals, subtotals, averages, percentages, and so on. They are controls with an expression as the data source.

Each type of control has specific characteristics you can change using the Properties feature. You can modify properties by right-clicking the control you want to modify, and then clicking Properties. In the controls property sheet, you can specify the characteristics you want to change. Although there are commands and buttons you can use to change a specific characteristic, using the Properties button is a fast way to see all of the characteristics for a control and make several changes at once.

Unbound control

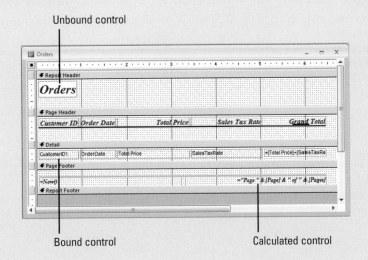

Bound control

Calculated control

Creating and Modifying a Report in Design View

Create or Modify a Report in Design View

1. Click the **Create** tab.

2. Do either of the following to create or modify a form:

   ◆ **Create.** Click the Report Design button, and then click the Design View button.

   ◆ **Modify.** Double-click the report you want to change in the Navigation pane, and then click the Design View button.

3. If necessary, click the **Add Existing Field** button on the Design tab under Report Design Tools to add a bound control.

4. Use Ribbon commands and the Field List to create or modify a report in Design view.

5. To view or hide headers and footers, click the **Arrange** tab, and then click **Report Header/Footer** or **Page Header/Footer** button.

Did You Know?

You can create an unbound report. Create a report without choosing a table or query on which it is based. Such reports are called unbound reports. A dialog box is an example of an unbound report.

When you create a report from scratch in Design view, three sections appear: Page Header, Detail, and Page Footer. Once you create the report, you need to populate it with data. You can add **bound controls**—fields of data from a table or query—directly from the Field List, or you can add other types of **unbound controls**—text boxes, labels, pictures, buttons, and so on—from the Ribbon. In Design view, you see two parts for every control: the control itself and its corresponding label. When you move a control, its corresponding label moves with it.

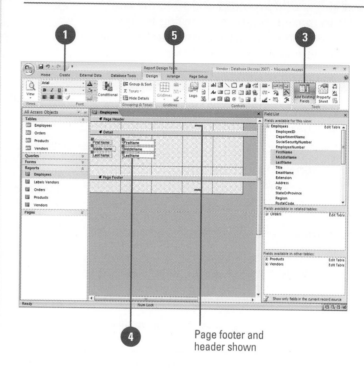

Page footer and header shown

Add a Bound or Unbound Control

1. Display the report in Design view.

2. Click the **Design** tab under Report Design Tools.

3. To add a bounded control, click the control button you want to add, such as a text box, and then drag to draw a box in the location where you want the control.

4. To add an unbounded control, select the fields you want to include from the Field List; press Shift or Ctrl while you click to select multiple fields. Drag the selected field or fields to the section in which you want the field to appear. Two boxes appear for each field: one containing the label and one for the field values.

Did You Know?

You can display or hide the ruler and grid. The ruler and grid provide guides to help you arrange your controls. Click the Arrange tab under Report Design Tools, and then click the Ruler or Show Grid button.

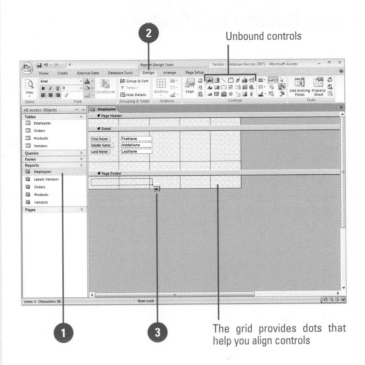

Unbound controls

The grid provides dots that help you align controls

Working With Controls

To	Do This
Change control font	Select a control, click the Font list arrow on the Home tab and then click the font name you want, or click the Bold, Italic, or Underline button on the Home tab.
Remove formatting	Select the control, and then click the button that corresponds to the formatting you want to remove.
Change the position of	Select the control, and then click the Align Left, text within a control Center, or Align Right button on the Home tab. If the control is in a header or footer, the control is aligned within the page margins.
Keep labels aligned with controls in the Detail section	When you adjust bound controls in the Detail section, be sure to make the same adjustments in the Header sections so that the headings appear directly over the data.

Using Buttons and Controls

Buttons and Controls

Button	Name	Description
`ab|`	Text Box	This button creates a text box in which the user can enter text (or numbers) for the selected field in the record. Use this control for fields assigned to a text or number data type.
`Aa`	Label	This button creates a text label. Because the other controls already include a corresponding label, use this button to create labels that are independent of other controls, such as text needed for user instructions or the name of the form or report in a heading.
	Command Button	This button creates a button that runs a macro or Microsoft Visual Basic function when the user clicks the button in the form or report.
	Combo Box	This button creates a combo box in which the user has the option to enter text or select from a list of options. You can enter your own options in the list, or you can display options stored in another table.
	List Box	This button creates a list box that allows a user to select from a list of options. You can enter your own options in the list, or can have another table provide a list of options.
	Subform/Subreport	This button inserts another form or report within the current form or report at the insertion point.
	Line	This button creates a line that you draw on the form or report.
	Rectangle	This button creates a rectangle or border that you draw on the form or report.
	Bound Object Frame	This button inserts an OLE object from another source within the same database. Use this button to insert an object that is linked to another source in the database and needs to be updated to reflect recent changes.
	Option Group	This button creates a box around a group of option buttons. The user is only allowed to make one selection from the buttons enclosed by a group box.
	Check Box	This button creates a check box that allows a user to make multiple yes or no selections. Use this control for fields assigned to the yes/no data type.
	Option Button	This button creates an option button (also known as a radio button) that allows the user to make a single selection from at least two choices. Use this control for fields assigned to the yes/no data type.

Buttons and Controls *(continued)*

Button	Name	Description
	Toggle Button	This button creates a button that allows the user to make a yes or no selection by clicking the toggle button. Use this control for fields assigned to the yes/no data type.
	Tab Control	This button creates a tab in your form. Creating tabs in a form gives your form the appearance of a dialog box in a program so that related controls can appear together on their own tab.
	Insert Page (**New!**)	This button inserts a page, in which you can insert additional information.
	Chart	This button inserts a chart using the Microsoft Chart OLE program. The program starts a wizard and steps you through the chart creation process.
	Unbound Object Frame	This button inserts an OLE object from another source. Use this button to insert an object that is linked to another program and needs to be updated to reflect recent changes.
	Image	This button inserts a frame, in which you can insert a graphic in your form or report. Use this control when you want to insert a graphic that remains the same in all the records displayed in a form or report, such as clip art or a logo.
	Page Break	This button forces the fields that start at the insertion point to appear on the next screen.
	Insert Hyperlink	This button insert a hyperlink to an existing file or Web page, object in a database, or e-mail address. This button uses the Insert Hyperlink dialog box.
	Attachment (**New!**)	This button inserts an attachment field that allows you to insert an attachment file into a form or report.
	Select	Click this button, and then click the control you want to select. To select multiple controls that are grouped together, click this button, and then drag a rectangle shape around all the controls you want to select.
	Control Wizards	Click to use control wizards when they are available.
	ActiveX (**New!**)	This button inserts an ActiveX control. Use this button to insert an ActiveX functionality installed on your computer, such as a Button Bar, Calendar, or Contact Selector.

Arranging Information

The information in a form or report is arranged according to the arrangement of the sections and controls in Design view. You can modify that arrangement by changing section heights and by moving and resizing controls. When you select a control on a form, sizing handles appear on the sides and at the corners of the control. You can drag the sizing handles to adjust the size of the control. You can also drag inside a selected control to move the control to a new location.

Change the Size of a Control

1. In Design view, click the control you want to resize.

2. Position the pointer over a sizing handle until the pointer shape changes to a two-headed arrow.

3. With the sizing pointer, drag to resize the control.

   For example, to make the control wider, drag the sizing handle on the center- right area of the control further to the right.

Sizing handles indicate control is selected

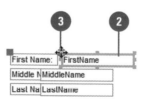

Move a Control

1. Display the report or form in Design view, and then display controls you want to move.

2. Select the control you want to format.

3. To move a control without a label, position the pointer over the large sizing handle in the upper-left corner of the control, and then drag to a new location.

   Only the label or control will move, not both.

4. To move a control, position the pointer over an edge of a control until the pointer changes to a four-headed arrow, and then drag to a new location.

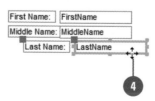

Adjust Page or Section Spacing

1. Display the report or form in Design view whose page or section size you want to change.

2. Position the pointer (which changes to a two-headed arrow) over the bottom of the section whose height you want to change.

3. Drag the border up or down in the appropriate direction to change the spacing. You can drag the border all the way to the previous or next section to hide that section.

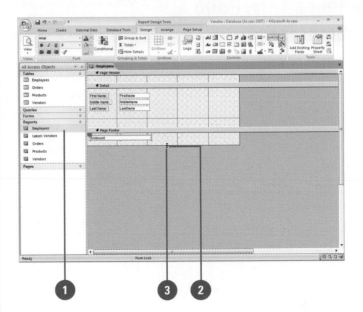

Did You Know?

You can change the size in two directions at once. You can change the height and width of a control at the same time by dragging a corner sizing handle.

You can select controls. To select controls that are next to each other, click the Select button on the Design tab, and then drag a rectangle around the controls you want to select. To select controls that are not next to each other, press and hold Shift as you click each control. You can also select a control by clicking the Object list arrow on the Home tab, and then clicking the control you want.

Inserting a Title, Page Numbers, or the Date and Time

When you create a report or form, you typically want to include a title, page number, and the date and time. If Access doesn't include a title, page number, or the date and time in a form or report, you can quickly add them using buttons on the Design tab (in Design view) or Formatting tab (in Layout view). These elements are added to the report or form header or footer by default, so they appear on every page. After you insert the elements, you can move them around and format them.

Insert a Title into a Report or Form

1. Display the report or form in Design or Layout view you want to insert a picture.

2. Click the **Design** tab (in Design view) or the **Formatting** tab (in Layout view).

3. Click the **Title** button.

4. Type the title you want.

5. Click a blank area of the report or form to deselect the title.

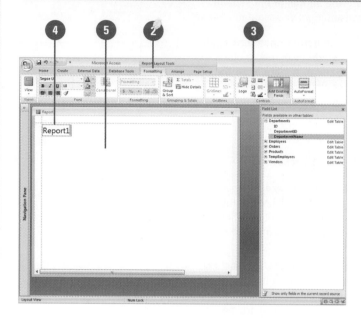

Insert Page Numbers into a Report or Form

1. Display the report or form in Design or Layout view you want to insert a picture.

2. Click the **Design** tab (in Design view) or the **Formatting** tab (in Layout view).

   ◆ You cannot insert page numbers on a form in Layout view, only in Design view.

3. Click the **Page Numbers** button.

4. Select a format and position option.

5. Click the **Alignment** list arrow, and then select an alignment option.

6. Select or clear the **Show Number on First Page** check box.

7. Click **OK**.

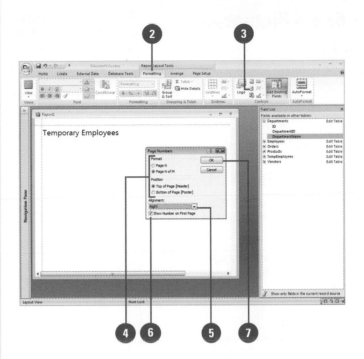

Insert the Date and Time into a Report or Form

1. Display the report or form in Design or Layout view you want to insert a picture.

2. Click the **Design** tab (in Design view) or the **Formatting** tab (in Layout view).

3. Click the **Date and Time** button.

4. To include the date, select the **Include Date** check box, and then select a date format option.

5. To include the time, select the **Include Time** check box, and then select a time format option.

6. Click **OK**.

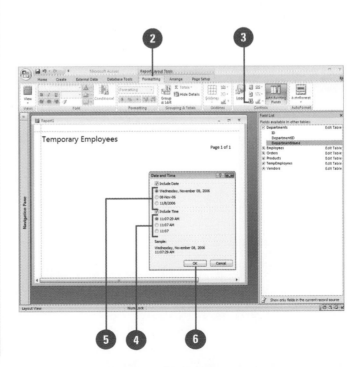

Inserting a Picture as a Logo

If you have pictures, graphics, scanned photographs, art, photos, or artwork from a CD-ROM or other program, you can insert them into a report or form to personalize your Access database. You can use the Logo button on the Design tab (in Design view) or Formatting tab (in Layout view) to quickly insert a picture on your hard disk drive, scanner, digital camera, or Web camera. The picture is inserted into the report or form header by default. You can move the picture to another location by dragging the image or resize it by dragging the edge.

Insert a Picture as a Logo from a File into a Report or Form

1. Display the report or form in Design or Layout view you want to insert a picture.

2. Click the **Design** tab (in Design view) or the **Formatting** tab (in Layout view).

3. Click the **Logo** button.

4. Click the **Look in** list arrow, and then select the drive and folder that contain the file you want to insert.

5. Click the file you want to insert.

6. Click **OK**.

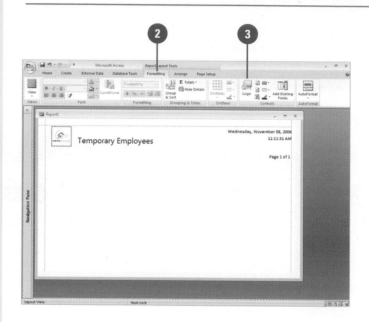

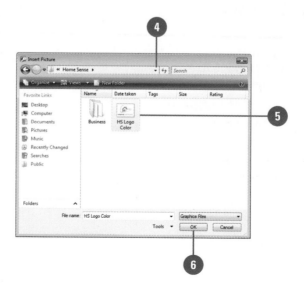

Setting Properties

Set Properties

1. In Design view, select the control, section, form, or report whose properties you want to modify.

2. Click the **Design** tab under Form or Report Design Tools.

3. Click the **Property Sheet** button.

4. Click the tab that contains the property you want to modify.

5. Click the property box for the property you want to modify, and then do one of the following.

   ◆ Type the information or expression you want to use.

   ◆ If the property box contains a list arrow, click the arrow and then click a value in the list.

   ◆ If a Builder button appears to the right of the property box, click it to display a builder or a dialog box giving you a choice of builders.

6. Click the **Close** button on the Property Sheet.

Every object has **properties**, or settings, that control its appearance and function. A form or report has properties; each section in a form or report has properties, and each control in a section has properties. When you work with a control in a form or report, you can open a property sheet that displays all the settings for that control.

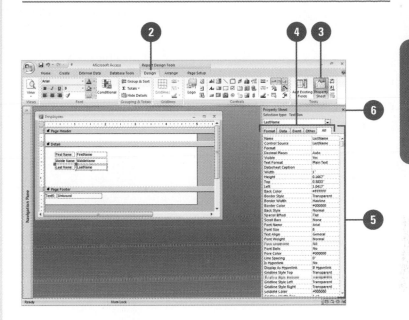

Did You Know?

You can open a subreport in a new window. When you open a report with a subreport, it opens in the subreport control by default. To open a subreport in a new window, open the subreport in Design view, select the subreport, click the Design tab, and then click the Subreport in New Window button.

Performing Calculations in Reports

When you create a report, you might want to include summary information or other calculations. The wizards often include built-in functions, but you can use the **Expression Builder** to create your own by clicking buttons for the arithmetic operators you want to use and including constant values as needed. For example, if you want to determine bonuses based on a percentage of sales, you can create an arithmetic expression to compute the results. When you generate the report, Access will perform the required calculations and display the results in the report. To display the calculations in the appropriate format, you can also use the Properties feature to specify formats for dates, currency, and other numeric data.

Choose Fields to Use in a Calculation

1. In Design view, create a text box control and position it where you want the calculated field to appear, or select an existing unbound control.

2. Click the **Design** tab under Report Design Tools.

3. Click the **Property Sheet** button.

4. Click the **Control Source** property box, which specifies what data appears in a control, and then click the **Expression Builder** button.

5. Click the equal sign (=) button, and then enter the values and operators you want to use.

   ◆ Click operator buttons to supply the most common operations.

   ◆ Double-click folders in the left pane to open lists of objects you can use in your expression, including existing fields, constants, operators, and common expressions.

   ◆ Manually type an expression.

6. Click **OK** to insert the calculation.

7. Click the **Close** button on the Property Sheet.

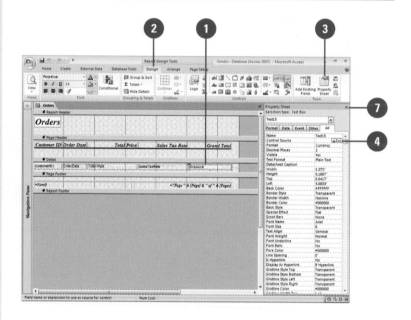

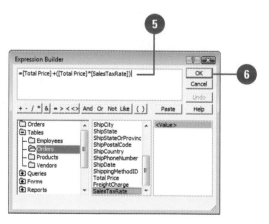

Format Values in a Report

1. In Design view, position the insertion point in the field whose format you want to change.

2. Click the **Design** tab under Report Design Tools.

3. Click the **Property Sheet** button.

4. On either the **All** tab or the **Format** tab of the property sheet, click the Format property box, click the list arrow that appears, and then click the format you want to use.

   The names of the formats appear on the left side of the drop-down list, and examples of the corresponding formats appear on the right side.

5. If you are formatting a number (rather than a date), and you do not want to accept the default, "Auto," click the Decimal Places property box, click the list arrow, and then click the number of decimal places you want.

6. Click the **Close** button on the Property Sheet.

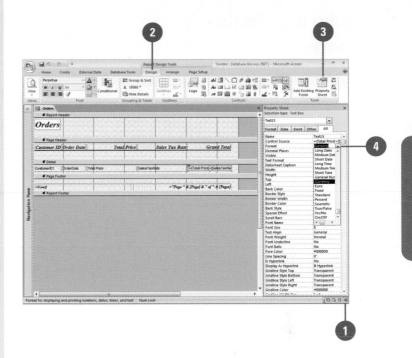

Did You Know?

You can use a builder. Access makes it easy to change many types of settings by providing builders, or tools that simplify tasks. The Expression Builder is just one of many builders in Access. You know a builder is available for a task when you click a property box and a Build button appears.

Grouping and Sorting in Reports

In Layout view, you can use the Group, Sort, and Total pane (**New!**) to create group levels and add totals. The Group, Sort, and Totals pane provides a visual interface to make it easy to understand, use, and navigate. In Layout view, you see group, sort, and total changes right when you make them, so you can quickly decide if you need to make any changes. You can quickly add simple grouping and sorting, or take a little more time to create complex ones. The Totals drop-down list (**New!**) makes it quick and easy to add a sum, average, count, maximum or minimum to report headers or footers.

Create a Group or Sort in a Report

1. Display the report you want to format in Layout view.

2. Click the **Formatting** tab under Report Layout Tools.

3. Click the **Group & Sort** button.

4. Click **Add a group** or **Add a sort**.

5. Click the **select field** list arrow on the Group on or Sort by bar.

6. Click the field you want to group or sort by.

   The grouping or sorting is applied to the report.

7. To create a more complex grouping or sorting, click the **More** arrow (toggles to Less) on the Group on or Sort by bar, click a list arrow with the criteria you want, and then select options.

8. When you're done, click the **Close** button on the Group, Sorting, and Totals pane.

Did You Know?

You can hide details in a group. To hide the records at the next lower level of grouping, display the report in Layout view, click the Formatting tab, and then click the Hide Details button.

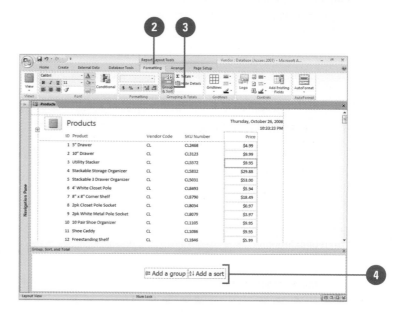

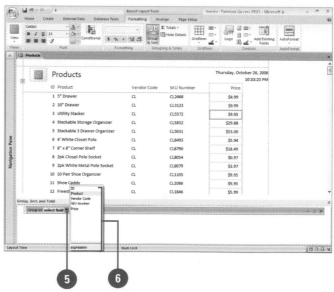

Change or Delete a Group or Sort in a Report

1. Display the report you want to format in Layout view.

2. Click the **Formatting** tab under Report Layout Tools.

3. Click the **Group & Sort** button.

4. To change the order of grouping and sorting, click the **Move Up** or **Move Down** button at the end of the Group on or Sort by bar.

5. To delete a grouping or sorting, click the **Delete** button at the end of the Group on or Sort by bar.

6. When you're done, click the **Close** button on the Group, Sorting, and Totals pane.

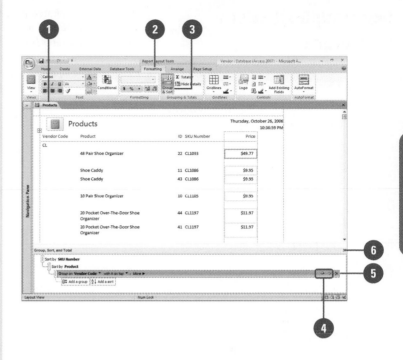

Add a Totals Function for a Group to a Report

1. Display the report you want to format in Layout view.

2. Click the **Formatting** tab under Report Layout Tools.

3. Click the field you want to use with a Totals function.

4. Click the **Totals** button, and then select the function you want.

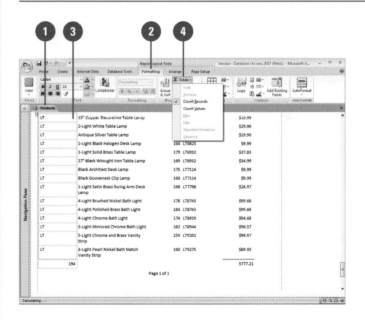

Inserting a Header or Footer

Most reports use headers and footers to help you keep track of where you are. A **header** is text printed in the top section of every page within a document. **Footer** text is printed in the bottom section. Commonly used headers and footers contain your name, the document title, the file name, the print date, and page numbers. You can also add a header and footer to a form.

Insert a Header or Footer

1. Display the report in Design view in which you want to insert a header or footer.

2. Click the **Design** tab under Report Design Tools.

3. Click the **Text Box** button.

4. Drag a text box control in the header or footer section.

5. Click the **Property Sheet** button.

6. Click the **All** tab, click the **Control Source** property box, which specifies what data appears in a control, and then click the **Expression Builder** button.

7. Double-click the **Common Expressions** folder.

8. Double-click the expression you want to use, such as Page Number, Total Pages, Page N of M, Current Date/Time, and so on.

9. Click **OK** to insert the expression.

10. Click the **Close** button on the Property Sheet.

See Also

See "Formatting a Form or Report" on page 222 for information on showing and hiding headers or footers.

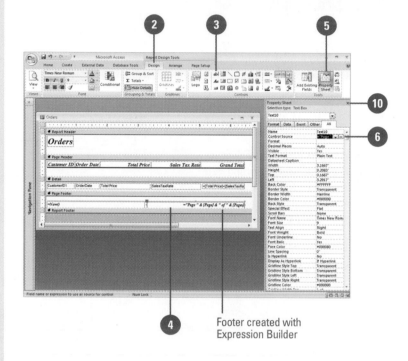

Footer created with Expression Builder

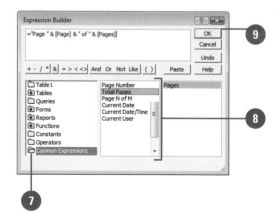

Assigning a Shortcut Key to a Control

You can make selecting a control easier in a form or report by assigning it a shortcut key (also known as an **access key**). When you assign an access key to a label or button on a form or report, you can press Alt + an underline character to move the focus to the control. If you have a data access page—a Web page published by an earlier version of Access—you can assign the access key to the control instead of the label attached to the control.

Assign an Access Key to a Control

1. Display the form or report with the label or button you want to assign an access key.

2. Click the **Design** tab under Form or Report Design Tools.

3. Select the label or button.

4. Click the **Property Sheet** button.

5. In the Caption property box, type an ampersand (**&**) immediately before the character you want to use as the access key.

6. Click the **Close** button on the Property Sheet.

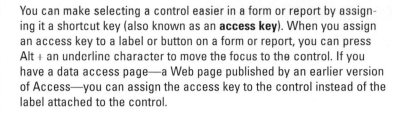

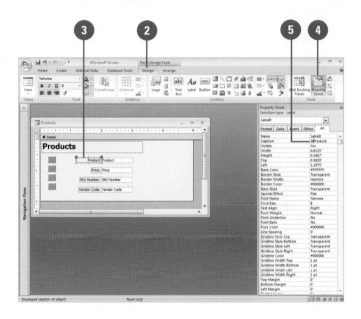

> ### Did You Know?
>
> **You can assign an access key to a control on a data access page.** In a data access page, select the control in which you want to assign a key, type the character you want in the Access Key property box.

Checking for Errors in Reports and Forms

AC07S-6.2.2

As you create reports and forms, Access helps you by catching common errors, such as controls being positioned outside the page size, as they happen. Error checking points out errors in a report or form, and provides you with options using a smart tag button for correcting them. When an error occurs, the Error Checking Options button appears, indicating a problem. Click the button to display a list of options to correct or ignore the problem.

Enable Error Checking

1. Click the **Office** button, and then click **Access Options**.

2. In the left pane, click **Object Designers**.

3. Select the **Enable error checking** check box.

4. To change the color of the error indicator, click the **Error indicator color** list arrow, and then select a color.

5. Select or clear check boxes for the specific errors in which you want to check.

   ◆ **Check for unassociated label and control.**

   ◆ **Check for new unassociated labels.**

   ◆ **Check for keyboard shortcut errors.**

   ◆ **Check for invalid control properties.**

   ◆ **Check for common report errors.**

6. Click **OK**.

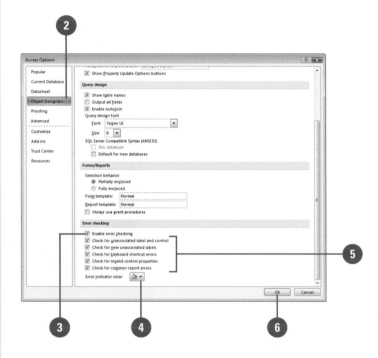

Error Checking Types

Type	Description
Unassociated label and control	A label and a control, such as a text box or list box, are not associated with each other. The Trace Error button appears instead of the Error Checking Options button.
New unassociated labels	A label to a form or report is not associated with any other control.
Keyboard shortcut errors	A control with an invalid shortcut key; either an unassociated label has a shortcut key, or a label or button has a duplicated shortcut key or a space character as its shortcut key.
Invalid control properties	A control with one or more properties is set to an invalid value.

Correct Errors in Reports and Forms

1 When an error indicator (small triangle) appears in a control, select the control.

2 Click the **Error Checking Options** button.

3 Click the option you want (options vary depending on the type of error found). Some of the common options include:

- ◆ **Help on this error.**
- ◆ **Ignore error or dismiss error.**
- ◆ **Error checking options.**

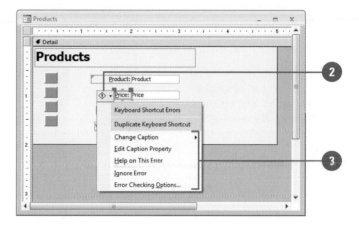

Unassociated label and control

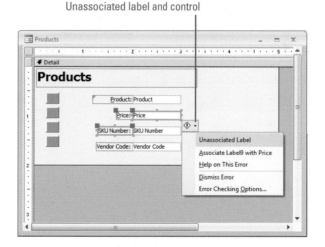

Changing the Page Setup

 AC07S-2.6.6

Once you have created a report or form, you can change the page setup, which includes the margin, paper size and orientation, and grid and column settings. Margins are the blank space between the edge of a page and the text. You can also select the page orientation (portrait or landscape) that best fits the entire document or any section. Portrait orients the page vertically (taller than it is wide), and landscape orients the page horizontally (wider than it is tall). When you shift between the two, the margin settings automatically change.

Change Page Setup Options

1. In the Navigation pane, click the report, form, table, query, or any data you want to preview.

2. Click the **Office** button, point to **Print**, and then click **Print Preview**.

3. To change margin settings, click the **Margins** button, and then click **Normal**, **Wide**, or **Narrow**.

4. To change paper settings, click the **Size** button, and then select the size you want.

5. To change paper orientation, click the **Portrait** or **Landscape** button.

6. To change column settings, click the **Columns** button, change or select the column and row grid settings, column size, and column layout (**Down**, **Then Across** or **Across**, **Then Down**) you want, and then click **OK**.

7. When you're done, click the **Close Print Preview** button.

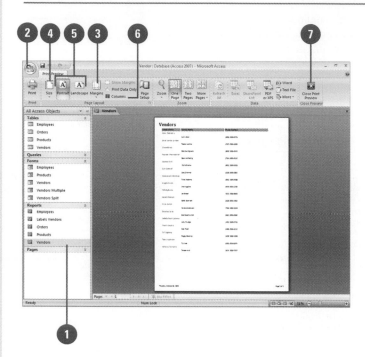

Change Default Print Margins

1. Click the **Office** button, and then click **Access Options**.

2. In the left pane, click **Advanced**.

3. Specify the default margin for datasheets, modules, and new forms and reports.

   ◆ **Left Margin.**

   ◆ **Right Margin.**

   ◆ **Top Margin.**

   ◆ **Bottom Margin.**

   You can use values from zero to the width or height of the printed page.

4. Click **OK**.

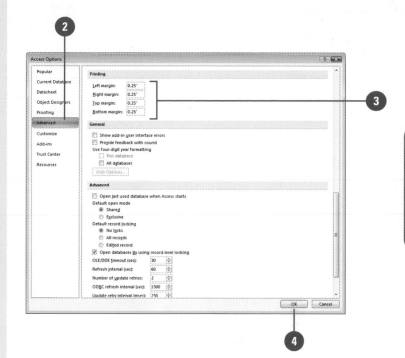

Did You Know?

You can export objects from Print Preview. Access allows you to export data from Print Preview. The available formats include Word RTF, text, PDF or XPS, Snapshot Viewer, HTML Document, XML File, Excel, SharePoint List, and Access Database. The available options vary depending on the objected displayed in Print Preview.

See Also

See "Creating a PDF Document" on page 300 or "Creating an XPS Document" on page 301 for information on using and saving a file with different formats.

Previewing Information

Microsoft Certified Application Specialist

AC07S-5.6

Before printing, you should verify that the data you want to print looks the way you want. You save time, money, and paper by avoiding duplicate printing. Print Preview shows you exactly how your data will look on each printed page. This is especially helpful when you have a multi-page report. Print Preview provides the tools, such as the One Page, Two Pages, Multiple Pages, Previous, and Next buttons, you need to proof the look of each page. Instead of printing the report, you can also use exporting tools in Print Preview to save the report in another format, including a PDF or XPS document.

Preview Data

1 In the Navigation pane, click the report, form, table, query, or any data you want to preview.

2 Click the **Office** button, point to **Print**, and then click **Print Preview**.

3 Use the **One Page**, **Two Page**, or **More Pages** buttons to view the data pages the way you want.

4 Use the record navigation buttons (**First**, **Previous**, **Record Selection** box, **Next**, and **Last**) to display pages.

5 To print from the Print Preview window, click the **Print** button, specify the options you want, and then click **OK**.

6 To export objects from Print Preview, use the export buttons.

7 When you're done, click the **Close Print Preview** button.

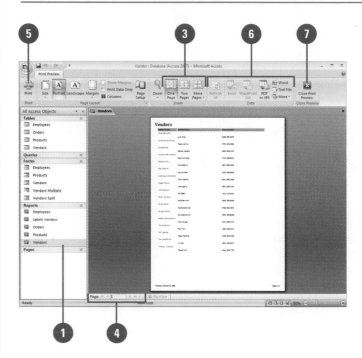

See Also

See Chapter 11, "Importing and Exporting Information," on page 279 for information on exporting data from Access.

Printing Information

Microsoft Certified Application Specialist AC07S-5.6

Printing a paper copy is one of the most common ways to share your data from Access. You can print a report, a table, a query, or any data in a single step using the Print button, in which case Access prints a single copy of all pages. If you want to print only selected pages or if you want to specify other printing options, use any of the Print commands on the Office menu.

Print Data

1 Display the report, form, table, query, or any data you want to format in Design View.

2 Click the **Office** button, point to **Print**, and then click **Print**.

In Print Preview, click the **Print** button.

TIMESAVER *To print an object using default settings (without the Print dialog box), click the Office button, point to Print, and then click Quick Print.*

3 If necessary, click the **Name** list arrow, and then select the printer you want to use.

4 Select the print range you want.

◆ To print all pages, click the **All** option.

◆ To print selected pages, click the **Pages** option, and then type the first page in the From box and the ending page in the To box.

◆ To print selected record, click the **Selected Record(s)** option.

5 Click **OK**.

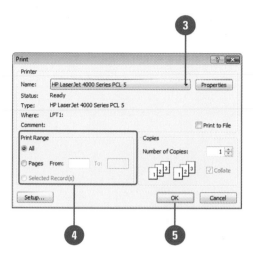

Improving the Appearance of Forms and Reports

9

Introduction

The objects in a database most "on display" are the forms and reports designed for those individuals responsible for data entry and those who receive reports from the database. For this reason, database designers often give extra attention to the visual appearance and clarity of those objects.

Microsoft Office Access 2007 offers database designers many aids in creating attractive data entry and display objects. The templates that create databases, forms, and reports format those objects attractively, but if you want to go beyond the design provided by a template, Access provides numerous formatting, layout, and style options. You can enhance the appearance of your forms and reports with different fonts and font styles, borders and lines, and judicious use of color. You can also add special effects to certain objects, giving them an embossed or 3-D effect. Access formatting features help you give your customized reports and forms the exact look you want. Although most design changes take place within Design view, you can make color, line, and other formatting changes from within a form or report using Layout view.

You can also insert pictures, charts, and graphs to enhance the appearance of database forms and reports. To help to work with pictures, you can use other tools, such as Microsoft Office Document Imaging and Microsoft Office Picture Manager, included with your Microsoft Office Access installation. Access allows you to insert Microsoft Excel charts and objects such as graphs created with other software programs that display data from database tables or queries. When you insert an object, you can edit the inserted information without having to leave Access.

What You'll Do

Format a Form or Report

Add Lines and Rectangles

Change Line Thickness and Colors

Apply Special Effects to Controls

Apply Conditional Formatting

Use the Format Painter

Change Tab Order

Resize and Move Controls

Align, Group, and Position Controls

Change Gridlines

Create a Tabular or Stacked Layout

Change Control Margins and Padding

Share Information Among Documents

Copy and Paste Objects

Insert Objects and Pictures

Scan and Manage Pictures

Insert Excel Charts and Worksheets

Insert and Format a Graph Chart

Move and Resize an Object

Set OLE Options

AutoFormatting a Form or Report

Format a Form or Report with AutoFormat

 Display the form or report you want to format in Design or Layout view.

2️⃣ Click the **Arrange** tab under Form or Report Design Tools (in Design view) or click the **Formatting** tab under Form or Report Layout Tools (in Layout view).

3️⃣ Select all or part of the form or report you want to format.

4️⃣ Click the **AutoFormat** button, and then click the style option you want.

Did You Know?

You can quickly select all controls and objects on a form or report. In Design view, display the form or report you want to use, click the Design tab, and then click the Select All button. You can also use the keyboard shortcut, Ctrl+A, to select everything on the page.

A fast way to format a form or report is with the AutoFormat button (**New!**), available in Design or Layout view. When you click this button, you can select from a variety of layouts and styles. After you make your selection, Access formats the selected portion of a report or form consistently for you. To have more control of the AutoFormat style you want to apply to a form or report, you can use the AutoFormat Wizard, which allows you to select options during the process.

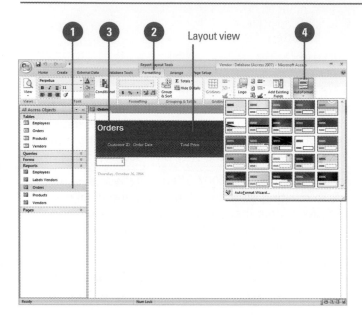

Layout view

Format a Form or Report Using the AutoFormat Wizard

1. Display the form or report you want to format in Design or Layout view.

2. Click the **Arrange** tab under Form or Report Design Tools (in Design view) or click the **Formatting** tab under Form or Report Layout Tools (in Layout view).

3. Click the **AutoFormat** button.

4. Click **AutoFormat Wizard**.

5. Click the style option you want.

6. To apply attributes (Font, Color, or Border), click **Options**, and then select or clear the options you want to apply with AutoFormat.

7. Click **OK**.

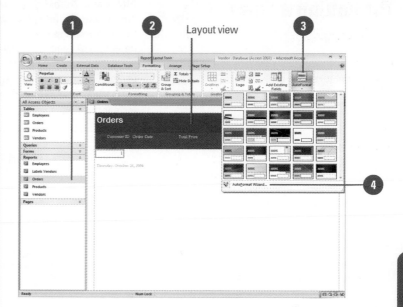

Layout view

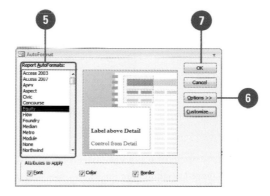

Formatting a Form or Report

After using AutoFormat, you can always make additional changes to the formatting using buttons on tabs under Report or Form Design Tools. If you don't see the header and footer sections, you can display them to add controls. When you select a control, sizing handles appear around the control, which you can drag to size it. You can also drag inside a selected control to move it to a new location. In Datasheet, and Form View, you can also select text and use the Mini-Toolbar (**New!**) to format the text.

Format a Form or Report Using Formatting Tools

1. Display the form or report you want to format in Design or Layout view.

2. Click the **Design** tab under Form or Report Design Tools (in Design view) or click the **Formatting** tab under Form or Report Layout Tools (in Layout view).

3. Select the item you want to format.

4. Use formatting buttons to apply the following:

   ◆ Font type, font size, text style, color, and alignment.

   ◆ Box fill and line/border color, and line/border width.

   ◆ Background fill color.

   ◆ Currency, percent, comma number, increase decimal, and decrease decimal.

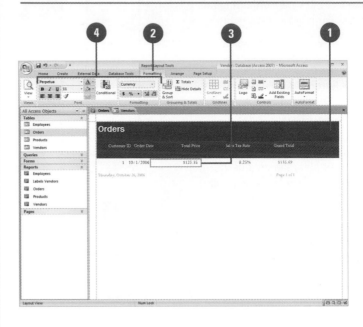

Did You Know?

You can wrap text in a field on a form or report. In Design view, right-click the field you want the text to wrap, click Properties, click the Format tab, and then set the CanGrow property to Yes.

Show and Hide Headers and Footers

1. Display the form or report in Design view.

2. Click the **Arrange** tab under Report Design Tools.

3. Click the Header/Footer button you want to show or hide:

   ◆ **Page Header/Footer.** Displays a header and footer for each page.

   ◆ **Form Header/Footer.** Displays a header and footer for the form.

4. If necessary, click **Yes** or **No** to delete the header/footer section.

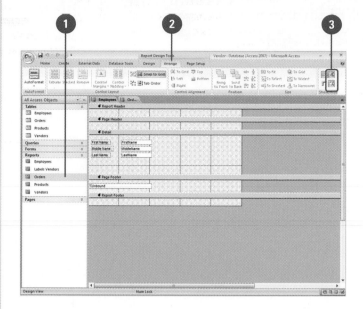

Adding Lines and Rectangles

You can make forms and reports that contain a lot of information easier to read by adding lines between sections or by adding rectangles around groups of controls. Lines and rectangles help organize the information so that reports are easier to read and forms are easier to fill out.

Add a Line to a Form or Report

1. Display the form or report in Design view.

2. Click the **Design** tab.

3. Click the **Line** button.

4. With the Line pointer, drag a line where you want the line to appear.

   Sizing handles appear.

5. To adjust the line length or angle, drag a sizing handle left, right, up, or down.

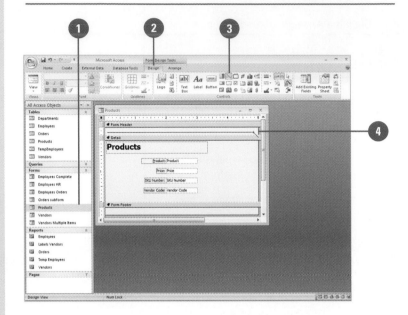

Add a Rectangle to a Form or Report

1. Display the form or report in Design view.

2. Click the **Design** tab.

3. Click the **Rectangle** button.

4. Drag a rectangle where you want the border to appear.

   Sizing handles appear at each corner and on each side of the border.

5. To adjust the position of the line or rectangle, point to the line (not a sizing handle), and then drag the object to a new position.

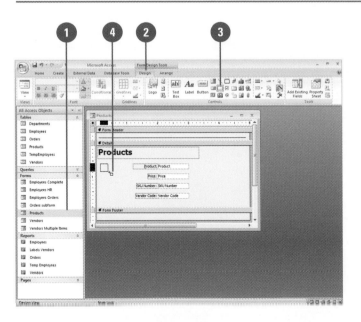

Changing Line or Border Thickness and Style

You can adjust the thickness and style of any line, shape, or field border with the Line Thickness and Line Type buttons. The Line Thickness button provides six different sizes, while the Line Type button provides eight different styles, including dots, dashes, and no style at all. You can modify field border thickness and type from Layout view, but to modify lines or rectangles, you must work in Design view.

Change Line or Border Thickness and Style

1 Display the form or report in Design view or Layout view.

2 Click the **Design** tab under Form or Report Design Tools (in Design view) or click the **Formatting** tab under Form or Report Layout Tools (in Layout view).

3 Select the line or border whose line thickness you want to adjust.

4 Click the **Line Thickness** button, and then select the thickness you want.

5 Click the **Line Type** button, and then select the type you want, such as dotted or dashed.

Did You Know?

You can set control defaults. When you create a control, you can set the initial formatting. Create a control, format the control the way you want, click the Design tab under Report or Form Design Tools, and then click Set Control Defaults.

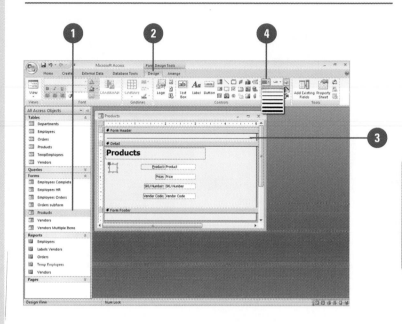

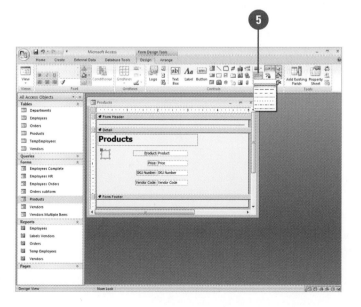

Changing Colors

Choosing appropriate colors for your form or report is an important formatting decision. For example, colors on forms can be used to assist users in correctly filling them out. Also, if you have a color printer available, you can significantly enhance the appearance of a report or form by adding color to lines or text. Other elements you can add color to include rectangles, backgrounds, headers, footers, or detail areas of a report or form.

Change Line or Border Color

1 Display the form or report in Design view or Layout view.

2 Click the **Design** tab under Form or Report Design Tools (in Design view) or click the **Formatting** tab under Form or Report Layout Tools (in Layout view).

3 Select the line or border whose color you want to change.

4 Click the **Line Color** button arrow, and then select the color you want. You can also select Transparent to make the border around a colored object disappear.

Did You Know?

You can quickly select a repeat color. After you select a color using the color palette on a color button, the color appears in the button. Instead of clicking the button arrow to select the same color, you can simply click the button.

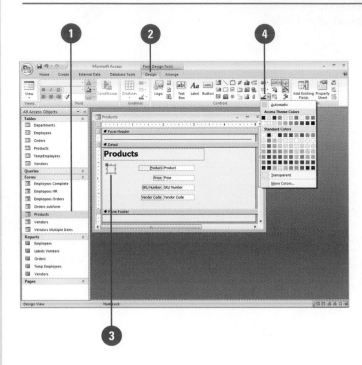

Change Fill Color

1. Display the form or report in Design view or Layout view.

2. Click the **Design** tab under Form or Report Design Tools (in Design view) or click the **Formatting** tab under Form or Report Layout Tools (in Layout view).

3. Select the object whose color you want to change.

4. Click the **Fill/Back Color** button arrow, and then select the color you want.

5. Click the **Alternate Fill/Back Color** button arrow, and then select the color you want.

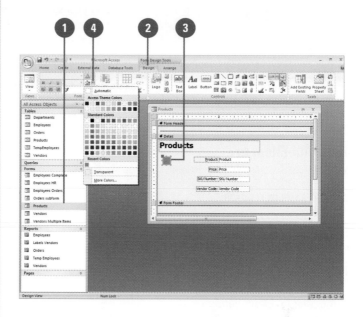

Change Text Color

1. Display the form or report in Design view or Layout view.

2. Click the **Design** tab under Form or Report Design Tools (in Design view) or click the **Formatting** tab under Form or Report Layout Tools (in Layout view).

3. Select the text box with the text whose color you want to change.

4. Click the **Font Color** button arrow, and then select the color you want.

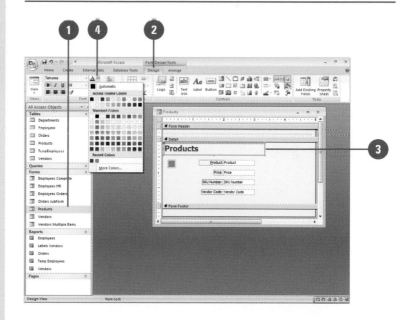

Applying Special Effects to Controls

You can apply special effects to one or more controls in a form or report to enhance the appearance of the form or report. For example, you can create three-dimensional effects, including flat (the default effect), raised, sunken, etched, shadowed, and chiseled. Use the effect that seems most appropriate for the tone of the form or report. For example, in a more formal financial report, you might choose the simple flat effect. In a report outlining future technology needs, consider using a high-tech shadowed effect.

Apply a Special Effect to a Control

1. Display the form or report in Design view.

2. Click the **Design** tab.

3. Select the control to which you want to apply a special effect.

4. Click the **Special Effect** button arrow, and then select the effect you want to use.

   Note that only the control's line or border is affected. Any text in the control is not affected by applying a special effect.

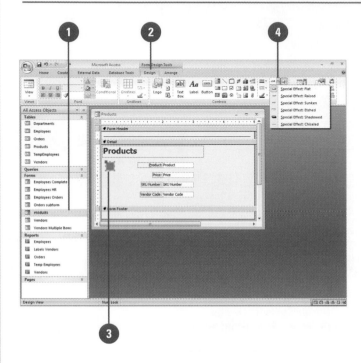

Applying Conditional Formatting

Microsoft Certified Application Specialist

AC07S-2.7.6

You can make your reports and forms more powerful by setting up conditional formatting. **Conditional formatting** allows you to format a field based on values the user enters. For example, you can use a conditional format to make negative values appear in red and positive values appear in black. The formatting is applied to fields only if the values meet the a condition that you specify. Otherwise, no conditional formatting is applied to the fields.

Apply Conditional Formatting to a Field

1. Display the form or report in Design view or Layout view.

2. Click the **Design** tab (in Design view) or click the **Formatting** tab (in Layout view).

3. Click the field to which you want to apply conditional formatting.

4. Click the **Conditional** button.

5. Specify the default format for the field.

6. Click the **Condition 1** list arrow, and then click **Field Value Is**.

7. Click the second list arrow, and then select a condition type.

8. Enter values for the condition.

9. Specify the format when this condition is true.

10. Click **Add**.

11. Click **OK** to apply the formatting.

Did You Know?

You can use expressions in a conditional format. For more complicated conditional formats, select the input field, click the Design or Formatting tab and then click the Conditional button. Click the Condition 1 list arrow, select Expression Is, type the conditional formatting expression, and then click OK.

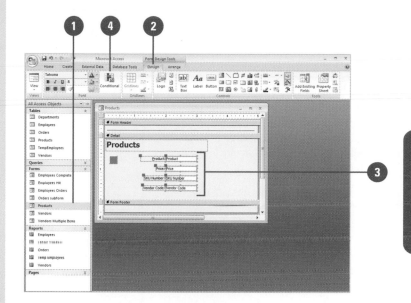

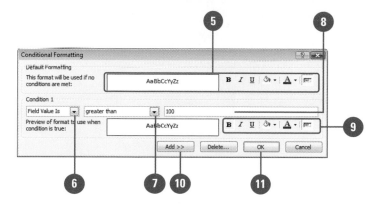

Using the Format Painter

After formatting an object or control in a form or report, you might want to apply those same formatting changes to other objects and controls. The Format Painter lets you "pick up" the style of one section and apply, or "paint" it to another. To apply a format style to more than one item, double-click the Format Painter button instead of a single-click. The double-click keeps the Format Painter active until you want to press Esc to disable it, so you can apply formatting styles to any text or object you want in your document.

Apply a Format Style Using the Format Painter

1. Display the form or report in Design view or Layout view.

2. Click the **Design** tab under Form or Report Design Tools (in Design view) or click the **Formatting** tab under Form or Report Layout Tools (in Layout view).

3. Click the object or control with the style you want to copy.

4. Click the **Format Painter** button.

   If you want to apply the format to more than one item, double-click the Format Painter button.

5. Click the object or control to which you want to apply the format.

6. If you double-clicked the Format Painter button, click another object or control to which you want to apply the format, and then click the **Format Painter** button again when you're done.

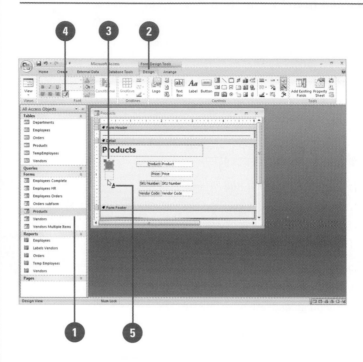

Changing Tabbing Order

Microsoft
Certified
Application
Specialist

ACO7S-2.7.3

Change Tab Order

1 Display the form or report in Design or Layout view.

2 Click the **Arrange** tab.

3 Click the **Tab Order** button

4 Click the section you want to change.

5 Click to select a row, or click and drag to select multiple rows.

6 Drag the selected rows to move them to the tab order you want.

7 Click **OK**.

Did You Know?

You can quickly preview the first 10 records on a form or report. In Design view, display the form or report you want to use, click the Design tab, and then click the First 10 Records Preview button. Access switches to Print Preview view and displays the first 10 records in your form or report.

In Design view, the order in which you create controls is the order in which you tab from field to field in Form, Report, or Layout views. As you change a form or report, you typically need to change the tab order too. You can use the Tab Order button on the Arrange tab in Design or Layout view to change tab order. You can change the tab order for specific sections in a form or report, such as the Page Header, Detail, or Page Footer.

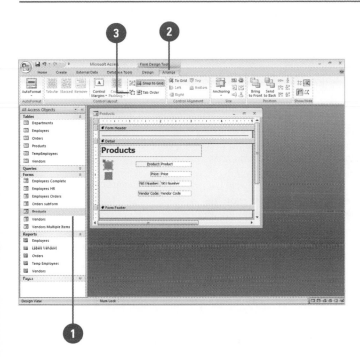

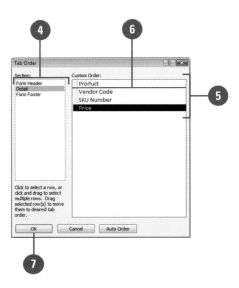

Resizing and Moving Controls

AC07S-2.7.5

When you select a control, sizing handles appear around the control, which you can drag to size it. You can also drag inside a selected control to move it to a new location. Access also provides tools to resize controls and objects relative to each other and anchor them to a section or another control. When you move or resize an anchored control, the item moves or resizes in conjunction with the movement or resizing of the parent.

Resize or Move a Control

1. Display the form or report in Design view.

2. Select the control you want to format.

   TROUBLE? *If you have trouble selecting a control or object, make sure the Select button on the Design tab is highlighted.*

3. To resize a control, position the pointer over a sizing handle, and then drag to a new location.

4. To move a control and a label, position the pointer over an edge of a control until the pointer changes to a four-headed arrow, and then drag to a new location.

   To move a control or a label, position the pointer over the brown square handle until the pointer changes to a four-headed arrow, and then drag to a new location.

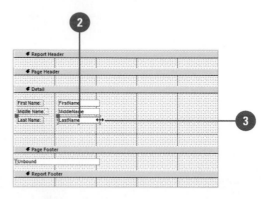

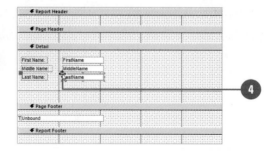

Change the Size of Controls and Objects

1. Display the form or report in Design view.

2. Select the controls and objects you want to resize.

3. Click the **Arrange** tab.

4. Click the sizing option button you want: **To Fit**, **To Grid**, **To Tallest**, **To Shortest**, **To Widest**, or **To Narrowest**.

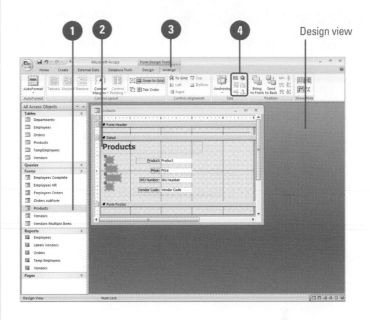

Design view

Anchor Controls and Objects

1. Display the form or report in Design view.

2. Select the controls and objects you want to anchor.

3. Click the **Arrange** tab.

4. Click the **Anchoring** button, and then select the anchoring position you want: **Top Left**, **Stretch Down**, **Bottom Left**, **Stretch Across Top**, **Stretch Down and Across**, **Stretch Across Bottom**, **Top Right**, **Stretch Down and Right**, or **Bottom Right**.

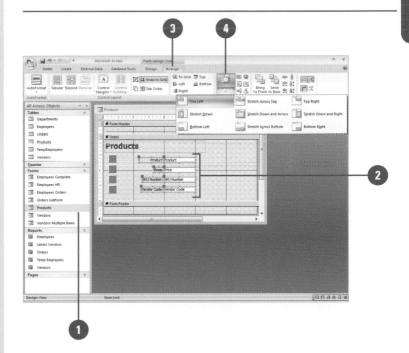

Aligning and Grouping Controls

Often when you work with multiple controls and objects, they look best when aligned with each other. You can manually align and group controls and objects to create your own layout. In Design and Layout view, the controls and other objects you create align themselves along an invisible grid as you move them. To gain control over the placement of elements, you can turn on and off the Snap to Grid option. When Snap to Grid is turned on, Access aligns the upper-left corner of the control to the grid. If you create a control by dragging, Access aligns all corners of the control to the grid.

Align Controls and Objects to Each Other

1. Display the form or report in Design or Layout view.

2. Select the controls and objects you want to align.

3. Click the **Arrange** tab.

4. To align controls to each other using the grid, click the **To Grid** button (in Design view only) to highlight it.

   ◆ To disable the command, click the **To Grid** button to unhighlight it.

5. Click the control alignment button you want: **Left**, **Right**, **Top**, or **Bottom**.

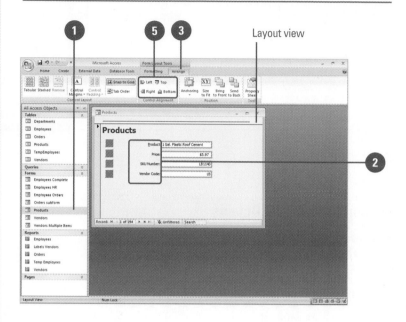

Layout view

Did You Know?

You can show or hide the ruler. In Design view, click the Arrange tab under Form or Report Design Tools, and then click the Ruler button to toggle the ruler on and off.

Enable or Disable Snap to Grid

1 Display the form or report in Design or Layout view.

2 Click the **Arrange** tab.

3 To enable the command, click the **Snap to Grid** button to highlight it.

4 To disable the command, click the **Snap to Grid** button to unhighlight it.

Did You Know?

You can temporarily override the current Snap to Grid setting. Hold down the Ctrl key while you're placing, moving, or resizing a control.

You can show or hide the grid. In Design view, click the Arrange tab under Form or Report Design Tools, and then click the Grid button to toggle the grid on and off.

You can change the grid dot spacing. In Design view, click the Design tab under Form or Report Design Tools, click the Property Sheet button, click the list arrow at the top of the Property Sheet pane, click Form or Report, click in the Grid X or Grid Y box, and then enter a number in dots per inch. The default is 24.

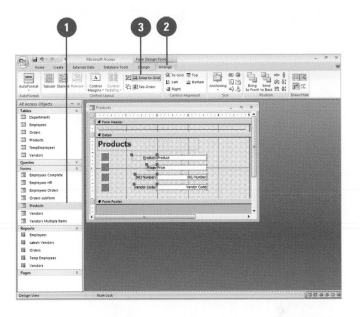

For Your Information

Grouping Objects

Objects can be grouped and ungrouped in a form or report. Rather than moving several objects one at a time, you can group the objects and move them all together. Grouped objects appear as one object, but each object in the group maintains its individual attributes. You can change an individual object within a group without ungrouping. This is useful when you need to make only a small change to a group, such as changing the color of a single field in the group. Simply select the object within the group, change the object or edit text within the object, and then deselect the object. However, if you need to move an object in a group, you need to first ungroup the objects, move it, and then group the objects together again. To group and ungroup objects, display the form or report in Design view, click the Arrange tab, select the objects you want to group or the one already in a group, and then click the Group or Ungroup button.

Positioning Controls

Microsoft
Certified
Application
Specialist

AC07S-2.7.5

Multiple objects in a form or report appear in a stacking order, like layers of transparencies. Stacking is the placement of objects one on top of another. In other words, the first object that you draw is on the bottom and the last object that you draw is on top. You can change the order of this stack of objects by using Bring to Front or Send to Back, commands on the Arrange tab. You can also change the horizontal and vertical spacing between controls and objects and resize controls and objects relative to each other and group them together.

Change Stacking Order of Objects and Controls

1. Display the form or report in Design or Layout view.

2. Select the controls and objects you want to align.

3. Click the **Arrange** tab.

4. Click the **Bring to Front** or **Send to Back** button.

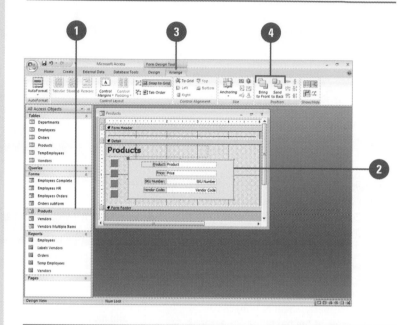

Change Horizontal or Vertical Spacing

1. Display the form or report in Design view.

2. Select the controls and objects whose spacing you want to change.

3. Click the **Arrange** tab.

4. Click the spacing option button you want. You can increase or decrease horizontal or vertical spacing or make horizontal or vertical spacing equal.

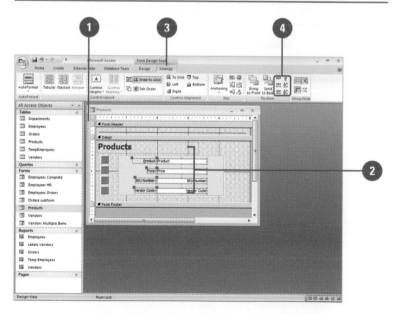

Changing Gridlines

If your controls are located in a control layout, you can add gridlines to provide a visual distinction between the controls. A control layout aligns your controls in a predefined layout, either tabular or stacked, to give your reports and forms a uniform appearance. You can quickly add gridlines to a control layout in a variety of different ways, including Horizontal, Vertical, Cross Hatch, Top, Bottom, and Outline. After you add a gridline, you can change the gridline width, style, and color.

Change Gridlines

1. Display the form or report in Design view or Layout view with the control layout you want to add or change gridlines.

2. Click the **Design** tab under Form or Report Design Tools (in Design view) or click the **Formatting** tab under Form or Report Layout Tools (in Layout view).

3. Select the control to which you want to apply gridlines.

4. Click the **Gridlines** button , and then select the style you want: **Both**, **Horizontal**, **Vertical**, **Cross Hatch**, **Top**, **Bottom**, **Outline**, or **None**.

5. To change line width, style, or color, use any of the following buttons:

   ◆ **Width.** Click to select a gridline thickness.

   ◆ **Style.** Click to select a gridline style.

   ◆ **Color.** Click to select a gridline color.

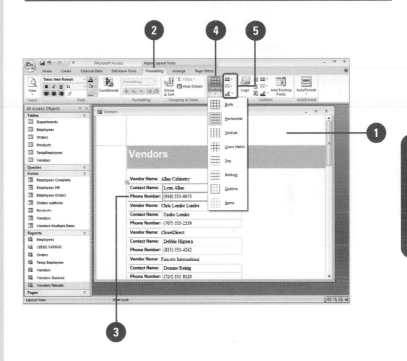

Creating a Tabular or Stacked Layout

Often when you work with multiple controls and objects, they look best when aligned with each other. You can quickly create a predefined tabular and stacked layout (**New!**), or you can manually align and group controls and objects to create your own layout. The tabular layout arranges controls in rows and columns like a spreadsheet with labels across the top. The stacked layout arranges controls vertically down the page with a label to the left of each control. You can also have more than one layout of each type. If you no longer want a tabular or stacked layout, you can quickly remove it.

Change Form or Report Fields to a Tabular Layout

1 Display the form or report in Design view or Layout view.

2 Select the controls you want to change.

3 Click the **Arrange** tab.

4 Click the **Tabular** button.

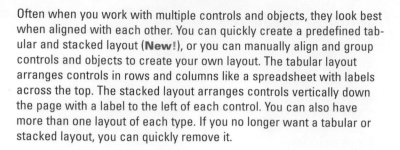

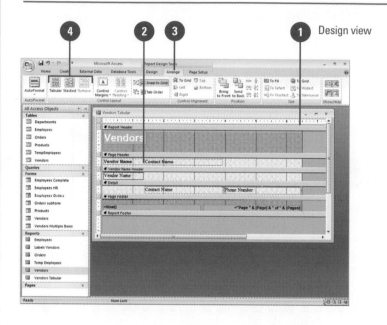

Design view

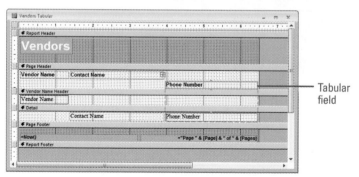

Tabular field

Change Form or Report Fields to a Stacked Layout

1. Display the form or report in Design view or Layout view.

2. Select the controls you want to change.

3. Click the **Arrange** tab.

4. Click the **Stacked** button.

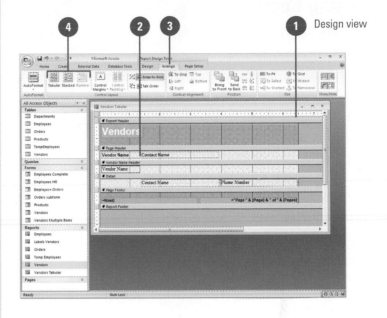

Design view

Remove a Tabular or Stacked Layout

1. Display the form or report in Design view or Layout view.

2. Select the fields with the tabular or stacked layout you want to remove.

3. Click the **Arrange** tab.

4. Click the **Remove** button.

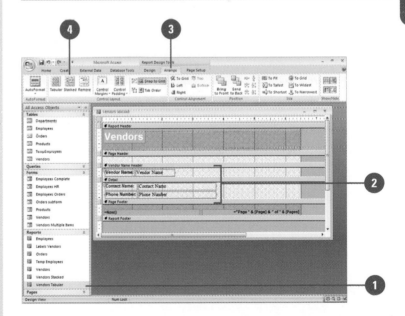

Changing Control Margins and Padding

In the same way you can adjust margins for a page, you can also adjust margins within a control. If the spacing between controls is to tight or large, you can change the spacing, known as padding, between them. You have three control margins and padding options from which to choose: Narrow, Medium, or Wide. If you no longer want to set control margins or padding, you can set either option to None.

Change Control Margins

1. Display the form or report in Design view or Layout view.

2. Select the controls you want to change.

3. Click the **Arrange** tab.

4. Click the **Control Padding** button, and then select the padding option you want: **None**, **Narrow**, **Medium**, or **Wide**.

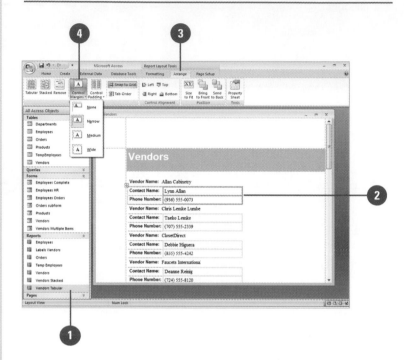

Change Control Padding

① Display the form or report in Design view or Layout view.

② Select the controls you want to change.

③ Click the **Arrange** tab.

④ Click the **Control Padding** button, and then select the padding option you want: **None**, **Narrow**, **Medium**, or **Wide**.

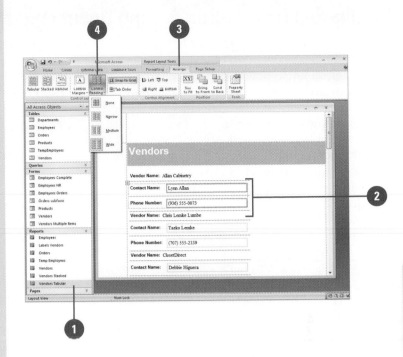

Sharing Information Among Documents

The ability to insert an object created in one program into a document created in another program allows you to create documents that meet a variety of needs. Access can convert data or text from one format to another using a technology known as **object linking and embedding (OLE)**. OLE allows you to move text or data between programs in much the same way as you move them within a program. The table below includes terms that you'll find useful in understanding how you can share objects among documents.

Embedding and Linking	
Term	**Definition**
Source program	The program that created the original object
Source file	The file that contains the original object
Destination program	The program that created the document into which you are inserting the object
Destination file	The file into which you are inserting the object

To better understand how these objects and terms work together, consider this example: If you place an Excel chart in an Access database, Excel is the source program and Access is the destination program. The chart is the source file; the database is the destination file.

There are three ways to share information in Windows programs: pasting, embedding, and linking.

Pasting

You can cut or copy an object from one document and then paste it into another using the Cut, Copy, and Paste buttons on the source and destination program tabs.

Embedding

When you embed an object, you place a copy of the object in the destination file. When you activate the embedded object, the tools from the source program become available in the destination file. For example, if you insert an Excel chart into an Access database, the Excel ribbons and tabs become available, replacing the Access tabs so you can edit the chart if necessary. With embedding, any changes you make to the chart in the database do not affect the original file.

Linking

When you link an object, you insert a representation of the object itself into the destination file. The tools of the source program are available, and when you use them to edit the object you've inserted, you are actually editing the source file. Moreover, any changes you make to the source file are reflected in the destination file.

Copying and Pasting Objects

When you copy or paste an object, Access stores the object in the Clipboard. You can paste the object into the destination file using the Clipboard task pane, Paste button, or Paste Special command, which gives you more control over how the object will appear in the destination file. When you use the Paste button, you are sometimes actually embedding. Because embedding can greatly increase file size, you might want to use Paste Special. You can select a format that requires minimal disk space and paste the object as a simple picture or text.

Paste an Object

1. Select the object in the source program.

2. Click the **Copy** button on the source program's Home tab.

3. Switch to Access and display the area where you want to paste the copied object.

4. Click the **Paste** button on the Home tab and position the object.

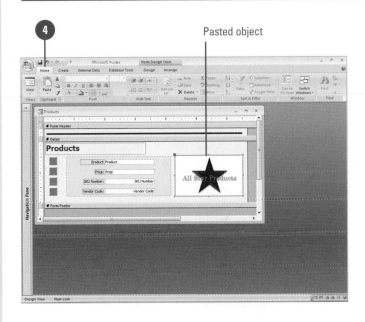

Pasted object

Paste Information in a Specified Format

1. Select the object in the source program.

2. Click the **Copy** button on the source program's Home tab.

3. Switch to Access and display the area where you want to paste the copied object.

4. Click the **Paste** button arrow, and then click **Paste Special**.

5. Click the object type you want.

6. Click **OK**.

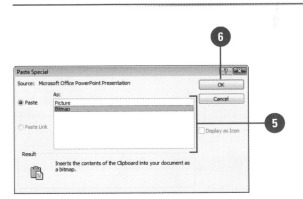

Inserting a New Object

You can create objects from scratch without leaving the Access program. After you drag to create a new unbound object frame control, the Insert Object dialog box appears, and you can select the program in which you want to create the graphic. The programs that appear correspond to the software installed on your computer. For example, if you want to create a picture in Microsoft Paint, a graphics accessory that accompanies the Microsoft Windows operating system, you can choose the Bitmap Image option.

Insert a New Object

1. Display the form or report in Design view.

2. Click the **Design** tab.

3. Click the **Unbound Object Frame** button.

4. With the Unbound Object pointer, drag a rectangle where you want the picture to appear. Make the rectangle approximately the same size as the picture you will insert.

5. Click the **Create new** option.

6. Double-click the program in which you want to create an object.

7. Create the new object using the tools that appear in the program you selected.

8. Click outside the window in which you created the unbound object.

   The program with which you created the object closes, and the new object is inserted in the form or report.

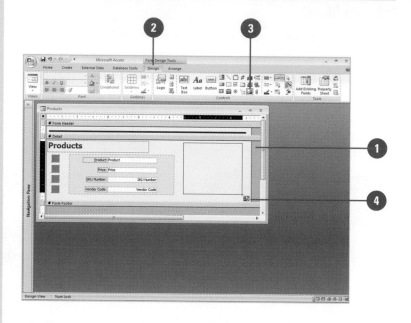

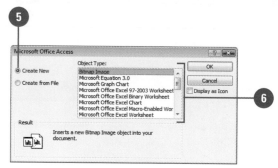

Did You Know?

You can edit the original graphic.
Double-click the graphic object you created to redisplay the program in which you created the object, and then modify the graphic. When you close the program, the modified graphic will be inserted in the form or report.

Inserting an Object from a File

There are several ways to embed or link an object from a file. If you want to embed a new object that you create from scratch, you can use the Insert Object command. If you want to insert an existing file, you can also use Insert Object and you can specify whether or not you want to link the object. If your object is already open in the program that created it, you can copy it, and in some cases, paste it into a form or report, automatically embedding it. Finally, you can use the Paste Special command to paste link a copied object—pasting and linking it at the same time.

Insert an Object from a File

1. Display the form or report in Design view.

2. Click the **Design** tab.

3. Click the **Unbounded Object Frame**, and then drag to create a frame.

4. Click the **Create from file** option, click **Browse**, select the file you want to insert, and then click **OK**.

5. To embed the object, make sure the **Link** check box is clear. To link it, select the **Link** check box.

6. Click **OK**.

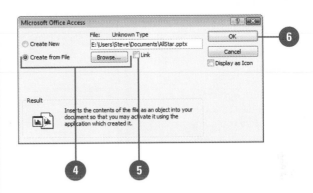

Paste Link an Object

1. In the source program, select the object you want to paste link.

2. Click the **Cut** or **Copy** button on the Home tab in the source program.

3. Switch to your database form or report.

4. Click the **Paste** button arrow, click **Paste Special**, and then click the **Paste Link** option.

5. Click the format you want, and then click **OK**.

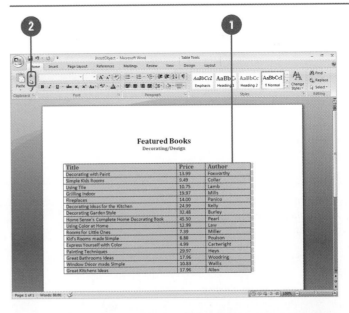

Inserting a Picture

You can insert interesting visuals, such as pictures, into your forms and reports or even fields. For example, in an employee table a field could contain employee photos. Or a field might contain a Word document that is a recent performance review. When you run a report that includes this field, the report will display the contents of the field. In Datasheet view, you can double-click the field to display the field's contents.

Insert a Graphic File

1. Display the form or report in Design view.

2. Click the **Design** tab.

3. Click the **Image** button.

4. Drag a rectangle where you want the picture to appear. Make the rectangle approximately the same size as the picture you will insert.

5. Click the **Look in** list arrow, and then locate the drive and folder containing the picture you want to insert.

    For example, if you want to insert a picture from the clip art collection provided with Office, open the Clip Art folder in the Office folder.

6. Click the file you want to insert, and then click **OK**.

7. If necessary, drag the sizing handles to resize the graphic as needed.

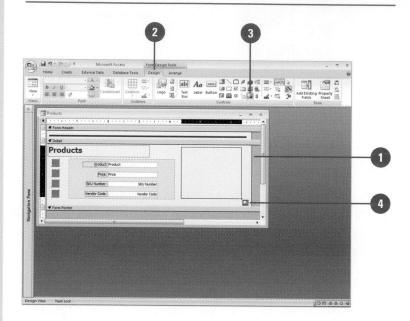

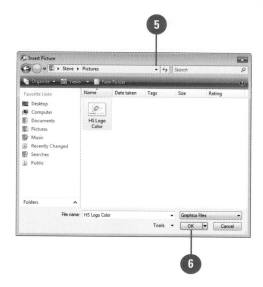

Did You Know?

You can crop parts of a graphic that you want to hide. Press and hold Shift, and then drag a sizing handle over the area you want to crop. To create more space around the graphic, drag the handle away (while holding down Shift) from the center of the graphic.

Insert a Clip Art Object

1. Click the **Start** button, point to **All Programs**, click **Microsoft Office**, click **Microsoft Office Tools**, and then click **Microsoft Clip Organizer**.

2. Use the Collection pane to locate the clip art you want to use.

3. Point to the clip art, and then click the image list arrow.

4. Click **Copy** on the submenu.

5. Click the **Close** button.

6. Display the form or report in Design view in which you want to paste.

7. Click the **Paste** button on the Home tab.

8. Use the sizing handles to resize the clip art object.

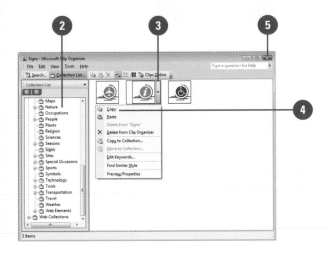

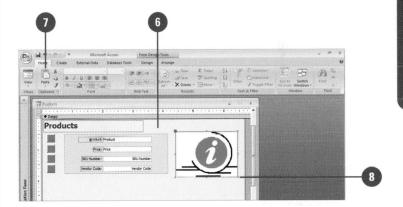

Did You Know?

You can resize an image inside the control on a form or report. In Design view, right-click the picture control, click Properties, click the Format tab, and then set the Size Mode property to Clip, Stretch, or Zoom. Clip stays the same regardless of control size. Stretch resizes to match control size. Zoom resizes to match control size with the original aspect ratio.

For Your Information

Adding Attachments to a Form or Report

If you have added an attachment field to a table, you can add the attachment control to a form or report. To add the attachment control, display the form or report in Design view, click the Design tab, click the Add Existing Fields button, drag the entire attachment field (the parent and child items: name.FileData, name.FileName, and name.FileType) from the list to your form or report, and then save your changes. After you add the attachment field to your form or report, you can add, edit, remove, and save attachments files directly from the form or report. When you select the attachment field in a form or report, a mini-toolbar appears, where you can use the Back and Forward buttons to scroll through attachments, or use the View Attachments button to open the Attachments dialog box.

Scanning Images and Documents

With Microsoft Office Document Imaging, you can scan and manage multiple page documents using the TIFF file format and recognize text in image documents and faxes as editable text by using Optical Character Recognition (OCR). You can copy scanned text and images into Microsoft Office programs as well as e-mail or fax the document over the Internet. If you need to add information to a document, such as a fax, you can add text as a note or comment, apply highlighting, draw shapes, and insert pictures by using the Annotation toolbar (**New!**).

Scan a Document Image

1. Click the **Start** button, point to **All Programs**, click **Microsoft Office**, click **Microsoft Office Tools**, and then click **Microsoft Office Document Imaging**.

2. Click the **Scan New Document** button on the toolbar.

3. Click **Scanner**, select your scanner hardware, and then click **OK**.

4. Click a preset scanning option.

5. Click the scanner options you want.

6. Click the **Scan** button.

   The document is scanned.

7. Click the **Save** button on the toolbar, specify a name and location, and then click **Save**.

8. When you're done, click **Close**.

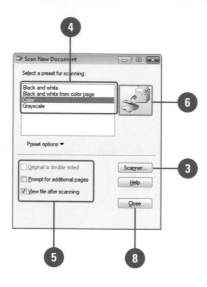

Did You Know?

You can open Microsoft Office Document Scanning program separately. Click the Start button, point to All Programs, click Microsoft Office, click Microsoft Office Tools, and then click Microsoft Office Document Scanning.

Perform OCR on a Document Image

1. Click the **Start** button, point to **All Programs**, click **Microsoft Office**, click **Microsoft Office Tools**, and then click **Microsoft Office Document Imaging**.

2. Click the **Open** button on the toolbar.

3. Click the **Look in** list arrow, and then navigate to the file.

4. Click the document image you want to open, and then click **Open**.

5. Click the **Recognize Text Using OCR** button on the toolbar.

6. To add annotations and comments, use the pen, highlighter, and comments buttons on the Annotation toolbar.

7. Select the text in the document. It appears with a red rectangle around it.

8. Click the **Edit** menu, and then click **Copy**.

9. Save and close the document.

10. Open or switch to Access, and then place the insertion point where you want to paste the text.

11. Click the **Paste** button on the Home tab.

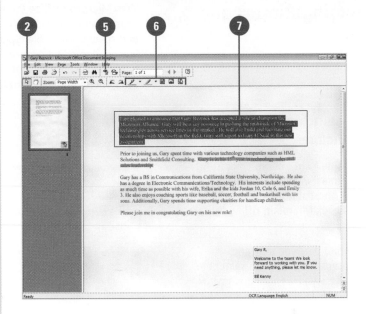

Managing Pictures

With Microsoft Office Picture Manager, you can manage, edit, and share your pictures. You can view all the pictures on your computer and specify which file type you want to open with Picture Manager. If you need to edit a picture, you can use Picture Manager to change brightness, contrast, and color, and to remove red eye. You can also crop, rotate and flip, resize, and compress a picture.

Open Picture Manager and Locate Pictures

1. Click the **Start** button, point to **All Programs**, click **Microsoft Office**, click **Microsoft Office Tools**, and then click **Microsoft Office Picture Manager**.

   The first time you start the program, it asks you to select the file types you want to open with Picture Manager. Select the check boxes with the formats you want, and then click **OK**.

2. If necessary, click **Add Picture Shortcut**.

3. Click **Locate Pictures**.

4. Click the **Look in** list arrow, and then select a location.

5. Click **OK**.

6. Use the **View** buttons to view your pictures.

7. When you're done, click the **Close** button.

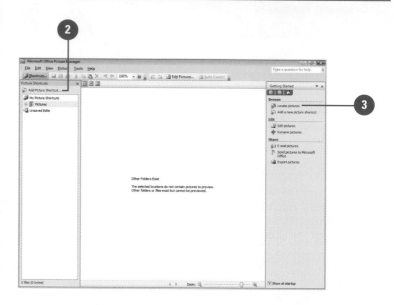

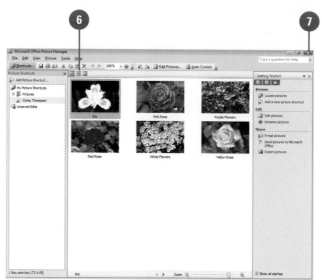

Edit Pictures

1. In Picture Manager, select the picture you want to edit.

2. Click the **Edit Pictures** button on the Standard toolbar.

3. Use the editing tools on the Edit Pictures task pane to modify the picture.

   - Brightness and Contrast
   - Color
   - Crop
   - Rotate and Flip
   - Red Eye Removal

4. Use the sizing tools on the Edit Pictures task pane to change the picture size.

   - Resize
   - Compress Pictures

5. Click the **Save** button on the Standard toolbar.

6. When you're done, click the **Close** button.

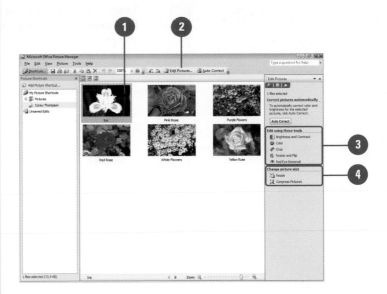

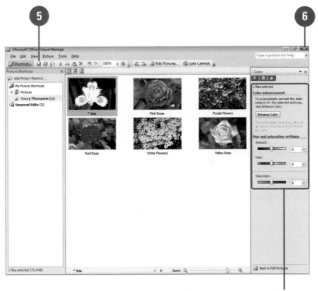

Color enhancing options

Did You Know?

You can discard changes to a picture. If you don't like the changes you make to a picture, click the Edit menu, and then click Discard Changes to restore the picture.

Inserting Excel Charts and Worksheets

There are several types of Excel objects that you can insert into your form or report. Two of the most common are worksheets and charts. You can insert a new Excel worksheet and then add data to it, or you can insert an existing Excel worksheet. You can also insert a chart from an Excel workbook.

Insert an Excel Chart

1 In Excel, click the chart you want to insert in the Access report or form.

2 In Excel, click the **Copy** button on the Home tab.

3 Switch to Access and display the form or report on which you want the chart in Design view.

4 Click the **Paste** button on the Home tab.

5 Click outside the chart to deselect it.

Did You Know?

You can drag and drop to Excel. You can drag objects from Excel right into Design view. Make sure that neither window is maximized and that both the object you want to drag and its destination are visible.

You can edit an inserted Excel worksheet. If you want to modify the worksheet, double-click it, and then use the Excel tools to edit. When you're done, click the Close button, and then click Yes to save changes.

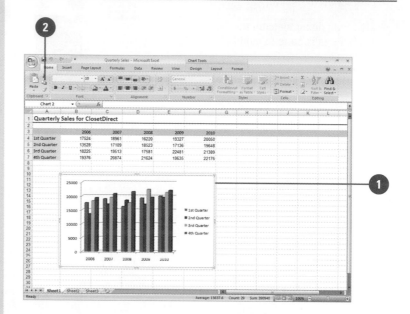

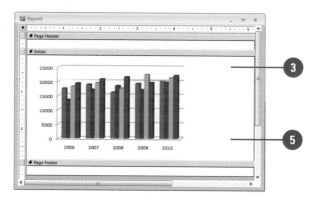

Insert an Excel Worksheet

1. Display the form or report in Design view into which you want to insert the Excel worksheet.

2. Click the **Design** tab.

3. Click the **Unbound Object Frame** button, and then drag to create a frame.

4. Click the **Create from file** option.

5. Click **Browse**, locate and select the worksheet, and then click **OK**.

6. Click **OK**.

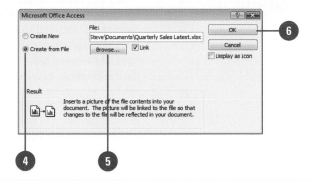

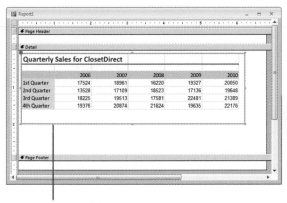

Excel worksheet

Inserting a Graph Chart

You can create a chart from data in a table or query using the Chart Wizard. The wizard steps you through the process to select the data and chart type. The Graph chart uses two views to display the information that makes up a graph: the datasheet, which is a spreadsheet-like grid of rows and columns that contains your data, and the chart, which is the graphical representation of the data. A datasheet contains cells to hold your data. A cell is the intersection of a row and column. Graph Chart comes with a gallery that lets you change the chart type and then format the chart to get the result that you want. You can also save your customized settings as a format to use when you create other charts.

Create a Graph Chart

1. Display the form or report in Design view.

2. Click the **Design** tab.

3. Click the **Insert Chart** button.

4. Drag the pointer to create a rectangle the size of the chart you want to create.

5. When the Chart Wizard appears, click a chart option, and then click the table or query you want to use to make the chart. Click **Next** to continue.

6. Click a field, and then click the **Add** button for each field you want to chart. Click **Next** to continue.

7. Click the chart type you want, and then click **Next** to continue.

8. Make any layout modifications that are desired, and then click **Next** to continue.

9. If you want the chart to change from record to record, select the fields that link the document and the chart, and then click **Next** to continue.

10. Enter a chart name, click the No option if you do not want to display the legend, and then click **Finish**.

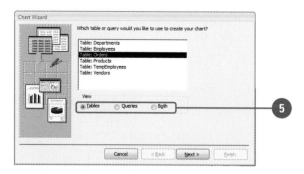

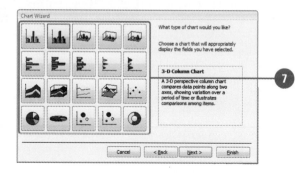

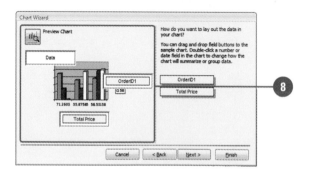

Change a Chart Type

1. In Design view, double-click the chart on your form or report.

2. Click the **Chart Type** button list arrow.

3. Click the button for the chart type you want.

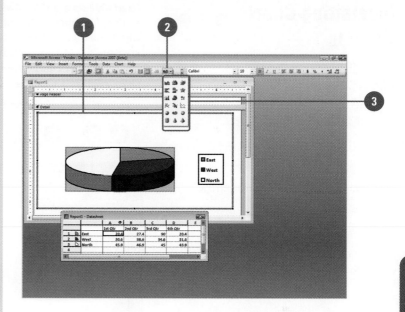

Save Chart Settings as a Custom Chart Type

1. In Design view, double-click the chart on your form or report.

2. Click the **Chart** menu, and then click **Chart Type**.

3. Click the **Custom Types** tab.

4. Click the **User-defined** option.

5. Click **Add**.

6. Type a name and description for the chart, and then click **OK**.

7. Click **OK**.

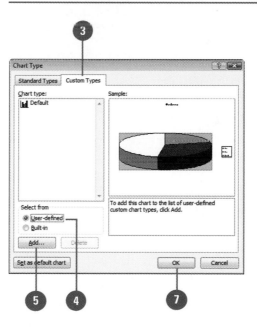

Formatting Chart Objects

Chart objects are the individual elements that make up a chart, such as an axis, the legend, or a data series. The **plot area** is the bordered area where the data are plotted. The **chart area** is the area between the plot area and the Microsoft Graph object selection box. To suit your needs, you can format chart objects and individual elements that make up a chart, such as an axis, legend, or data series.

Select a Chart Object

1. In Design view, double-click the chart on your form or report.

2. Click the **Chart Objects** list arrow.

3. Click the chart object you want to select.

   When a chart object is selected, selection handles appear.

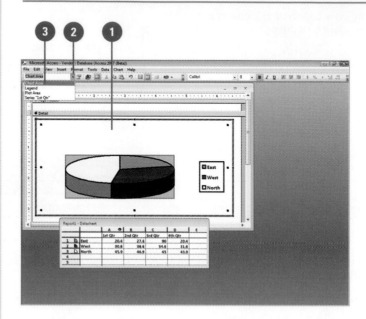

Format a Chart Object

1. In Design view, double-click the chart on your form or report.

2. Double-click the chart object you want to format, such as an axis, legend, or data series.

3. Click the tab corresponding to the options you want to change. Tabs differ depending on the chart object.

4. Select the options to apply.

5. Click **OK**.

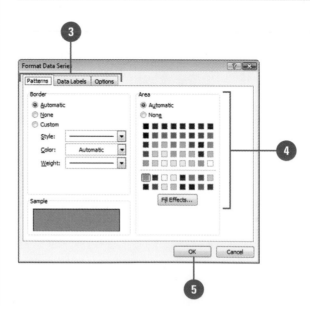

Customize a Chart

1. In Design view, double-click the chart on your form or report.

2. If necessary, select the chart object.

3. Click the **Chart** menu, and then click **Chart Options**.

4. Click the tab (**Titles**, **Axes**, **Gridlines**, **Legend**, **Data Labels**, or **Data Table**) corresponding to the chart object you want to customize.

5. Make your changes.

6. Click **OK**.

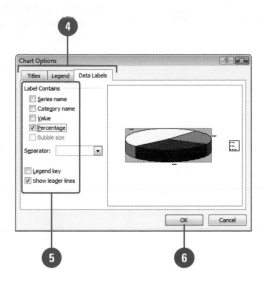

Change the View of a 3-D Chart

1. In Design view, double-click the chart on your form or report.

2. Select the 3-D chart you want to change.

3. Click the **Chart** menu, and then click **3-D View**.

4. Click the left or right rotation button.

5. Click the up or down elevation button.

6. Click **OK**.

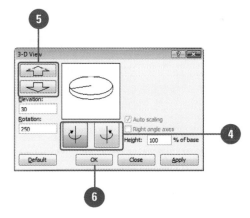

Moving and Resizing an Object

After you insert a graphic object, you can resize or move it with its selection **handles**, the little squares that appear on the edges of the object when you click the object to select it. If you need to select more than one object, you can drag a selection rectangle around the objects, or press and hold down the Shift key, and then click each object to select it.

Move an Object

1. In Design view, select an object you want to move.

2. Position the mouse pointer over the object, and then when the mouse pointer changes to a hand, drag it to move the outline of the object to a new location.

   Do not click a handle or else you will resize the object.

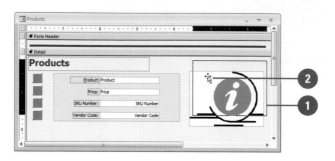

Resize an Object

1. In Design view, select the object you want to resize.

2. Position the mouse pointer over one of the handles.

3. When the pointer changes to a two-headed arrow, drag the handle until the object is the size you want.

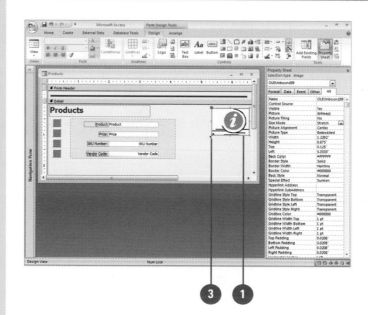

258

Setting OLE Options

When you insert an OLE object, also known as a DDE (Dynamic Data Exchange) object, into a database, you are creating a link to another program. When you open a database with a linked object, Access checks the link to make sure it's working properly. If the linked object is not located in the linked location, Access keeps trying to re-establish the link until the specified timeout period in Access Options. If you don't want other programs to use Access as an OLE object, you can ignore requests from other programs. When linked information changes, you can enable or disable the option to refresh the data.

Set OLE Options

1. Click the **Office** button, and then click **Access Options**.

2. In the left pane, click **Advanced**.

3. Select or clear check boxes for the following OLE options:

    ◆ **OLE/DDE timeout (sec).** Specify the interval after which Access retries a failed OLE or DDE attempt. The default value is 30. You can set a range from zero to 300.

    ◆ **Ignore DDE requests.** Access ignores DDE requests from other applications.

    ◆ **Enable DDE refresh.** Enables Access to update DDE links at the interval specified in the Refresh interval (sec) box.

4. Click **OK**.

Working on the Web

10

Introduction

The Internet and the Web have become an integral part of computing today. By providing quick and easy communication and data sharing to users around the world, the Internet has made it possible for data to have a global, rather than simply local, application. Microsoft Office Access 2007 provides support for the Web in four ways:

- ◆ By allowing database tables, queries, forms, and reports to contain links to objects on the Web

- ◆ With tools to navigate the Web from within the database

- ◆ With the ability to import and export tables, queries, forms, and reports as HTML documents.

Each of these features makes it easier for you to work with data from the Web in your database and makes your data available to the outside world.

If you have access to a Microsoft Windows or Office SharePoint 2007 site, you can share information from Access with other people using the Web site. For example, you can create a table or import data from SharePoint site and export or move data to a SharePoint site (**New!**). You can also publish Access data to a SharePoint Document Management Server (**New!**) in a similar way that you save a database on your hard disk.

Integrating Access and the Internet

One of the chief uses of computers today lies in accessing the **Internet**, a structure of millions of interconnected computers that allows users to communicate and to share data with one another. In its early years, the Internet was limited to a small community of university and government organizations. This was due, in part, to the sometimes difficult commands needed to navigate the Internet.

However, the introduction of the World Wide Web in the early 1990s led to an explosion in Internet use by businesses and the general public. The Web made Internet navigation easy by replacing arcade commands with a simple point-and-click interface within an application called a **Web browser**. The Web made data accessible to a wider audience than ever before. Companies could create Web sites containing product information, stock reports, and information about the company's structure and goals. Later innovations allowed businesses to accept and process orders online and to enter those orders into databases containing inventory and customer information.

Because of the importance of these developments, Microsoft has worked to integrate Access more tightly with the Internet and the Web. You can now navigate the Web from inside Access. Access databases can contain links to Internet resources, and you can save tables, forms, and reports as Web documents. These features make it possible for you to manage Access data locally and across the globe.

Creating Hypertext Links

The Web is a giant structure of documents connected together through hypertext links. **Hypertext links**, or **hyperlinks**, are elements on a Web page that you can activate, usually with a click of your mouse, to retrieve another Web document, which is called the **target** of the link. For example, a document about the national park system might contain a hypertext link whose target is a page devoted to Yosemite National Park. The great advantage of hypertext is that you don't have to know where or how the target is stored. You need only to click the hyperlink to retrieve the target. A target is identified by its **Uniform Resource Locator (URL)**, an address that uniquely identifies the location of the target on the Internet.

Access incorporates hypertext in two ways. First, through **hypertext fields**, fields in tables that contain hyperlinks, you can view and click a link and retrieve the link's target. Second, Access allows you to insert hyperlinks as elements within forms and reports. A footnote on a form, for example, could be a link to a Word document.

The targets of these links need not be pages on the Web. You can also direct the links to target other files on a hard disk drive, to an object within the current database, or to a different database altogether.

Creating Web Pages

Web pages are created in a special language called **HTML (Hypertext Markup Language)**, a cross-platform language which any operating system, including Microsoft Windows, Macintosh, and UNIX, can use to access a Web page. The cross-platform nature of HTML is one reason for the popularity of the Web.

Static Web Pages

Access allows you to export reports, forms, and tables to HTML format. Once you export these database objects, you can publish them as Web pages for others to view. These Web pages are **static Web pages** because their content is unchanged until you export the database object again. You have some control over the appearance of the Web page through the use of **HTML templates**, files that consist of HTML commands describing the page's layout. The templates can be used to insert company logos, graphics, and other elements. However, Access does not supply the templates for you, and you must have some working knowledge of HTML to create your own.

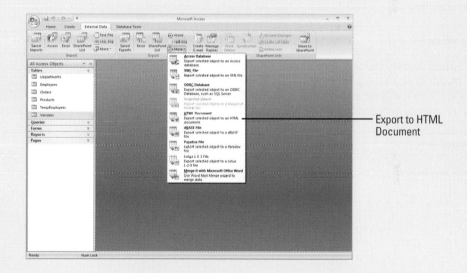

Export to HTML Document

Creating a Hyperlink Field

The Hyperlink data type allows you to create a Hyperlink field, a field that can store hyperlinks. The hyperlink can be a path to a file on your hard disk drive or network, or it can be a link to a page on the Web. When you click a Hyperlink field, Access jumps to the target specified by the link. For example, if you have a Clients table, and most of your clients have their own Web pages, you might want to create a Hyperlink field that contains links to each client Web page.

Create a Hyperlink Field in a Table

1. Display the table in Design view.

2. Create a new field in which you want to store a hyperlink.

3. Click the **Data Type** list arrow, and then click **Hyperlink**.

4. Click the **Save** button on the Quick Access Toolbar to save the changes to the table.

See Also

See "Viewing Field Properties" on page 75 and "Changing Field Properties" on page 76 for more information on working with data types.

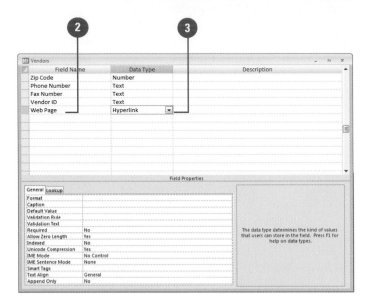

Inserting a Hyperlink to a File or Web Page

Use the Insert Hyperlink button to create a hyperlink within a Hyperlink field or as hypertext within a form or report. A hyperlink consists of the text that the user sees that describes the link, the URL of the link's target, and a ScreenTip that appears whenever the pointer passes over the link. If you have created a Hyperlink field for client Web pages, you can use this method to add a URL for each client's Web page.

Insert a Hyperlink to a File or Web Page

1. Within a Hyperlink field or while editing a form or report in Design view, click the **Design** tab.

2. Click the **Insert Hyperlink** button.

3. Click **Existing File or Web Page** on the Link to bar.

4. Enter the hyperlink text.

5. Specify the linked document by either:

   ◆ Entering the file name or URL of the linked document

   ◆ Choosing the linked document from the Recent Files, Browsed Pages, or Inserted Links list

6. Click **ScreenTip** to create a ScreenTip that will be displayed whenever the mouse pointer moves over the hyperlink.

7. Click **OK**.

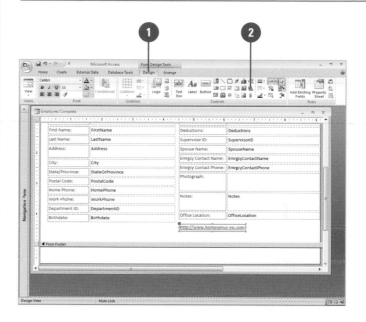

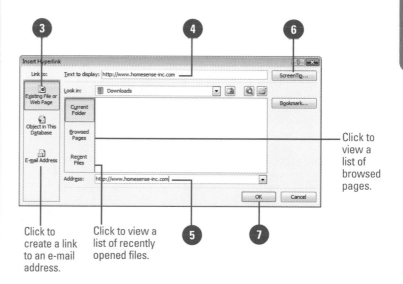

Click to view a list of browsed pages.

Click to create a link to an e-mail address.

Click to view a list of recently opened files.

Did You Know?

You can remove a hyperlink. Right-click the hyperlink in Design view, point to Hyperlink, and then click Remove Hyperlink.

You can edit a hyperlink. Right-click the hyperlink in Design view, point to Hyperlink, and then click Edit Hyperlink.

Linking to an Object in a Database

You can create hyperlinks that target forms, tables, and reports within the current database. You can also link to objects in other databases by specifying the database's file name and selecting the form, table, or report you want to target. You will have immediate access to those objects by clicking the hyperlink you insert.

Link to a Database Object in the Database

1. Within a Hyperlink field or while editing a form or report in Design view, click the **Design** tab.

2. Click the **Insert Hyperlink** button.

3. Click **Object in This Database** on the Link to bar.

4. Enter the hyperlink text.

5. Select the database object.

6. Click **OK**.

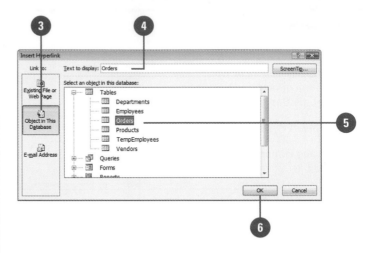

Link to an Object in Another Database

1. Within a Hyperlink field or while editing a form or report in Design view, click the **Design** tab.

2. Click the **Insert Hyperlink** button.

3. Click **Existing File or Web Page** on the Link to bar.

4. Enter the hyperlink text.

5. Enter the database file name or click **Browse** to locate and select a database file name.

6. Click **Bookmark**.

7. Select the database object.

8. Click **OK**.

9. Click **OK**.

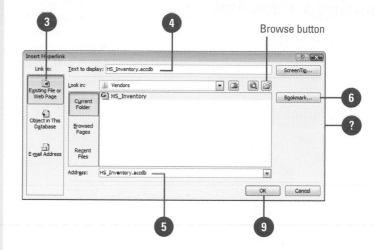

Browse button

Inserting a Hyperlink with an E-mail Address

You can use the Insert Hyperlink button to create a hyperlink with an e-mail address. When you click the hyperlink with an e-mail address, Access starts Outlook and creates a new message with the e-mail address you specified in the hyperlink. In the Insert Hyperlink dialog box, Access adds *mailto:* in front of the e-mail address, which commands Access to open your mail program.

Insert a Hyperlink to an E-mail Address

1. Within a Hyperlink field or while editing a form or report in Design view, click the **Design** tab.

2. Click the **Insert Hyperlink** button.

3. Click **E-mail Address** on the Link to bar.

4. Enter the e-mail address, or select an recently used e-mail address.

5. Enter a subject for use in the e-mail.

6. Enter the text you want to display for the e-mail address in a form or report.

7. Click **ScreenTip** to create a ScreenTip that will be displayed whenever the mouse pointer moves over the hyperlink.

8. Click **OK**.

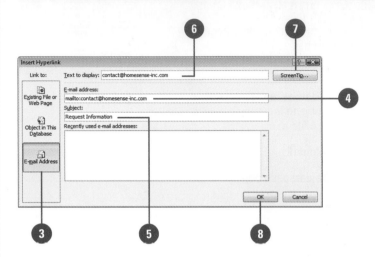

Navigating Hyperlinks

When you have added a hyperlink to a form, report, or table, you can activate the link by clicking it with the mouse in Form, Report, or Datasheet view. As the pointer moves over the hyperlink, the pointer changes to a hand, which indicates the presence of the link. If you have supplied a ScreenTip when you created the link, the tip appears, giving additional information about the link.

Navigate a Hyperlink

1. Open a table, form, or report containing a hyperlink.

2. Move the pointer over the hyperlink so that the pointer shape changes to a hand.

3. Click the hyperlink to display the linked document.

Did You Know?

You can remove or edit a hyperlink. To remove or edit a Hyperlink field, right-click the link, point to Hyperlink, and then click Remove Hyperlink or Edit Hyperlink. To remove or edit a hypertext link from a form or report, right-click the link in Design view, and then click Remove or Edit.

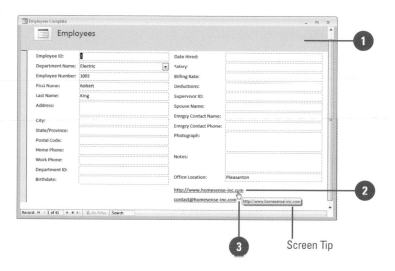

Screen Tip

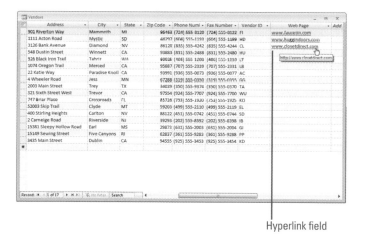

Hyperlink field

Exporting Database Objects to HTML

In Access, the Export HTML Document command allows you to save a table, query, form, or report as a Web page. If the page is saved in HTML format, it represents a snapshot of the data at the time you created the file. If your data changes, you must export it again if you want the Web page to be current.

Export to an HTML File

1 In the Navigation pane, select or open a table, query, form, or report.

2 Click the **External Data** tab.

3 If you want to export selected records, select them.

4 Click the **More** button (in the Export group), and then click **HTML Document**.

5 Click **Browse**, select a location, enter a name, and then click **Save**.

6 Select the options you want:

   ◆ **Export data with formatting and layout**.

   ◆ **Open the destination file after the export operation is complete**.

   ◆ **Export only the selected records**.

7 Click **OK**.

8 If you want to use a HTML template, select the **Select a HTML Template** check box, and then specify the template location.

9 Click **OK**, and then click **Close**.

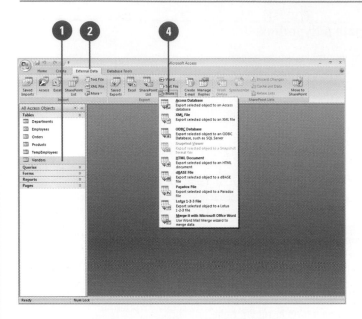

Did You Know?

You can use HTML templates.
Templates are usually stored in the *C:\Program Files\Microsoft Office\ Templates\1033\Access* folder. See online Help for more information on creating your own templates.

Importing or Linking to an HTML File

In Access, the Import HTML Document command allows you to import a HTML data into a table. You can import the source data into a new table in the current database, append a copy of imported records to a table, or link to the data source by creating a linked table. Access uses the Import HTML Wizard to help you specify how you want to import the HTML data into your database.

Import or Link to an HTML Document

1. Click the **External Data** tab.

2. Click the **More** button (in the Import group), and then click **HTML Document**.

3. Enter the complete path to the HTML document or click **Browse**, select the HTML document, and then click **OK**.

4. Specify the option how and where you want to store the data in the database:

   ◆ **Import the source data into a new table in the current database.**

   ◆ **Append a copy of the records to the table.**

   ◆ **Link to the data source by creating a linked table.**

5. Click **OK**.

6. Follow the Import HTML wizard instructions to specify how to import the HTML data.

7. When you're done, click **Finish**, and then click **Close**.

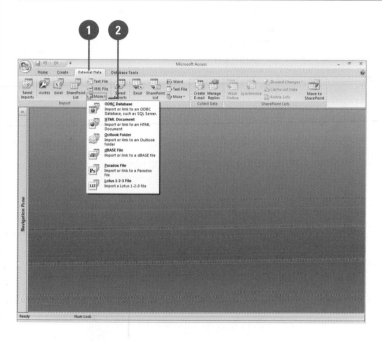

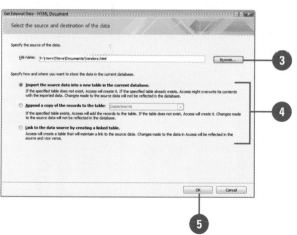

Viewing a Data Access Page

Access 2007 no longer supports data access pages. Instead, you can connect your data to a Microsoft SharePoint site and use the tools provided by Access and the site to import and export data to share it with others on the Web. If you open a database created with an earlier version of Access with a data access page, you can view the pages in Internet Explorer.

View a Data Access Page

1. In the Navigation pane, click **Pages** on the Objects bar.

2. Double-click the data access page you want to view.

3. If necessary, click the **Update Link**, locate and select the HTML file, and then click **OK**.

   Access starts your Web browser, loading the data access page.

Did You Know?

You can choose a Web browser for your data access page. You must use Internet Explorer 5.0 or later to view a data access page.

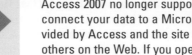

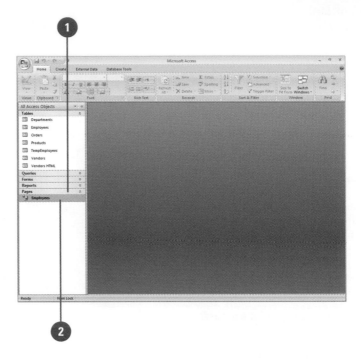

Data access page in a Web browser

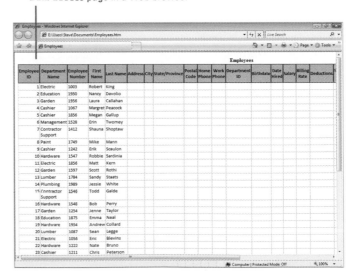

Creating a Table Using SharePoint

If you have access to a Microsoft Office SharePoint Services site, you can import a SharePoint list (**New!**) into an Access database as a table. A SharePoint Services site is a server application that uses Web site templates to create, organize, and share information. To access a SharePoint Services site, you might need access privileges. See your network administrator for a user name and password. Access provides several SharePoint list table templates including: Contacts, Tasks, Issues, Events, Custom, and Existing SharePoint List.

Create a Table Using a SharePoint List

1. Click the **Create** tab.

2. Click the **SharePoint List** button.

3. Click the SharePoint list template (**Contacts**, **Tasks**, **Issues**, **Events**, **Custom**, or **Existing SharePoint List**) you want.

4. Enter a SharePoint site address or select an existing one.

5. Type a name and description.

6. To open the list, select the **Open the list when finished** check box.

7. Click **OK**.

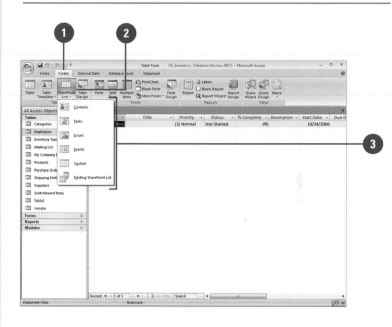

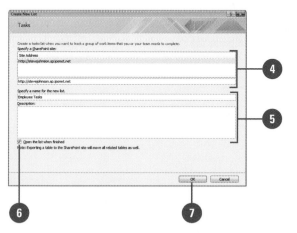

Importing or Linking to SharePoint Data

If you have access to a Microsoft Office SharePoint Services site, you can import SharePoint data (**New!**) into an Access database as a new or linked table. A wizard takes you step-by-step through the process and asking you to select a SharePoint list and other import options. To access a SharePoint Services site, you might need access privileges. See your network administrator for a user name and password.

Import SharePoint Data

1. Click the **External Data** tab.

2. Click the **Import SharePoint List** button.

3. Enter a SharePoint site address or select an existing one.

4. Click the **Import the source data into a new table in the current database** or **Link to the data source by creating a linked table** option.

5. Click **Next** to continue.

6. Select the lists you want to import or link.

7. If you're importing, select the view you want for each selected list, and then select or clear the **Import display values instead of IDs for fields that look up values stored in another list** check box.

8. Click **OK**, and then complete the rest of the wizard.

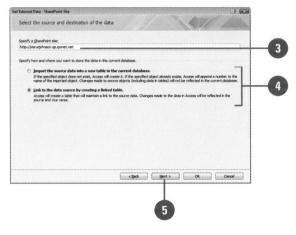

Did You Know?

You can take SharePoint data offline.
If you link a table to SharePoint, you can work offline on a local copy. Open the database, click the External Data tab, and then click the Work Offline button. Click the Work Offline button again to reconnect. Click Synchronize button to update lists with data from SharePoint. Click the Discard Changes button to discard your offline changes.

Exporting Data to SharePoint

If you have access to a Microsoft Office SharePoint Services site, you can export your data to a SharePoint list (**New!**), which can be shared with others over the Web. A wizard takes you step-by-step through the process and creates a SharePoint list for each table and then links each list back to your existing database. To access a SharePoint Services site, you might need access privileges. See your network administrator for a user name and password.

Export Data to a SharePoint Site

1. Open the table you want to move to a SharePoint site.

2. Click the **External Data** tab.

3. Click the **Export to SharePoint List** button.

4. Enter a SharePoint site address or select an existing one.

5. Type a name and description.

6. To open the list, select the **Open the list when finished** check box.

7. Click **OK**, and then complete the rest of the wizard.

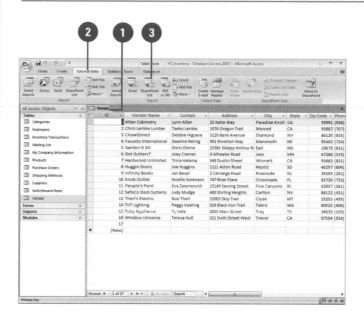

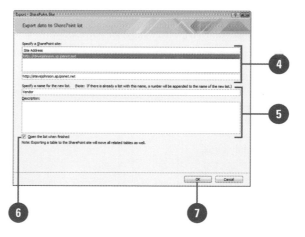

Moving Data to SharePoint

If you have access to a Microsoft Office SharePoint Services site, you can move your data to a SharePoint list (**New!**), which can be shared with others over the Web. A wizard takes you step-by-step through the process and creates a SharePoint list for each table and then links each list back to your existing database. To access a SharePoint Services site, you might need access privileges. See your network administrator for a user name and password.

Move Data to a SharePoint Site

1. Open the table you want to move to a SharePoint site.

2. Click the **External Data** tab.

3. Click the **Move to SharePoint** button.

4. Enter a SharePoint site address or click **Browse**, select an existing one, and then click **OK**.

5. To open the list, select the **Save a copy of my database to the SharePoint site and create shortcut to my Access forms and reports** check box.

6. Click **Next**.

7. Follow the remaining instructions to complete the wizard.

Did You Know?

You can create and link a new database to a SharePoint. Click the Office button, click New, select a database template, select the Create and link your database to a Windows SharePoint Services Site check box, click Download, and then follow the SharePoint wizard instructions.

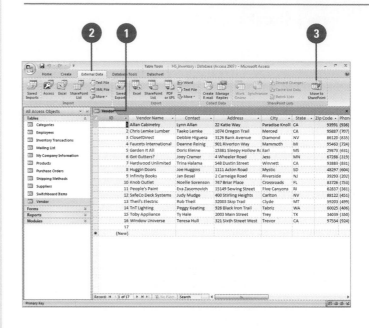

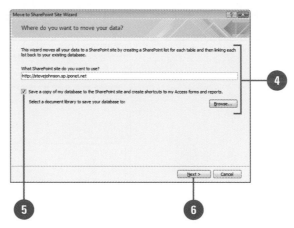

Publishing a Database to SharePoint

You can save an Access database to a Document Management Server (**New!**), such as a Document Library on an Office SharePoint site, in a similar way that you save a database on your hard disk. After you save the data for the first time using the Document Management Server command, you can use the Document Management Server command again to republish the database to update the document on the site. If you save a file to a library that requires you to check documents in and out, the SharePoint site checks it out for you. However, you need to check the document in when you're done with it. If the site stores multiple content types, you might be asked to specify the content type.

Publish Data to a Document Management Server

① Open the database you want to save to a Document Management Server.

② Click the **Office** button, point to **Publish**, and then click **Document Management Server**.

③ Navigate to the network folder location on the SharePoint server where you want to save the file.

④ Type a file name.

⑤ If necessary, click the **Save as type** list arrow, and then click **Microsoft Office Access 2007 Database**.

⑥ Click **Save**.

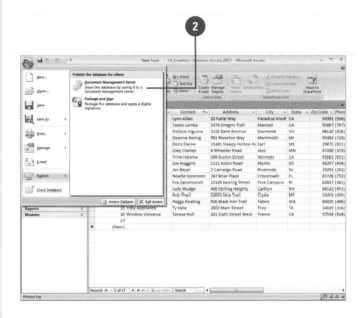

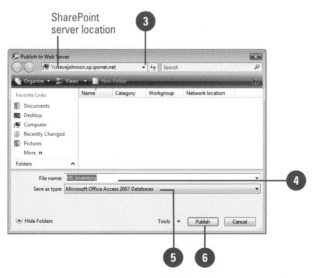

SharePoint server location

Viewing and Navigating a SharePoint Site

Introducing Sites and Workspaces

Microsoft Office SharePoint Server 2007 is a server application that uses Web site templates to create, organize, and share information. Since this is a Web based system, everyone can access this with a simple Web browser. Office SharePoint Server allows you to create several different types of sites including: Team Site, Wiki Site, Document Workspace, Meeting Workspace, or Blog. A **Team Site** is a template for teams to create, organize, and share information; a **Wiki Site** (New!) is a template where users can quickly and easily add, edit, and link information, such as a brainstorming session; a **Document Workspace** is a template for team members to work together on documents; a **Meeting Workspace** (New!) is a template for users to plan, organize, and track meetings; and a **Blog** (New!) is a template for users to post information and comment on it. You can also use other site templates to communicate and track information, such as announcements, contacts, discussion boards, links, calendars, tasks, project tasks, issues, and surveys. You can create these and many other sites by using the Site Actions menu, which provides easy access to commands that allow you to create and edit content pages and manage all site settings. Click the Site Actions menu, click Create, click the element you want to create, and then fill in the page.

You can navigate within an Office Share-Point site by clicking links on the **Quick Launch** in the left navigation pane, clicking linked tabs, such as Home, on the **Top link bar**, clicking the page name in the horizontal list above the page name, or using the Back and Forward buttons on your Web browser toolbar. You can click View All Site Content at the top of the Quick Launch to display a list of all content available on the site. To customize site navigation and the display, click the Site Actions menu, click Site Settings, and then click the option you want to change under Look and Feel.

Administering Sites Settings

The administrator of an Office SharePoint Server site controls the ability to create, access, and contribute to a site. With Administrator permissions, you can administer all aspects of an Office SharePoint site from a centralized location on the Site Settings page. To display the Site Settings page, navigate to the main or subsite Home page where you want to make changes, click the Site Actions menu, and then click Site Settings. The **Site Settings page** displays five different categories with a list of options: Users and Permissions, Look and Feel, Galleries, Site Administration, and Site Collection Administration.

You can access an Office SharePoint Server by entering a URL or network location in a Web browser, and then providing a user name (include a domain name\user name, if necessary) and password. If you do not have access information to the Office SharePoint Server, contact your Systems Administrator.

Importing and
Exporting Information

11

Introduction

Microsoft Office Access 2007 allows you to incorporate information from a variety of sources into a database and exchange information from a database into other sources. You can use the Access import and export features to easily move data between your database and other databases and programs.

When you get data from other sources, you have the choice to import the data into a new table or link an existing table of the data to the database. When you import data, Access converts and copies the data into the database file. When you link to the data in another program, the data stays separate from the Access database. You can import data or link to data from several sources, including Microsoft Access, other databases (such as Paradox), HTML (a standard Web format), Microsoft Office Excel, Microsoft Exchange, Microsoft Office Outlook, and SharePoint Services.

If you work with XML (Extensible Markup Language), Access allows you to import and export XML data as well as transform the data to and from other formats using XML related files. XML is a new standard that enables you to move information across the Internet and programs where the data is stored independently of the format so you can use the data more seamlessly in other forms.

The data sharing techniques in Access allow you to exchange data with other Microsoft Office programs. For example, you can merge your Access data with Microsoft Office Word to create form letters, or you can use Microsoft Office Excel's analysis tools on your Access data.

If you need to send database objects to others, which cannot be changed, Access provides the option to save a database object as an XPS or PDF file (**New!**), which are secure fixed-layout formats.

Importing and Linking Data

If you have data in other forms, yet need the information in Access, you can import the data into a new table or link the data to the database. When you import data, Access converts and copies the data into the database file. When you link to the data in another program, the data stays separate from the database, yet you can view and edit the data in both the original program and in the Access database.

If you need to use the data in different programs and sources, linking data is the most efficient way to keep the data up-to-date. However, if you plan to use your data only in Access, importing data is the most effective way. Access works faster and more efficiently when you import the data.

In addition to Access databases and projects, you can import or link data using the most common data formats from other programs, such as Microsoft Excel spreadsheets, Lotus 1-2-3 spreadsheets, Paradox for Windows databases, dBASE files, Microsoft SharePoint Services, Microsoft Exchange, Outlook folders, text files, HTML, XML (Extensible Markup Language), and SQL tables with ODBC (Open Database Connectivity).

When you import data, you cannot append data to an existing table unless you import a spreadsheet or text files. When you link data, you can read and update the external data without altering the external data format in the original data source. Access uses different

Import options

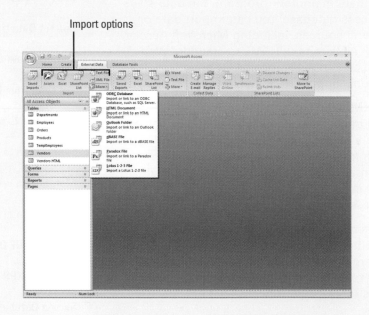

icons to represent linked tables and nonlinked tables. A diamond shape indicates a linked table.

If you no longer need a linked table, you can delete the linked table from the Access window. When you delete a linked table, you are deleting only the information that Access uses to open the table. You can re-link to the table again at any time.

You can also import or link data in Access using commands in the Import group on the External Data tab. When you choose one of these commands, the Get External Data dialog box opens, displaying a dialog box similar to a wizard. Use the Browse to select the file you want to import or link, and other options to determine how you want to store the data in the current database.

Get External Data dialog box   Browse button

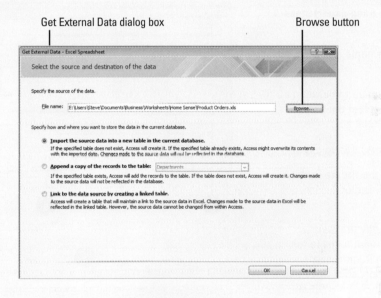

Import Spreadsheet Wizard

Saving Import and Export Settings

Microsoft Certified Application Specialist

AC07S-3.5.3,
AC07S-5.4.3

When you import or export data in Access, you can save your import and export settings (**New!**) for use again in the future. In the final screen of an import or export wizard, you have the option to save settings. When you select the Save import steps option, additional fields and options appear where you can type a name and description and set specifications to perform the import or export operation at fixed intervals by creating tasks in Outlook. After you save import or export settings, you can use the Manage Data Tasks dialog box to run or delete them, or create an Outlook tasks.

Save Import or Export Settings

1. In the final screen of an import or export wizard, select the **Save import steps** or **Save export steps** check box.

2. Enter a Save as name and a description.

3. To perform this import operation at fixed intervals, select the **Create Outlook Task** check box.

4. Click **Save Import** or **Save Export**.

5. If you selected the Create Outlook Task check box, Outlook starts and creates a task.

    Review and modify the task settings. If you want to make the task recur, click **Recurrence**. When you're done, click **Save and Close**.

Did You Know?

You can run a saved task from Outlook. In Outlook, click Tasks in the Navigation pane, and then double-click the Access task. Click the Task tab, and then click Run Import. Switch to Access, and then open the imported table in Datasheet view and check the data for errors.

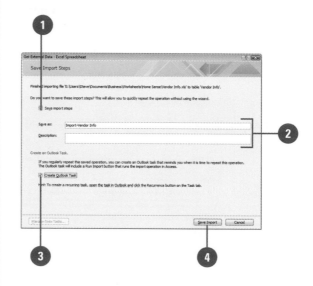

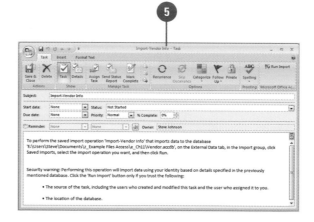

Manage Existing Saved Import and Export Settings

1. Click the **External Data** tab.

2. Click the **Saved Import** or **Saved Export** button.

3. To switch between import and export settings, click the **Saved Imports** or **Saved Exports** tab.

4. Select the saved settings you want to manage.

5. Click the button option you want:

    ◆ **Run.** Executes the saved import or export settings.

    ◆ **Create Outlook Task.** Creates a recurring task to perform the saved import or export settings.

    ◆ **Delete.** Removes the import or export saved settings.

6. Click **Close**.

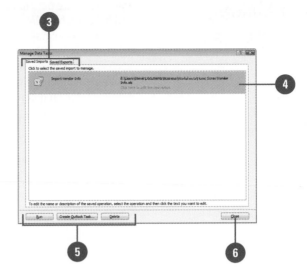

Importing or Linking Data from an Access Database

You can create new tables from other Access databases by importing and linking tables. When you import a table, you copy data from a table in one Access database and place it in a new table in your database. When you link a table, the data stays in its original location, but you can display and access that data from within your database. If data in the original database changes, the changes will appear in your linked database, too. You can also import data from other programs.

Import or Link Data from an Access Database

1. Open the database in which you want to import or link data.

2. Click the **External Data** tab.

3. Click the **Import Access Database** button.

4. Click **Browse**, locate and select the database file that contains the data you want to import, and then click **Open**.

5. Click the import or link option you want.

6. Click **OK**.

7. Click the tab with the database object you want to import or link.

8. Click the objects you want. To deselect an object, click it.

9. Click **OK**.

10. To save import steps, select the **Save import steps** check box, enter a name and description, and then click **Save Import**.

    Otherwise, click **Close**.

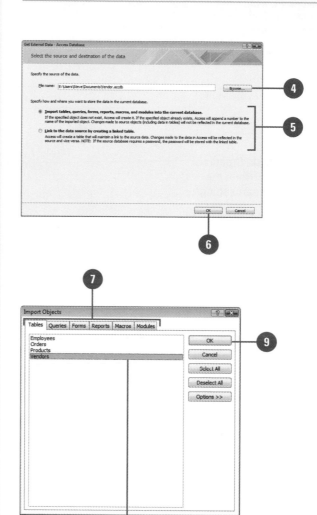

Did You Know?

You can delete the link to a linked table. In the Navigation pane, click Tables, click the linked table you want to delete, and then press Delete.

284

Convert a Linked Table to a Nonlinked Table

1. In the Navigation pane, select the linked table you want to convert.

2. Click the **Home** tab.

3. Click the **Copy** button.

4. Click the **Paste** button.

5. Type a name for the new table.

6. Click the **Structured Only (Local Table)** or **Structure and Data (Local Table)** option.

7. Click **OK**.

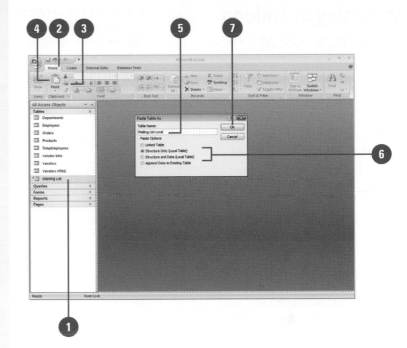

Importing or Linking Data from Excel

Microsoft Certified Application Specialist   AC07S-3.5.1, AC07S-3.5.2

If you have data in an Excel spreadsheet, you can use the information in an Access database. You can import or link all the data from a spreadsheet or specific data from a named range. When you import or link data, Access normally creates a new table for the information. For Excel spreadsheet data, you can also append data to an existing table as long as the table field's and spreadsheet column headings match. After you import or link data, you should check to make sure Access assigned the appropriate data type to the imported fields.

Import or Link Data from an Excel Spreadsheet

1. Open the database in which you want to import or link data.

2. Click the **External Data** tab.

3. Click the **Import Excel Spreadsheet** button.

4. Click **Browse**, locate and select the Excel spreadsheet file you want to import or link, and then click **Open**.

5. Click the import, append, or link option you want.

6. Click **OK**.

7. Follow the wizard instructions; some of the requested information includes:

   ◆ A worksheet or named range

   ◆ First row column heading

   ◆ A new or existing table

   ◆ Field information

   ◆ Primary key

   ◆ Table name

8. When you're done, click **Finish**.

9. To save import steps, select the **Save import steps** check box, enter a name and description, and then click **Save Import**.

   Otherwise, click **Close**.

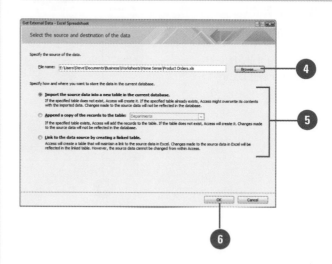

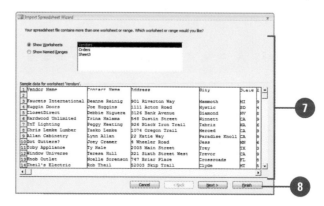

Importing or Linking Data from a Mail Program

If you have data in a mail program, such as Microsoft Exchange or Microsoft Outlook, you can use the Import From Exchange/Outlook Wizard or the Link To Exchange/Outlook Wizard to import or link your Contacts folder. You can use the information from your Contacts folder to create form letters and mailing labels by merging the data using the Microsoft Word Mail Merge Wizard. You need to have Microsoft Outlook, Outlook Express, or Microsoft Exchange installed on your computer to use these wizards to import or link data.

Import or Link Data from Microsoft Exchange or Outlook

1. Open the database in which you want to import or link data.

2. Click the **External Data** tab.

3. Click the **More** button, and then click **Outlook Folder**.

4. Click the import, append, or link option you want.

5. Click **OK**.

   The Import or Link Exchange/ Outlook Wizard dialog box opens.

6. Click the **Contacts** folder icon (use the plus and minus signs to display folders), and then click **Next**.

7. Follow the remaining wizard instructions; some of the requested information includes:

   - A worksheet or named range
   - First row column heading
   - A new or existing table
   - Field information
   - Primary key
   - Table name

8. When you're done, click **Finish**.

9. To save import steps, select the **Save import steps** check box, enter a name and description, and then click **Save Import**.

   Otherwise, click **Close**.

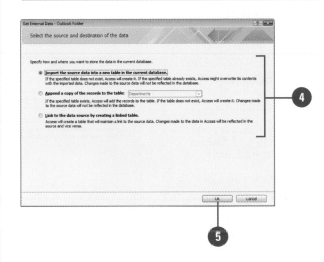

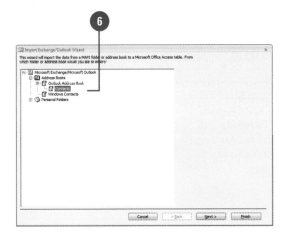

Collecting Data Using E-mail

If you need to conduct a survey, get report status, or organize an event, you can use Access to help you gather data from people using e-mail. Access 2007 works with Outlook 2007 to help you create and send an e-mail message that includes a data entry form. When recipients receive the e-mail message, fill out the forms and reply back to you, the message data in the form is added to the appropriate table in your database. The Collect Data Through E-mail Messages Wizard (**New!**) takes you through the process step-by-step.

Collect Data Using E-mail

1. Open the database in which you want to collect data.

2. Click the **External Data** tab.

3. Click the **Create E-mail** button.

   ◆ You can also right-click a table or query, and then click **Collect and Update Data via E-mail**.

4. Read the getting started screen, and then click **Next** to continue.

5. Select the type of data entry form option you want: **HTML form** or **Microsoft Office InfoPath form**. Click **Next** to continue.

6. Select the option to collect new information or update existing information. Click **Next** to continue.

7. Use the arrow buttons to select the form fields you want to use, and then click the **Move Up** and **Move Down** buttons to rearrange the fields in the order you want. Click **Next** to continue.

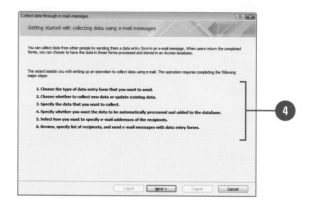

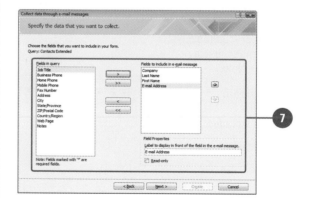

8 Select or clear the **Automatically process replies and add data to** *table name* check box, and then click **Next** to continue.

9 Select the option to specify where to get e-mail addresses, and then click **Next** to continue.

10 Enter a subject and message for the e-mail message, and then click **Next** to continue.

11 Click **Create**.

Outlook creates an e-mail message with a form.

12 Address the e-mail, and then click **Send**.

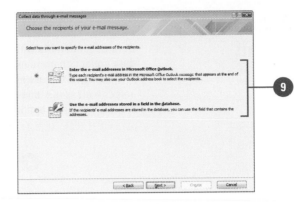

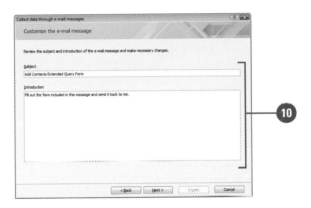

Did You Know?

You can rmanually process data collection replies. In Outlook, right-click the reply message, click Export data to Microsoft Office Access, review the details of the reply in the Export data to Microsoft Access dialog box, and then click OK.

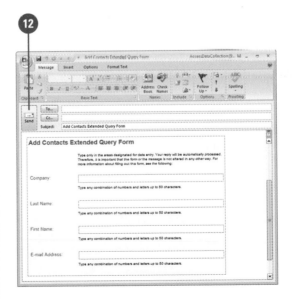

Managing Data Collection E-mail Replies

After you create and send an e-mail form to gather information, such as a survey, report status, or event organization, you can use the Manage Data Collection Messages dialog box (**New!**) to help you work with the data collection messages and the replies in your Outlook 2007 Inbox. The dialog box displays the messages saved in your database. You can select a message, and then review the message details, view or change message options, resend the message, or delete the message.

Collect Data Using E-mail

1. Open the database in which you want to collect data.

2. Click the **External Data** tab.

3. Click the **Manage Replies** button.

4. Select the message you want to manage.

5. To resend the message, click **Resend this E-mail Message**.

6. To delete the message, click **Delete this E-mail Message**.

7. To set message options, click **Message Options**, change the options you want, and then click **OK**. Select or specify any of the following options:

   ◆ Automatically process replies and add data to the database.

   ◆ Discard replies form those to whom you did not send the message.

   ◆ Set the number of replies to be processed and the date and time to stop.

8. Click **Close**.

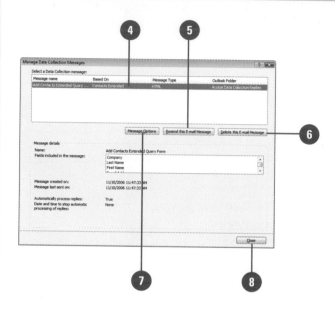

Message options

Getting Data from Other Programs

When you import data, you insert a copy of one file into another program—in this case, Access. When you import data into Access, Access creates a new table to store the data, using labels from the first row of a worksheet or table for the new table. If you need to keep the data in a separate file for use in other programs, you can also link your data to a table in Access, which allows you to keep both updated. You can import or link data from a variety of sources, such as dBase, Microsoft Excel, Microsoft Exchange, Microsoft Outlook, HTML, Lotus 1-2-3, Paradox, SharePoint Services, and text files. Access commands help you edit and format the imported data.

Import or Link Data from Another Source

1. Open the database into which you want to import data.

2. Click the **External Data** tab.

3. Click the **More** button, and then click the command for the type of file you import or link.

4. If requested, click **Browse**, locate and select the file you want to import or link, and then click **Open**.

5. Click the import, append (if available), or link option you want.

6. Click **OK**.

7. If necessary, follow the instructions in the Import Wizard to set up the data as an Access table.

8. Edit the imported information using Access commands and features, if necessary.

9. To save import steps, select the **Save import steps** check box, enter a name and description, and then click **Save Import**.

   Otherwise, click **Close**.

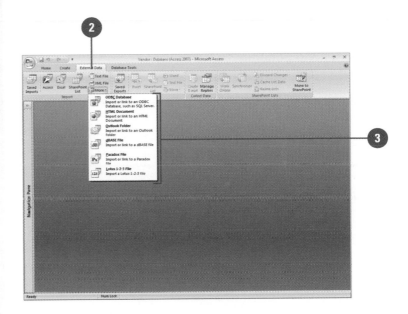

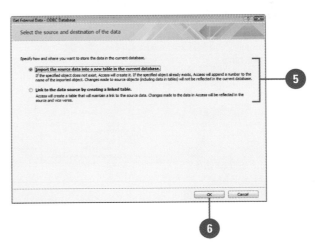

Importing and Exporting XML Data

XML (Extensible Markup Language) is a universal language that enables you to move information across the Internet and programs where the data is stored independently of the format so you can use the data more seamlessly in other forms. XML is fully supported in Office 2007 through Word, Excel, and Access. Access allows you to import and export XML data as well as transform the data to and from other formats using XML related files, such as Extensible Stylesheet Language (XSL). This provides a flexible and consistent way to present your data. When you import and export XML data, you can use an XML Schema (XSD)—a set of rules that defines the elements and content used in an XML file—to ensure the data conforms to a defined structure. XML schemas and XSL transformations are created by developers who understand XML.

Import Data and Schema from XML

1. Open the database in which you want to import.

2. Click the **External Data** tab.

3. Click the **Import XML File** button.

4. Click **Browse**, locate and select the XML data or schema file you want to import, and then click **Open**.

5. Click **OK**.

6. If available, click **Options**, and then click an import option: **Structure Only**, **Structure and Data**, or **Append Data to Existing Table(s)**.

7. To select a transform, click **Transform**, click a transform, and then click **OK**.

8. Click **OK**.

9. Click **OK** again.

10. To save import steps, select the **Save import steps** check box, enter a name and description, and then click **Save Import**.

    Otherwise, click **Close**.

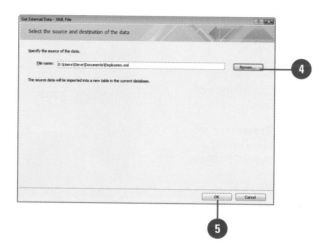

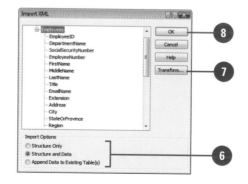

Export XML Data

1. Open the database containing the object you want to export, and then select the database object.

2. Click the **External Data** tab.

3. Click the **More** button, and then click **XML File**.

4. Click **Browse**, select a location, enter a name, and then click **Save**.

5. Click **OK**.

6. Select the export check boxes you want.

    ◆ **Data (XML).**

    ◆ **Schema of the data (XSD).**

    ◆ **Presentation of your data (XSL)**

7. Click **More Options**.

8. Click the tabs (Data, Schema, and Presentation) with the export type you want, and then select the related options you want.

9. Click **OK**.

10. To save export steps, select the **Save exports step** check box, enter a name and description, and then click **Save Import**.

    Otherwise, click **Close**.

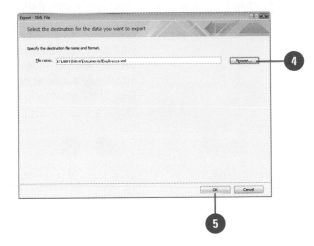

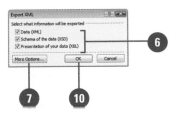

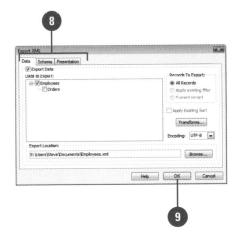

Exporting Data to Other Programs

Microsoft
Certified
Application
Specialist

AC07S-5.4.1,
AC07S-5.4.2

When you **export** Access data, you save a database object in a new format so that it can be opened in a different program. For example, you might export a table to an Excel worksheet. Or you might want to save your database as an earlier version of Access so someone who hasn't yet upgraded to Access 2007 can edit, format, and print it. You can also attach any database object to an e-mail message as an Excel (.xls), Rich Text Format (.rtf), or Hypertext Markup Language (.html) file.

Export an Object to Another Program

1. Open the database containing the object you want to export, and then select the database object.

2. Click the **External Data** tab.

3. Click the **More** button, and then click the command for the type of file you export.

4. Click **Browse**, select a location, enter a name, and then click **Save**.

5. If requested, click the export options you want to use.

6. Click **OK**.

7. If requested, select the options you want, and then click **OK**.

8. To save export steps, select the **Save exports step** check box, enter a name and description, and then click **Save Import**.

   Otherwise, click **Close**.

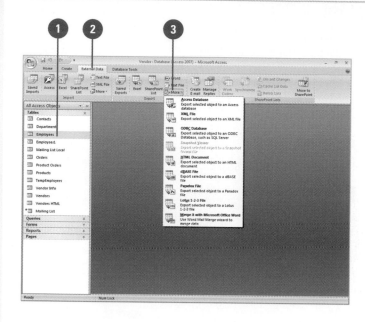

See Also

See "Exporting Database Objects to HTML" on page 270 for information on exporting data to the Web.

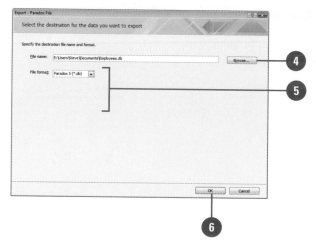

294

Attach a Database Object to an E-Mail Message

1. In the Navigation pane, click the object you want to attach to an e-mail message.

2. Click the **Office** button, and then click **Mail**.

3. Click the file format you want.

4. Click **OK**.

5. Log on to your e-mail system if necessary, and then type your message.

   Access attaches the object to the message in the format you selected.

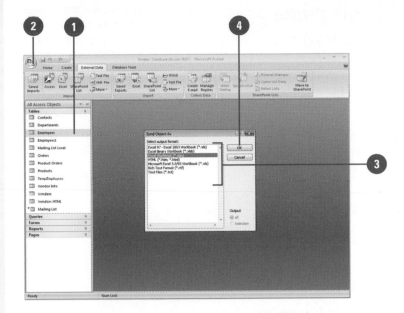

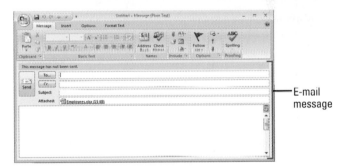

E-mail message

Merging Data with Word

Microsoft Certified Application Specialist

AC07S-5.4.1, AC07S-5.4.2

Access is a great program for storing and categorizing large amounts of information. You can combine, or **merge**, database records with Word documents to create tables or produce form letters and envelopes based on names, addresses, and other Access records. For example, you might create a form letter in Word and personalize it with an Access database of names and addresses. Word uses the Mail Merge task pane to step you through the process. Mail merge is the process of combining names and addresses stored in a data file with a main document (usually a form letter) to produce customized documents.

Insert Access Data into a Word Document

1. In the Navigation pane, click the table or query that you want to insert in a Word document.

   IMPORTANT *The database cannot be in exclusive mode.*

2. Click the **External Data** tab.

3. Click the **More** button, and then click **Merge it with Microsoft Office Word**.

4. Click the export options you want to use.

5. Click **OK**.

   If you selected the option for linking to an existing Word document, open the document.

6. In Word, follow the step-by-step instructions in the Mail Merge task pane to create a letter or mailing list using the data from Access.

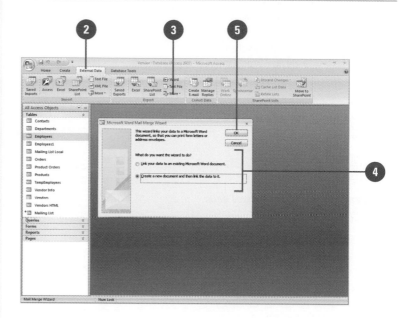

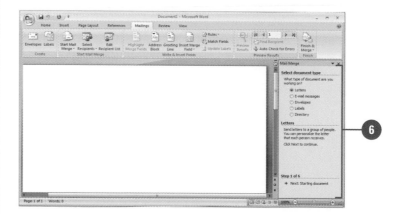

Create a Word Document from an Access Database

① In the Navigation pane, click the table, query, report, or form that you want to save as a Word document.

② Click the **External Data** tab.

③ Click the **Export to RTF File** (.rtf file) or **Export to Text File** (.txt file) button.

④ Click **Browse**, select a location, enter a name, and then click **Save**.

⑤ Click the export options you want to use.

⑥ Click **OK**.

Word opens and displays the document.

⑦ Edit the document using Word commands and features.

Did You Know?

You can save in Rich Text Format. A Rich Text Format file (.rtf) retains formatting, such as fonts and styles, and can be opened from Word or other word processing or desktop publishing programs.

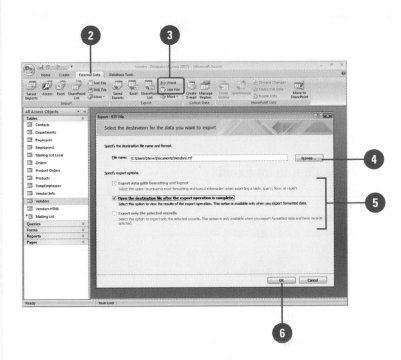

Access data in a Word document

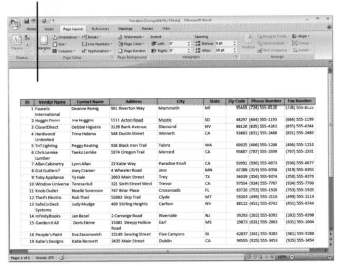

ID	Vendor Name	Contact Name	Address	City	State	Zip Code	Phone Number	Fax Number
1	Faucets International	Deanne Reinig	901 Riverton Way	Mammoth	MI	55463	(724) 555-8120	(724) 555-8122
2	Huggin Doors	Ira Huggins	1111 Acton Road	Mystic	SD	48297	(604) 555-1193	(604) 555-1199
3	ClosetDirect	Debbie Higuera	3126 Bank Avenue	Diamond	NV	86120	(835) 555-4242	(835) 555-4244
4	Hardwood Unlimited	Trina Halama	548 Dustin Street	Winnett	CA	93883	(831) 555-2488	(831) 555-2480
5	TnT Lighting	Peggy Keating	926 Black Iron Trail	Tabriz	WA	60025	(406) 555-1208	(406) 555-1210
6	Chris Lemke Lumber	Taeko Lemke	1074 Oregon Trail	Merced	CA	95887	(707) 555-2339	(707) 555-2331
7	Allan Cabinetry	Lynn Allan	22 Katie Way	Paradise Knoll	CA	93991	(936) 555-0073	(936) 555-0077
8	Got Gutters?	Joey Cramer	4 Wheeler Road	Jess	MN	67288	(319) 555-0350	(319) 555-0355
9	Toby Appliance	Ty Hale	2003 Main Street	Trey	TX	34039	(350) 555-9374	(350) 555-0370
10	Window Universe	Teresa Hull	321 Sixth Street West	Trevor	CA	97554	(524) 555-7707	(924) 555-7700
11	Knob Outlet	Noelle Sorenson	747 Briar Place	Crossroads	FL	83726	(753) 555-1920	(753) 555-1925
12	Theil's Electric	Rob Theil	52003 Skip Trail	Clyde	MT	59203	(499) 555-2110	(499) 555-2119
13	SafeCo Deck Systems	Judy Mudge	400 Stirling Heights	Carlton	NV	88122	(451) 555-0742	(451) 555-0744
14	InfinityBooks	Jan Besel	2 Carneige Road	Riverside	NJ	39293	(202) 555-8392	(202) 555-8398
15	Garden It All	Doris Eleine	15381 Sleepy Hollow Road	Earl	MS	29873	(631) 555-2003	(631) 555-2004
16	People's Paint	Eva Zasomovich	15149 Sewing Street	Five Canyons	RI	62837	(361) 555-9283	(361) 555-9288
19	Katie's Designs	Katie Bennett	3435 Main Street	Dublin	CA	94555	(925) 555-3453	(925) 555-3454

Exporting Data to Excel

Microsoft
Certified
Application
Specialist

AC07S-5.4.1,
AC07S-5.4.2

Information you want to analyze may not always exist in an Excel workbook; you might have to retrieve it from another Office program, such as Access. Access table data can be easily converted into Excel worksheet data. Before you can analyze Access data in a workbook, you must convert it to an Excel file. You can either use the Excel command in Access to export data as an Excel table file, or use the PivotTable or PivotChart and PivotTable Report option in Excel to use the Access data as a PivotTable, a table you can use to perform calculations with or rearrange large amounts of data.

Export a Table into an Excel Workbook

1. In the Navigation pane, click the table or query that you want to export to Excel.

2. Click the **External Data** tab.

3. Click the **Export to Excel Spreadsheet** button.

4. Click **Browse**, select a location, enter a name, and then click **Save**.

5. Specify the file format.

6. Specify the export options you want.

7. Click **OK**, and then click **Close**.

8. Use Excel tools to edit and analyze the data.

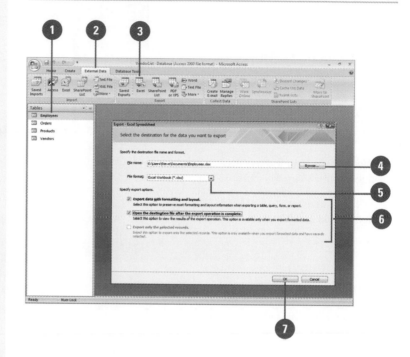

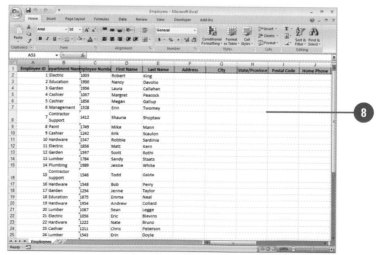

Create an Excel Workbook PivotTable from an Access Database

1. In Excel, click the **Data** tab.

2. Click the **From Access** button.

3. Click the table from Access you want to use.

4. Click **OK**.

5. Click the **PivotTable Report** or **PivotChart and PivotTable Report** option.

6. Click the **Existing worksheet** option, and then specify a cell location, or click the **New worksheet** option.

7. To set refresh, formatting, and layout options for the imported data, click **Properties**, make the changes you want, and then click **OK**.

8. Click **OK**.

9. Use tabs under PivotChart Tools to create and format the PivotChart.

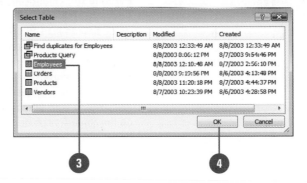

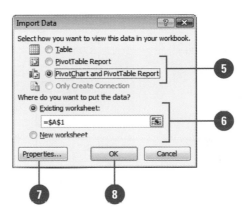

Creating a PDF Document

Portable Document Format (PDF) is a fixed-layout format developed by Adobe Systems that retains the form you intended on a computer monitor or printer. A PDF is useful when you want to create a document primarily intended to be read and printed, not modified. Access allows you to save database objects as a PDF file (**New!**), which you can send to others for review in an e-mail. To view a PDF file, you need to have Acrobat Reader—free downloadable software from Adobe Systems—installed on your computer. If the PDF or XPS command is not available on the Save As submenu (use Find add-ins for other formats), you'll need to download and install the Publish as PDF or XPS add-in for Microsoft Office 2007 from the Microsoft Web site.

Save a Database Object as a PDF Document

1. In the Navigation pane, select the object you want to save.

2. Click the **Office** button, point to **Save As**, and then click **PDF or XPS**.

3. Click the **Save as type** list arrow, and then click **PDF**.

4. Click the **Save in** list arrow, and then click the drive or folder where you want to save the file.

5. Type a PDF file name.

6. To open the file in Adobe Reader after saving, select the **Open file after publishing** check box.

7. Click the **Standard** or **Minimize size** option to specify how you want to optimize the file.

8. Click **Options**.

9. Select the publishing options you want, such as what to publish, range to publish, whether to include non-printing information, or PDF options.

10. Click **OK**.

11. Click **Publish**.

12. If necessary, install Adobe Acrobat Reader and related software as directed.

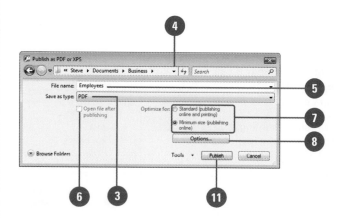

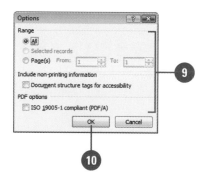

Creating an XPS Document

XML Paper Specification (XPS) is a secure fixed-layout format developed by Microsoft that retains the form you intended on a monitor or printer. An XPS is useful when you want to create a document primarily intended to be read and printed, not modified. Access allows you to save database objects as an XPS file (**New!**), which you can send to others for review in an e-mail. The XPS format also preserves live links with documents, making files fully functional. To view an XPS file, you need to have a viewer—free downloadable software from Microsoft Office Online—installed on your computer. If the PDF or XPS command is not available on the Save As submenu (use Find add-ins for other formats), you'll need to download and install the Publish as PDF or XPS add-in for Microsoft Office 2007 from the Microsoft Web site.

Save a Database Object as an XPS Document

1. In the Navigation pane, select the object you want to save.

2. Click the **Office** button, point to **Save As**, and then click **PDF or XPS**.

3. Click the **Save as type** list arrow, and then click **XPS Document.**

4. Click the **Save in** list arrow, and then click the drive or folder where you want to save the file.

5. Type an XPS file name.

6. To open the file in viewer after saving, select the **Open file after publishing** check box.

7. Click the **Standard** or **Minimize size** option to specify how you want to optimize the file.

8. Click **Options**.

9. Select the publishing options you want, such as what to publish, range to publish, or whether to include non-printing information.

10. Click **OK**.

11. Click **Publish**.

12. If necessary, click **Install** to download and install the Microsoft .NET Framework.

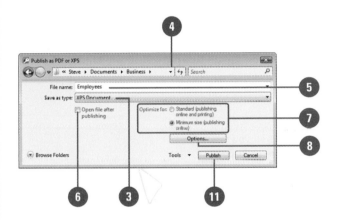

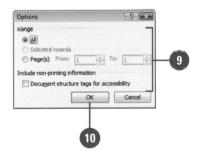

Saving a Database Object

AC07S-5.5

If you have a database object that is similar to a new object you want to create, you can can use the Save Object As command on the Save As submenu on the Office menu to create a new one with a different name, and then make the changes you want. You can also convert a database object to a different type. For example, you can convert a form to a report. However, not all objects can be converted to different types of objects. For example, a report can not be converted to another type, or a query can not be converted to a table. If an object can not be converted, the option in the Save As is grayed out or not available.

Save a Database Object as a New Object

1. In the Navigation pane, select the object you want to save.

2. Click the **Office** button, point to **Save As**, and then click **Save Object As**.

3. Type a name for the new object.

4. Click the **As** list arrow, and then select the object type you want: **Table**, **Query**, **Form**, or **Report**.

5. Click **Save**.

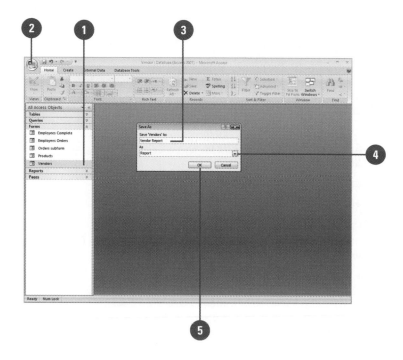

Managing a Database

12

Introduction

Access provides tools that help your database operate more efficiently. This includes the ability to compact your database file and to repair it if it is damaged, or split up your database to reduce its size. You can also use Access to analyze the design of your database and tables in order to improve performance and reliability. In addition, Access helps you keep tabs on all the elements in a database with the Documenter utility.

Add-ins are additional programs, designed to run seamlessly within Access. Some add-ins are installed when you run the Access Setup program, while others can be purchased from third-party vendors. The Add-ins Manager makes it easy to add and remove add-ins.

Finally, if you're interested in making your database easier to use, Access provides a Switchboard Manager that can put a user-friendly face on your database. With a switchboard, new users can access database reports and forms with a single click of a button, and you can control what parts of the database you want users to be able to access. You can also customize your database application by adding a title and an icon that appears in the Windows title bar.

Backing Up a Database

AC07S-6.1.2

Back up an Access Database

1. Save and close all objects in a database.

2. Click the **Office** button, point to **Manage**, and then click **Back Up Database**.

3. Click the **Save in** list arrow to select a location for the back up copy.

4. Specify a different backup name.

5. Click **Save**.

See Also

See "Splitting a Database" on page 314 for information on splitting up a database to reduce the size.

It is vital that you make back up copies of your database on a regular basis so you don't lose valuable data if your computer encounters problems. Access makes it easy to create a back up copy of a database with the Back Up Database command, which works like the Save As command. When you make a back up copy of your database, save the file to a removable disk or network drive to make sure the file is safe if your computer encounters problems. If you need the back up copy of the database, you can use the Open button to restore and view your data.

Compacting and Repairing a Database

Microsoft Certified Application Specialist

AC07S-6.1.3

What do you do when your database starts acting erratically, or when even the simplest tasks cause Access to crash? Problems of this type can occur when a database gets corrupted or when the database file becomes too large. A database can become corrupted when, for example, Access suffers a system crash. Access can repair many of the problems associated with a corrupted database. The size of the database file may also be the trouble. When you delete objects such as forms and reports, Access does not reclaim the space they once occupied. To use this space, you have to **compact** the database, allowing Access to rearrange the data, filling in the space left behind by the deleted objects.

Compact and Repair a Database

1. Make sure all users close the database, and then open the database you want to compact and repair.

2. Click the **Office** button, and then point to **Manage**.

3. Click **Compact and Repair Database**.

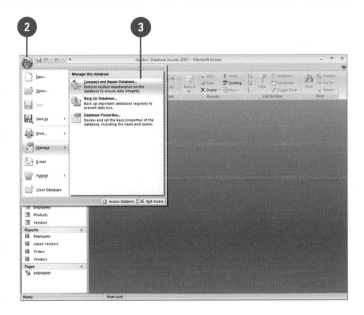

Did You Know?

You can automatically compact and repair a database when you close. Click the Office button, click Access Options, click Current Database in the left pane, select the Compact on Close check box and then click OK.

See Also

See "Splitting a Database" on page 314 for information on splitting up a database to reduce the size.

Changing Database Properties

You can use document properties—also known as **metadata**—to help you manage and track files. Search tools can use the metadata to find a database using your search criteria, such as title, subject, author, category, keywords, or comments. You can create advanced custom properties to associate more specific criteria for search tools to use. If you associate a database property to an item, the database property updates when you change the item.

Change Database Properties

1. Click the **Office** button, point to **Prepare**, and then click **Database Properties**.

2. Click the tabs to view and add information:

   ◆ **General**. To find out file location or size.

   ◆ **Summary**. To add title and author information.

   ◆ **Statistics**. To display details about the database.

3. Click the **Custom** tab.

4. Type the name for the custom property or select a name from the list.

5. Select the data type for the property you want to add.

6. Type a value for the property.

7. Click **Add** or **Modify**.

8. Click **OK**.

Did You Know?

You can remove personal information from file properties when you save. Click the Office button, click Access Options, click Current Database in the left pane, select the Remove personal information from file properties on save check box and then click OK. Close and reopen the database.

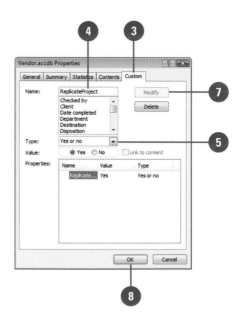

Documenting a Database

Microsoft Certified Application Specialist

AC07S-6.2.3

Document a Database

1. Click the **Database Tools** tab.

2. Click the **Database Documenter** button.

3. Click the **All Object Types** tab.

4. Select the check boxes for the objects you want to document.

5. Click **Options**.

6. Click the definitions you want to print for the selected object(s).

7. Click **OK**.

8. Click **OK**.

9. Check how many pages will print. If necessary, click the **Office** button, click **Print Preview**, and then click the **Print** button to print the pages.

Did You Know?

You can save the Documenter output.
To save the summary report created by the Documenter, click the Word or Text File button on the Print Preview tab. Access will then export the report to a Word or text file. Other export options are available, including PDF or XPS, Snapshot Viewer, HTML Document, XML File, Excel, SharePoint List, or Access Database.

Complex databases can include many tables, forms, relationships, and user information. Access helps you keep tabs on all the elements in a database with the **Documenter** utility. You can use Documenter to print all the information about a database in a summary report. After the Documenter creates a report, Access displays it in Print Preview, where you can print the report or export it to another format, such as a PDF or an XPS document, or a Word document.

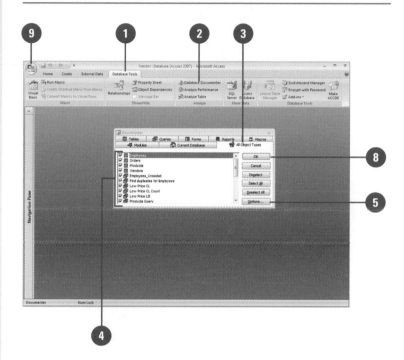

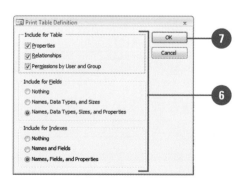

Analyzing a Database

Microsoft
Certified
Application
Specialist

AC07S-2.3.2

From time to time, you should analyze your database to ensure that it works as efficiently as possible. Begin by running the **Performance Analyzer**, which provides ways to organize your database optimally and helps you make any necessary adjustments. Whenever you determine that several fields in a table store duplicate information, run the **Table Analyzer** to help you split the data into related tables (a process called normalization), but leave the original table intact.

Optimize Database Performance

1. Click the **Database Tools** tab.

2. Click the **Analyze Performance** button.

3. Click the **All Object Types** tab.

4. Select the check boxes for the objects whose performance you want to analyze.

5. Click **OK**.

   If the Performance Analyzer has suggestions for improving the selected object(s), it displays them in its analysis results.

6. Click each item, and then review its analysis notes.

7. Press and hold Ctrl, and then click the suggested optimizations you want Access to perform.

8. Click **Optimize**.

9. Click **Close**.

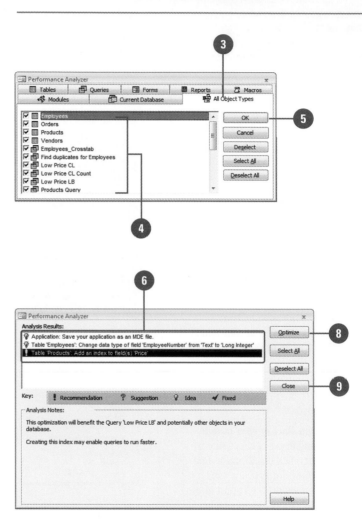

Analyze the Design of Your Tables

① Click the **Database Tools** tab.

② Click the **Analyze Table** button.

③ If an explanation screen for the Table Analyzer Wizard opens, read it, click **Next** to continue, and then read the second explanation screen. Click **Next** to continue.

④ Click the table you want to analyze. Click **Next** to continue.

⑤ Click the option for letting the wizard decide which fields to place in which tables. Click **Next** to continue.

⑥ Continue following the wizard instructions for naming the new tables, specifying the primary key for the new tables, and so on.

⑦ Click **Finish**, or click **Cancel** if the wizard recommends not to split the table.

Did You Know?

You can apply performance Analyzer results. The Performance Analyzer returns recommendations, suggestions, and ideas. You should have Access perform the recommended optimizations. Suggested optimizations have potential tradeoffs, and you should review the possible outcomes in the Analysis Notes box before having Access perform them. You can perform idea optimizations manually by following the instructions in the Analysis Notes box.

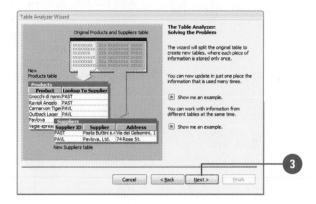

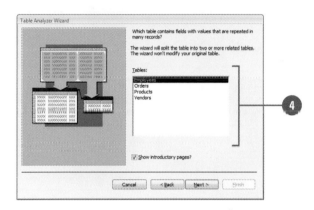

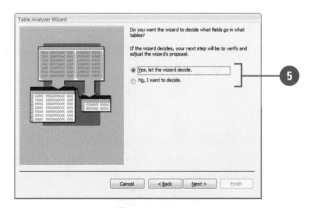

Using Add-Ins

Add-ins are additional programs, designed to run seamlessly within Access. Some add-ins are installed when you run the Access Setup program, while others can be purchased from third-party vendors. One of these add-ins is the Switchboard add-in, used to create and manage database switchboards. Another add-in, the Linked Table Manager, helps users work with linked tables in their database. To work with add-ins, Access provides the **Add-In Manager**, a utility to install and remove your add-in files.

Install and Uninstall Add-Ins

1. Click the **Database Tools** tab.

2. Click the **Add-ins** button, and then **Add-In Manager**.

3. Click **Add New**, and then locate and open the add-in you want to install.

4. Double-click the available add-in you want install.

5. Click any installed add-in you want to remove, and then click **Uninstall**.

6. Click **Close**.

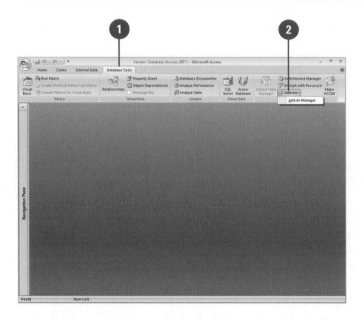

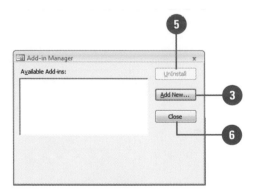

Creating a Database Switchboard

Switchboards are forms that provide easy access to many of your database's features. With a properly designed switchboard, your database users can display forms, print reports, and run macros with a single click of an action button. You can even hide all the other features of Access, making your switchboard the only thing the users see when interacting with your database. To help you create a switchboard, Access provides the Switchboard Manager add-in. The Switchboard Manager makes it easier to create new switchboards or edit the content of existing switchboards.

Create a Switchboard

① Click the **Database Tools** tab.

② Click the **Switchboard Manager** button.

③ Click **Yes** when you are asked to create a switchboard.

④ Click **Edit** to edit the content of the switchboard's main page.

⑤ Type a name for the main page.

⑥ Click **New** to add an action button.

⑦ Enter text for the button.

⑧ Click the **Command** list arrow, and then select a command.

⑨ Click the **Report** list arrow, and then select a form, report, macro, switchboard or function name.

⑩ Click **OK**.

⑪ Repeat steps 6 through 10 to add additional action buttons to the switchboard.

⑫ Click **Close**.

⑬ Click **Close**.

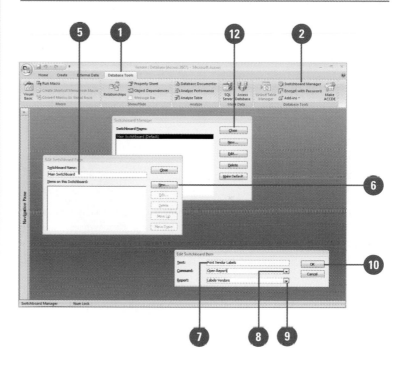

Did You Know?

You can edit the switchboard design.
To edit your switchboard's design, open the switchboard form in Design view or Layout view.

Managing a Switchboard

After you create a switchboard, you can edit it using the same Switchboard Manager command you used to create it in the first place. In your revisions, you may want to add extra pages to the switchboard or delete action buttons you've previously created. You can also edit action buttons so that they perform new tasks. The switchboard can thereby grow and change as your database changes.

Add a Switchboard Page

1 Click the **Database Tools** tab.

2 Click the **Switchboard Manager** button.

3 Click **New**.

4 Type a name for the new page.

5 Click **OK**.

6 Select the new page from the Switchboard Pages list, and then click **Edit** to edit the page's content.

7 Click **Close**.

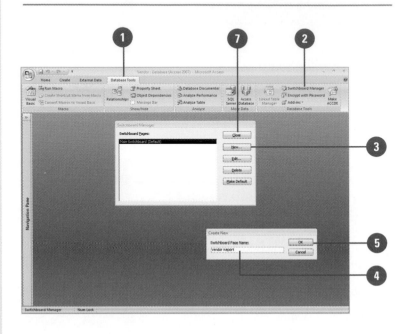

Define the Default Switchboard Page

1 Click the **Database Tools** tab.

2 Click the **Switchboard Manager** button.

3 Select the page that you want to act as the default.

4 Click **Make Default**.

5 Click **Close**.

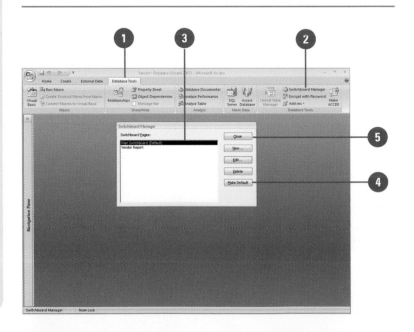

Adding a Database Title and Icon

For each Access database, you can set specific options that don't effect other Access databases. You can customize your database application by adding a title and an icon that appears in the Windows title bar. If you add an icon, you can also enable the Use as Form and Report Icon option to place the icon in the document tabs for forms and reports.

Add a Database Title and Icon

1. Click the **Office** button, and then click **Access Options**.

2. In the left pane, click **Current Database**.

3. Type an application title for your database.

4. Click **Browse**, locate and select the application icon file, either a bitmap (.bmp) or icon (icon), you want to use.

5. To place the application icon in the tabs atop the forms and reports in the current database, select the **Use as Form and Report Icon** check box.

6. Click **OK**.

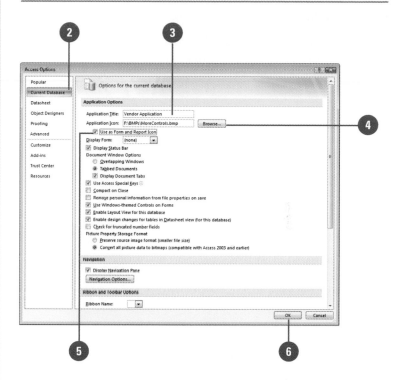

Splitting a Database

Microsoft
Certified
Application
Specialist

AC07S-1.4

You can reduce the size of a database file by splitting the database. When Access **splits** a database, it places the tables in one file, called the **back-end database**, and the other database objects, like forms and reports, in the current database file. This technique stores all of the data in one location, while allowing each user to create his or her own forms and reports in his or her own database files.

Split a Database

1. Make sure all users close the database, and then close the switchboard, if necessary. Open the database with administrative privileges.

2. Click the **Database Tools** tab.

3. Click the **Access Database** button.

4. Click **Split Database**.

5. Click the **Save in** list arrow, and then specify a location for the split database.

6. Enter the name of the back-end database that contains the database tables.

7. Click **Split**.

8. Click **OK**.

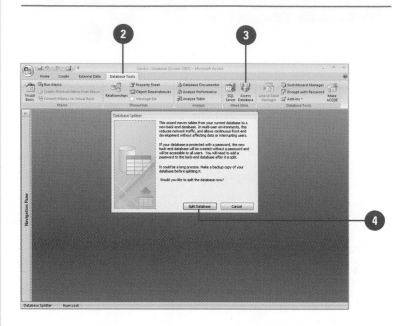

Did You Know?

You can make a backup copy of your database. It is a good idea to back up your database before compacting or splitting it. If an error occurs during either process and data is lost, you can retrieve data from your backup.

See Also

See "Backing Up a Database" on page 304 for information on backing up a database.

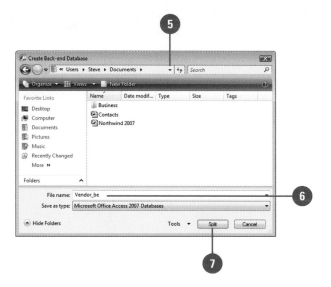

Protecting and Securing a Database

13

Introduction

Adding a password to protect your database is not only a good idea for security purposes, it's an added feature to make sure that changes to your database aren't made by unauthorized people. When you add database protection, you'll be asked to supply a password, and then enter it again when you want to work on the file. If you need to validate the authenticity of a database, you can package the database in a file and add an invisible digital signature, an electronic secure stamp of authentication on a database.

The Trust Center (New!) is a place where you set security options and find the latest technology information as it relates to document privacy, safety, and security from Microsoft. The Trust Center allows you to set security and privacy settings and provides links to Microsoft privacy statements, a customer improvement program, and trustworthy computing practices.

Adding Security Encryption to a Database

Microsoft
Certified
Application
Specialist

AC07S-6.2.1

File encryption is additional security you can apply to a database. File encryption scrambles your password to protect your document from unauthorized people from breaking into the file. You don't have to worry about the encryption, Office handles everything. All you need to do is remember the password. If you forget it, you can't open the file. Password protection takes effect the next time you open the document. Before you can encrypt a database in Access, you need to open the database in Exclusive mode, which allows Access to encrypt the database without any outside connections. You can set the database to Exclusive mode by using the Advance pane in Access Options.

Apply File Encryption

1. Click the **Office** button, and then click **Open**.

2. Locate and select the database you want to encrypt.

3. Click the **Open** button arrow, and then click **Open Exclusive**.

4. Click the **Database Tools** tab.

5. Click the **Encrypt with Password** button.

6. Type a password.

7. Type the password again.

8. Click **OK**.

Did You Know?

You should use strong passwords.
Hackers identify passwords as strong or weak. A strong password is a combination of uppercase and lowercase letters, numbers, and symbols, such as Grea8t!, while a weak one doesn't use different character types, such as Hannah1. Be sure to write down your passwords and place them in a secure location.

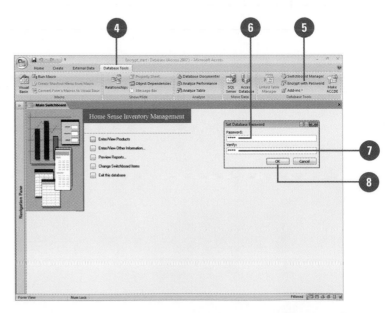

Decrypt and Open a Database

① Click the **Office** button, click **Open**, navigate to a database with password encryption, and then click **Open**.

② Type a password.

③ Click **OK**.

Change or Remove the Password Encryption

① Click the **Office** button, click **Open**, navigate to a database with password encryption, and then click **Open**.

② Type a password.

③ Click **OK**.

④ Click the **Database Tools** tab.

⑤ Click the **Decrypt Database** button.

⑥ Type the password.

⑦ Click **OK**.

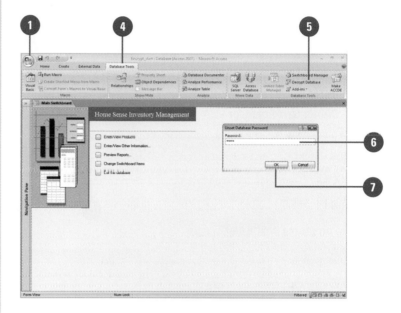

Creating a Digital Certificate

After you've finished a database, you might consider adding an invisible digital signature—an electronic, secure stamp of authentication on a document. Before you can add a digital signature, you need to get a **digital ID**, or **digital certificate**, which provides an electronic way to prove your identity. A digital certificate checks a public key to validate a private key associated with a digital signature. To assure a digital signature is authentic, it must have a valid (non expired or revoked) certificate issued by a reputable certification authority (CA), and the signing person must be from a trusted publisher. If you need a verified authenticate digital certificate, you can obtain one from a trusted Microsoft partner CA. If you don't need a verified digital certificate, you can create one of your own, known as a self-signed certificate. If someone modifies the file, the digital signature is removed and revoked.

Create a Self-signed Certificate

1. Click the **Start** button, point to **All Programs**, click **Microsoft Office**, click **Microsoft Office Tools**.

2. Click **Digital Certificate for VBA Projects**.

3. Enter a name.

4. Click **OK**.

5. Click **OK**.

   Office programs trust a self-signed certificate only on the computer that created it.

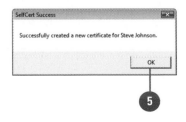

Adding a Digital Signature to a Database Project

If you want to add a digital signature to a presentation with a macro, you need to add it using the Visual Basic editor. If you open a presentation that contains a signed macro project with a problem, the macro is disabled by default and the Message Bar appears to notify you of the potential problem. You can click Options in the Message Bar to view information about it. For more details, you can click Show Signature Details to view certificate and publisher information. If a digital signature has problems—it's expired, not issued by a trusted publisher, or the presentation has been altered—the certificate information image contains a red X. When there's a problem, contact the signer to have them fix it, or save the presentation to a trusted location, where you can run the macro without security checks.

Sign a Database Project

1. Open the database you want to sign, and then click the **Database Tools** tab.

2. Click the **Visual Basic** button to open the Visual Basic window.

3. Click the **Tools** menu, and then click **Digital Signature**.

4. Click **Choose**.

5. Select a certificate in the list.

6. To view a certificate, click **View Certificate**, and then click **OK**.

7. Click **OK**.

8. Click **OK** again.

9. Click the **Save** and **Close** button in the Microsoft Visual Basic window.

Packaging and Digitally Signing a Database

The Package and Sign command (**New!**) allows you to package, digitally sign, and distribute an Access database. Access saves the database you want in the Access Deployment file format (.accdc), signs the package, and then stores the digitally signed package where you want. Other users can extract the database from the package and work directly in the database.

Create a Signed Package

1. Open the database you want to package and sign.

2. Click the **Office** button, point to **Publish**, and then click **Package and Sign**.

3. Select a digital certificate.

4. Click **OK**.

5. Click the **Save in** list arrow, and then click the drive or folder where you want to save the signed database package.

6. Type a name for the signed database package.

7. Click **Create**.

Extract and Use a Signed Package

1. Click the **Office** button, and then click **Open**.

2. Click the **Files of type** list arrow, and then click **Microsoft Office Access Signed Packages (*.accdc)**.

3. If the file is located in another folder, click the **Look in** list arrow, and then navigate to the file.

4. Click the .accdc file you want.

5. Click **Open**.

6. Do one of the following:

   ◆ If you chose to trust the digital certificate, the Extract Database To dialog box opens. Go to the next step.

   ◆ If you have not chosen to trust the digital certificate, click **Open** to trust the database, or click **Trust All From Publisher** to trust any certificate from the publisher. The Extract Database To dialog box opens. Go to the next step.

7. If necessary, click the **Save in** list arrow, select a location for the extracted database, and then type a different name for the extracted database.

8. Click **OK**.

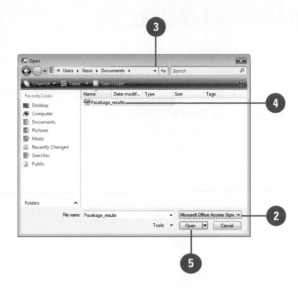

Avoiding Harmful Attacks

Spreading Harmful Infections

Many viruses and other harmful attacks spread through file downloads, attachments in e-mail messages, and data files that have macros, ActiveX controls, add-ins, or Visual Basic for Applications (VBA) code attached to them. Virus writers capitalize on people's curiosity and willingness to accept files from people they know or work with, in order to transmit malicious files disguised as or attached to benign files. When you start downloading files to your computer, you must be aware of the potential for catching a computer virus, worm, or Trojan Horse. Typically, you can't catch one from just reading a mail message or downloading a file, but you can catch one from installing, opening, or running an infected program or attached code.

Understanding Harmful Attacks

Phishing is a scam that tries to steal your identity by sending deceptive e-mail asking you for bank and credit card information online. Phishers spoof the domain names of banks and other companies in order to deceive consumers into thinking that they are visiting a familiar Web site.

Phishers create a Web address that looks like a familiar Web address but is actually altered. This is known as a **homograph**. The domain name is created using alphabet characters from different languages, not just English. For example, the Web site address "www.microsoft.com" looks legitimate, but what you can't see is that the "i" is a Cyrillic character from the Russian alphabet.

Don't be fooled by spoofed Web sites that looks like the official site. Never respond to requests for personal information via e-mail; most companies have policies that do not ask for your personal information through e-mail. If you get a suspicious e-mail, call the institution to investigate and report it.

Spam is unsolicited e-mail, which is often annoying and time-consuming to get rid of. Spammers harvest e-mail addresses from Web pages and unsolicited e-mail. To avoid spam, use multiple e-mail addresses (one for Web forms and another for private e-mail), and opt-out and remove yourself from e-mail lists. See the Microsoft Windows and Microsoft Outlook Help system for specific details.

Spyware is software that collects personal information without your knowledge or permission. Typically, spyware is downloaded and installed on your computer along with free software, such as freeware, games, or music file-sharing programs. Spyware is often associated with **Adware** software that displays advertisements, such as a pop-up ad. Examples of spyware and unauthorized adware include programs that change your home page or search page without your permission. To avoid spyware and adware, read the fine print in license agreements when you install software, scan your computer for spyware and adware with detection and removal software (such as Ad-aware from Lavasoft), and turn on Pop-up Blocker. See the Microsoft Windows Help system for specific details.

Avoiding Harmful Attacks Using Office

There are a few things you can do within any Office 2007 program to keep your system safe from the infiltration of harmful attacks.

1) Make sure you activate macro, ActiveX, add-in, and VBA code detection and notification. You can use the Trust Center to help protect you from attached code attacks. The Trust Center checks for trusted publisher and code locations on your computer and provides security options for add-ins, ActiveX controls, and macros to ensure the best possible protection. The Trust Center displays a security alert in the Message Bar when it detects a potentially harmful attack.

2) Make sure you activate Web site spoofing detection and notification. You can use the Trust Center to help protect you from homograph attacks. The *Check Office documents that are from or link to suspicious Web sites* check box under Privacy Options in the Trust Center is on by default and continually checks for potentially spoofed domain names. The Trust Center displays a security alert in the Message Bar when you have a database open and click a link to a Web site with an address that has a potentially spoofed domain name, or you open a file from a Web site with an address that has a potentially spoofed domain name.

3) Be very careful of file attachments in e-mail you open. As you receive e-mail, don't open or run an attached file unless you know who sent it and what it contains. If you're not sure, you should delete it. The Attachment Manager provides security information to help you understand more about the file you're opening. See the Microsoft Outlook Help system for specific details.

Avoiding Harmful Attacks Using Windows

There are a few things you can do within Microsoft Windows to keep your system safe from the infiltration of harmful attacks.

1) Make sure Windows Firewall is turned on. Windows Firewall helps block viruses and worms from reaching your computer, but it doesn't detect or disable them if they are already on your computer or come through e-mail. Windows Firewall doesn't block unsolicited e-mail or stop you from opening e-mail with harmful attachments.

2) Make sure Automatic Updates is turned on. Windows Automatic Updates regularly checks the Windows Update Web site for important updates that your computer needs, such as security updates, critical updates, and service packs. Each file that you download using Automatic Update has a digital signature from Microsoft to ensure its authenticity and security.

3) Make sure you are using the most up-to-date antivirus software. New viruses and more virulent strains of existing viruses are discovered every day. Unless you update your virus-checking software, new viruses can easily bypass outdated virus checking software. Companies such as McAfee and Symantec offer shareware virus checking programs available for download directly from their Web sites. These programs monitor your system, checking each time a file is added to your computer to make sure it's not in some way trying to change or damage valuable system files.

4) Be very careful of the sites from which you download files. Major file repository sites, such as FileZ, Download.com, or TuCows, regularly check the files they receive for viruses before posting them to their Web sites. Don't download files from Web sites unless you are certain that the sites check their files for viruses. Internet Explorer monitors downloads and warns you about potentially harmful files and gives you the option to block them.

Using the Trust Center

The **Trust Center** (**New!**) is a place where you set security options and find the latest technology information as it relates to document privacy, safety, and security from Microsoft. The Trust Center allows you to set security and privacy settings—Trusted Publishers, Trusted Locations, Add-ins, ActiveX Settings, Macro Settings, Message Bar, and Privacy Options—and provides links to Microsoft privacy statements, a customer improvement program, and trustworthy computing practices.

View the Trust Center

1 Click the **Office** button, and then click **Access Options**.

2 In the left pane, click **Trust Center**.

3 Click the links in which you want online information at the Microsoft Online Web site.

◆ **Show the Microsoft Office privacy statement.** Opens a Microsoft Web site detailing privacy practices.

◆ **Microsoft Office Online privacy statement.** Opens a Microsoft Web site detailing privacy practices.

◆ **Customer Experience Improvement Program.** Opens the Microsoft Customer Experience Improvement Program (CEIP) Web site.

◆ **Microsoft Windows Security Center.** Opens Windows Security Center on your computer.

◆ **Microsoft Trustworthy Computing.** Opens a Microsoft Web site detailing security and reliability practices.

4 When you're done, close your Web browser or dialog box, and return to Access.

5 Click **OK**.

For Your Information

Working with Security Levels

If you open a database from an earlier version of Access in Office Access 2007 with a user-level security, the settings remain in place as long as the file format remains the same. If you convert the database to the Microsoft Office Access 2007 file format, the user-level security settings are stripped away and you can set new security settings in Access 2007.

Selecting Trusted Publishers and Locations

The Trust Center security system continually checks for external potentially unsafe content in your documents. Hackers can hide Web beacons in external content—images, linked media, data connections and templates—to gather information about you or cause problems. When the Trust Center detects potentially harmful external content, the Message Bar appears with a security alert and options to enable or block the content. Trusted publishers are reputable developers who create application extensions, such as a macro, ActiveX control, or add-in. The Trust Center uses a set of criteria—valid and current digital signature, and reputable certificate—to make sure publishers' code and source locations are safe and secure. If you are sure that the external content is trustworthy, you can add the content publisher and location to your trusted lists (**New!**), which allows it to run without being checked by the Trust Center.

Modify Trusted Publishers and Locations

1 Click the **Office** button, and then click **Access Options**.

2 In the left pane, click **Trust Center**.

3 Click **Trust Center Settings**.

4 In the left pane, click **Trusted Publishers**.

5 Select a publisher, and then use the **View** and **Remove** buttons to make the changes you want.

6 In the left pane, click **Trusted Locations**.

7 Select a location, and then use the **Add new location**, **Remove**, and **Modify** buttons to make the changes you want.

8 Select or clear the **Allow Trusted Locations on my network (not recommended)** check box.

9 Select or clear the **Disable all Trusted Locations, only files signed by Trusted Publishers will be trusted** check box.

10 Click **OK**.

11 Click **OK**.

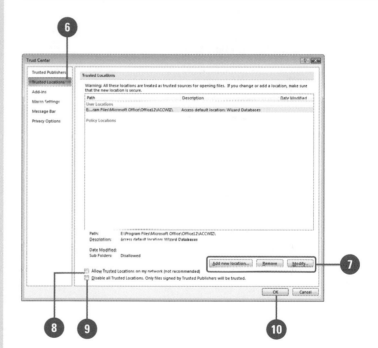

Setting Add-in Security Options

An add-in, such as smart tags, extends functionality to Microsoft Office programs (**New!**). An add-in can add buttons and custom commands to the Ribbon. Since add-ins are software code added to Microsoft Office programs, hackers can use them to do malicious harm, such as spreading a virus. The Trust Center uses a set of criteria—valid and current digital signature, reputable certificate and a trusted publisher—to make sure add-ins are safe and secure. If it discovers a potentially unsafe add-in, it disables the code and notifies you in the Message Bar. If you're not sure whether an add-in is disabled, you can use the Trust Center to display disabled items and enable them one at a time to help you pin point any problems. If the add-in security options are not set to the level you need, you can change them in the Trust Center.

Set Add-in Security Options

1. Click the **Office** button, and then click **Access Options**.

2. In the left pane, click **Trust Center**.

3. Click **Trust Center Settings**.

4. In the left pane, click **Add-ins**.

5. Select or clear the check boxes you do or don't want.

   ◆ **Require Application Add-ins to be signed by Trusted Publisher.** Select to check for a digital signature on the .dll file.

   ◆ **Disable notification for unsigned add-ins (code will remain disabled).** Only available if the above check box is selected. Select to disable unsigned add-ins without notification.

   ◆ **Disable all Application Add-ins (may impair functionality).** Select to disable all add-ins without any notifications.

6. Click **OK**.

7. Click **OK**.

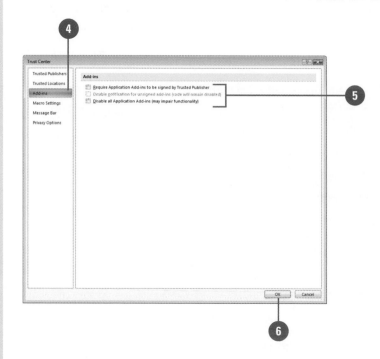

View Disabled Items

1. Click the **Office** button, and then click **Access Options**.

2. In the left pane, click **Add-Ins**.

3. Click the **Manage** list arrow, and then click **Disabled Items**.

4. Click **Go**.

5. In the dialog box, you can select an item, click **Enable** to activate and reload the add-in, and then click **Close**.

6. Click **OK**.

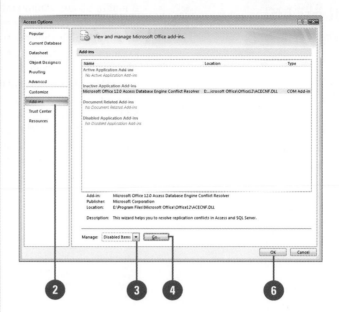

Setting Macro Security Options

A macro allows you to automate frequently used steps or tasks to save time and work more efficiently. Macros are written using VBA (Visual Basic for Applications) code, which opens the door to hackers to do malicious harm, such as spreading a virus. The Trust Center uses a set of criteria—valid and current digital signature, reputable certificate and a trusted publisher—to make sure macros are safe and secure. If the Trust Center discovers a potentially unsafe macro, it disables the code and notifies you in the Message Bar. You can click Options on the Message Bar to enable it or set other security options. If the macro security options are not set to the level you need, you can change them in the Trust Center (**New!**).

Change Macro Security Settings

1. Click the **Office** button, and then click **Access Options**.

2. In the left pane, click **Trust Center**.

3. Click **Trust Center Settings**.

4. In the left pane, click **Macro Settings**.

5. Click the option you want for macros in documents not in a trusted location.

   ◆ **Disable all macros without notification.**

   ◆ **Disable all macros with notification.** (default)

   ◆ **Disable all macros except digitally signed macros.**

   ◆ **Enable all macros (not recommended, potentially dangerous code can run).**

6. Click **OK**.

7. Click **OK**.

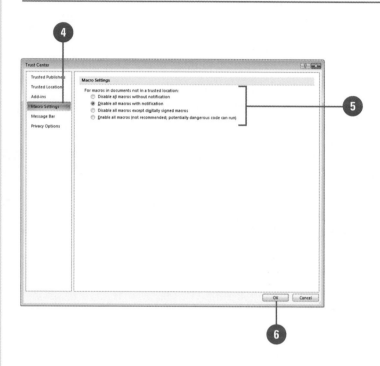

Changing Message Bar Security Options

The Message Bar (**New!**) displays security alerts when Office detects potentially unsafe content in an open document. The Message Bar appears below the Ribbon when a potential problem arises. The Message Bar provides a security warning and options to enable external content or leave it blocked. If you don't want to receive alerts about security issues, you can disable the Message Bar.

Modify Message Bar Security Options

1. Click the **Office** button, and then click **Access Options**.

2. In the left pane, click **Trust Center**.

3. Click **Trust Center Settings**.

4. In the left pane, click **Message Bar**.

5. Click the option you want for showing the Message bar.

   ◆ **Show the Message Bar in all applications when content has been blocked.** (default)

   This option is not selected if you selected the Disable all macros without notification check box in the Macros pane of the Trust Center.

   ◆ **Never show information about blocked content.**

6. Click **OK**.

7. Click **OK**.

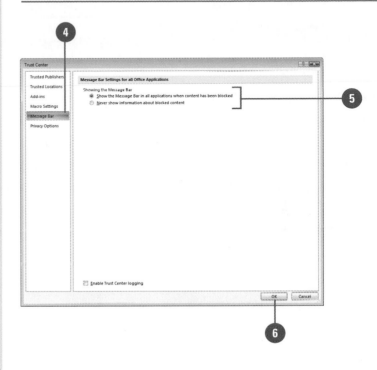

Setting Privacy Options

Privacy options in the Trust Center allow you to set security settings that protect your personal privacy online. For example, the *Check Office documents that are from or link to suspicious Web sites* option checks for spoofed Web sites and protects you from phishing schemes (**New!**). If your kids are doing research online using the Research task pane, you can set Privacy Options to enable parental controls and a password to block sites with offensive content.

Set Privacy Options

1 Click the **Office** button, and then click **Access Options**.

2 In the left pane, click **Trust Center**.

3 Click **Trust Center Settings**.

4 In the left pane, click **Privacy Options**.

5 Select or clear the check boxes you do or don't want.

- ◆ **Search Microsoft Office Online for Help content when I'm connected to the Internet.** Select to get up-to-date Help content.

- ◆ **Update featured links from Microsoft Office Online.** Select to get up-to-date headlines and featured templates.

- ◆ **Download a file periodically that helps determine system problems.** Select to have Microsoft request error reports, update trouble-shooting help, and accept downloads from Office Online.

- ◆ **Sign up for the Customer Experience Improvement Program.** Select to sign-up.

- ◆ **Check Microsoft Office documents that are from or link to suspicious Web sites.** Select to check for spoofed Web sites.

6 Click **OK**.

7 Click **OK**.

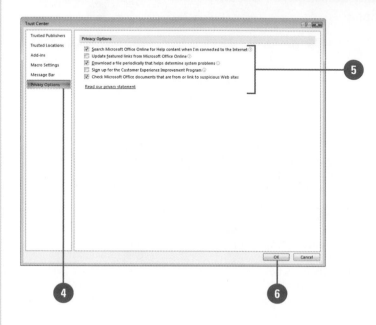

Locking a Database

The Make ACCDE button on the Database Tools tab allows you to lock a database file, and prevent users from viewing or modifying VBA code and making changes to forms or reports. The command changes the database file extension from .accdb to .accde. If the Access 2007 database .accdb file contains any VBA code, only the compiled (or executable) code is include in the new .accde file. When you open a .accde file, Access creates and opens a temporary locking file with the file extension .laccdb to prevent conflicts. When you close the file, Access automatically deletes the temporary file.

Create a Locked Database

1. Open the Access 2007 .accdb database file you want to save as an .accde file.

2. Click the **Database Tools** tab.

3. Click the **Make ACCDE** button.

4. Click the **Save in** list arrow, and then click the drive or folder where you want to save the .accde file.

5. Type a name for the .accde file.

6. Click **Save**.

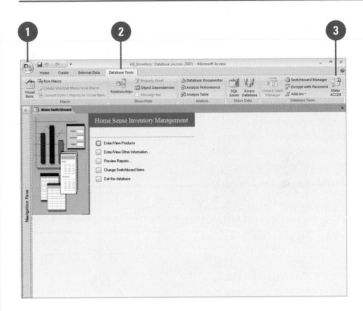

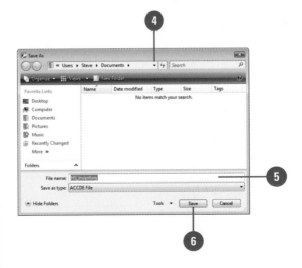

Did You Know?

You can only replicate a database created in a previous version. Replication is not supported in Office Access 2007. However, you can still use Office Access 2007 to replicate a database created in a previous version of Access.

You can use Workgroup Information files in Access 2007. Workgroup Information files (.mdw) store information for secure databases. The Office Access 2007 Workgroup Manager creates .mdw files, which are the same as those created in Access 2000 through 2003.

Locking Database Records

AC07S-6.1.1

In a multi-user environment, several users could attempt to edit the same record simultaneously. Access prevents conflicts of this sort using **record locking**, ensuring that only one user at a time can edit data. You can also prevent conflicts by opening the database in **exclusive mode**, preventing all other users from accessing the database while you're using it. This technique is useful for administrators who need sole access to the system while making changes to the database itself.

Set Record Locking

1 Click the **Office** button, and then click **Access Options**.

2 In the left pane, click **Advanced**.

3 Click the **Shared** or **Exclusive** option to indicate whether the default strategy for opening the database is shared (allowing simultaneous access by other users) or exclusive (keeping out other users).

4 Click the Default Record Locking strategy option you want to use: **No locks**, **All records**, or **Edited record**.

5 Select the **Open databases by using record-level locking** check box.

6 Click **OK**.

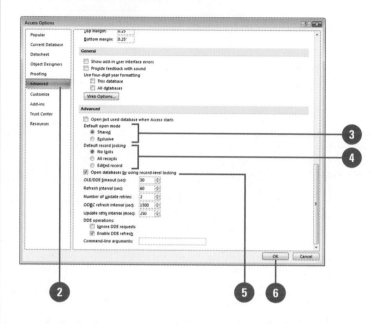

Record Locking Strategies	
Locking Type	**Description**
No Locks	Access does not lock the record you're editing. When you save changes, Access gives you the option to overwrite another user's changes, copy your version to the clipboard, or discard your changes.
All Records	Access locks all records in the table for the entire time you have it open, so no one else can edit or lock the records.
Edited Record	Access locks the record you're currently editing and displays a locked record indicator to other users who may try to edit the record.

Customizing Access

14

Introduction

There are several ways you can customize Microsoft Office Access 2007 to meet your needs and the needs of those who will use the databases you create. You can use Access options to set display, editing, and object design options. Some of the other Access customization features allow you to set a default font and related attributes to use when you are typing text or numbers. Other defaults might be the color or line style of a shape object that you create. You can change the location of the Ribbon and the configuration of the Quick Access Toolbar to include commands not available on the Ribbon.

Access also allows you to create macros, stored collections of actions that perform a specific task. Macros allow you to create new commands designed to work with a particular database. You can attach macros to button and form controls or the Quick Access Toolbar. You can write a macro so that it executes its actions only if a particular condition is met.

When you install Microsoft Office 2007, you also install a set of Microsoft Office Tools, which includes Microsoft Office 2007 Language Settings.

Setting Current Database Options

You can customize the way Access appears when you work on a database. If you need more room to view another row of data, you can hide the Status bar or Navigation pane. To customize the way you work with database objects, you can choose to display them as tabbed documents (**New!**) for easy access or overlapping windows for a custom interface. Tabbed documents display one object at a time and uses tabs to allow you to switch between them. You can also display Layout view (**New!**), which allows you to make design changes while you browse a form or report. You can choose display options you want for the open database on the Current Database pane in Access Options.

Change Display Options

1. Click the **Office** button, and then click **Access Options**.

2. In the left pane, click **Current Database**.

3. Select or clear the check boxes or options to change display options. Some options include:

   ◆ **Display Form**. Select the form to automatically open when you start this database. (Default is (none).

   ◆ **Display Status Bar**. Show or hide the Status bar. (Default on).

   ◆ **Document Window Options.** Select the Overlapping Windows or Tabbed Documents option. If you select Tabbed Documents, select or clear the Display Document Tabs check box. (Default is Tabbed Documents).

   ◆ **Use Access Special Keys.** Enables or disables shortcut keys. (Default on).

   F11 to show or hide the Navigation pane; Ctrl+G to show the Immediate window in the Visual Basic Editor; Alt+F11 to start the Visual Basic Editor; and Ctrl+Break to stop retrieving records in an Access project.

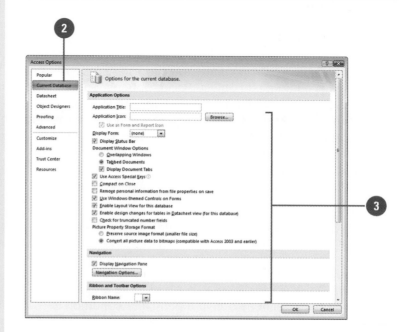

◆ **Use Windows-themed Controls on Forms.** Uses your Windows theme on controls in forms and reports. (Default on).

◆ **Enable Layout View for this database.** Show or hides the Layout View button on the Status bar. (Default on).

◆ **Enable design changes for tables in Datasheet view (for this database).** Allows you to change the design of tables in Datasheet view. (Default on).

◆ **Display Navigation Pane.** Show or hide the Navigation pane. (Default on).

◆ **Navigation Options.** Click this button to customize the Navigation pane. You can show or hide objects, group objects, change categories, or show the Search bar.

◆ **Ribbon Name.** Select the name of a custom Ribbon group. (Default on).

◆ **Shortcut Full Menus.** Set or change the default menu bar for shortcut menus. (Default is Default).

◆ **Allow Full Menus.** Enable or disable full menus, instead of frequently-used menus. (Default on).

◆ **All Default Shortcut Menu.** Enable or disable the shortcut pop-up menu. (Default on).

4 Click **OK**.

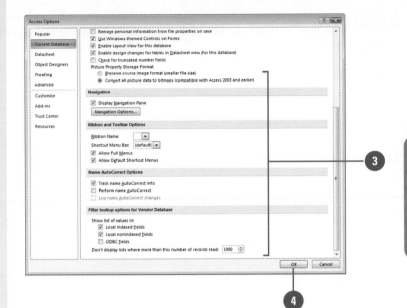

Setting Object Designers Options

Creating and working with tables, queries, forms, and reports are an important part of creating a database. You can change specific options for each database object type to help you customize Access to match the way you work. For example, you can set the default field type, default text field size, or default number field size in new tables. For queries, you can set the default font type and size. For new forms and reports, you can specify selection behavior or templates. Object design options are available on the Object Designers pane in Access Options.

Change Table Object Designer Options

1. Click the **Office** button, and then click **Access Options**.

2. In the left pane, click **Object Designers**.

3. Specify the Table design options you want. Some options include:

   ◆ **Default field type.** Set the default data type for fields in new tables and fields (Default is Text).

   ◆ **Default text field size.** Set the maximum number of characters for a field. (Default is 255)

   ◆ **Default number field size.** Set the integer type for fields with the Text data type. (Default is Long Integer)

   ◆ **AutoIndex on Import/Create.** Enter beginning or ending characters to match fields for indexing.

   ◆ **Show Property Update Options buttons.** Show or hide the Property Update Options button. (Default on)

4. Click **OK**.

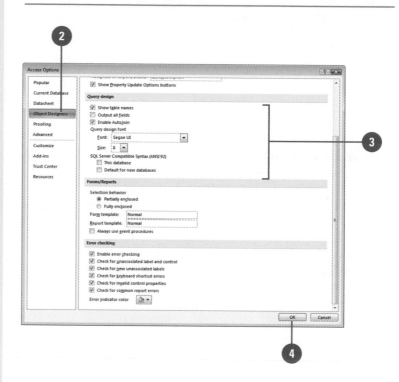

Change Query Object Designer Options

① Click the **Office** button, and then click **Access Options**.

② In the left pane, click **Object Designers**.

③ Specify the Query design options you want. Some options include:

◆ **Show table names.** Show or hide the table row in the query design grid. (Default on).

◆ **Enable Autojoin.** Select to automatically define a relationship between two tables (Default on).

◆ **Query design font.** Select the font style and size for query design.

④ Click **OK**.

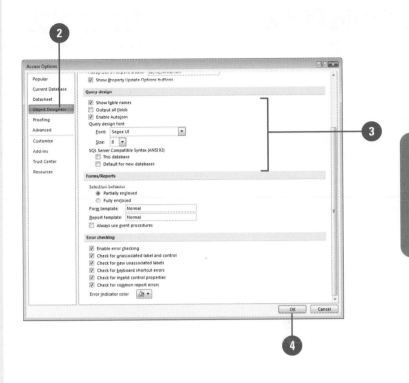

Change Forms/Reports Object Designer Options

① Click the **Office** button, and then click **Access Options**.

② In the left pane, click **Object Designers**.

③ Specify the Forms/Reports design options you want. Some options include:

◆ **Selection behavior.** Specify how the selection rectangle selects objects. (Default is Partially enclosed).

◆ **Form or Report Template.** Enter the name of an existing form or report. The form or report becomes the template for all new forms or reports. (Default template is "Normal").

④ Click **OK**.

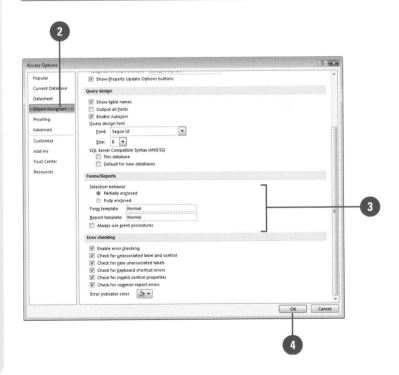

Setting Editing Options

If you spend a lot of time modifying database fields, you can set editing options in Access to customize the way you work. You can set options to specify the move direction after pressing Enter, the behavior when you enter a field or use the Find or Replace command, the arrow key direction, and whether to ask for confirmation when you make changes for certain types of tasks. Editing options are available on the Advanced pane in Access Options.

Change Edit Options

① Click the **Office** button, and then click **Access Options**.

② In the left pane, click **Advanced**.

③ Select or clear the check boxes or options to change editing options. Some options include:

- ◆ **Move after enter.** (Default is Next field).

- ◆ **Behavior entering field.** (Default is Select entire field)

- ◆ **Arrow key behavior.** (Default is Next field).

- ◆ **Default find/replace behavior.** (Default is Fast search).

- ◆ **Confirm.** Confirm record changes, document deletions, or action queries. (Default is all on).

- ◆ **Default direction.** Display direction for objects. (Default is Left-to-right).

- ◆ **General alignment.** Display character alignment based on language. (Default is Interface mode).

- ◆ **Cursor movement.** Language based cursor movement. (Default is Logical).

④ Click **OK**.

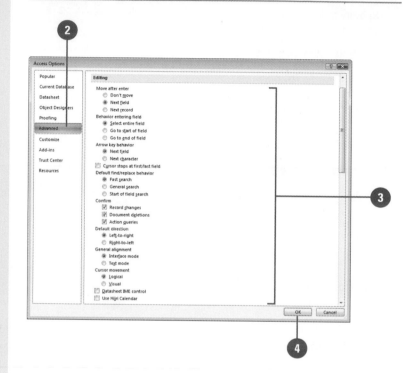

Changing Datasheet Formatting Options

If you want to print a datasheet, you can use formatting tools to make it look better than the standard display. You can apply special effects to cells, change the background, alternate background (**New!**), and grid-line color, and modify border and line styles. The alternate background color shades alternate rows in a datasheet. If you don't want to show the gridlines, you can hide either the horizontal or vertical gridlines, or both. The default display for a datasheet is to display the columns from left to right. If you prefer, you can change the column display to appear from right to left.

Change Datasheet Default Formatting Options

1 Click the **Office** button, and then click **Access Options**.

2 In the left pane, click **Datasheet**.

3 Select the default colors you want: Font color, Background color, Alternate background color, or Gridlines color.

4 Select the default gridlines and cell effects you want.

5 Select the default font and style you want.

6 Click **OK**.

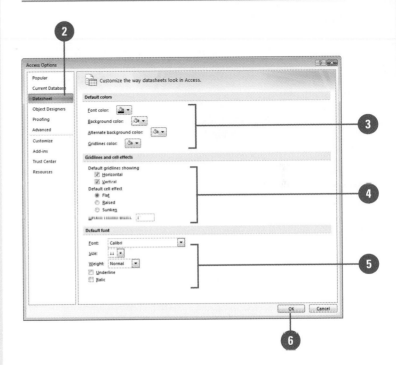

Accessing Commands Not in the Ribbon

If you don't see a command in the Ribbon that was available in an earlier version of Access, you might think Microsoft removed it from the product. To see if a command is available, check out the Customize section in Access Options. The Quick Access Toolbar gives access to commands not in the Ribbon (**New!**), which you can add to the toolbar. For example, you can add the following commands: Filter By Selection, Filter Excluding Selection, OLE/DDE Links, Split, Subform, Size to Fit Form, or Revert.

Add Commands Not in the Ribbon to the Quick Access Toolbar

1. Click the **Customize Quick Access Toolbar** list arrow, and then click **More Commands**.

2. Click the **Choose command from** list arrow, and then click **Commands Not in the Ribbon**.

3. Click the **Customize Quick Access Toolbar** list arrow, and then click **For all documents** (Default).

4. Click the command you want to add (left column).

   TIMESAVER *Click <Separator>, and then click Add to insert a separator line between buttons.*

5. Click **Add**.

6. Click the **Move Up** and **Move Down** arrow buttons to arrange the commands in the order you want them to appear.

7. Click **OK**.

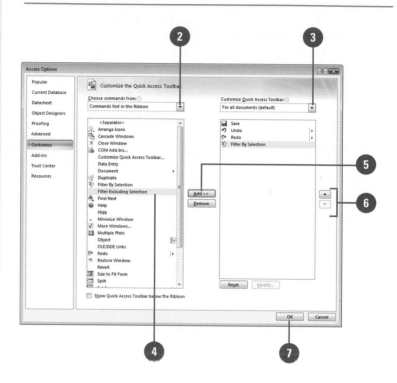

Learning About Macros

A **macro** is a stored collection of actions that perform a particular task, such as opening a specific form and report at the same time or printing a group of reports. You can create macros to automate a repetitive or complex task or to automate a series of tasks. Using a macro to automate repetitive tasks guarantees consistency and minimizes errors caused when you forget a step. Using a macro can also protect you from unnecessary complexity. You can perform multiple tasks with a single button or keystroke. For whatever reason you create them, macros can dramatically increase your productivity when working with your database.

Macros consist of actions or commands that are needed to complete the operation you want to automate. Sorting, querying, and printing are examples of **actions**. **Arguments** are additional pieces of information required to carry out an individual action. For example, an Open Table macro action would require arguments that identify the name of the table you want to open, the view in which to display the table, and the kinds of changes a user would be able to make in this table. Because there are no wizards to help you make a macro, you create a macro by entering actions and arguments directly in Design view. After creating a macro, make sure you save your work and give the macro a meaningful name.

Actions that make up the macro

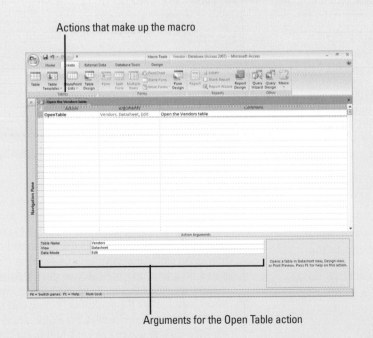

Arguments for the Open Table action

Creating a Macro

Before you begin creating a macro, you should plan the actions required to complete the tasks you want to automate. Practice the steps needed to carry out the operation and write them down as you go. Finally, test your written instructions by performing each of the steps yourself. You can use the New Object button on the Create tab (**New!**) to quickly create a new macro. The name on the New Object button displays the last object created, either Macro, Module, or Class Module.

Create and Save a Macro

1. Click the **Create** tab.

2. Click the **New Object** button arrow, and then click **Macro**.

   ◆ The name on the New Object button displays the last object created, either Macro, Module, or Class Module.

3. Click the **Action** list arrow, click the action you want to use, and then press Tab twice.

4. Type a comment if you want to explain the action.

5. Click the table name in the first Action Arguments box, click the list arrow, and then select a value.

6. To add more actions to the macro, click the right side of a new Action row, and repeat steps 2 through 5. The macro will carry out the actions in the order in which you list them.

7. Click the **Save** button on the Quick Access Toolbar.

8. Enter a descriptive macro name that helps identify the tasks the macro carries out.

9. Click **OK**.

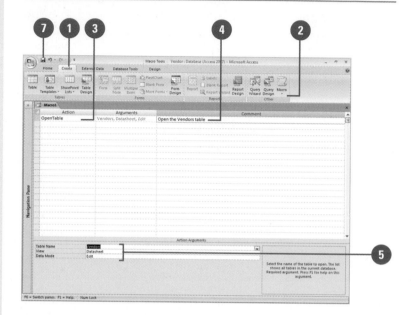

For Your Information

Creating an Embedded Macro

An embedded macro (**New!**) is stored in the event property of a form, report, or control instead of the Navigation pane under Macros. An embedded marco is used when you want to copy, import, or export a form or report object, because the embedded macro stays with the object. An embedded macro runs each time the event property is triggered. To create an embedded macro, right-click the form or report you want to use, click Design View, click the Design tab, click the Property Sheet button, click the control or section that contains the event you want to embed a macro, click the Event tab, click the event property, click the Builder button (...), click Macro Builder, and then click OK. Click the first row of the Action column, click the list arrow, and then click the action you want. You can add other actions as desired. When you're done, click the Save button and then click the Close button.

Edit an Existing Macro

1. In the Navigation pane, click **Macros** on the Objects bar.

2. Right-click the macro you want to edit, and then click **Design View**.

3. Change the actions and arguments you want.

   ◆ To insert a new action, click the **Insert Rows** button.

   ◆ To remove an action, select the action row, and then click the **Delete Rows** button.

4. Click the **Save** button on the Quick Access Toolbar.

5. Click the **Close** button.

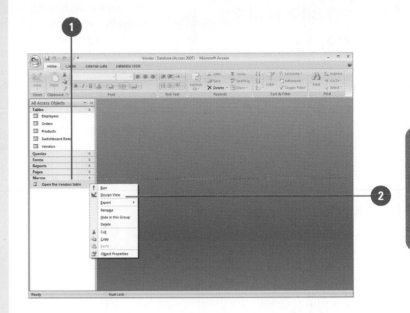

Did You Know?

You can create a new macro based on an existing one. Open the macro in Macro Design view, click the Office button, point to Save As, and then click Save Object As. Give the macro a new name, and then modify the new macro as needed.

You can use conditions to control macro actions. You can use any True/False or Yes/No expression in a condition. The macro action executes if the condition is True or Yes. To enter a condition for a macro action, display the Condition column in the Macro Builder, click the Design tab, click the Conditions button, type an expression in the Condition column that doesn't start with an equal sign (=). For example, [ZipCode]="94566'. To make the condition apply to several actions at once, type ... (three periods) in each row below it.

Running and Testing a Macro

To have a macro perform its actions, you must run it, or instruct it to execute its actions. There are two ways to run a macro. You can have the macro perform all the steps in a sequence at once, or you can test a macro by running it to perform one step at a time, allowing you to review the results of each step. By testing your macro, you might discover that it did not perform all its tasks in the way you expected. If so, you can make changes and retest the macro as you continue to make adjustments in Macro Design view. Keep in mind that a macro will perform only the actions that are appropriate in the currently active view, so be sure to display the correct view before you run the macro; you can have the first action in the macro display the view in which you want to run the macro.

Run a Macro in a Sequence

① Display the macro you want to run in Macro Design view.

② Click the **Design** tab.

If your macro does not automatically switch you to the correct view, switch to the view in which you want to run the macro.

③ Click the **Run** button.

If the macro encounters an action it cannot perform, a message box appears, indicating a problem.

④ If necessary, click **OK** to close the message box.

⑤ Click **Stop All Macros** to stop the macro.

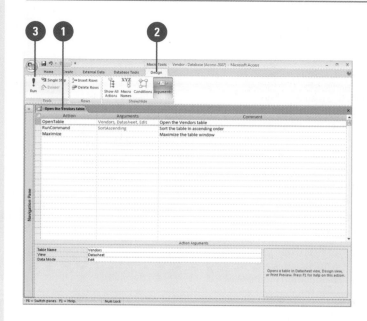

Did You Know?

You can run a macro from the Navigation pane. In the Navigation pane, click the Macros bar, and then double-click the name of the macro you want to run.

Test a Macro Step-by-Step

1. Display the macro you want to run in Macro Design view.

2. Click the **Design** tab.

3. Click the **Single Step** button.

   If necessary, switch to the view in which you want to run the macro.

4. Click the **Run** button.

5. Click **Step** to perform the first action in the macro.

6. Repeat step 4 until the macro finishes.

   If the macro encounters an action it cannot perform, you see a message box stating the action it could not carry out.

7. Click **OK** to close the message box.

8. Click **Stop All Macros** to stop the macro.

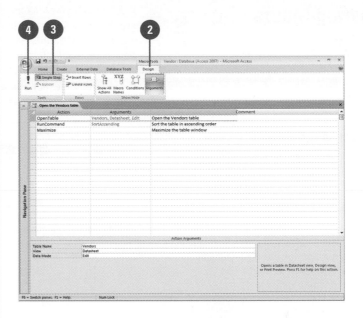

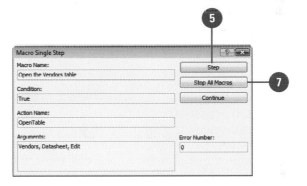

Did You Know?

You can stop the macro before it finishes. In the Macro Single Step dialog box, click Halt.

You can run all steps in a macro. If the Single Step button on the Macro Design toolbar is active, you can still run all the steps in the macro without stopping. In the Macro Single Step dialog box, click Continue.

Creating Macro Groups

If you have numerous macros, grouping related macros in macro groups can help you to manage them more easily. When Access runs a macro group, the first macro in the group starts with the first action, continuing until it reaches a new macro name or the last action in the window. To run a macro group, use the macro group name followed by the macro name. For example, you can refer to a macro group named Report1 in the Employees macro as Report1.Employees.

Create a Macro Group

1. Display the macro you want to run in Macro Design view.

2. Click the **Design** tab.

3. Click the **Macro Names** button.

4. Type a name for the macro group next to the first action in the Macro Name column.

5. Click the **Save** button on the Quick Access Toolbar.

6. Click the **Close** button.

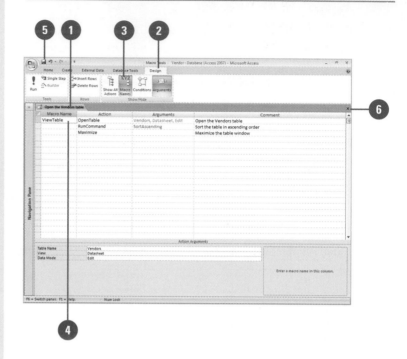

> ## Did You Know?
>
> ***You can display the Macro Name column.*** Display the Macro Name column by clicking the Macro Names button on the Design tab under Macro Tools.

Creating Conditional Macros

Sometimes you may want a macro to run only if some prior condition is met. For example, you could create a macro that prints a report only if the number of records to print is greater than zero. You can do this by creating a **conditional expression**, an expression that Access evaluates as true or false. If the condition is true, Access carries out the actions in the macro.

Create a Macro Condition

① Display the macro you want to run in Macro Design view.

② Click the **Design** tab.

③ Click the **Conditions** button.

④ Click the **Builder** button to open the Expression Builder.

⑤ Enter an expression that Access could evaluate as either true or false.

⑥ Click **OK**.

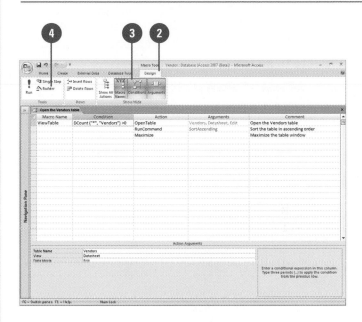

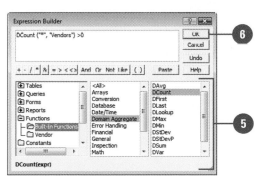

Assigning a Macro to an Event

An **event** is a specific action that occurs on or with a certain object. Clicking a button is an event, called the Click event. The Click event in this case occurs on the button object. Other events include the Dbl Click event (for double-clicking) and the On Enter event, which occurs, for example, when a user "enters" a field by clicking it. If you want to run a macro in response to an event, you have to work in the object's property sheet. The property sheet lists all of the events applicable to the object. You can choose the event and then specify the macro that will run when it occurs, or create a new macro in the Macro window.

Assign a Macro to an Event

1. In Design view, click the object in which the event will occur.

2. Click the **Design** tab.

3. Click the **Property Sheet** button.

   TIMESAVER *You can double-click an object to open the Property Sheet.*

4. Click the **Event** tab.

5. Click the box for the event you want to use.

6. Click the list arrow, and then click the macro you want to use.

7. Click the **Close** button.

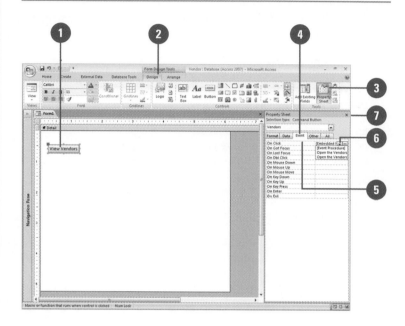

Create a New Macro for an Event

1 In Design view, click the object in you want the event to occur.

2 Click the **Design** tab.

3 Click the **Property Sheet** button.

> **TIMESAVER** *You can double-click an object to open the Property Sheet.*

4 Click the **Event** tab.

5 Click the specific event to which you want to assign the macro.

6 Click the **Builder** button.

7 Click **Macro Builder**.

8 Click **OK**.

9 Enter the actions for the new macro, and then close the Macro window.

10 Click the **Save As** button.

11 Enter a name for the new macro, and then click **OK**.

12 Click the **Close Master View** button.

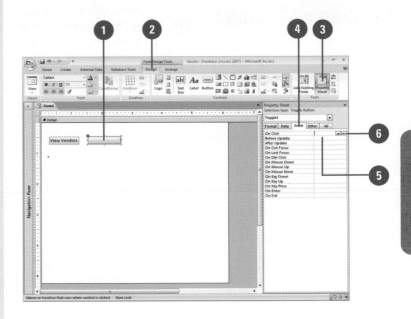

Creating a Message Box

When you create a macro, you may want to give database users information about how the macro works as it runs. You can create message boxes for your macros that, for example, ask the user if he or she wants to proceed. You do this with the MsgBox action. The MsgBox action allows you to specify the text of the message, whether or not a beep sounds when the box is displayed, the type of box that appears, and the box's title. Access supports five different types of message boxes. Each one has a different icon. The icons convey the importance of the message box, ranging from merely being informative to indicating a serious error.

Create a Message Box

1. In the Navigation pane, display the macro in Design view to which you want to add a message box.

2. Click the **Design** tab.

3. Click in an action box, and then type **MsgBox**.

4. Specify the text you want contained in the message box.

5. Indicate whether a beep will accompany the message.

6. Specify the box type.

   ◆ Critical

   ◆ Warning?

   ◆ Warning!

   ◆ Information

   ◆ None

7. Enter the box title.

8. Click the **Close** button.

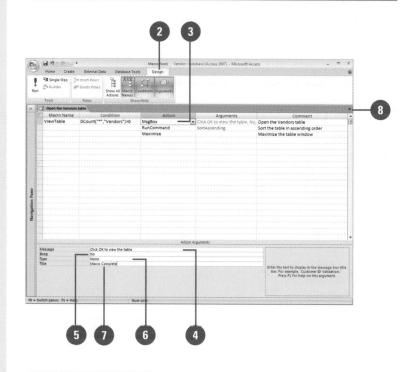

Message box

Assigning a Macro to a Button

Database designers often attach macros to form controls, particularly buttons, so that when a user clicks the button, the macro is activated. If you create a button, you can use the Command Button Wizard to specify the action that will occur when the button is clicked. If you want to assign a macro to a button, you choose the action of running the macro.

Assign a Macro to a Button

1. In Design view for a form, click the **Design** tab under Form Design Tools.

2. Click the **Command Button** tool.

3. Click the **Control Wizards** button.

4. Drag the image onto the form, report, or page.

5. Click **Miscellaneous**.

6. Click **Run Macro** and then click **Next** to continue.

7. Choose the macro you want to run, and then click **Next** to continue.

8. Specify the text or image that will appear on the button, and then click **Next** to continue

9. Enter a name for the command button control, and then click **Finish**.

10. Save the form or report, and then test the button to verify that your macro runs when the button is clicked.

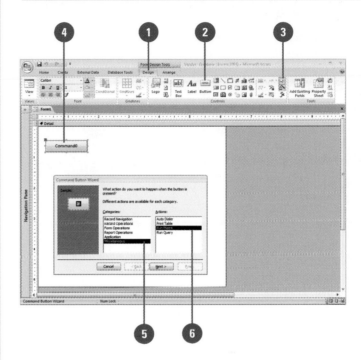

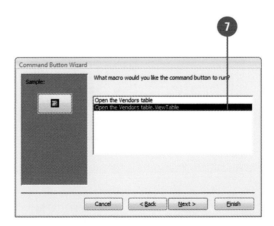

Assigning a Macro to a Toolbar

After you create a macro, you can add the macro to the Quick Access Toolbar (**New!**) for easy access. When you create a macro, the macro name appears in the list of available commands when you customize the Quick Access Toolbar in Access Options. When you point to a macro button on the Quick Access Toolbar, a ScreenTip appears, displaying Macro: *database name*!*macro name*.

Assign a Macro to a Toolbar

1. Click the **Customize Quick Access Toolbar** list arrow, and then click **More Commands**.

2. Click the **Choose command from** list arrow, and then click **Macros**.

3. Click the **Customize Quick Access Toolbar** list arrow, and then click **For all documents** (default).

4. Click the macro you want to add (left column).

5. Click **Add**.

6. Click the **Move Up** and **Move Down** arrow buttons to arrange the commands in the order you want them to appear.

7. Click **Modify**.

8. Type a name for the button.

9. Click an icon in the symbol list.

10. Click **OK**.

11. Click **OK**.

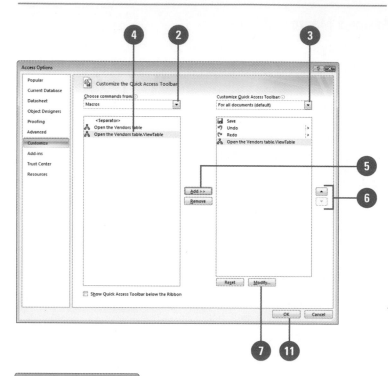

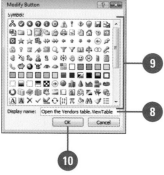

Macro button

Using Multiple Languages

International Microsoft Office users can change the language that appears on their screens by changing the default language settings. Users around the world can enter, display, and edit text in all supported languages—including European languages, Japanese, Chinese, Korean, Hebrew, and Arabic—to name a few. You'll probably be able to use Office programs in your native language. If the text in your document is written in more than one language, you can automatically detect languages or designate the language of selected text so the spelling checker uses the right dictionary.

Add a Language to Office Programs

1 Click **Start** on the taskbar, point to **All Programs**, click **Microsoft Office**, click **Microsoft Office Tools**, and then click **Microsoft Office 2007 Language Settings**.

> **TIMESAVER** *In Access, click the Office button, click Access Options, click Popular, and then click Language Settings.*

2 Select the language you want to enable.

3 Click **Add**.

4 Click **OK**, and then click **Yes** to quit and restart Office.

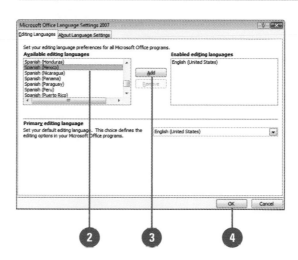

Did You Know?

You can check your keyboard layout. After you enable editing for another language, such as Hebrew, Cyrillic, or Greek, you might need to install the correct keyboard layout so you can enter characters for that language. In the Control Panel, double-click the Regional And Language icon, click the Language tab, and then click Details to check your keyboard.

Enhancing a Database with Programming

15

Introduction

If you want to create customized Microsoft Office Access 2007 applications, you'll need to learn how to work with the Microsoft Office 2007 programming language, **Microsoft Visual Basic for Applications**, or **VBA**. VBA is more powerful and more flexible than Access macros, and you can use it in all major Office applications.

To create a VBA application, you have to learn VBA conventions and syntax. Access provides extensive online Help available to assist you in this task. Office 2007 makes VBA more user-friendly by providing the Visual Basic Editor, an application that includes several tools to help you write error-free VBA applications.

With VBA you can create applications that run when the user initially opens a database, or you can link applications to buttons, text boxes, or other controls. You can even use VBA to create your own custom functions, supplementing Access's library of built-in functions. VBA may be a difficult language for the new user, but its benefits make the effort of learning it worthwhile.

Enhancing a Database with VBA

Office 2007 applications like Access, Excel, and Word share a common programming language: VBA. With VBA, you can develop applications that combine tools from these Office 2007 products, as well as other programs that support VBA. Because of the language's power and flexibility, programmers often prefer to use VBA over Access macros to customize their Access applications.

Introducing the Structure of VBA

VBA is an **object-oriented** programming language because, when you develop a VBA application, you manipulate objects. An object can be anything within your database, such as a table, query, or a database. Even Access itself is considered an object. Objects can have properties that describe the object's characteristics. Text boxes, for example, have the Font property, which describes the font Access uses to display the text. A text box also has properties that indicate whether the text is bold or italic.

Objects also have methods, actions that can be done to the object. Deleting and inserting are examples of methods available with a record object. Closely related to methods are events. An **event** is a specific action that occurs on or with an object. Clicking a form button initiates the Click event for the button object. VBA also refers to an event associated with an object as an event property. The form button, for example, has the Click event property. You can use VBA to either respond to an event or to initiate an event.

Writing VBA Code

Unlike Access macros, which are created in the Macro Design window, the VBA programmer types the statements, or **code**, that make up the VBA program. Those statements follow a set of rules, called **syntax**, that govern how commands are formulated. For example, to change the property of a particular object, the command follows the general form:

Object.Property = Expression

where **Object** is the name of a VBA object, **Property** is the name of a property that object has, and **Expression** is a value that will be assigned to the property. The following statement sets the Caption property of the Departments form:

Forms!Departments.Caption="Department Form"

You can use Access's online Help to learn about specific object and property names. If you want to apply a method to an object, the syntax is:

Object.Method arg1, arg2, ...

where **Object** is the name of a VBA object, **Method** is the name of method that can be applied to that object, and **arg1**, **arg2**, ... are optional **arguments** that provide additional information for the method operation. For example, to move to page 2 of a multipage form, you could use the GoToPage method as follows:

Forms!Departments.GoToPage 2

Working with Procedures

You don't run VBA commands individually. Instead they are organized into groups of commands called **procedures**. A procedure either performs an action or calculates a value. Procedures that perform actions are called **Sub procedures**. You can run a Sub procedure directly, or Access can run it for you in response to an event, such as clicking a button or opening a form. A Sub procedure initiated by an event is also called an **event procedure**. Access provides event procedure templates to help you easily create procedures for common events. Event procedures are displayed in each object's event properties list.

A procedure that calculates a value is called a **function procedure**. By creating function procedures you can create your own function library, supplementing the Access collection of built-in functions. You can access these functions from within the Expression Builder, making it easy for them to be used over and over again.

Working with Modules

Procedures are collected and organized within **modules**. Modules generally belong to two types: class modules and standard modules. A **class module** is associated with a specific object. For example, each form or report can have its own class module, called a **form module** or **report module**. In more advanced VBA programs, the class module can be associated with an object created by the user.

Standard modules are not associated with specific objects, and they can be run from anywhere within a database. This is usually not the case with class modules. Standard modules are listed in the Navigation pane on the Modules Object list.

Building VBA Projects

A collection of modules is further organized into a **project**. Usually a project has the same name as a database. You can create projects that are not tied into any specific databases, saving them as Access add-ins that provide extra functionality to Access.

Using the Visual Basic Editor

You create VBA commands, procedures, and modules in Office's **Visual Basic Editor**. This is the same editor used by Excel, Word, and other Office applications. Thus, you can apply what you learn about creating programs in Access to these other applications.

The Project Explorer

One of the fundamental tools in the Visual Basic Editor is the Project Explorer. The **Project Explorer** presents a hierarchical view of all of the projects and modules currently open in Access, including standard and class modules.

The Modules Window

You write all of your VBA code in the **Modules** window. The Modules window acts as a basic text editor, but it includes several tools to help you write error-free codes. Access also provides hints as you write your code to help you avoid syntax errors.

The Object Browser

There are hundreds of objects available to you. Each object has a myriad of properties, methods, and events. Trying to keep track of all of them is daunting, but the Visual Basic Editor supplies the **Object Browser**, which helps you examine the complete collection of objects, properties, and methods available for a given object.

Creating a Module

All modules in a database are listed in the Modules section of the Navigation pane. You can open a module for editing or create a new module. When you edit a module or design a new one, Access automatically starts the Visual Basic Editor. You can use the New Object button on the Create tab (**New!**) to quickly create a new module. The name on the New Object button displays the last object created, either Macro, Module, or Class Module.

Create a New Standard Module or Class Module

1. Click the **Create** tab.

2. Click the **New Object** button arrow.

   ◆ The name on the New Object button displays the last object created, either Macro, Module, or Class Module.

3. Click **Module** or **Class Module**.

   Access starts the Visual Basic Editor, opening a new module window.

Did You Know?

You can open the Visual Basic Editor.
You can open the Visual Basic Editor directly by pressing and holding Alt while you press F11. You can also toggle back and forth between Access and the Visual Basic Editor by pressing and holding Alt while you press F11.

See Also

See "Enhancing a Database with VBA" on page 356 for information on modules.

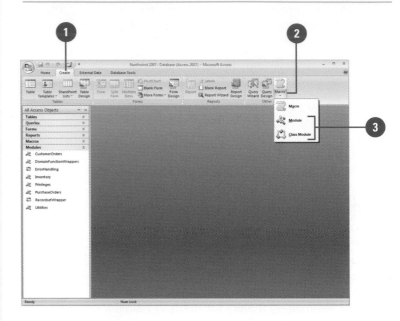

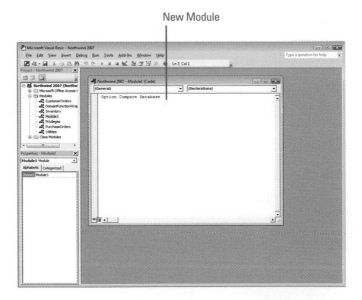

New Module

Understanding Parts of the Visual Basic Editor

The Project Explorer displays a hierarchical list of all open projects and modules.

The Modules window allows you to enter VBA commands.

VBA project

VBA project

The Properties window displays properties for selected objects.

VBA statement

The Object Browser displays a list of available objects, properties, methods, and events.

Method

Objects   Properties

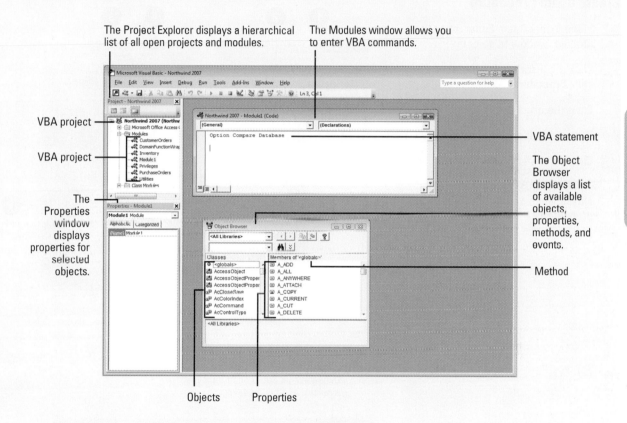

Creating a Sub Procedure

You can either type a Sub procedure directly into the Modules window, or the Visual Basic Editor can insert it for you. Sub procedures all begin with the line: Sub ProcedureName( ) where ProcedureName is the name of the Sub procedure. If the Sub procedure includes arguments, enter them between the opening and closing parentheses. Not every Sub procedure requires arguments. After entering the first line, which names the procedure, you can insert the procedure's VBA commands. Each Sub procedure ends with the line: End Sub.

Create a Sub Procedure

1. In the Visual Basic Editor, click the Module window to select it.

2. Click the **Insert** menu, and then click **Procedure**.

3. Enter the procedure's name.

4. Click the **Sub** option, if necessary.

5. Click **OK**.

   The Editor inserts the opening and closing lines of the new Sub procedure.

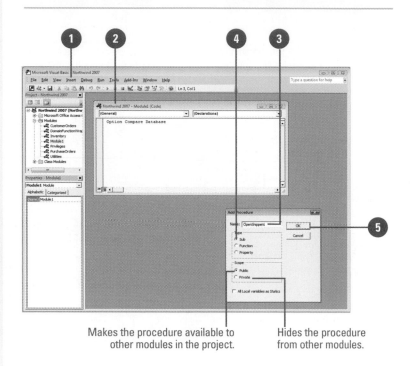

Makes the procedure available to other modules in the project.

Hides the procedure from other modules.

Indicates that Sub procedure is available to other modules.

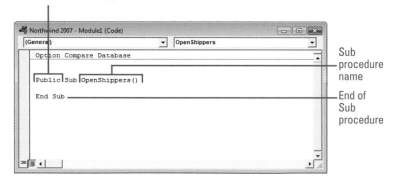

Sub procedure name

End of Sub procedure

Writing VBA Commands

You insert VBA commands by typing them into the appropriate place in the Module window. This, of course, requires some knowledge of VBA. Access provides online Help to assist you in writing VBA code. The Visual Basic Editor also helps you with hints that help you complete a command accurately. If you have entered a command incorrectly, the Editor notifies you of the error and may suggest ways of correcting the problem. One of the most useful VBA objects you'll encounter in writing VBA code is the DoCmd object, which represents Access commands. You can use DoCmd in your commands to perform basic operations, like opening tables, reports, and forms.

Write a VBA Command to Open a Table

1. Click the Modules window to activate it.

2. Click a blank line after the Sub *ProcedureName* command in the Modules window.

3. Type **DoCmd.** Make sure you include the period.

4. Double-click **OpenTable** in the list box that appears, and then press the Spacebar.

5. As indicated by the hints supplied by the Editor, type the name of a table from the current database. Make sure you enclose the name in quotation marks.

6. Type a comma.

7. Double-click **acViewNormal** to open the table in Normal view.

8. Type a comma.

9. Double-click **acReadOnly** to open the table in Read-only mode.

10. Press Enter to add a new blank line below the command.

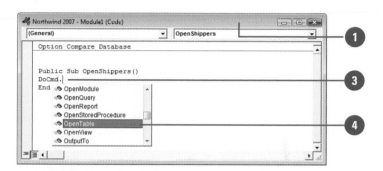

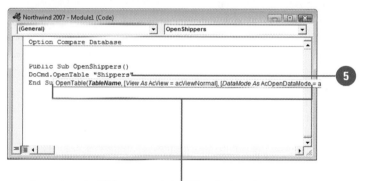

As you type the VBA command, the Editor displays the correct syntax. Optional arguments are enclosed in square brackets [ ].

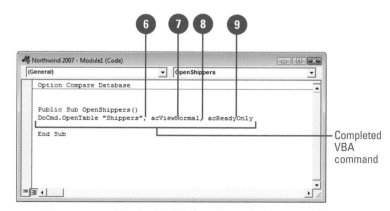

Completed VBA command

Running a Sub Procedure

After writing a Sub procedure, you may want to test it. You can run a Sub procedure from within the Visual Basic Editor, but you might have to return to Access to view the results. If the Sub procedure is a long one, you can also click buttons to pause it or to stop it altogether.

Run a Sub Procedure

1. Click the **Save** button on the toolbar to save changes to the VBA project.

2. Enter a name for your module, if requested.

3. Click anywhere within the Sub procedure that you want to run.

4. Click the **Run Sub/User Form** button on the toolbar.

   If the Macros dialog box appears, select the macro you want to run, and then click **Run**.

5. Return to Access, if necessary, to view the results of your Sub procedure.

Did You Know?

You can rename a module. If you want to rename a module, select the module from the Project Explorer, and then enter a new name in the Name box, located in the Properties window.

You can run a procedure from the keyboard. You can also run a Sub procedure by pressing F5. If you need to halt the procedure, press the Ctrl and the Break keys simultaneously.

Click to pause the procedure.

Click to stop the procedure.

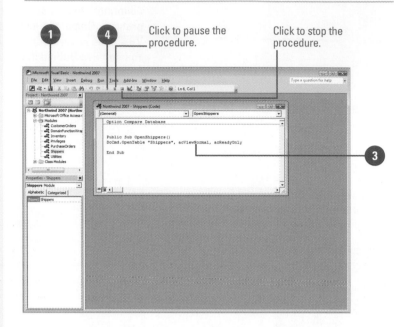

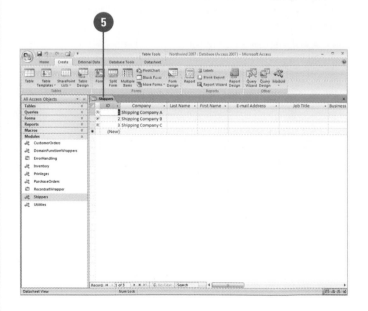

Copying Commands from the Object Browser

The Object Browser displays a hierarchical list of all of the objects, properties, methods, and events available to VBA procedures. The browser organizes these different objects into libraries. The list of libraries is not limited to those built into Access itself. It also includes libraries from other Access projects and add-ins. You can use the Object Browser as a reference tool, or you can copy and paste commands from the browser directly into your Sub procedures.

Insert an Object from the Object Browser

1. In the Visual Basic Editor, click the **Object Browser** button on the toolbar to display the Object Browser.

2. Click the **Libraries** list arrow, and then select the library that contains your object.

3. Select the object you want to insert.

4. Click the **Copy** button.

5. Return to the Sub procedure in the Modules window.

6. Click the location in the Sub procedure where you want to paste the object name.

7. Click the **Paste** button on the toolbar.

Did You Know?

You can search for objects. The Object Browser contains a search tool that helps you locate an object's name.

Enter a search string for an object, property, method, or event.

Click to search for an object, property, method, or event.

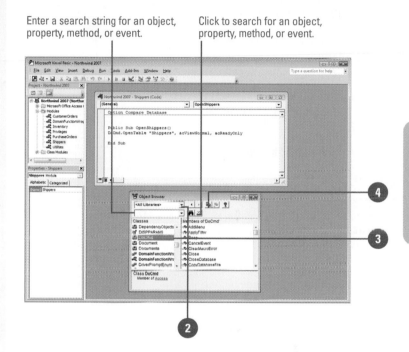

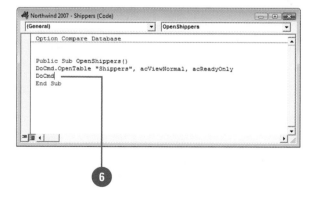

Creating a Custom Function

In addition to Sub procedures, you can also create function procedures that Access uses as custom functions. Each function procedure begins with the line: FunctionName( ) where FunctionName is the name of the function procedure. Within the parentheses, place any variables needed for the calculation of the function. You can learn more about variables from Access's online Help. After statement of the function's name and variables, add VBA commands to calculate the result of the function. The function concludes with the End Function line.

Create a Custom Function

① In the Visual Basic Editor, open a Modules window, click the **Insert** menu, and then click **Procedure**.

   ◆ To create a new module, click the **Insert** menu, and then click **Module**.

② Enter the function's name.

③ Click the **Function** option.

④ Click **OK**.

   The Editor inserts the opening and closing lines of your new custom function.

⑤ Enter variable names needed for the function.

⑥ Enter VBA commands required to calculate the function's value.

⑦ Insert a line assigning the calculated value to a variable with the same name as the function.

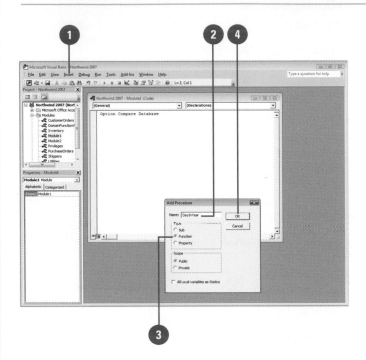

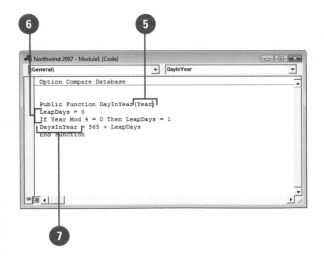

Running a Custom Function

Once you've completed a custom function, you can use it in any Access query, report, or form. The easiest way to access the function is through the Expression Builder. After you open the Expression Builder, you can access the custom function using the Functions folder.

Run a Custom Function

1 Open Expression Builder from any query, report, or form.

2 Double-click the **Functions** folder.

3 Double-click the name of the project containing your custom function (usually the name of the current database).

4 Click the module containing the custom function.

5 Double-click the name of the custom function.

6 Edit the function, replacing the variable names within the parentheses with the appropriate field names or constants.

7 Click **OK**.

8 Test your query, form, or report to verify the values returned by the custom function.

6 The variable name is replaced with a reference to the Year field in the Years table.

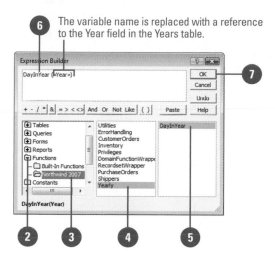

> **Did You Know?**
>
> **You can save a module.** Save changes to your module before using a customized function. Otherwise, the function will not appear in the Expression Builder.

Creating a Class Module for a Form or Report

Similar to the standard modules that you create, you can also create class modules with Access using the Create tab or the Visual Basic Editor. You usually begin a class module in Design view for a form or report. In most cases, class modules are associated with events such as clicking a form button or opening the form. You can access class modules in the Modules Object list in the Navigation pane or from within the Project Explorer.

Create a Class Module for a Form or Report

1. Display a form or report in Design view.

2. Click the **Design** tab.

3. Click the control or object within the form or report in which you want to create a class module.

4. Click the **Property Sheet** button.

5. Click the **Event** tab.

6. Click the event box that you want to associate with a VBA procedure.

7. Click the **Builder** button.

8. Click **Code Builder**.

9. Click **OK**.

   The Visual Basic Editor opens a Modules window and automatically creates an Event procedure for the control and event you selected.

10. Enter the VBA commands you want.

> ### See Also
>
> *See "Creating a Module" on page 358 for information on creating a class module using the Create tab.*

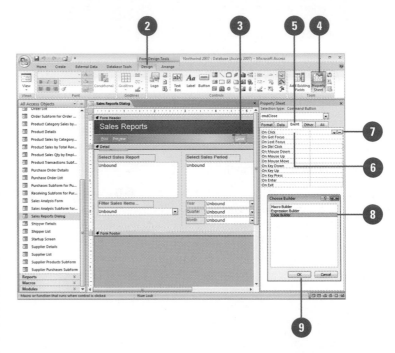

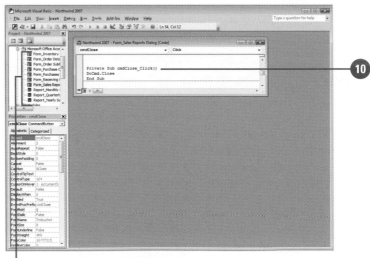

The Project Explorer lists all of the forms and report modules, as well as other class modules.

Setting Project Properties

By default, Access assigns the same name to the project containing your VBA modules and procedures as your database's name. You can change the project's name to make it more descriptive. You can also password-protect your VBA project to keep other users from accessing and changing your procedures.

Set Project Properties

① Open the Visual Basic Editor by pressing and holding Alt while pressing F11.

② Select your project from the list of projects in Project Explorer.

③ Click the **Tools** menu, and then click *ProjectName* Properties, where *ProjectName* is the current name of your project.

④ Click the **General** tab.

⑤ Enter a new name for your project, if necessary.

⑥ Enter a description of your VBA project.

⑦ Click the **Protection** tab.

⑧ Click the **Lock project for viewing** check box if you want to keep others from viewing your project's source code.

⑨ Enter a password to unlock the project for viewing.

⑩ Confirm the unlocking password.

⑪ Click **OK**.

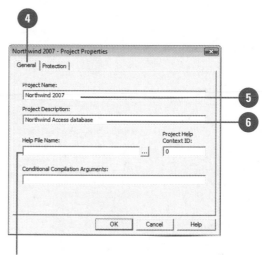

If you've created a Help file for your project, enter the name and location of the file here.

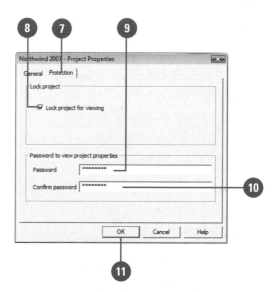

Did You Know?

You need to remember your project password. Save your password. If you lose it, you will not be able to open your code to edit it later.

Debugging a Procedure

The Visual Basic Editor provides several tools to help you write error-free code. However, sometimes a procedure does not act the way you expect it to. To deal with this problem, you can use the Editor's debugging tools to help you locate the source of the trouble. One the most common approaches to debug failed code is to "walk through" the procedure step by step, examining each thing the procedure does. In this way, you can try to locate the exact statement that is causing you trouble.

Stepping Through a Procedure

① Click the **View** menu, point to **Toolbars**, and then click **Debug**.

② Click the first line of the procedure you want to debug.

③ Click the **Step Into** button on the Debug toolbar to run the current statement and then to move to the next line in the procedure.

④ Continue clicking the **Step Into** button to move through the procedure one line at a time, examining the results of the procedure as you go.

⑤ Click the **Stop** button on the Debug toolbar to halt the procedure at a specific line.

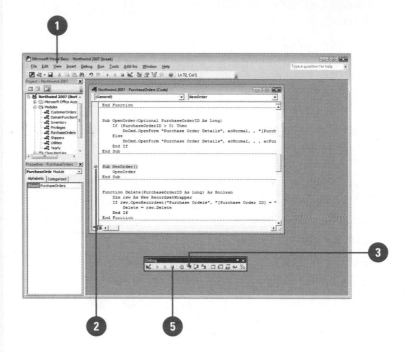

Identifying VBA Debugging Tools

Click to open the Immediate window.

Click to open the Locals window.

Click to Open the Watch window.

The Locals window shows the value and type of all variables used in your VBA procedure. You can use the Locals window to check the effect of your VBA procedure on all variables.

You can enter VBA commands into the Immediate window and then view the results of those commands immediately. The Immediate window saves you the time and effort of creating a VBA procedure and then running it.

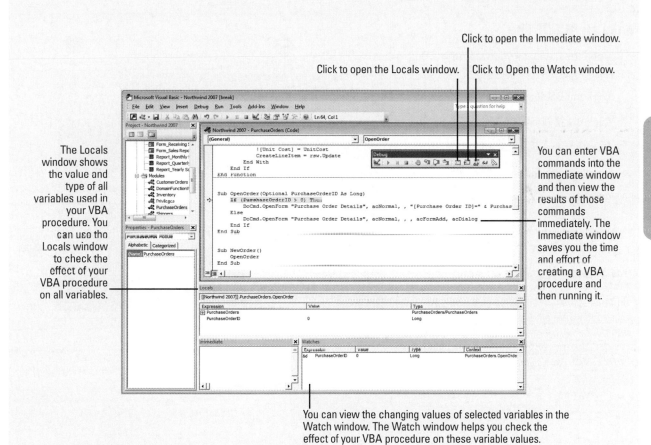

You can view the changing values of selected variables in the Watch window. The Watch window helps you check the effect of your VBA procedure on these variable values.

Optimizing Performance with an ACCDE File

If you share your modules with others, you may want to convert the database file to ACCDE format. In creating an ACCDE file, Access removes the editable source code and then compacts the database. Your VBA programs will continue to run, but others cannot view or edit them. There are several advantages to converting a database to ACCDE format. In ACCDE format, a database is smaller, and its performance will improve as it optimizes memory usage. However, you should create an ACCDE file only after the original database has been thoroughly tested.

Make an ACCDE File

1. Open the database you want to save as an ACCDE database.

2. Click the **Database Tools** tab.

3. Click the **Make ACCDE** button.

4. Specify a location.

5. Enter a name for the ACCDE file.

6. Click **Save**.

Did You Know?

You can save the original database. Make a backup copy of the original database. You'll need it if you have to edit your VBA modules or add new ones.

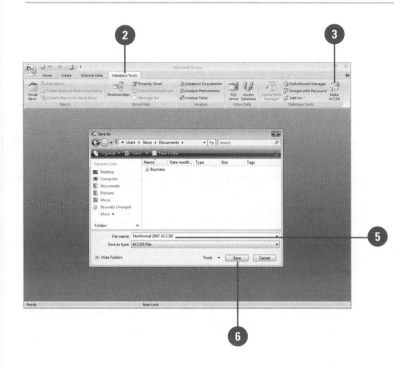

Working Together on Office Documents

16

Introduction

Microsoft Office Groove 2007 is a new addition to the Microsoft Office 2007 Enterprise system that enables teams to set up collaborative workspaces. With Office Groove 2007 (**New!**), you can bring the team, tools, and information together from any location to work on a project. After creating documents with Microsoft Office programs, you can use Groove for file sharing, document reviews, co-editing and co-reviewing Word documents, and for co-viewing Access databases.

Instead of using a centralized server—like Office SharePoint Server 2007—to store information and manage tasks, Office Groove stores all your workspaces, tools, and data right on your computer. You don't need to connect to a network to access or update information. While you're connected to the Internet, Groove automatically sends the changes you make in a workspace to your team member's computers, and any changes they make get sent to you. Office Groove uses built-in presence awareness, alerts, and unread marks to see who is working online and what team members are doing without having to ask.

Office Groove uses tools and technology from other Microsoft Office system products to help you work together and stay informed. With the Groove SharePoint Files tool, you can check out documents from Microsoft Office SharePoint 2007 into a Groove workspace, collaborate on them, and then check them back in when you're done. With the Groove InfoPath Forms tool, you can import form solutions created in Office InfoPath 2007, or design your own.

Configuring Groove

The first time you launch Microsoft Office Groove 2007, the Account Configuration Wizard appears, asking you to create a new Groove account or use an existing one already created on another computer. During the wizard process, you'll enter your Groove Account Configuration Code—for network purposes only—and Groove Account Information, including name, e-mail address, and password. If you want your Groove account to be listed in a Public Groove Directory, you can also select that option during the wizard process.

Start, Configure, and Exit Groove

1. For the first time, click the **Start** button, point to **All Programs**, click **Microsoft Office**, and then click **Microsoft Office Groove 2007**.

2. Click the **Create a new Groove account** option.

3. Click **Next**.

4. Click the Account Configuration Code option you want, and then click **Next**.

5. Enter account information, including name, e-mail address, and password.

6. Click **Next**.

7. Click an option to list your account in the Public Groove Directory, either **No Listing** (default), **Name Only**, and **All Contact Information**.

8. Click **Finish**.

9. Click **Yes or No** to watch a movie about Groove.

10. To exit Groove, click the **Close** button on the title bar.

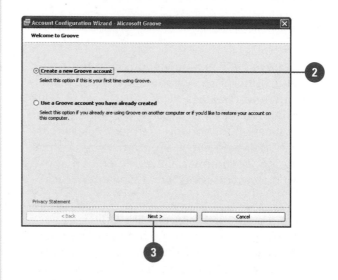

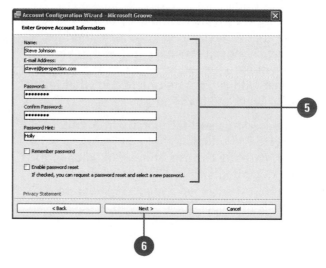

Did You Know?

You can use your account on another computer. Click the Options menu, click Invite My Other Computers, click OK, and then copy the account file for use on another computer.

Launching Groove

Microsoft Groove 2007 allows teams to securely work together over the Internet or corporate network as if they were in the same location. Teams using Groove can remotely work with shared files and content, even when they are offline. You can launch Groove 2007 from the Start menu or from the notification area. When you start Groove, the Launchbar window opens, displaying two tabs: one for creating and managing workspaces, and one for adding and managing contacts. If you are having difficulty launching Groove, check to make sure Groove is configured as a Windows Firewall exception.

Launch Groove from the Start Menu and Login

1 Click the **Start** button on the taskbar, point to **All Programs**, click **Microsoft Office**, and then click **Microsoft Office Groove 2007**.

> **TIMESAVER** *Click the Groove icon in the notification area, and then click Open Groove.*

2 Enter your password, and then click **Login**.

3 To logoff, click the **File** menu, and then click **Log Off Account**.

Add Groove as a Firewall Exception

1 In Windows, click **Start**, and then click **Control Panel**.

2 Double-click the **Windows Firewall** icon.

3 Click the **Exceptions** tab.

4 Click **Add Program**.

5 Click **Browse**, navigate to the Programs Files folder, Microsoft Office folder, Office 12 folder, click **Groove.exe**, and then click **Open**.

6 Click **OK**.

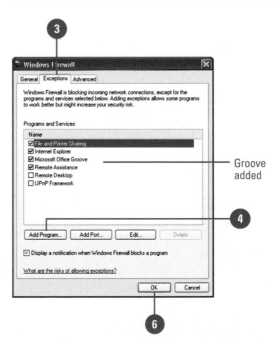

Groove added

Viewing the Groove Window

Workspace   Workspace selector   Workspace members   Launcher

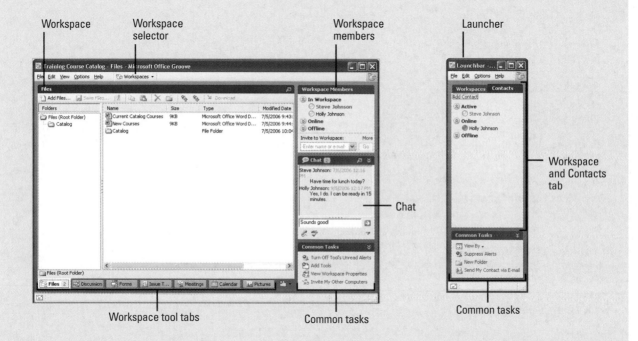

Chat

Workspace and Contacts tab

Workspace tool tabs   Common tasks   Common tasks

Setting General Preferences

Groove makes it easy to set program preferences all in one place by using the Preferences dialog box. You can select from six different tabs —Identities, Account, Security, Alerts, Options, and Synchronization—to specify startup and application settings, alert levels, communication policies, file and workspace restrictions, account privileges, and identity information. The Options tab allows you to set general preferences to startup Groove and related applications, like Launchbar and Workspace Explorer, and scan for viruses.

Set General Preferences

1. In the Launchbar, click the **Options** menu, and then click **Preferences**.

2. Click the **Options** tab.

3. Select or clear the **Launch Groove when Windows starts up** and the **Integrate messenger Contacts** check boxes.

4. Click an application (Launchbar or Workspace Explorer by default), and then click **Settings**, select start up and display options, and then click **OK**.

5. Select or clear the **Discard Groove messages from unknown contacts** check box.

6. Select or clear the **Send e-mail invitations using Microsoft Outlook** check box.

7. Specify the online presence settings you want.

8. Select or clear the **Scan incoming and outgoing files for viruses** check box.

9. Click **OK**.

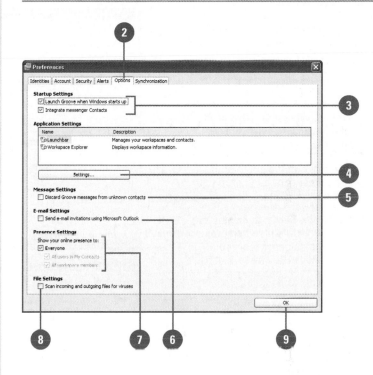

Did You Know?

You can set workspace properties. In the workspace, click View Workspace Properties under Command Tasks, click the tab and select the properties you want, and then click OK.

Creating a Groove Workspace

A Groove workspace is a special site template that provides you with tools to share and update documents and to keep people informed about the current status of the documents. After you create a workspace, you can use Files and Discussion Tools to share files, exchange messages, and collaborate with a team. In a Groove workspace, you can point to the Files or Discussion tab to display the contacts currently using a tool.

Create a Workspace

1. In the Launchbar, click the **File** menu, point to **New**, and then click **Workspace**.

2. Click a workspace option:

   ◆ **Standard.** Select to display the Groove Workspace Explorer and initially include the Files and Discussion Tools.

   ◆ **File Sharing.** Select to share the contents of a folder in your Windows system.

   ◆ **Template.** Select to display the Groove Workspace Explorer with the selected tools you want. Click Browse to visit a Groove Web site, where you can download templates.

3. Type a new name for the workspace.

4. Click **OK**.

   The new workspace opens in another window.

Did You Know?

You can delete a workspace. In the workspace, click the File menu, point to Delete Workspace, and then click From This Computer or For All Members.

You can save a workspace as a template or back it up. In the workspace, click the File menu, point to Save Workspace As, and then click Template or Archive.

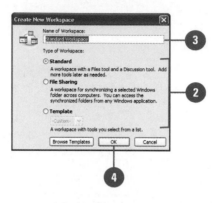

New workspace

Inviting Others to a Workspace

Before you can invite someone to a Groove workspace, they need to be a Groove user. Each person you invite to a Groove workspace needs to have a role, either Manager, Participant, or Guest. Each role comes with a set of permissions that allow a user to perform certain tasks. Mangers can invite others, edit existing files, and delete files or the entire workspace. Participants can edit and delete files. Guests can view existing data, but not make changes. After you send an invitation to join a workspace, check for Groove alerts in the notification area to see if the user has accepted your invitation.

Invite Users to a Workspace

1. Open the workspace, click the **Options** menu, and then click **Invite to Workshop**.

2. Click the **To** list arrow, and then select a user.

    If the user you want is not there, click **Add More**, click **Search for User**, type part of the user's name, click **Find**, select the user's name you want, and then click **Add**, and then click **OK**.

3. Click the **Role** list arrow, and then click a role: **Manager**, **Participant**, or **Guest**.

4. Enter a message.

5. Select the **Require acceptance confirmation** check box as a security recommendation.

6. Click **Invite**.

    Monitor your Groove alerts for status and acceptance.

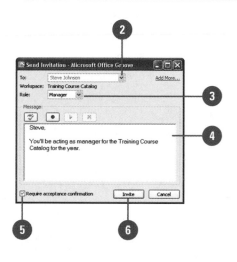

Groove alert with invitation

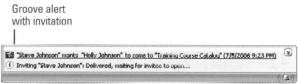

Did You Know?

You can change workspace roles and permissions. In the Launchbar, click Set Roles under Common Tasks. To adjust permissions for a tool, right-click the tool tab, and then click Properties/Permissions.

Dealing with Groove Alerts

Groove alerts appear as blinking messages in the lower right corner of Windows. You can check for Groove alerts by resting the pointer on the Groove icon in the notification area. Groove alerts notify you about updates and work status. For example, Groove sends you an alert when someone accepts an invitation to a workspace, sends a message, changes an existing file or adds a new file. If you're getting more alerts than you want, you can set alert options in the Preferences dialog box.

Check for Groove Alerts

1. Look for a blinking message or Groove icon in the notification area.

2. Point to the **Groove** icon in the notification area to display the alert.

3. Click the alert to open Groove.

Set Alert Options

1. In the Launchbar, click the **Options** menu, and then click **Preferences**.

2. Click the **Alerts** tab.

3. Drag the slider to select an alert level:

   ◆ **Auto.** Similar to the High alert level, but auto-dismissed ignored unread alerts.

   ◆ **High.** Highlight unread content with an icon and display an alert for all unread content.

   ◆ **Medium.** Highlight unread content with an icon.

   ◆ **Off.** Don't display an alert for new or modified content.

4. Specify the number of days you want to keep unread alerts from being removed.

5. Click **OK**.

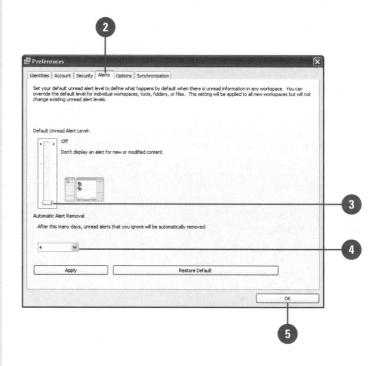

Sharing Files in a Workspace

The Files Tool in Groove allows you to share and collaborate on different types of files, including files from Microsoft Office programs. All team members of a workspace can open files that appear in the Files Tool. When a team member opens, changes, and saves a file to the workspace, Groove automatically updates the file for all other team members. When several team members work on the same file at the same time, the first person to save changes to the workspace updates the original file. If another team member saves changes to the original version, Groove creates a second copy with the editor's name.

Share Files in a Workspace

1. In Launchbar, double-click the workspace you want to share.

2. Click the **Files** tab.

3. Click the **Add Files** button.

4. Locate and select the files you want to add to the workspace.

5. Click **Open**.

   The selected files appear in the file list in the workspace.

Manage Tools

◆ **New Files**. Select a folder, click the File menu, point to New, and then click a file type.

◆ **Open Files**. Double-click it, make and save changes, and then click Yes or No to save changes in Groove.

◆ **Delete Files**. Right-click, and then click Delete.

◆ **New Folder**. Select a folder, click the File menu, point to New, click Folder, type a name, and then press Enter.

◆ **Alerts**. Right-click a folder or file, click Properties, click the Alerts tab, drag slider, and then click OK.

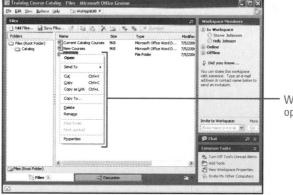

Workspace file options

Holding a Discussion

The Discussion Tool in Groove allows users to post an announcement, news item, or other information for everyone working together in a standard workspace. Team members can add and view discussion items as a threaded conversation. Since the discussions are entered into a different area than the shared document, users can modify the document without affecting the collaborative discussion. Users can add changes to read-only documents and allow multiple users to simultaneously create and edit discussion items.

Start and Participate in a Discussion

1. In Launchbar, double-click the workspace from which you want to hold a discussion.

2. Click the **Discussion** tab.

3. Click the **New** button, and then click **Topic**.

   A new topic opens.

4. Type the Subject.

5. Click the **Category** list arrow, and then select a category.

   If the category you want is not available, click the plus (+) sign, enter a category name, and then click OK.

6. Enter a message in the discussion box.

7. Click **Save** to post the message or click **Save and Create Another** to post and create a new topic.

   The new discussion is displayed in the workspace.

8. To participate in a discussion, double-click the discussion within the workspace in order to respond.

   When you're online, Groove synchronizes the discussion, so all workspace participants can see all new postings and topics.

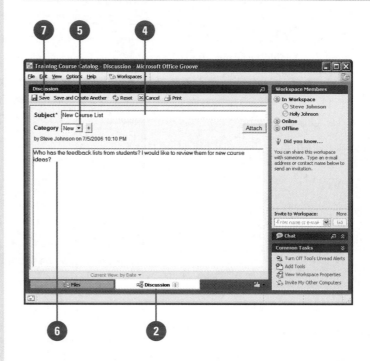

Adding Tools to a Workspace

Like many other Office programs, Groove allows you to add functionality. Groove already comes with the Files and Discussion Tools. You can add other tools, such as InfoPath Forms, Issue Tracking, or SharePoint Files. The InfoPath Tool allows you to collect and view data. The Issue Tracking Tool lets you report on and track the status of issues and incidents. If you have access to an Office or Windows SharePoint Server, the SharePoint Files Tool allows you to synchronize files on a workspace with those on a SharePoint site, document library, or folder.

Add Other Tools to a Workspace

1. In Launchbar, double-click the workspace you want to open.

2. Under Command Tasks, click **Add Tools**.

   TIMESAVER *Click the Add a tool to this workspace button, and then click the tool you want.*

3. Select the check box next to each tool you want to add.

4. Click **OK**.

   A button tab for each tool appears at the bottom of the workspace.

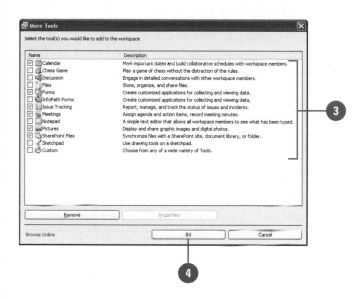

Manage Tools

- **Delete**. Right-click the tool tab, click Delete, and then click Yes.

- **Rename**. Right-click the tool tab, click Rename, enter a new name, and then click OK.

- **Move**. Drag a tool tab name to the left or right.

- **Open in Window**. Right-click the tool tab, and then click Open in New Window.

- **Properties**. Right-click the tool tab, and then click Properties. Click a tab—General, Permissions, Alerts—to view or change properties.

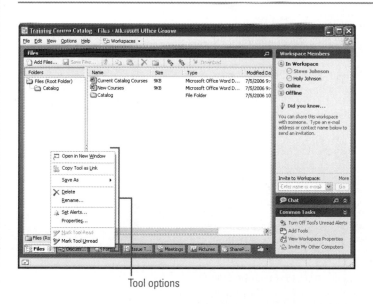

Tool options

Setting Calendar Appointments

Using the Calendar Tool, you can manage your time by doing much more than circling dates. The Calendar collects important information for team members by providing them with critical dates for the completion of a project. Among its many features, the Groove Calendar lets you schedule and manage project appointments and customize the Calendar view to help everyone stay on track.

Add an Appointment

1. In Launchbar, double-click the workspace you want to open, and then click the **Calendar** tab.

2. Click the **New Appointment** button.

    TIMESAVER *To create an appointment with pre-selected dates and times, drag across the range of dates and times you want.*

3. Enter an appointment subject.

4. Fill in the start and end date and a start and end time.

5. Click **OK**.

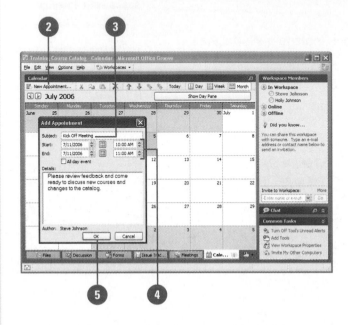

Manage Appointments and the Calendar

- **View**. Point to an appointment to display a text window.

- **Delete**. Select the appointment, and then press Delete.

- **Edit**. Double-click the appointment, make changes, and then click OK.

- **Navigate**. Click Navigate Previous or Next Appointment buttons on the toolbar, or click Navigate Previous or Next Unread buttons on the toolbar.

- **Navigate Calendar Days**. Click the Previous/Next buttons in the Calendar's title bar.

- **Change Calendar Display**. Click the Day, Week, or Month icons.

Navigate days   Change display

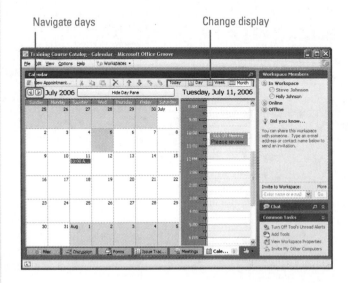

Managing Meetings

The Groove Meetings Tool helps you organize, conduct, and record meetings. Every Groove meeting includes a Meeting profile (start and end times, location, and description), Attendees list, Agenda, Minutes, and Actions, which are displayed as tabs for easy access. You can use a wizard to quickly create a meeting, and then manage all aspects of it.

Create a Meeting

1. In Launchbar, double-click the workspace you want to open, and then click the **Meetings** tab.

2. Click the **New Meeting** button to start the wizard.

3. Enter the subject, start and end times, location and details.

4. Click **OK**.

5. Use the **Attendees** tab to select meeting attendees and appoint a chairperson and minutes-taker.

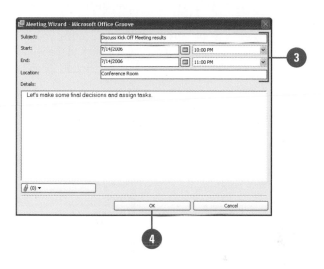

Manage a Meeting

◆ **Agenda**. Click the Agenda tab, click New Topic, fill in the form, and then click OK.

◆ **Action Items**. Click the Actions tab, click New Action Item, fill in the form, and then click OK.

◆ **Record Minutes**. Click the Minutes tab, click Edit, type in text or click Insert Agenda, and then save or discard your work.

◆ **Attendees**. Click the Attendees tab, click Edit, make changes, and then click Save and Close.

◆ **Navigate**. Click the Date of range options button, and then select a range of dates, or click the Previous/Next arrows.

◆ **Attachments**. Select a profile, agenda, or action, click Edit, click Attachments list arrow, and then click Add, Delete, Save all, or file name you want to open.

Meeting options

Working with Forms

If you need to collect data as part of your project, you can use the Groove Forms Tool to create custom forms in the workspace window, or use the InfoPath Forms Tool to import forms you have already created using Microsoft Office InfoPath 2007. With Designer Access privileges, you can use the Groove Forms Tool to name the form, choose the fields, select the form style, and create a form view to view the data. You create and layout form elements in the design sandbox, which multiple team members can use to help with the design. Like working with files in Groove, your form designs are stored locally until you publish them back to the workspace.

Create a Form and View

1. In Launchbar, double-click the workspace you want to open, and then click the **Forms** tab.

2. Click the **Designer** button, and then click **Create New Form**.

   ◆ On first run, click **Start Here**.

3. On the Basics tab, enter form name.

4. Select the check boxes with the system fields you want.

5. To create new fields, click **Create New Field** in the left pane, click the field type you want, click **Next**, click a property in the left pane, enter information or select options, and then click **Finish**.

6. Click the **Style Form** button, and then select a style.

7. Click **Column Number** button, and then select a number.

8. Select other options for defining the behavior of the fields and form.

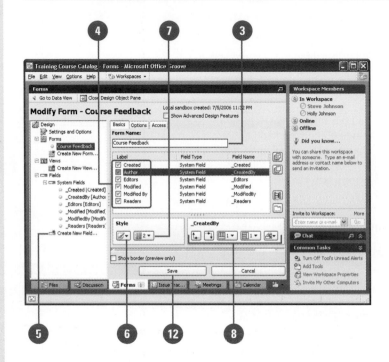

Did You Know?

You can revise a form. In the workspace, click the Forms tab, click the Designer button, point to Modify Form, click a form name, make changes, click Save, and then click Publish Sandbox to update the workspace.

9. In the left pane, click **Create New View**.

10. Click the **Basics** tab, and then enter a view name.

11. Select the check boxes with the fields you want, and other options.

12. Click **Save**.

13. Click the **Publish Sandbox** or **Discard Sandbox** button.

Did You Know?

You can change form settings and access. In the workspace, click the Forms tab, click the Designer button, point to Modify Form, click a form name, click the Options or Access tab, select options, click Save, and then click Publish Sandbox.

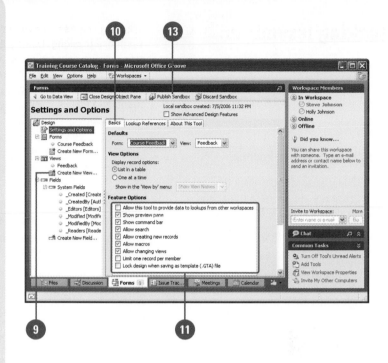

Create and Manage a Form Record

1. In Launchbar, double-click the workspace you want to open, and then click the **Forms** tab.

2. Click the **New** button, and then click the form name.

3. Enter form data.

4. Click the **Save** or **Save and Create Another** button.

5. To edit a form record, double-click it, make changes, and then click **Update**.

6. To delete a form record, click the form record, and then click the **Delete** button.

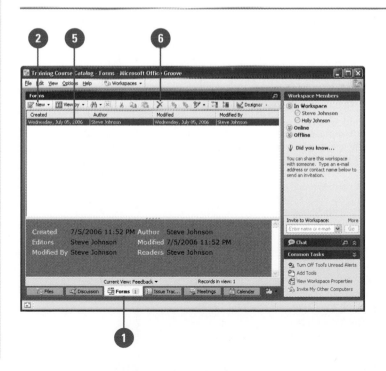

Tracking Issues

Tracking issues is useful for managing all phases of issue reporting and response tracking. Users can create reports, assign ownership, and track status over time. Issue Tracking is a tool designed using the Groove Forms Tool, which includes two basic form types: Issue and Response. The Issue form records issue information, owner assignment, and tracks status. The Response form records a response to an issue record.

Track Issues Using Forms

1. In Launchbar, double-click the workspace you want to open, and then click the **Issue Tracking** tab.

2. Click the **New** button, and then click **Issue**.

3. Click the **Original Report** tab.

4. Enter a title for the issue.

5. Click the list arrow next to each, and then select or add an item.

   ◆ Category.

   ◆ Subcategory.

   ◆ Originated by: Organization.

   ◆ Individual.

6. Enter a description.

7. If you want to attach a file and work with it, use the Attachment buttons.

8. Click the **Current Status** tab.

9. Click the list arrow next to each, and then select or add an item.

   ◆ Status.

   ◆ Priority.

   ◆ Assigned to: Organization.

   ◆ Individual.

10. Enter ongoing remarks.

11. Click the **Save** or **Save and Create Another** button.

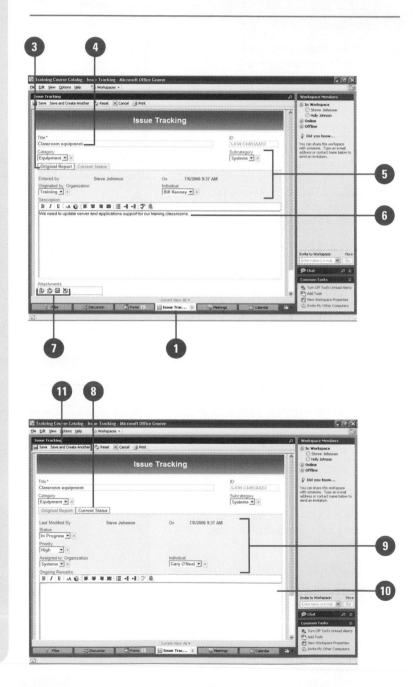

Manage Tools

◆ **Edit**. Double-click the issue, make changes, and then click Update.

◆ **Delete**. Select the issue record, and then click the Delete button on the toolbar.

◆ **Update Assignments**. As a manager, click the Run Macros button on the toolbar, and click Update Assignment - manager only.

◆ **Sort**. Click the column heading you want to sort by.

◆ **View by**. Click the View By button on the toolbar, and then select a view, such as Assignment, Category, Originator, Priority, and Status.

◆ **Search**. Click the Search button on the toolbar, click Search, enter the search criteria you want, and then click Search.

When you're done with the results, click the **Clear Results** button on the toolbar.

Did You Know?

You can set alerts for tools. In the workspace, click any tool tab, click Set Tool Alerts under Command Tasks, drag the slider to select an alert level, and then click OK. To turn alerts off, click Turn Off Tool's Unread Alerts under Common Tasks.

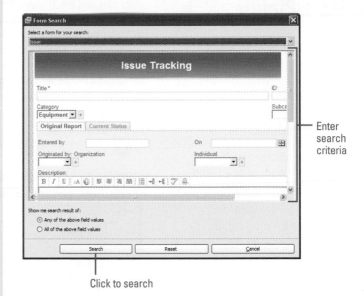

Enter search criteria

Click to search

Creating a Picture Library

You can add the Groove Pictures Tool to a workspace to display and share picture files in JPEG (.jpg) or bitmap (.bmp) format. You can view a list of picture files that you or other team members have added to the Pictures Tool. The list also includes status information about the picture files, such as type, size, modified date, and last editor. The Pictures Tool automatically scales all pictures you add to fit the current size of the picture viewer window.

Add and View Pictures

1. In Launchbar, double-click the workspace you want to open, and then click the **Pictures** tab.

2. To add pictures, click **Add Pictures**, and then drag and drop files into the list or copy and paste files into the list.

3. To show or hide picture details, click the **Show Pictures Details** or **Hide Picture Details** button.

4. To view pictures, click the **Previous** or **Next** buttons.

Manage Pictures

- **Edit**. Right-click a picture, and then click Open. Your graphics program opens. Edit and save the picture, and then Yes to update in Groove.

- **Rename**. Select the picture, click the Rename button on the toolbar, type a new name, and then click OK.

- **Export**. Select the picture file, click the Export button on the toolbar, select a location, and then click Save.

- **Delete**. Select one or more pictures, and then press Delete.

Toolbar to manage pictures

Adding a Contact

In order to send messages or have a chat with other Groove team members, you need to add them as contacts. In the Launchbar, you can quickly and easily check for the online presence of a contact. By default, each contact appears on the Contacts tab based on status, either Active, Online, or Offline. Each icon next to a contact also indicates whether the member is online, away or offline. In a Groove workspace, you can point to the Files or Discussion tab to display the contacts currently using a tool.

Add a Contact

① In Launchbar, click the **Contacts** tab.

② Click the **Add Contact** button.

The Find User window opens.

③ Type part of the user's name.

④ Click **Find**.

⑤ Select the user's name you want to add as a contact.

⑥ Click **Add**.

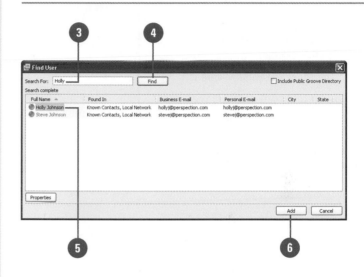

Check the Presence of a Contact

◆ In the Launchbar, click the **Contacts** tab. By default, each contact appears in the Launchbar based on status, either Active, Online, or Offline. Each icon next to a contact also indicates whether the member is online, away or offline.

> **TIMESAVER** To change order, click the Options menu, point to View Contacts By, and then click a sort method.

◆ In a Groove workspace, the tabs at the bottom of the workspace display the number of people who are actively using the tool, either Files or Discussion. To see the names of the people using a Tool, point to the tab.

Contacts

Sending a Message

You can send messages to other Groove contacts at any time even if you or your contact are not online. If you or your contact are offline, Groove sends the message and alerts you of delivery, when it's opened, and when your contact replies as soon as you and your contact are online.

Send a Message

1. In Launchbar, click the **Contacts** tab.

2. Right-click a contact, and then click **Send Message**.

   The Send Message window opens.

   TIMESAVER *Press Shift-Shift to open a new instant message window or bring up your next unread instant message from your inbox.*

3. Type a message.

4. Click **Send**.

   An alert appears, indicating your message was sent. Monitor Groove alerts for more message status.

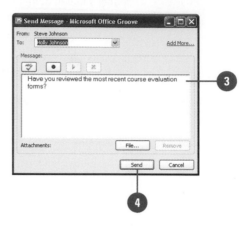

Receive and Reply to a Message

1. When a Groove alert appears, indicating you have received a message, click it.

2. Enter your reply to the message.

3. Click **Send**.

   An alert appears, indicating your message was sent. Monitor Groove alerts for more message status.

   When the original sender received back the message, the sender can Reply, Forward, or Close the message.

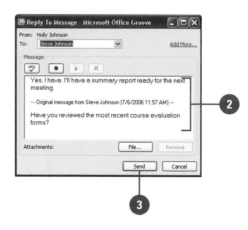

Chatting with Others

A chat is an ongoing conversation you type and send, or post. Each Groove workspace includes a chat tool, where you can communicate with others in real time or offline. The number of team members currently involved in a chat appears on the title bar. When you post a new message in the chat tool, a Groove alert notifies other team members. As each team members post messages in a workspace chat, the ongoing conversation is saved in the workspace for reference until the workspace is deleted.

Chat with Other Workspace Team Members

1 In Launchbar, double-click the workspace you want to open, and then click **Expand Chat** button next to Chart, if necessary.

IMPORTANT *If you are using Groove on a Tablet PC, the chat window may open by default in Ink mode. To switch to Text mode, click the Options menu (Down Arrow), and then click Switch to Text Mode.*

2 Click in the blank box at the bottom of the chat tool, located on the right side of the workspace, and then type a message.

3 To check spelling, click the **Check Spelling** button, and then correct any mistakes.

4 Click **Go**.

Your message is added to the ongoing conversation.

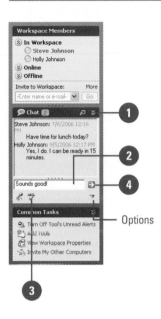

Options

Did You Know?

You can use a microphone. With a microphone installed on your computer, click the Microphone button, and then reply to the Audio Tuner wizard questions.

Sharing Files with SharePoint

If you have access to an Office or Windows SharePoint Server 3.0 site, (workspace collaboration using a Web server), you can synchronize file content between Groove and SharePoint libraries. Groove uses the SharePoint Files Tool as a centralized location to work on SharePoint files and with people outside your workspace. The SharePoint Files Tool synchronizes data with workspace members in the same way as the standard File Tool. The one who sets up the SharePoint connection is the synchronizer, and is typically the workspace Owner. The synchronizer has two options: manual or automatic based on a time interval. Simply double-click a SharePoint file to edit it in its native program. As the synchronizer, you can also check out/in files to avoid conflicts with other SharePoint users while you edit a file.

Set Up a SharePoint Connection

1. In Launchbar, double-click the workspace you want to open, and then click the **SharePoint Files** tab.

2. Click **Setup**.

3. Enter the SharePoint Server Web address, and then press Enter.

   See your Network Administrator for specifics.

4. Click the library in which you want to connect.

5. Click **Select**.

   All the files in the SharePoint library are synchronized with the Groove workspace.

Did You Know?

You can get more information about SharePoint. To download a complete chapter about Office SharePoint, go to *www.perspection.com*.

You can set file permissions for SharePoint files. In the workspace, right-click the SharePoint Files tab, click Properties, click the Permissions tab, select a role, select the permissions you want, and then click OK.

Check Out and In Files to Edit

1. In Launchbar, double-click the workspace you want to open, and then click the **SharePoint Files** tab.

2. Select the file you want to check out.

3. Click the **Check In/Out** button on the toolbar, and then click **Check Out from SharePoint**.

4. To edit a file, double-click the file to open it in its native program, make changes, save and close it.

5. In Groove, click **Yes** to save changes.

6. Click the **Check In/Out** button on the toolbar, and then click **Check In from SharePoint**.

7. Describe your changes, and then click **OK**.

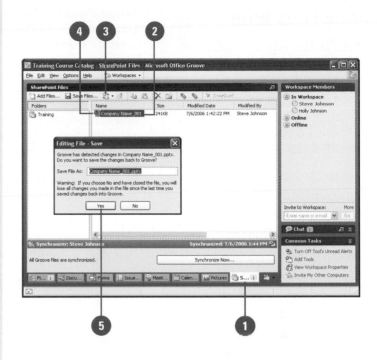

Synchronize Files

1. In Launchbar, double-click the workspace you want to open, and then click the **SharePoint Files** tab.

2. To set synchronization options, click the **Calendar** icon, click the **Manually** or **Automatically** option, and then if necessary, specify an interval, and then click **OK**.

3. To manually synchronize files, click **Synchronize Now**.

   The Preview Synchronization dialog box opens.

4. Click **Synchronize Now**.

   Resolve any conflicts that arise. If necessary, click Resolve, select another file version, and then click OK.

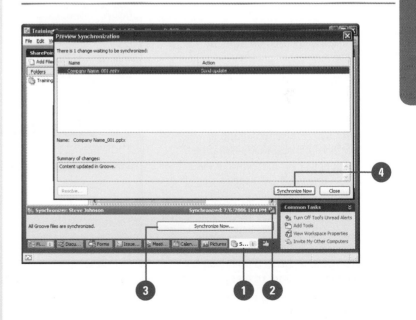

Sharing Files with Synchronizing Folders

Instead of using the File Tool in Groove, you can use Groove Folder Synchronization (GFS) in Windows to make sure all changes within a folder are shared between users and kept up-to-date. You create GFS folders in your Windows file system using Windows Explorer. GFS folders are separate from workspaces and currently have a 2 gigabyte size limit. Files shared in Groove workspaces are stored in an encrypted format, while files in a GFS folder are only encrypted during transmission between computers. Any new files added to a synchronized folder are automatically shared with other team members to ensure a secure environment. In Windows Explorer, you can use the Groove Folder Synchronization pane to view the details of the file sharing workspace, view members of the workspace, send workspace invitations, and set workspace and folder properties.

Synchronize Local Folders

1. In Windows Explorer, click the folder you want to share as a GFS folder.

2. Click the **Folder Sync** button.

   The Groove Folder Synchronization pane replaces the Windows Folder pane.

3. Click **Start synchronizing** *foldername*.

4. Click **Synchronize Now**, if necessary, to continue from the preview synchronization.

5. Click **Yes** to confirm the folder share.

6. Use commands in the Groove Folder Synchronization pane to view the details of the file sharing workspace, view members of the workspace, send workspace invitations, mark folders read or unread, and set workspace and folder properties.

7. In Groove, click the **Workspace** tab to access the GFS folder, and view read and unread files.

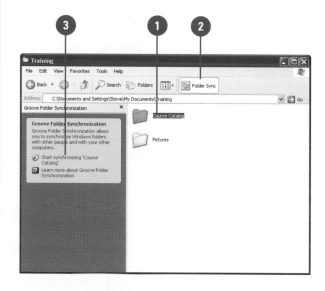

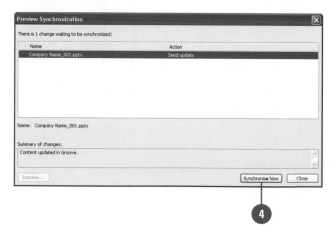

New! Features

Microsoft Office Access 2007

Microsoft Office Access 2007 is a database program that allows you to store an almost limitless amount of information, organize and retrieve information in a way that makes sense for how you work, create forms that make it easier to enter information, and generate meaningful and insightful reports that can combine data, text, graphics, and other objects.

Only New Features

If you're already familiar with Microsoft Office Access 2003, you can access and download all the tasks in this book with Microsoft Office Access 2007 New Features to help make your transition to the new version simple and smooth. The Microsoft Access Office 2007 New Features as well as other 2003 to 2007 transition helpers are available on the Web at *www.perspection.com.*

What's New

If you're searching for what's new in Office 2007, just look for the icon: New!. The new icon appears in the table of contents and throughout this book so you can quickly and easily identify a new or improved feature in Office 2007. The following is a brief description of each new feature and it's location in this book.

Office 2007

◆ **Ribbon (p. 6, 340)** The Ribbon is a new look for Office 2007. It replaces menus, toolbars, and most of the task panes found in Office 2003. The Ribbon is comprised of tabs with buttons and options that are organized by task.

◆ **KeyTip (p. 6)** If you prefer using the keyboard instead of the mouse to access commands on the Ribbon, you can use KeyTips. Simply press and release the Alt or F10 key to display KeyTips over each feature, and then continue to press the letter shown in the KeyTip until you press the one that you want to use.

◆ **Office button and menu (p. 7)** The Office button and menu replaces the File menu with a revised list of commands and options, such as the Recent Documents list.

- ◆ **Quick Access Toolbar and Mini-Toolbar** (p. 8-9, 222, 352) Office includes its most common commands, such as Save and Undo, on the Quick Access Toolbar. The Mini-Toolbar appears above selected text and provides quick access to formatting tools.

- ◆ **Dialog Box Launcher** (p. 10, 19) Dialog Box Launchers are small icons that appear at the bottom corner of some groups on the Ribbon. When you point to a Dialog Box Launcher, a ScreenTip with a thumbnail of the dialog box appears to show you which dialog box opens when you click the Dialog Box Launcher.

- ◆ **Status bar (p. 11)** The Status bar displays the on/off status of features, such as signatures and spelling, and determines what information appears on the bar.

- ◆ **Recent Documents list** (p. 14-15) Office Similar to the Windows Start menu, the Recent Documents list allows you to quickly access recently used database files.

- ◆ **View selector (p. 17, 44)** You can quickly switch between program views using buttons in the lower-right corner of the program window or on the Ribbon.

- ◆ **Diagnose problems (p. 26-27)** The Diagnose command improves performance by diagnosing and repairing problems, such as missing files from setup, corrupted file by malicious viruses, and registry settings.

- ◆ **Message Bar (p. 31)** The Message Bar appears based on Trust Center security settings to protect your computer from harmful attacks.

- ◆ **Common spell checking and dictionary (p. 116-118)** Microsoft Office 2007 programs share a common spell checker and dictionary, so you only need to make additions and changes once.

- ◆ **Microsoft Office Document Imaging (p. 248-249)** With Microsoft Office Document Imaging, you can now add annotations to a scanned document image, such as a fax.

- ◆ **Document Management Server and SharePoint (p. 273-278)** You can save your documents to a Document Management Server, such as a Document Library on an Office SharePoint site that provides you with tools to share and update documents and to keep people informed about the current status of the documents using a workflow and validation process.

- ◆ **Create a PDF or XPS (p. 300-301)** You can now save a database object as a PDF or an XPS file, which is a fixed-layout format that retains the form you intended on a computer monitor or printer.

- ◆ **Trust Center (p. 324-330)** The Trust Center is a place where you set security options and find the latest technology information as it relates to document privacy, safety, and security from Microsoft. The Trust Center allows you to set security and privacy settings, including Trusted Publishers, Trusted Locations, Add-ins, Macro Settings, Message Bar, and Privacy Options.

- ◆ **Microsoft Office Groove (p. 371-394)** With Office Groove 2007 (an enterprise program), you can bring a team, tools, and information together from any location to work on a project.

Access 2007

◆ **Getting Started with Microsoft Access page (p. 5)** The Getting Started with Microsoft Office Access 2007 window displays when you start Access or create a new database, where you can quickly create a database using the built-in templates.

◆ **Spotlight (p. 5)** The Spotlight section at the bottom of the Getting Started with Microsoft Office Access 2007 window, highlights new content from Microsoft Office Online.

◆ **Save file format (p. 12-13, 16, 22-24)** You can save an Access database in the .accdb format (for Access 2007) or .mdb format (for Access 2000 or 2002-2003). When you save a database, Access 2007 saves Access 97-2003 files in their older format. The database stays in the original file format until you convert it to the Access 2007 file format.

◆ **Navigation pane (p. 17, 19)** The area on the left side of the window that displays database objects. The Navigation pane replaces the Database window from previous versions of Access. You can also hide, show, and minimize the Navigation pane.

◆ **Tabbed documents (p. 17, 334-335)** Database objects, such as tables, queries, forms, reports, and macros, display as tabbed documents for easy access and navigation.

◆ **Layout view (p. 17, 170-173, 334-336)** Layout view allows you to make common design changes while you view a live form or report. Instead of switching between Design view and Form view, you can use Layout view.

◆ **Help (p. 20-21)** You can access end-user and developer help from the same Help viewer window.

◆ **Add New Field (p. 50, 52)** In a table, click the Add New Field column to quickly enter data. Access automatically determines the data type.

◆ **Table templates (p. 50, 53)** A table template is a predefined table with fields you can quickly insert and use in a database.

◆ **Field Templates pane (p. 50, 70-71)** A field template is a design for a field, complete with a name, data type, length, and properties. You can drag the fields you want from the Field Templates pane.

◆ **Field List pane (p. 50, 70-71)** The Field List pane now includes fields from other tables. When you use a field from another table, Access automatically creates a relationship between the two table objects.

◆ **Automatic calendar for data picking (p. 74, 82)** For date fields and controls, a calendar button automatically appears to the right of the date to let you quickly find and choose a date.

◆ **Change field data types (p. 76)** In Datasheet view, you can quickly set the field data type and format.

◆ **Rich text in memo field** (p. 81)   You can format text with options, such as bold, italic, and other formatting, and store the text in a Memo field in an HTML-based format.

◆ **Totals row** (p. 85)   You can use the Totals row to calculate values using functions such as sum, count, average, maximum, minimum, standard deviation, or variance.

◆ **Multivalue fields** (p. 97)   You can create a field that holds multiple values. This is useful when you work with a SharePoint list that contains multivalue field types.

◆ **Data attachment** (p. 98-99)   Attachment data type allows you to store and compress all types of data files, such as pictures, graphics, and Office files.

◆ **Sort and filter** (p. 128-129)   You can quickly find matching values using the AutoFilter context menu. AutoFilter options automatically change the data, so you can view the results.

◆ **Create tab** (p. 157, 160, 342, 358)   The Create tab allows you to quickly create new forms, reports, tables, SharePoint lists, queries, macros, and modules from one place.

◆ **Automatic forms and reports** (p. 160, 190)   Use buttons on the Create tab to quickly create professional looking forms and reports.

◆ **Split form** (p. 162)   You can create a form that combines a Datasheet view and a Form view.

◆ **Multiple Items form** (p. 165)   A form that shows multiple records in a datasheet, with one record per row. The data on the form appears in rows and columns.

◆ **PivotTable or PivotChart** (p. 168-169)   You can use the improved PivotTable or PivotChart layout to determine what fields and criteria you want to use to summarize the data and how you want the resulting table to look.

◆ **Controls** (p. 198-199)   You can insert a page, attachments, or ActiveX controls in a form or report. These controls are available on the Design tab under Form or Report Design Tools.

◆ **Group, sort, and total** (p. 208-209)   The Group, Sort, and Total pane in Layout view allows you to quickly add a group level, sort the data, and perform a calculation, such as a sum, average, count, maximum, or minimum.

◆ **AutoFormat** (p. 220-221)   A fast way to format a form or report. The improved AutoFormat button allows you to select from a variety of layouts and styles.

◆ **Stacked and tabular layout** (p. 238-239)   These layouts group controls in a column or row format to create a form or report. The controls are grouped together so you can work with them as one unit.

◆ **Save import or export settings** (p. 282-283)   When you import or export data in Access, you can save your import and export settings for use again in the future.

- **Collect data using Outlook 2007 (p. 288-291)** The Data Collection option allows you to create an HTML or InfoPath 2007 form and embed it in an e-mail message and send it to Outlook or Access contacts.

- **Connect with SharePoint (p. 273-278)** Use the SharePoint List button to import a SharePoint list or use the Move to SharePoint Site wizard to automatically migrate Access data to SharePoint.

- **Package and digitally sign (p. 320-321)** The Package and Sign command allows you to package, digitally sign, and distribute an Access database.

- **Alternate background color (p. 339)** The alternate background color shades alternate rows in a datasheet.

- **Embedded macros (p. 342)** An embedded macro are trusted to be safe and stored in a property and is part of the object.

What Happened To . . .

- **File menu** The File menu has been replaced by the Office button and menu with a revised list of commands and options.

- **Options command** The Options command on the Tools menu has been replaced by the Access Options button on the Office menu.

- **Detect and Repair** The Detect and Repair command has been replaced by Microsoft Office Diagnostics, which provides additional detection and repair capabilities.

  ➤ Click the **Office** button, click **Access Options**, click **Resources**, and then click **Diagnose**.

- **Web Toolbar** The Web toolbar is not available. However, you can still use some of the commands on the toolbar. You can add the Back and Forward buttons to the Quick Access Toolbar.

- **Data access pages** Access 2007 no longer supports data access pages. Instead, you can connect your data to a Microsoft SharePoint site and use the tools provided by Access and the site to import and export data to share it with others on the Web.

Microsoft Certified Applications Specialist

About the MCAS Program

The Microsoft Certified Applications Specialist (MCAS) certification is the globally recognized standard for validating expertise with the Microsoft Office suite of business productivity programs. Earning an MCAS certificate acknowledges you have the expertise to work with Microsoft Office programs. To earn the MCAS certification, you must pass a certification exam for the Microsoft Office desktop applications of Microsoft Office Word, Microsoft Office Excel, Microsoft Office PowerPoint, Microsoft Office Outlook, or Microsoft Office Access. (The availability of Microsoft Certified Applications Specialist certification exams varies by program, program version, and language. Visit *www.microsoft.com* and search on *Microsoft Certified Applications Specialist* for exam availability and more information about the program.) The Microsoft Certified Applications Specialist program is the only Microsoft-approved program in the world for certifying proficiency with Microsoft Office programs.

What Does This Logo Mean?

It means this book has been approved by the Microsoft Certified Applications Specialist program to be certified courseware for learning Microsoft Office Access 2007 and preparing for the certification exam. This book will prepare you for the Microsoft Certified Applications Specialist exam for Microsoft Office Access 2007. Each certification level has a set of objectives, which are organized into broader skill sets. Throughout this book, content that pertains to a Microsoft Certified Applications Specialist objective is identified with the following MCAS certification logo and objective number below the title of the topic:

Microsoft Certified Application Specialist   AC07S-1.1
AC07S-2.2

Access 2007 Objectives

Objective	Skill	Page
AC07S-1	**Structuring a Database**	
AC07S-1.1	**Define data need and types**	
AC07S-1.1.1	Define table fields	74-75
AC07S-1.1.2	Define appropriate table field data types for fields in each table	74-75
AC07S-1.1.3	Define tables in databases	50-51
AC07S-1.2	**Define and print table relationships**	
AC07S-1.2.1	Create relationships	60-63
AC07S-1.2.2	Modify relationships	60-63, 66
AC07S-1.2.3	Print table relationships	64-65
AC07S-1.4	Split databases	314
AC07S-1.3	**Add, set, change or remove primary keys**	
AC07S-1.3.1	Define and modify primary keys	50, 56-57, 59
AC07S-1.3.2	Define and modify multi-field primary keys	50, 59
AC07S-2	**Creating and Formatting Database Elements**	
AC07S-2.1	**Create databases**	
AC07S-2.1.1	Create databases using templates	12-13
AC07S-2.1.2	Create blank databases	12-13
AC07S-2.2	**Create tables**	
AC07S-2.2.1	Create custom tables in Design view	52, 58
AC07S-2.2.2	Create tables by copying the structure of other tables	102-103
AC07S-2.2.3	Create tables from templates	53
AC07S-2.3	**Modify tables**	
AC07S-2.3.1	Modify table properties	100
AC07S-2.3.2	Evaluate table design using the Table Analyzer	308-309
AC07S-2.3.3	Rename tables	102-103
AC07S-2.3.4	Delete tables	102-103
AC07S-2.3.5	Summarize table data by adding a Total row	85
AC07S-2.4	**Create fields and modify field properties**	
AC07S-2.4.1	Create commonly used fields	74, 76-77
AC07S-2.4.2	Modify field properties	75-77
AC07S-2.4.3	Create and modify multivalued fields	97

C

Access 2007 Objectives *(continued)*

Objective	Skill	Page
AC07S-2.4.4	Create and modify attachment fields	98-99
AC07S-2.5	**Create forms**	
AC07S-2.5.1	Create forms using Design view	174-175
AC07S-2.5.2	Create datasheet forms	164
AC07S-2.5.3	Create multiple item forms	165
AC07S-2.5.4	Create split forms	162
AC07S-2.5.5	Create subforms	182-183
AC07S-2.5.6	Create PivotTable forms	168-169
AC07S-2.5.7	Create forms using Layout view	166
AC07S-2.5.8	Create simple forms	160
AC07S-2.6	**Create reports**	
AC07S-2.6.1	Create reports as a simple report	190-191
AC07S-2.6.2	Create reports using the Report wizard	190-191
AC07S-2.6.3	Create reports using Design view	196-197
AC07S-2.6.4	Define group headers	194, 196-197
AC07S-2.6.5	Create aggregate fields	144-145
AC07S-2.6.6	Set print layout	214-215
AC07S-2.6.7	Create labels using the Label Wizard	193
AC07S-2.7	**Modify the design of reports and forms**	
AC07S-2.7.1	Add controls	70-71, 176-179, 271
AC07S-2.7.2	Bind controls to fields	195-199
AC07S-2.7.3	Define the tab order of controls	231
AC07S-2.7.4	Format controls	222
AC07S-2.7.5	Arrange controls	232-236
AC07S-2.7.6	Apply the change conditional formatting on controls	229
AC07S-2.7.7	Apply AutoFormats to forms and reports	220-221
AC07S-3	**Entering and Modifying Data**	
AC07S-3.1	Enter, edit, and delete records	56-57
AC07S-3.2	Navigate among records	56-57
AC07S-3.3	Find and replace data	114-115
AC07S-3.4	Attach documents to and detach from records	98-99
AC07S-3.5	**Import data**	

Access 2007 Objectives *(continued)*

Objective	Skill	Page
AC07S-3.5.1	Import data from a specific source	286, 291
AC07S-3.5.2	Link to external data sources	286
AC07S-3.5.3	Save and run import specifications	282-283
AC07S-4	**Creating and modifying queries**	
AC07S-4.1	**Create queries**	
AC07S-4.1.1	Create queries based on single tables	133, 138, 148
AC07S-4.1.2	Create queries based on more than one table	136-139, 149
AC07S-4.1.3	Create action queries	150-151
AC07S-4.1.4	Create crosstab queries	154-155
AC07S-4.1.5	Create sub queries	136-137
AC07S-4.1.6	Save filters as queries	128-129
AC07S-4.2	**Modify queries**	
AC07S-4.2.1	Add tables to and remove tables from queries	135, 138-139
AC07S-4.2.2	Add criteria to queries	140-141, 146-147
AC07S-4.2.3	Create joins	62-63
AC07S-4.2.4	Create calculated fields in queries	144-145
AC07S-4.2.5	Add aliases to query fields	136-137, 144-145
AC07S-4.2.6	Create sum, average, min/max, and count queries	144-145
AC07S-5	**Presenting and sharing Data**	
AC07S-5.1	**Sort data**	
AC07S-5.1.1	Sort data within tables	124-125
AC07S-5.1.2	Sort data within queries	124-125
AC07S-5.1.3	Sort data within reports	124-125
AC07S-5.1.4	Sort data within forms	124-125
AC07S-5.2	**Filter data**	
AC07S-5.2.1	Filter data within tables	128-129
AC07S-5.2.2	Filter data within queries	128-129
AC07S-5.2.3	Filter data within reports	128-129
AC07S-5.2.4	Filter data within forms	128-129
AC07S-5.2.5	Remove filters	128-129
AC07S-5.3	**Create and modify charts**	
AC07S-5.3.1	Create charts	254-255

Access 2007 Objectives (continued)

Objective	Skill	Page
AC07S-5.3.2	Format charts	256-257
AC07S-5.3.3	Change chart types	254-255
AC07S-5.4	**Export data**	
AC07S-5.4.1	Export data from tables	294-299
AC07S-5.4.2	Export data from queries	294-299
AC07S-5.4.3	Save and run export specifications	282-283
AC07S-5.5	Save database objects as other file types	300-302
AC07S-5.6	Print database objects	216-217
AC07S-6	**Managing and Maintaining Databases**	
AC07S-6.1	**Perform routine database operations**	
AC07S-6.1.1	Open databases	14, 332
AC07S-6.1.2	Back up databases	304
AC07S-6.1.3	Compact and repair databases	305
AC07S-6.1.4	Save databases as a previous version	22-24
AC07S-6.2	**Manage Databases**	
AC07S-6.2.1	Encrypt databases using passwords	316-317
AC07S-6.2.2	Configure database options	212-213, 334-335
AC07S-6.2.3	Set database properties	306
AC07S-6.2.4	**Identify object dependencies**	
AC07S-6.2.4.1	Advanced tools tab	67 68
AC07S-6.2.5	Print database information using the Database Documenter	307
AC07S-6.2.6	Reset or refresh table links using the Linked Table Manager	105

Preparing for a MCAS Exam

Every Microsoft Certified Applications Specialist certification exam is developed from a list of objectives based on how Microsoft Office programs are actually used in the workplace. The list of objectives determine the scope of each exam, so they provide you with the information you need to prepare for MCAS certification. Microsoft Certified Applications Specialist Approved Courseware, including the On Demand series, is reviewed and approved on the basis of its coverage of the objectives. To prepare for the certification exam, you should review and perform each task identified with a MCAS objective to confirm that you can meet the requirements for the exam.

Taking a MCAS Exam

The Microsoft Certified Applications Specialist certification exams are not written exams. Instead, the exams are performance-based examinations that allow you to interact with a "live" Office program as you complete a series of objective-based tasks. All the standard ribbons, tabs, toolbars, and keyboard shortcuts are available during the exam. Microsoft Certified Applications Specialist exams for Office 2007 programs consist of 25 to 35 questions, each of which requires you to complete one or more tasks using the Office program for which you are seeking certification. A typical exam takes from 45 to 60 minutes. Passing percentages range from 70 to 80 percent correct.

The Exam Experience

After you fill out a series of information screens, the testing software starts the exam and the Office program. The test questions appear in the exam dialog box in the lower right corner of the screen.

- ◆ The timer starts when the first question appears and displays the remaining exam time at the top of the exam dialog box. If the timer and the counter are distracting, you can click the timer to remove the display.

- ◆ The counter at the top of the exam dialog box tracks how many questions you have completed and how many remain.

- ◆ If you think you have made a mistake, you can click the Reset button to restart the question. The Reset button does not restart the entire exam or extend the exam time limit.

- ◆ When you complete a question, click the Next button to move to the next question. It is not possible to move back to a previous question on the exam.

- ◆ If the exam dialog box gets in your way, you can click the Minimize button in the upper right corner of the exam dialog box to hide it, or you can drag the title bar to another part of the screen to move it.

Tips for Taking an Exam

◆ Carefully read and follow all instructions provided in each question.

◆ Make sure all steps in a task are completed before proceeding to the next exam question.

◆ Enter requested information as it appears in the instructions without formatting unless you are explicitly requested otherwise.

◆ Close all dialog boxes before proceeding to the next exam question unless you are specifically instructed otherwise.

◆ Do not leave tables, boxes, or cells "active" unless instructed otherwise.

◆ Do not cut and paste information from the exam interface into the program.

◆ When you print a document from an Office program during the exam, nothing actually gets printed.

◆ Errant keystrokes or mouse clicks do not count against your score as long as you achieve the correct end result. You are scored based on the end result, not the method you use to achieve it. However, if a specific method is explicitly requested, you need to use it to get credit for the results.

◆ The overall exam is timed, so taking too long on individual questions may leave you without enough time to complete the entire exam.

◆ If you experience computer problems during the exam, immediately notify a testing center administrator to restart your exam where you were interrupted.

Exam Results

At the end of the exam, a score report appears indicating whether you passed or failed the exam. An official certificate is mailed to successful candidates in approximately two to three weeks.

Getting More Information

To learn more about the Microsoft Certified Applications Specialist program, read a list of frequently asked questions, and locate the nearest testing center, visit:

www.microsoft.com

Index

A

ACCDB files, 12, 22
    Blank.accdb files, 48
ACCDC files, 320-321
ACCDE files, 22
    for VBA projects, 370
ACCDR files, 22
ACCDT files, 22
Access Deployment files (ACCDC), 320-321
access keys. *See* shortcuts
Account Configuration Wizard, 372
Acrobat Reader, 300
Action Items for meetings, 383
action queries, 132
actions, 341
ActiveX controls
    Trust Center settings, 324
    viruses and, 322
Add Existing Fields button, 247
adding/removing. *See also* deleting
    Navigation pane custom category, 35
    query fields, 138
    Quick Access Toolbar, items from, 9
Add-In Manager, 310
add-ins
    disabled items, viewing, 327
    installing/uninstalling, 310
    Publish as PDF or XPS add-in, 300, 301
    security options, setting, 326-327
    Trust Center settings, 324, 326-327
    viruses and, 322
Add New Field column, Datasheet view, 50, 70
Add or Remove features, 27
Address Book switchboard, 32
Adobe Systems. *See* PDF files
ADP files, 3

alerts. *See also* Groove; Message Bar
    for macros, 31
aligning
    controls/objects, 234-235
    form fields, 238-239
    options, 338
    report fields, 238-239
Allow Zero Length property, 75, 76
analyzing database, 308-309
anchoring controls/objects, 232-233
AND
    filters, 130
    function, 146
    operator, 142
Annotation toolbar, 248-249
appending
    data to tables, 102-103
    query, creating, 151
arguments, 341
arrow key behavior, 338
ascending order sorts, 124-125
Assets table template, 53
Attachment fields, 98-99
Attachment Manager, 323
attachments
    database objects as, 294
    field records, attaching files to, 98-99
    forms, adding to, 247
    Groove meeting agendas as, 383
    reports, adding to, 247
    security issues with, 323
AutoCorrect
    adding and editing entries, 111
    database objects, renaming, 35
    replacing text as you type, 110, 111
    as smart tag, 112
    with spell-checking, 116-117
    for tables, 110-111

D

reports, changing font color in, 227

footers. *See* headers and footers

foreign keys, 60

Format Painter
    in forms, 230
    in reports, 230

Format property, 75, 76

formatting. *See also* reports
    chart objects, 256
    conditional formatting in reports/forms, 229
    currency values, 84
    datasheets, 119, 339
    date/time formats, 82-83
    Format Painter, 230
    form input boxes, 172
    memo text, 81
    number values, 84
    pasting information in formats, 106
    pasting in specified formats, 243
    query fields, 141
    for report controls, 197
    Rich Text format, 81
    symbols, 80
    text data, 80

Form button, 34, 158

form controls
    adding, 176, 178
    aligning controls/objects, 234-235
    all controls, selecting, 220
    anchoring, 232-233
    colors for gridlines, changing, 237
    combo boxes, creating, 180-181
    in Design view, 159
    editing, 177, 179
    flat effect in, 228
    gridlines, changing, 237
    list boxes, creating, 180-181
    margins, changing, 240
    modifying, 179
    moving, 232-233
    padding, changing, 240-241
    positioning for, 236
    Properties feature, 159
    resizing, 232-233
    Snap to Grid option, 234-235
    spacing, adjusting, 236

special effects, applying, 228

stacking, 236, 238-239

tabbing order, changing, 231

3-D effects in, 228

types of, 159

Form Design Tools, 176

form modules in VBA, 357

forms, 2. *See also* Groove; hyperlinks; images; subforms; switchboards
    adding fields and controls to, 176
    attachments, adding, 247
    AutoFormat for, 220-221
    blank forms, creating, 166
    borders
        colors, changing, 226-227
        thickness, changing, 225
    class modules, creating, 366
    colors of lines/borders, changing, 226-227
    conditional formatting in, 229
    creating, 158
    data entry for, 41
    datasheet forms, 164
    defined, 157
    deleting
        records, 171
        stacked layout, 239
        tabular layout, 239
    dependency information, 67
    Design view, working in, 170, 174-175
    dialog forms, creating, 167
    editing, 176-177
        controls, 179
        in Design view, 175
        form controls, 177
        records, 171
    entering records in, 40
    error checking, 212-213
    existing forms, creating split forms from, 162-163
    fill color, changing, 227
    filters, creating, 130
    font color, changing, 227
    Format Painter in, 230
    formatting tools for, 222-223
    Form Wizard, creating forms with, 161
    headers and footers, showing and hiding, 223